THE AMBIGUOUS EMBRACE

NEW FORUM BOOKS

Robert P. George, Series Editor

A list of titles

in the series appears

at the back of

the book

THE AMBIGUOUS EMBRACE

GOVERNMENT AND FAITH-BASED SCHOOLS
AND SOCIAL AGENCIES

Charles L. Glenn

With a foreword by Peter L. Berger

PRINCETON UNIVERSITY PRESS

PRINCETON, NEW JERSEY

COPYRIGHT © 2000 BY PRINCETON UNIVERSITY PRESS

PUBLISHED BY PRINCETON UNIVERSITY PRESS, 41 WILLIAM STREET,

PRINCETON, NEW JERSEY 08540

IN THE UNITED KINGDOM: PRINCETON UNIVERSITY PRESS, CHICHESTER, WEST SUSSEX

LIBRARY OF CONGRESS CATALOGING-IN-PUBLICATION DATA

GLENN, CHARLES LESLIE, 1938–

THE AMBIGUOUS EMBRACE : GOVERNMENT AND FAITH-BASED SCHOOLS

AND SOCIAL AGENCIES / CHARLES L. GLENN ; WITH A FOREWORD

BY PETER L. BERGER.

P. CM.—(NEW FORUM BOOKS)

INCLUDES BIBLIOGRAPHICAL REFERENCES AND INDEX.

ISBN 0-691-04852-5 (ALK. PAPER)

1. HUMAN SERVICES—CONTRACTING OUT—UNITED STATES. 2. HUMAN SERVICES—
CONTRACTING OUT—EUROPE. 3. CIVIL SOCIETY—UNITED STATES. 4. CIVIL SOCIETY—EUROPE.
5. CHURCH AND STATE—UNITED STATES. 6. CHURCH AND STATE—EUROPE. 7. CHURCH
CHARITIES—UNITED STATES. 8. CHURCH CHARITIES—EUROPE. 9. CHURCH SCHOOLS—
UNITED STATES. 10. CHURCH SCHOOLS—EUROPE. I. TITLE. II. SERIES.

HV95.G54   2000

361.7′5′0973—dc21   99-035074   CIP

THIS BOOK HAS BEEN COMPOSED IN JANSON TEXT TYPEFACE

THE PAPER USED IN THIS PUBLICATION MEETS THE MINIMUM REQUIREMENTS

OF ANSI/NISO Z39.48-1992 (R1997) (PERMANENCE OF PAPER)

HTTP: //PUP.PRINCETON.EDU

PRINTED IN THE UNITED STATES OF AMERICA

1   3   5   7   9   10   8   6   4   2

*To those in faith-based schools, social agencies,
and other organizations who provide loving care,
with high expectations, in the name
of a loving and righteous God.*

CONTENTS

FOREWORD

THE PROBLEM discussed in Charles Glenn's book should be seen against the background of an intriguing paradox: By any reasonable measure, the United States is the most religious country in the community of Western democracies; yet, as the result of court decisions beginning in the 1960s, it also has the most rigorous definition of the separation of church and state—more rigorous even than that prevailing in France, the country that conceived the idea of *laïcisme*. This is not the place to delve into the reasons for this paradox, nor to enter into a philosophical debate over its merits. But the paradox has become very significant in the current debates over the future of educational and social policy in America, and these debates cannot be pushed forward in a constructive way unless the paradox is taken into account and resolved in a politically practical manner.

The reason for this is really quite simple: Throughout the Western world it has become clear that the modern welfare state (which in America made its debut considerably later than in Europe but by now has attained only slightly lesser magnitude) must be modified if it is to continue being affordable. A very plausible formula for such a modification has suggested that functions of the welfare state (including education) should be devolved onto institutions of civil society. These are the institutions that Richard John Neuhaus and I, in the little book generously mentioned by Glenn in his introduction, called the "mediating structures"—institutions that stand between the personal lives of individuals and the megastructures of modern society (including, above all, the structures of the state). In America these institutions have been especially powerful, grounded in a specifically American genius for voluntary association—a cultural trait that already Alexis de Tocqueville perceived as an explanation for the vitality of American democracy. In Catholic social thought these are the institutions subsumed under the principle of "subsidiarity," which suggests that the state should hold back from activities that can be more effectively undertaken by smaller units in the society. So far, so good. But the formula for devolution runs into a simple fact: *A very large number of these intermediate institutions are religiously defined.* At this point the question of how the state should relate to religion attains a new urgency.

No politically significant body of opinion in America favors the abolition of the separation of church and state. Rather, the argument revolves around the definition of this separation. People favoring the maintenance of the current rigorous definition rightly fear developments that would make the state support this or that religious community, thus infringing on the rights of those who do not belong to or possibly are even inimical to such a community. Consequently, they are fearful of any inclusion of religiously defined institutions in the process of devolution from the welfare state to civil society. But people who would in principle be friendly to state support for religiously defined institutions have another concern—namely, that with state support would come a mass of regulatory interventions that might undermine the religious character of these institutions and thus undermine religious liberty. To simplify matters a bit, one could say that one side fears the sacralization of the state, while the other side fears the secularization of the churches. An objective observer is likely to conclude that neither fear is without grounds, given the history of state-church relations in modern societies. What is clearly called for is a process of thorough and open-minded rethinking.

Another important point should be made: In this and in other areas of domestic policy, the American debates are peculiarly parochial. The issues are debated as if the United States were the only country facing them. Admittedly, America is a very large country, with very distinctive features. Yet comparison is almost always useful. There are lessons to be learned— some positive, some negative—from the way in which the modification of the welfare state and its relation to religiously defined institutions has been approached in other democracies.

Charles Glenn's book makes a magisterial contribution to this particular debate. It is thoroughly informed about the minutiae of the issue in this country (which Glenn knows not only as a scholar but as an active participant). It is also very informed about the issue as it has developed in Europe, not only in the countries on this side of what used to be the Iron Curtain, but also in the new democracies in the formerly Communist countries. And Glenn deals with the issue in an admirably evenhanded manner, carefully avoiding any sort of ideological dogmatism. His book will have to be required reading for anyone who is concerned with the future of social policy and the well-being of religion in America.

It gives me great satisfaction that the work resulting in this book was sponsored by the Institute for the Study of Economic Culture at Boston University, with funds generously provided by the Lynde and Harry Bradley Foundation.

Peter L. Berger
Director, Institute for the Study of Economic Culture
Boston University

ACKNOWLEDGMENTS

P ETER BERGER suggested that I undertake this study, and I am deeply grateful for his insights and for his patience with the delays occasioned by my other obligations. It has been exciting to work in parallel and to exchange ideas with Stephen Monsma, Jim Skillen, Stanley Carlson-Thies, and Amy Sherman through the Center for Public Justice. Emily Nielsen Jones (who coauthored the interlude on the Salvation Army) and Karen Bohlin did valuable fieldwork in and around Boston, as did Heinz-Dieter Meyer, Silke Tollmien, Andreas Flegel, Oliver Schwarz, and Suzanne Moeller in Germany. Others who have made suggestions include Jaap Dronkers and Anton Zijderveld in the Netherlands, Robert Whelan in Britain, José Luis Martínez López-Muñiz in Spain, Jan De Groof in Belgium, Jacques Georgel in France, and John Hiemstra in Canada, as well as others too many to mention here who took part in our discussions in Rotterdam and in Boston. Lawrence D. Weinberg has helped me to keep my legal citations in order, while researching his dissertation on a related topic.

Financial support for this project was provided by the Lynde and Harry Bradley Foundation, through the Institute for the Study of Economic Culture at Boston University. Additional support for the colloquia was provided by the Erasmus University of Rotterdam and the German-American Academic Council.

THE AMBIGUOUS EMBRACE

INTRODUCTION

T HIS STUDY has not one starting point, but three. Or are these, in some sense, the same issue meeting me over a dozen years in different guises? Working as a state education official responsible for civil rights and urban education, and then teaching educational policy, I have puzzled over the relationship between schools and families, between the wider world in which children must learn to live and the deeper world in which they will always to some extent be rooted. But if this is the continuing theme, I have come upon it (or it has come at me) in three different forms.

Mediating Structures

The first can be identified with some precision: a little book by Peter Berger and Richard John Neuhaus called *To Empower People*. Berger and Neuhaus called the attention of policymakers to the importance of "mediating structures," the "value-generating and value-maintaining agencies" that mediate between individuals and the state. They urged that public policy make greater use of these organizations associated with community, church, family, and voluntary associations.

> The proposal is that if these institutions could be more imaginatively recognized in public policy, individuals would be more "at home" in society, and the political order would be more "meaningful." Without institutionally reliable processes of mediation, the political order becomes detached from the values and realities of individual life. Deprived of its moral foundation, the political order is "delegitimated." Our belief is that human beings, whoever they are, understand their own needs better than anyone else—in, say, 99 percent of all cases. The mediating structures under discussion here are the principal expressions of the real values and the real needs of people in our society. They are, for the most part, the people-sized institutions. Public policy should recognize, respect, and, where possible, empower these institutions. . . . The paradigm of mediating structures aims at empowering poor people to do the things that the more affluent can already do.[1]

Berger and Neuhaus were of course by no means the first to stress the significance of what is commonly called "civil society," but they wrote at a time when American social policy was ripe for a change of course. Disillu-

---

[1] Berger and Neuhaus, *To Empower People*.

sionment over the failure of Great Society programs to deliver on their promises was growing on the Left, while to the Right it seemed obvious that the unanticipated consequences of these programs had made matters worse. Many across the political spectrum were ready for a new approach that put services and decisions about services closer to those being served . . . even in their own hands.

It seems fair to say that the first part of the Berger-Neuhaus argument—that government policies designed to meet human needs should make more use of the ways in which people organize their own lives—was heard more readily than was the warning with which they followed it. "We should learn," they wrote, "to ask about the effects of public policies on mediating structures," since "there is a real danger that such structures might be 'co-opted' by the government in a too eager embrace that would destroy the very distinctiveness of their function."[2] Proponents of community-based programs, education vouchers, and government collaboration with what came to be called the "third sector" of nonprofit organizations saw Berger and Neuhaus as valuable allies but paid insufficient attention to their concern about the corrupting effects of such collaboration.

It was in fact easy to misread their advocacy of the role of mediating structures as a call to return to the "community action programs" under the War on Poverty, programs that sought to use federal dollars to mobilize the poor through grassroots organizations and ended up corrupting and eventually destroying many of the grassroots organizations, often faith-based, that already existed and had done good work in their quiet way.

The most unfashionable aspect of their case, in the context of the seventies, was the high value they placed upon religious institutions as significant participants in the health of American society. They were in effect echoing Tocqueville's famous observation, "Religion, which never intervenes directly in the government of American society, should . . . be considered as the first of their political institutions, for although it does not give them the taste for liberty, it singularly facilitates their use thereof."[3]

I came across *To Empower People* several years after it was published, when I was well into my twenty-one-year career as the state official responsible for urban education and civil rights in Massachusetts. While it did not cause me to abandon my convictions about the desirability of racial integration, or my belief that the state has an important role to play in education, it made me wonder whether we were going about our work in a way that destroyed much else of value. Berger and Neuhaus wrote, for example, that their "preference for the parents over the experts . . . is a bias based upon the simple, but often overlooked, consideration that virtually all par-

[2] Ibid., 163.
[3] Tocqueville, *Democracy in America*, 292.

ents love their children. Very few experts love, or can love, most of the children in their care. . . . In addition, the parent, unlike the expert, has a long-term, open-ended commitment to the individual child. . . . virtually any structure is better for children than what experts or the state can provide." They insisted upon "perhaps the most fundamental human right—the right to make a world for one's children," and I could not help wondering whether they were correct that, by taking decisions out of the control of the family, "schools teach contempt for the parents and, ultimately, self-contempt." Could a system of vouchers, which I had never considered seriously until then, "enhance the diversity of American life by fostering particularist communities of value—whether of life style, ideology, religion, or ethnicity"?[4]

School Choice

The second starting point for this study was the growing movement in support of public policies to allow and encourage parents to choose the schools their children attend. This idea is often considered libertarian, but in fact was first implemented on a large scale under government auspices as part of the racial integration effort. In 1974, the Massachusetts Legislature took away the State Board of Education's authority to order student reassignment plans for racial balance, and in its place provided millions of dollars to encourage parent choices that would serve to integrate schools. Over the next seventeen years I was able to grant about half a billion dollars for magnet schools and other choice initiatives. Meanwhile, I served as official monitor for choice-based school assignments in Chicago, and advised Mobile and Albuquerque, San Diego and Tel Aviv, on putting school choice in place. Working with hundreds of magnet schools turned me into a strong advocate of the merits of school diversity and parent choice for their own sake.

Unlike the many supporters and opponents of school choice as a theory, we were forced to work out specific policies and procedures to ensure that it functioned within a framework balancing the general good with individual choices. Eventually, I came to believe that school choice could not realize its full potential unless the supply of schools among which to choose was opened up more radically, by charter schools and even by vouchers.[5] The bureaucratic constraints imposed by government-operated school systems are inconsistent with good education.

---

[4] Berger and Neuhaus, *To Empower People*, 179–81.
[5] Glenn, "Controlled Choice in Massachusetts," 88–105.

Norm-Maintaining Institutions

The third starting point of this study is the growing concern that I share with many others about the weakening of those institutions in the society that generate a sense of moral obligation. The triumph of the market as the metaphor for relationships, even the most intimate, and the ever-expanding activity of the welfare state have between them undermined individual moral and civic responsibility.

As my Boston University colleague Alan Wolfe has pointed out, "rather than following narrowly inscribed rules that are expected to be applied strictly and with little tolerance for ambiguity, modern liberal democrats find themselves facing unprecedented moral dilemmas without firm agreement, not merely about what their moral codes *are*, but even about where they can be *found*."[6] Neither the market nor the state can "revive [the] notions of moral agency associated with civil society." Only by recognizing the obligations associated with and derived from "the gift of society" can we recapture the appropriate balance of freedom and rootedness that will allow us—and our children—to learn this all-important lesson.

This is why the revival of civil society in the post-Communist countries of Eastern Europe has been so profoundly important for their freedom as well as their prosperity. In *Educational Freedom in Eastern Europe*, I showed how the totalitarian devastation of civil society is being reversed in part through initiatives taken by teachers and parents in hundreds, if not thousands, of communities—from Estonia to Bulgaria and from Prague to the Urals and beyond—to educate children with integrity and effectiveness in nongovernment schools that they have created. This seemed a confirmation of the prediction of Václav Havel, in 1978, that "the official structures—as agencies of the post-totalitarian system, existing only to serve its automatism and constructed in the spirit of that role—[will] simply begin withering away and dying off, to be replaced by new structures that have evolved from 'below' and are put together in a fundamentally different way."[7]

Schools have been among the most common "new structures" emerging during the last years of Communist rule and in a flood since its collapse. Groups of parents and teachers began at once to re-create education through school-level initiatives, many involving new autonomous schools. Post-Communist education policy debates focused, even more than in the United States, on whether such initiatives should be merely tolerated as an

---

[6] Wolfe, *Whose Keeper?* 3.
[7] Havel, *Living in Truth*, 108.

expression of freedom or welcomed and supported in the interest of society as a whole.[8]

Such initiatives are an essential aspect of educational reform in societies where, as Jiří Musil put it, "a rich network of independent institutions and organizations has to be formed, that are neither state-directed nor state-controlled, that are autonomous social, political, and cultural entities. . . . Seeking and constituting such social, cultural, political forces, capable of attaining such independence and balance, is the process which will decide whether a postcommunist regime is successful in its efforts to achieve democracy."[9] Schools are ideally situated to serve as the occasion for new habits of cooperation, for the development of trust as adults work together in the interest of their children.

Here, surely, is an example of mediating structures at work and teaching profound lessons about moral obligation and citizenship.

Two other colleagues at Boston University, Kevin Ryan and Edwin Delattre, helped me to understand how crucial it is that we nourish opportunities for children—and adults as well—to develop the sense of moral obligation and the settled disposition to act virtuously. No social policy question could be more crucial than whether the public assistance, crisis intervention, and criminal justice systems teach those lessons effectively, and no educational policy question could be more crucial than whether schools, early childhood programs, and education of youth and adults based in social agencies do the same.

The question is especially sensitive in the American context because religion—the source for most Americans of their moral compass—has been chased vigorously out of public schools and out of publicly funded nonprofit institutions, leaving what Neuhaus has called a "naked public square." Teachers and youth leaders have been discouraged from offering any but prudential reasons for refraining from conduct that earlier generations would have called immoral; this has had a coarsening effect on the public conscience.

Putting Them Together

Three themes, then, which can be put together in several ways that make evident their intimate relationship. Mediating structures should be used to deliver education and social services because they are better than government at generating the sense of moral obligation that is essential to both. Parent choice of schools can help to nourish new and existing mediating

---

[8] See the country-by-country account in Glenn, *Educational Freedom*.
[9] Musil, "Czechoslovakia in Transition," 189–90.

structures. Despite ferocious resistance by well-organized public employees, there is a growing willingness among elected officials to adopt policies that encourage the use of mediating structures. There is even a new willingness to contemplate partnerships between government and faith-based organizations.

In November 1996 the Institute for the Study of Economic Culture at Boston University cosponsored, with the Erasmus University of Rotterdam, a colloquium to explore these connections, with participants from Belgium, Canada, Germany, the Netherlands, Spain, Switzerland, the United Kingdom, and the United States. We took the appropriate role and limits of government as a normative rather than merely as a technical question and explored the possibility of a "remoralizing" of society through institutions with the authority and integrity to overcome excessive individualism and inadequate socialization. As Jan De Groof pointed out, Belgian law recognizes religious associations because of their social and moral importance to the public order. The basis of their position, then, is not simply religious freedom or individual conscience as guaranteed on constitutional or human rights principles, but a policy decision that they contribute to the general good. Similarly, legislators manifest an understanding that they should protect viewpoint-pluralism not only in society but, above all, in public services, that such pluralism is a positive social good that requires institutional support.

In a follow-up session held at Boston University in November 1997 (with additional support from the German-American Academic Council), an overlapping group continued this discussion. The growing support, in policy circles, for measures promoting greater autonomy of schools and social agencies was seen as opening the possibility of greater focus and responsiveness, but also as presenting new dangers for social goals and also for independent institutions.

Perhaps the most promising manifestation of this new spirit in American policy developments is the language introduced, by Senator Ashcroft of Missouri, into the federal law reforming the public assistance program. The so-called Charitable Choice provision requires that, if states choose to contract for social services with federal welfare funds, they must allow faith-based organizations to compete on equal terms and may not impose conditions that affect their religious practices. This innovative approach—and parallels in other government programs—will be discussed further in chapter 4.

Another indication of a new willingness to enter into partnership with faith-based organizations is the adoption, by Wisconsin, Ohio, and Puerto Rico, of educational voucher programs that are intended to include religious schools chosen by parents. The decision by the Supreme Court, in November 1998, not to consider a constitutional challenge to the Wisconsin programs create new forms of possibility. Voucher programs are being introduced in other states on a regular basis by legislators who are willing to brave the strong opposition of the teacher unions.

In the excitement over these developments, however, it is well to remember the warning expressed by Berger and Neuhaus twenty years ago, that "there is a real danger that such structures might be 'co-opted' by the government in a too eager embrace that would destroy the very distinctiveness of their function." Government support of choice among educational and social programs could come with so many strings attached that they would no longer offer real alternatives, function as mediating structures, or promote a coherent sense of moral obligation. We are already seeing this begin to happen in the short life of the charter school movement. Nongovernment organizations receiving public funds, even faith-based ones, could become indistinguishable from government programs. The civil society, as a result, could end up weaker than before. It is with these dangers that my study is concerned.

The most immediate question for my own work in educational policy has to do with whether vouchers or other mechanisms for extending public support to faith-based schools would lead to new injustices or would inevitably corrupt the schools. This danger has been raised both by Evangelical supporters of church-sponsored schools and by libertarian opponents of government intervention in the civil society. Some, indeed, consider that public funding is likely to be a *fatal* embrace.

The question cannot be answered directly from American experience, since there are very few examples of such support. We have had a great deal of speculation based on very little real evidence.

Focus of the Study

Fortunately, two forms of indirect evidence *are* available. The first derives from public funding of forms of faith-based social and educational services other than K-12 schools. We can ask to what extent the religious purposes and the distinctive character of these organizations and their ministries have been subverted as a result of government support. If they have been, we can ask whether that was the result of explicit regulation, of expectations associated with public funding, of professionalization of their staff, or of developments in the organizations themselves and the services they provide. Or of all of these factors together.

The world of nonprofit organizations in the United States and other Western democracies is a large one. In 1991 there were 133,357 "charitable organizations" in the United States, in addition to 257,648 religious congregations. Of the former, 48,793 were concerned with some form of human services, and 18,175 with education. The majority of the charitable organizations—56.7 percent—were founded between 1971 and 1990, many of them in response to government funding of nonprofit agencies to provide services. Of the charitable organizations providing human services, "41 percent reported receiving government grants and 27 [percent] reported receiving fees from government agencies."[10]

While only eighteen thousand or so of the charitable organizations identified themselves as affiliated with a religious denomination, "over nine out [of] ten religious congregations [reported that they] offered programs across most major activity areas of charitable organizations. . . . For the most part, these services were offered to their members as well as to other people in their communities."[11] Services provided by these civil society institutions are often invisible to social policy gurus, but they do much to sustain American society. This massive but almost invisible activity of congregations involved 1,194,985 paid staff, as well as 13,764,529 volunteers working an average of more than ten hours a month in 1989.[12]

Very few of the human service activities of congregations receive public funding, but Amy Sherman has documented the growing interest in policy circles in the possibility that congregations can play a more visible part in how our society addresses human needs.[13] It is becoming clear that "the natural affinity between religious belief and improving the human condition is probably much stronger than most people think. Almost as many congregations offered programs in human services as offered religious services and religious education."[14]

This, then, is the universe of nongovernment social services in the United States: thousands of "charitable organizations" or "nonprofits" (many of them religious) engaged in providing human services, and several hundred thousand religious congregations that include one form or several of human services among their activities. While our primary focus will be upon the first group (including Teen Challenge and the Salvation Army), and especially those that receive public funds, we will also keep in mind the less visible work of congregation-based human services, and how it might be included in public policy.

The other source of evidence is the experience of other Western democracies with political and cultural systems similar to our own. Most provide public funding—often full funding—for faith-based schools; they also regulate those schools much more closely than nonpublic schools are regulated in the United States. We can ask whether the close regulation neces-

---

[10] Hodgkinson et al., *Portrait of Independent Sector,* 9–14, 31.
[11] Ibid., 35.
[12] Hodgkinson et al., *From Belief to Commitment,* 21.
[13] Sherman, *Restorers of Hope.*
[14] Hodgkinson et al., *From Belief to Commitment,* 105.

sarily follows from the funding, and what strains and what distortions have occurred as a result. We can also ask (as occurs too seldom) whether American policymakers can learn any lessons from that experience.

It is significant that none of the European programs—apart from Margaret Thatcher's initiatives in England—has been justified by confidence in "markets." European policymakers have long been convinced that freedom and social solidarity require recognition of the role of religion in sustaining the civil society. Through considering their experience we explore how, as Berger and Neuhaus put it, "a common purpose can be achieved through the enhancement of myriad particular interests."[15]

Outline of This Book

Here is how the study is organized. First we consider the rise of the welfare state and some of the criticisms that have been directed against it. Government's intervention into domains that had traditionally been the business of civil society—education and social services—has, arguably, weakened the "mediating structures" upon which a healthy social and political order depend. Civil society institutions, and especially those based on religious themes, can transform lives and generate a sense of moral obligation.

Chapter 2 reviews the ways in which government *already* oversees faith-based organizations providing educational and social services, quite apart from funding them. Not all the threats of interference come attached to public funds, and some can be justified in the general interest. We will consider how government regulates or attempts to exert authority over faith-based schools that do *not* receive public funds—especially in relation to their ability to express a worldview at variance with that promoted by public schools.

In our first "interlude," we discuss the success of Teen Challenge and other faith-based programs that deal with addictions, and their conflicts with government regulators.

Government has in many cases gone beyond regulation to make use of faith-based organizations, especially to provide services for the homeless and the elderly, for pregnant girls, for young children, and for college students, and—in a cautious and controversial way—for certain pupils in K-12 schools. We review, in chapter 3, the convoluted reasoning that the American courts have used in placing much more severe restrictions on public funding of schools than on other educational services to youth, and recent evidence of change. Efforts to demonstrate that they are not "pervasively sectarian" and thus eligible to receive public funding could create problems for the integrity of faith-based schools and agencies.

---

[15] Berger and Neuhaus, *To Empower People*, 205.

We go on to review, in chapter 4, mechanisms by which government support can be extended to nongovernment organizations, and the problems associated with each. The arrangements for providing public funds to faith-based schools in France, Spain, Germany, and the Netherlands are discussed by way of contrast.

The second interlude discusses "neocorporatism" in the Netherlands and Germany, and the ways in which those political systems have made room for the active participation of religious organizations in providing schooling and early childhood programs.

In chapter 5 we ask whether pressures from government are the whole story in the drift of some of these organizations away from their original vision, or whether there are other influences at work, both external and internal to the organizations themselves that can turn them from their original mission and make them, over time, essentially indistinguishable from secular organizations. In particular, we consider the role of professional norms and training in making the religious mission of such organizations seem unimportant to many of their staff, and the conflicts that arise over whether the norms or the mission should prevail.

Professional norms operate, in part, through incorporation into the regulatory and funding requirements set by government as a result of the efforts of professional associations. Chapter 6 discusses the constraints, including nondiscrimination requirements, that are placed upon the employment practices of faith-based schools and agencies and affect their ability to appoint staff who support their core mission.

The Salvation Army, which has struggled consistently against this pressure to secularize, is the subject of the third interlude.

The influence of government and of professional norms is not always resisted by faith-based organizations. Chapter 7 considers how many become willing collaborators in their own seduction through detachment from their constituencies and through loss of nerve. Research on Catholic schooling in the United States demonstrates the importance of explicit foundational commitments and the community that is formed around them through voluntary participation. Evidence is presented on how nonprofit organizations experience government interference, and on its relationship to the religious activities that they may consider part of their work. Efforts in the Netherlands to renew the distinctiveness of faith-based schooling illustrate some of the considerations that arise in a secularized society.

Finally, chapter 8 identifies government policies, in this and other countries, that have succeeded in ensuring that funding faith-based organizations can result in a genuine partnership and serve the common good. Specific recommendations are offered for how faith-based schools and agencies can protect their integrity as they enter such partnerships.

1

REACHING OUT TO CIVIL SOCIETY

> It is obvious that the trend toward the comprehensive welfare
> state, whether nurtured by directly totalitarian or by demo-
> cratic-humanitarian motives, is a movement towards the
> omnipotent state. . . . The state as universal father *[Allvater]*,
> the state which intervenes in all things, exploiting even the
> inner powers of man (his dispositions and convictions) and
> registering everything and laying claim to everything, trans-
> gresses its allotted sphere.
>
> (Thielicke, *Theological Ethics*)

Challenges to the Welfare State

OVER THE last half century, governments in Western democracies have collected an increased share of national wealth through
taxation, and in turn have distributed it for such nonmilitary purposes as income subsidies, schooling, health care, and many other activities
that in the past were carried out by voluntary efforts, local institutions, and
for-profit organizations. This shift was most dramatic in Britain, which
until World War II had a relatively inactive government compared with its
Continental neighbors.

The consolidation of the British welfare state in the mid-1940s was partly an
extension of the all-pervasive powers assumed by the state in World War II
and partly a response to moderate socialist thinking. In particular, there were
ideological objections to the notion of patronizing, top-down charity and to
its particularism. There were strong calls, instead, for universal entitlement,
progressive taxation, and minimally acceptable standards of service. The balance of responsibility therefore shifted away from the voluntary sector and
onto the state as the main provider of a basic level of welfare in health, education, housing, unemployment benefits, and personal social services.[1]

That a government should be concerned about whether citizens have
access to education and employment and health care and housing and
enough to eat is now generally accepted, though there is nothing like
agreement about the extent to which a government should guarantee any

---

[1] Beckford, "Great Britain," 36.

or all of these. Wide-ranging debate continues about the level of benefits to which such a guarantee might extend. Should every family be guaranteed an apartment, or just a place in a homeless shelter? Should every young person of sufficient ability be guaranteed free elementary, or secondary, or higher education? The first is universal in the Organisation for Economic Cooperation and Development (OECD) nations, the second broadly available to some level in most, the third available in much of Western Europe (though tuitions are rising as the proportion of youth in universities increases), but not in Japan or the United States with their large private university sectors. Should government guarantee employment, or just make available training and counseling for private-sector employment? Or should it simply let the market determine who will work and at what wages? Personal characteristics and the decisions that people make affect their ability to benefit from education, employment, and the other dimensions of successful participation in the society; to what extent should government concern itself with changing the way people are, with how they think and what they value?

We are not concerned here with policy choices about which benefits government should guarantee or to what level, but with the second-order decisions following from almost any level of government concern with social welfare. Should government itself operate the schools and the hospitals, the housing and soup kitchens and counseling centers through which needs are met? Or should it provide funding for private initiatives— whether nonprofit or for-profit—to meet those needs? Or simply enable people in need to shop for a provider through income transfers or vouchers, as they can sometimes do for day care and housing and groceries?

The Inescapable Welfare State

The account of the welfare state in a standard British reference work on political thought is one of the shortest articles and surprisingly casual. Here it is in full:

> The term describes collectively a range of social policies that aim to provide basic services such as health and education according to need, and normally free of charge, through state funding. It is sometimes extended more loosely to areas such as social security in which individuals are legally required to make substantial contributions in order to receive the benefit. The term came into use during the 1940s at a time when (in Britain especially) the role of government in this field was expanding rapidly.
>
> The existence of some form of welfare state is now accepted across most of the political spectrum, and radically challenged only by libertarians, for whom it represents a violation of the rights of those who are taxed to provide its funding (see LIBERTARIANISM). The major point of debate is whether it should

be regarded as a safety-net, establishing a minimum level of welfare below
which no one is allowed to fall, or as an agency of redistribution from rich to
poor, fostering greater social equality. These alternatives broadly mirror the
division between traditional LIBERALISM and SOCIAL DEMOCRACY.[2]

This definition may serve us well enough, if we note that is says nothing
about the *delivery* of the services that are to be provided, emphasizing only
government responsibility for ensuring that (some undefined menu of) services and benefits are generally available. This may be done in different
ways, even within the same political system. The rise of the British welfare
state, for example, was epitomized by the National Health Act 1946, which
took over hundreds of private hospitals (and their endowments) to integrate them into a government-run system.

While the principle of government concern about social welfare may be
generally unchallenged, there are strong objections from various quarters
to government itself providing a full range of services. Some object to the
cost and inefficiency of government programs, to the elaborated procedures and bureaucracy that are required by the need for political accountability, and to the lack of a "bottom-line" and competitive discipline. The
strengths of government provision of social services and schooling are offset by significant weaknesses; European (like American) experience provides many examples of both. These weaknesses notwithstanding, it is next
to impossible to persuade citizens to give up any of the benefits once provided by the welfare state. In Britain, "despite a decade of Thatcherism,
the British Social Attitudes Surveys showed not diminishing, but strongly
growing support for a centralised, tax-financed welfare state." American
government actually grew under Ronald Reagan, all rhetoric to the contrary, and the British welfare state "remained remarkably unrolled-back
thirteen years after Margaret Thatcher took power."[3]

As a result, reformers have increasingly turned to seeking ways to deliver
the publicly guaranteed benefits to which we have all grown accustomed,
but in a manner that avoids the worst effects of the welfare state as we have
come to know them over the past half century.

Bureaucratic Ineffectiveness

There are some things—like administering justice and waging war—that
only government should be allowed to do, and there are other things—
like distributing Social Security checks—that government does efficiently.
Bureaucracy provides "strong integrating pressures for coherent overall

[2] Miller, "Welfare State," 548.
[3] Timmins, *The Five Giants*, 479, 508.

policy; its hierarchical structure brings maximum responsiveness to the day-to-day demands of political chiefs; while its tenure and recruitment rules for permanent officials are designed to minimize the influence of favoritism and political 'pull' in recruitment, dismissal and promotion, at least below the topmost levels."[4] It is inconceivable that any modern state would want to deny itself the advantages provided by a well-organized bureaucracy.

But bureaucracy also has well-known disadvantages. The elaboration of rules and procedures that is of the essence of its rational and routinized approach, to prevent arbitrary actions and favoritism, can choke initiative. The "behavioral codes, established practices, and standard operating procedures . . . lay a heavy weight on the selection, assignment, and promotion of personnel, the procurement process, and the delivery of government services to private citizens. The defensive instincts of bureaucrats, their desire to make what have been called 'declarations of innocence,' may represent one important source of these self-generated, or at least self-reinforced, rules."[5] Civil servants develop "an extremely risk-averse ethos because punishment for mistakes is more certain than advancement for successes, leading to difficulties in motivating innovative behaviour."[6] Activities that require flexibility and on-the-spot responsiveness do not lend themselves to bureaucratic control. Rule-driven teaching and counseling and other forms of "human care of human beings" can be as ineffective as are routine-guided business decisions.

Since at least the mid–nineteenth century critics of bureaucracy have questioned the supposed efficiency and effectiveness of centralized planning and control. Herbert Spencer's judgment in 1853 on what were then comparatively tiny government operations would be echoed by many today: "Strong as it looks at the outset, state-agency perpetually disappoints every one. Puny as are its first stages, private effort daily achieves results that astound the world."[7]

To repeat: bureaucratic codes and procedures serve an important purpose; they are in fact indispensable in a complex modern society. Among other functions, they help to ensure that publicly guaranteed educational and social services are provided universally and that the public funds appropriated to that end are spent as intended. As we will see, even the nonprofit organizations that undertake to provide services at public expense are obliged to take on some of the characteristics of bureaucracy in order to meet their management and reporting obligations. A certain degree of ad-

[4] Hood and Folke Schuppert, *Delivering Public Services*, 15.
[5] Garvey and DiIulio, "Sources of Overregulation," 22–23.
[6] Hood and Folke Schuppert, *Delivering Public Services*, 15.
[7] Spencer, "Over-Legislation," in *Man versus State*, 298.

ministrative elaboration is probably unavoidable. But when impersonality and routinization begin to infect the way the services themselves are rendered, it is likely that they will be rendered ineffectively.

If this were the only concern about government's role in providing education and social services, reformers might be content to propose administrative decentralization, more decision making by those staff who provide the services, and other measures to make government more flexible and responsive. Many of the recent changes in the organization of public education, in this and other countries, have been along these lines, and they have begun to do some good. School-based management, charter schools, and other reforms address these concerns. But there is another set of concerns that they cannot address.

Overstepping the State's Appropriate Limits

There are other critics of the welfare state who see dangers precisely in its effectiveness and are concerned that it has come to trespass upon the role of the civil society. They ask, with sociologist Alan Wolfe, "Will families be able to function well when government assumes some of their most important functions, including the raising of small children? What will happen to individual altruistic instincts if private charity is replaced by collective benefits administered impersonally?"[8] A German ethicist with direct experience of a totalitarian regime warned, after World War II, about "the general movement towards social perfection and its political expression in the welfare state. This movement is an alarming phenomenon even from a purely political standpoint inasmuch as the totalitarian state and the democratic state are both caught up in it, each in its own way: the totalitarian state because it necessarily seeks to penetrate every sphere of life and hence to take over the care of children, the chronically ill, the sick, and the aged; the democratic state because it hopes to validate itself from a humanitarian standpoint as the representative of social concern."[9]

The concern that government will overstep the limits of its appropriate role and begin to have an inappropriate influence upon its citizens is most strongly felt with respect to education. Put another way, popular schooling is the instrument that an activist government is most tempted to employ to bring about social transformation and that, having started to use, it is most likely to use ever more deliberately and extensively.[10]

[8] Wolfe, *Whose Keeper?* 22.
[9] Thielicke, *Theological Ethics*, 289.
[10] This is the central theme of Glenn, *Myth of Common School*.

This fear of state overreaching is a theme reaching back two centuries, expressed in the horrified reaction to events under the French Revolution and especially the Jacobin program of remolding citizens through schooling. German statesman Wilhelm von Humboldt wrote that "the State must wholly refrain from every attempt to operate directly or indirectly on the morals and character of the nation . . . everything calculated to promote such a design, and particularly all special supervision of education, religion, sumptuary laws, etc., lies wholly outside the limits of its legitimate activity."[11] Humboldt, in turn, influenced John Stuart Mill, who famously wrote that "a general State education is a mere contrivance for moulding people to be exactly like one another; and as the mould in which it casts them is that which pleases the predominant power in the government . . . in proportion as it is efficient and successful, it establishes a despotism over the mind, leading by natural tendency to one over the body."[12]

Efforts to use popular schooling as an instrument of government—and resistance to such use—is a theme with a long history, reaching back the anti-Huguenot measures of Louis XIV and to the "enlightened despots" of Austria and Prussia in the eighteenth century. More recently, government-provided social services, and especially those that entail counseling or efforts to change life-orientations (such as attitudes toward work or sexual behavior), have raised many of the same issues. In both cases, the state is in effect absorbing into itself the traditional value-shaping mission of churches and other institutions of the civil society and is tempted to do so in a fashion that drives those competitors in value-formation from the field. It is a natural progression from deciding that the state is competent to shape virtuous citizens through mandatory schooling to concluding that competing forms of socialization pose too great a risk. After all, why—by this logic—should the state tolerate competitors to its universalistic claims?

It is equally seductive to seek, as John Dewey put it in 1908, "to converge all the instrumentalities of the social arts, of law, education, economics and political science upon the construction of intelligent methods of improving the common lot."[13] Experts in human improvement, those with what Dewey and others liked to call "organized intelligence," would work through the state to guide social and individual development. In place of the wasteful bungling of civil society institutions, working often at cross purposes with one another, humanity would enter a new era of progress and harmony. Educators and social planners would lead the way "toward a socialized cooperative democracy," Dewey wrote during the depression,

---

[11] Humboldt, *Limits of State Action*, 81.
[12] Mill, *On Liberty*, 98.
[13] Dewey, "Intelligence and Morals," 45.

once they had rid themselves of "this incubus" of control by laypeople, noneducators, nonexperts.[14]

Herbert Spencer noted the tendency of government to see itself as all-competent, quoting a "Cabinet Minister who, addressing his constituents, speaks slightingly of the doings of philanthropic societies and religious bodies to help the poor, and says that 'the whole of the people of his country ought to look upon this work as being their own work.' "[15] Or, as some might now put it, "it takes a whole village to raise a child"! This temptation is hard to resist for those who believe themselves endowed with an extra measure of insight into how individuals and society as a whole could be improved. "It is not easy even for a democratic state to be content with a minimal role and to accept only the essentially negative task of restraining evil and preserving external order. The state is more inclined to press on to positive ideas which will sustain life and provide an intellectual under-girding for society. Nor is it easy to say whether these are legitimate duties or dangerous temptations, or both."[16]

So prevalent has the assumption of government omnicompetence become that an official of Catholic Charities, in telling a reporter that there had been "a remarkable upsurge in the number of donations and volunteers for the organization's work with the homeless, drug addicts, and others in need," expressed some regret about this turn of events. "This reflects a failure of government," he said. "In a more just society, these needs would be handled through government programs."[17]

Government and Education

Concern to extend the role of government into every area of education is to some extent related to—or at least justified by—a belief that secularization of consciousness and loosening of family and community bonds are inevitable processes under conditions of modernity, and that therefore the state must for its own protection seek to provide secular alternatives to the socializing effects of religious and community institutions, and of the family.

As societies become more diverse in worldview, the task of creating a common ground that is somehow above the squabbling seems all the more urgent, and government's pretensions to represent that higher ground of neutrality among all its citizens translates into the claim that government-

---

[14] Dewey, "Toward National System," 358.
[15] Spencer, "The New Toryism," in *Man versus State*, 25.
[16] Thielicke, *Theological Ethics*, 261.
[17] Neuhaus, foreword to *Welfare Reformed*, xix.

operated schools and social agencies are somehow neutral in contrast with those operated by religious or secular organizations. The myth that secularism is a neutral position between belief and unbelief is widely accepted, despite its inherent absurdity. The controversies over public school curriculum and over content standards in the United States reflect the fact that many parents and other citizens do not find their own values reflected in what those schools are teaching—and sometimes find values opposed to their own being taught to their children.[18]

There is widespread concern in the United States and other Western nations about what seems to be widespread moral relativism and irresponsible behavior, especially among youth, and this has led to the demand that schools do more to inculcate an understanding of the behavior that society expects and depends upon, and the underlying dispositions that make it second nature. Efforts to include moral development among the measurable standards by which schools are evaluated have, however, met widespread resistance among parent groups and conservative policy institutes. Critics of "outcome-based education" (OBE) insist that many of the legitimate goals of education should not be the concern of government, but only of parents and those to whom they entrust their children.[19]

Not that schools should limit their mission to value-neutral instruction! While much of the anti-OBE rhetoric has insisted that values are the exclusive concern of parents, in fact most want the school their children attend to make the development of character an important part of its mission. That does not mean that these parents want government to dictate what forms the development of character will take. Parents tend to make a distinction between their children's school, even though it may be government-operated, and government itself. They want to trust the school—it would be hard to send their children off each morning if they did not—but that trust does not generally extend to the educational system of which it is a part. New social movements based upon identity and lifestyle have found it easy to influence centralized decision-making into adopting their agendas for education.

Support for charter schools—independent public schools—reflects a growing awareness that conflict over the content of schooling is inevitable under a monopoly system. Your agenda seems virtuous to you, as mine seems virtuous to me, but education should not be imposed on my children in a form that undermines how I am seeking to raise them, just because you have been more successful in promoting your agenda. Majorities do not rule, under our system, when fundamental rights are at stake, nor do influential minorities. The Supreme Court addressed this question eloquently in one of its most important decisions: "The fundamental theory

[18] Glenn, "Religion, Textbooks."
[19] See Glenn, "Outcome-Based Education."

of liberty upon which all governments in this Union repose excludes any general power of the state to standardize its children. . . . The child is not the mere creature of the state; those who nurture him and direct his destiny have the right, coupled with the high duty, to recognize and prepare him for additional obligations."[20]

Government may turn to nonprofit organizations to provide services "in areas where direct government control is held to be undesirable"— broadcasting is a good example—because they involve the formation of opinions and values, especially if there are deep divisions in the society over what worldview should be promoted.[21] This is why most industrialized democracies have recognized that a government monopoly on tax-supported schooling is inconsistent with freedom. It is also why those who would remake society through changing opinions and values are always tempted to make use of compulsory schooling to that end, and why educational freedom has not been achieved without a struggle that in some cases extended over many decades.

Thielicke reminds us of Luther's insistence that "the state must not concern itself with man's salvation. . . . the state must limit itself to matters of secular order, to life and property, and leave the soul alone. To use the terms of our present discussion, the whole man is not entrusted to it. Wherever the state attempts to do more than this, it must be resisted."[22]

The State's Appropriate Role

Humboldt, Mill, and others who warned against the use of schooling as an instrument of state influence upon the opinions of future citizens were not necessarily opposed to active government concern to promote universal schooling. Humboldt would become one of the shapers of the Prussian educational system greatly admired by American and French educational reformers in the 1830s. Mill endorsed government responsibility to ensure that children were educated, without concluding that government should therefore be the educator:

> Is it not almost a self-evident axiom, that the State should require and compel the education, up to a certain standard, of every human being who is born its citizen? . . . if the parent does not fulfil this obligation, the State ought to see it fulfilled, at the charge, so far as possible, of the parent. . . . If the government would make up its mind to require for every child a good education, it might save itself the trouble of providing one. It might leave to parents to obtain the education where and how they pleased, and content itself with helping to pay the school fees of the poorer classes of children, and defraying the entire school

---

[20] *Pierce v. Society of the Sisters of the Holy Names of Jesus and Mary*, 268 U.S. 510 (1923).
[21] Hood et al., "Institutional Arrangements," 61.
[22] Thielicke, *Theological Ethics*, 269.

expenses of those who have no one else to pay for them. The objections which are urged with reason against State education do not apply to the enforcement of education by the State, but to the State's taking upon itself to direct that education, which is a totally different thing. . . . if the country contains a sufficient number of persons qualified to provide education under government auspices, the same persons would be able and willing to give an equally good education on the voluntary principle, under the assurance of remuneration afforded by a law rendering education compulsory, combined with State aid to those unable to defray the expense.[23]

As we will see in the chapters that follow, defining the right balance between the autonomy that allows schools or social agencies to function with sufficient coherence to be effective, on the one hand, and provisions for public accountability, on the other, is more complex than Mill imagined. We now have many decades of experience with different arrangements, and these vary considerably among countries with generally similar political and social conditions.[24] Much can be learned from this experience; it is therefore curious that the debates (for example, over the effects of allowing parents to choose schools) tend to offer, for and against, abstract scenarios that cannot be tested empirically.

There are good reasons for government to continue an active role—perhaps even more active, in some respects, than at present—in ensuring that educational and social services are adequate and accessible, even as it turns to civil society institutions to deliver those services. Nor is it necessary that an active government role trench severely upon the distinctive character of faith-based schools and agencies, provided that the limits of government's agenda are clearly and explicitly set. As we will see in chapters 5 through 7, the greater danger may be that those working in the schools and agencies lose their nerve and their sense of having a distinctive mission, surrendering to secular norms and assumptions while under no compulsion to do so.

Those who wish to expand the role of civil society institutions should not be enemies of effective government. Even Herbert Spencer, one of the most powerful critics of overextended government, insisted, "Far from contending for a *laissez-faire* policy in the sense which the phrase commonly suggests, I have contended for a more active control of the kind distinguishable as negatively regulative. One of the reasons I have urged for excluding State-action from other spheres, is, that it may become more efficient within its proper sphere. And I have argued that the wretched performance of its duties within its proper sphere continues, because its time is chiefly spent over imaginary duties."[25]

[23] Mill, *On Liberty*, 97–99.
[24] Glenn, "Common Standards."
[25] Spencer, "Specialized Administration," in *Man versus State*, 480.

Government's role in generating revenues equitably from the entire society, protecting the interests of the poor and vulnerable in the name of justice, promoting common standards (carefully!), and stimulating activity where it has not arisen spontaneously is entirely consistent with a vigorous civil society. Osborne and Gaebler, while calling for a larger role of the "third sector" of nonprofit organizations in providing services, point out that "the public sector tends to be better, for instance, at policy management, regulation, ensuring equity, preventing discrimination or exploitation, ensuring continuity and stability of services, and ensuring social cohesion."[26] They describe the appropriate role of the democratic process and thus of government as "steering" rather than "rowing" the boat. Government, they urge, should set general directions but leave it up to the third sector—the institutions of civil society—to implement them in a variety of ways. Or, as Berger and Neuhaus put it, "the goal of public policy in a pluralistic society is to sustain as many particularities as possible, in the hope that most people will accept, discover, or devise one that fits."[27]

What the Civil Society Strategy Is Not

The proposal to assign a larger role to the mediating structures of civil society, to those associations, institutions, and informal networks that are the "value-generating and value-maintaining agencies in society,"[28] should not be confused with other policy proposals that seem superficially to move in the same direction. Among these are *administrative decentralization, market strategies*, and *organizational flexibility*.

Administrative Decentralization

Decentralization of decision making to the public school or agency level has often been proposed as a remedy for bureaucratic deadlock, but it is a remedy that does not work with sufficient power. Several decades of experience with school-based management within existing structures have made it clear that a more fundamental shift of perspective is needed. This should not be surprising, since the environments within which schools function affect them profoundly, and these environments include not only a social class and physical context but also a context of authority and accountability. There is reason to believe that "the freer schools are from external control—the more autonomous, the less subject to bureaucratic constraints—

[26] Osborne and Gaebler, *Reinventing Government*, 45.
[27] Berger and Neuhaus, *To Empower People*, 206.
[28] Ibid., 163.

the more likely they are to have effective organizations"[29]—though of course some autonomous schools are highly ineffective!

Administrative decentralization may lead to efficiencies by shortening the hierarchical lines of control, but it leaves in place the subordinate situation of the school as a unit within a large organization constrained by bureaucratic rules, rewards and sanctions, and culture. There is a fundamental difference between *decentralization* within the institutional structures of the welfare state, and true *subsidiarity* that places primarily responsibility for "the human care of human beings" upon civil society institutions, with government playing a watchdog role on behalf of the vulnerable, and subsidizing services through its ability to raise and distribute revenue from the entire society. Either decentralization or subsidiarity could be characterized as measures promoting "autonomy," but the advantages of the first are limited to the greater efficiency that decentralization may bring, while promoting subsidiarity is intended to change the *nature* of the services provided.

Civil society institutions are able to have a more powerful effect in shaping character and giving direction to lives than can institutions that must comply with bureaucratic rationality. The movement toward greater autonomy of educational institutions in most Western democracies should be understood as an attempt to preserve the gains of the welfare state while drawing upon the energies and the freely chosen commitments characteristic of the associations of civil society. Their significance goes beyond efficiency to address the heart of the educational enterprise.

An extensive review of the research on school-based management (SBM) concluded that "the enthusiasm for SBM, expressed in hundreds of articles and papers, does not, on the whole, stem from positive student achievement results. . . . [The] conclusion of this review is that there is no collective evidence of positive effects."[30] This is not to say that decentralization may not, under some circumstances, have positive effects by bringing decision making closer to the point where accurate information is available and decisions must be implemented, but "teachers themselves appear to be an unlikely source of instructionally oriented reform in schools,"[31] except under exceptional circumstances. The same may be said of government social workers and others who have accommodated themselves to working within a bureaucratic structure that relieves them of responsibility for exercising creative problem-solving.

Decentralization of an ineffective monopolistic system—like a large public school district—may simply protect the lower levels from any pressure to change and become more effective.

[29] Chubb and Moe, *Politics, Markets*, 19, 187.
[30] Summers and Johnson, "Effects," 76.
[31] Hannaway, "Management Decentralization," 100.

Market Strategies

There has been a considerable vogue, over the last twenty years, for introducing competition into public services, with or without privatization of ownership. Civil servants (including teachers) would, it is contended, behave very differently if they were forced to attract and to satisfy "customers" for their services, and those who were not able to do so would quickly go out of business.

This is not the place to argue the merits of competition and privatization in education and other services; indeed, a vast literature has grown up around this debate.[32] Privatization of spheres of activity like education and social work and youth services that had been absorbed into the welfare state is in some sense a precondition for enlisting the energies of civil society in solving problems that government has not been able to address successfully. New forms of competition are likely to result from such a devolution of responsibility from government to mediating structures, and this could produce some efficiencies. What we are calling the civil society strategy is not primarily concerned with vindicating the market, however, nor does it assume that market forces should be allowed free rein in education and social services.

The conviction behind the civil society strategy is, rather, that "mediating structures . . . are the principal expressions of the real values and the real needs of people in our society. They are, for the most part, the people-sized institutions. Public policy should recognize, respect, and, where possible, empower these institutions"[33] and, in so doing, will ensure that social services and education are provided more effectively. Market forces, as Alan Wolfe has pointed out, are incapable of generating the sense of moral obligation that is essential to good education and effective social services.

Organizational Flexibility

Political scientists John Chubb and Terry Moe, in a controversial book, argued that the ineffectiveness of most urban public schools is a consequence of their embeddedness in a spider's web of regulations and reporting requirements. It is inherent in the democratic control of education that many different groups—apart from parents, who have no special rights—seek to have their own agendas reflected in curriculum and school practices. As a result,

[32] See, for example, James and Levin, *Comparing Schools*.
[33] Berger and Neuhaus, *To Empower People*, 164.

detailed formal specifications in legislative mandates and administrative regulations are voluminously imposed on all concerned, so that the schools' scope for discretionary action is sharply narrowed—and the discretion that remains is then insulated from political control through extensive reliance on civil service, tenure, (nominal) professionalism, and other structural means. Schools are thus subject to democratic control, but they are purposely made difficult to control. Schools are filled with "professionals," but their personnel are systematically and intentionally denied the discretion they need to act as professionals. Schools give the appearance of substantial autonomy, but what they have is insulation without discretion, which is really not autonomy at all.[34]

The constraining effects of politically generated and bureaucratically mediated expectations are exacerbated by the unionization that has come to be more prevalent in public-sector employment than in manufacturing, much less in nongovernmental services. "Unions do not really favor school autonomy," Chubb and Moe point out. "They favor teacher autonomy, which is very different indeed. They want teachers to be free from control by organizational superiors, including the principals who are charged with running the schools. Their pursuit of autonomy thus leads them to wage a war of formalization against principals."

Bureaucratization will be most elaborated in relation to schools that serve the most vulnerable children, since government multiplies its efforts to protect, through regulation, pupils who are handicapped, poor, or members of minority groups. "Precisely where the problems are the greatest—in poor urban areas—and thus where strong leadership, professionalism, clear missions, and other aspects of effective organization are most desperately needed, public authority will be exercised to ensure that schools are highly bureaucratized"[35] and thus ineffective.

Nor is this problem limited to schools; it is in part to escape the overregulation of government operations and personnel procedures, as we will see in chapter 4, that states have increasingly turned to contracting and other arrangements with nonprofit organizations to provide services.[36] It has become apparent that the reforms that began in the United States in the Progressive Era, early in this century, have led to unanticipated consequences: the professionalization of administration, the belief that there is "one best system"[37] that those who have received the appropriate training will infallibly establish and maintain, a system so perfect that it would be irresponsible to allow inferior alternatives. This insistence upon a single

---

[34] Chubb and Moe, *Politics, Markets,* 45.

[35] Ibid., 49, 65.

[36] See Hill, Pierce, and Guthrie, *Reinventing Public Education.*

[37] Tyack, *The One Best System.*

model, elaborately regulated, has led to rigidification of the social service and educational systems.

There is certainly a congruence between the concern to bring a greater measure of organizational flexibility to schools and social agencies, on the one hand, and what we have called the civil society strategy, on the other. Reliance upon nonprofit organizations and voluntary associations—including nonpublic schools—to play a more important role in meeting human needs of all kinds, within the guarantees underwritten by the state, would undoubtedly lead to a less sclerotic system of provision than does the present quasi monopoly. As a study of faith-based social service programs in late-Victorian Britain points out,

> It was the need to be always trying out new approaches, to see which would work most effectively, which gave these private charities their greatest advantage over blanket systems of state welfare. They were able to initiate new approaches which could be quickly abandoned if they were unsuccessful, or expanded to meet a growing demand. It was within the sphere of the evangelical charities that social work was first developed as a profession, together with the idea that training was necessary for both professional and voluntary charity workers.[38]

But, as we will see, the civil society strategy is concerned not only with organizational forms and dynamics—the theme of Chubb and Moe's book—but also with the spirit and the values that may animate schools or social agencies. What they do and how they treat those entrusted to them is, for good or ill, the expression of deeply held beliefs about human life. Thielicke points out that "the state—if it is not to be an ideological and totalitarian state—dare not have a specific view of man."[39] But arguably a school or social agency that does *not* have such a view, shared by all or most of its participants, cannot be fully effective.

The Promised Contribution of Voluntary Associations

It has been suggested that the United States and other industrialized nations are "in the midst of a global 'associational revolution.' "[40] Through calling upon—and funding—nonprofit agencies and organizations to provide an ever-increasing range of public services, government is able to maintain the expansive dynamic of a welfare state based upon entitlements without a concomitant (and politically undesirable) expansion of its own staff, and to address sensitive problems that government officials are reluc-

---

[38] Whelan, *The Corrosion of Charity*, 17.
[39] Thielicke, *Theological Ethics*, 259.
[40] Salamon and Anheier, *The Emerging Nonprofit Sector*, xi.

tant to touch, for fear of criticism. For example, "Government funding of nonprofit agencies socializes the risk associated with these problems but maintains community delivery mechanisms. Since these social problems are sensitive and sometimes controversial issues that require intervention in the family and individual life, the use of nonprofit organizations is seen as consistent with protecting the privacy and freedom of families and individuals from government interference."[41]

There is of course nothing new about voluntary associations providing a wide range of social services and education; after all, that was the norm throughout the nineteenth century, and nongovernment organizations have never ceased to play a major role in countries spared from totalitarian rule. Today, these include not only independent schools (more than twenty-six thousand in the United States) but hospitals, clinics, community organizations, advocacy groups, day care centers, relief organizations, nursing homes, homeless shelters, family counseling agencies, environmental groups and many other forms on nongovernmental activity that meet social needs. This "third sector" has been expanding rapidly as policymakers have lost confidence in the ability of direct government interventions to cope successfully with "the interrelated challenges of persistent poverty, environmental degradation, and social change,"[42] as well as schools that are less effective than those of most of our trading partners.

A strong impetus was given to government contracting with nonprofit associations and agencies in the United States, during the 1960s, by the need to get "community action" programs going quickly in thousands of communities across the country, and by amendments to federal legislation that encouraged states to purchase social services rather than attempt to provide them directly. As a result, "almost 60 percent of all social service providers are nonprofit organizations. These organizations offer child day care, counseling, information and referral services, family services, adoption assistance, and a host of similar activities."[43] Federal legislation in 1967 and again in 1988 called for nonprofit organizations to supply job training, remedial education, job finding, and child care at public expense. "Indeed, when public officials—state, local, and federal—want to provide social services today, they expect to seek out nonprofit organizations to provide them."[44] The federal reform of the welfare system in 1996—as we will see in chapter 4—went even further to ensure that faith-based agencies could participate in social service programs funded by government.

---

[41] Smith and Lipsky, *Nonprofits for Hire*, 18.
[42] Salamon and Anheier, *The Emerging Nonprofit Sector*, xi.
[43] Ibid., 101.
[44] Smith and Lipsky, *Nonprofits for Hire*, 160.

It did seem, for some decades, as though the ever-expanding reach of the welfare state might make nongovernmental provision of services redundant and inefficient. In the countries with Communist regimes, there was a largely successful drive to eliminate associations independent of state and Party.[45] In the West, they were expected to wither away spontaneously as society evolved.

Announcement of the impending death of voluntary associations and institutions, however, was premature. Alan Wolfe has pointed out the importance, to a healthy society, of a sense of moral obligation, nourished by a variety of voluntary organizations as it cannot be by government provision of social services, much less by reliance upon the market to provide those functions. This "third sector . . . is continually being rediscovered because it serves as a symbol of obligations to strangers."[46]

It was his recognition of the dynamic and sustaining role of civil society associations that led Humboldt, two centuries ago, to write that "the best efforts of the State should . . . aim at bringing men into such a condition by means of freedom that associations would arise with greater ease, and so take the place of political regulations in these and many kinds of similar instances."[47] This theme was reiterated by Tocqueville in his account of American society for a European audience that had grown—he argued— too dependent upon the state to solve every problem. In France, where Jacobin excesses had reinforced ancien régime absolutism, he warned, "it is the government alone which has inherited all the prerogatives snatched from families, corporations, and individuals; so the sometimes oppressive but often conservative strength of a small number of citizens has been succeeded by the weakness of all."[48] As a result, there was no sphere within which freedom and civic virtue could be practiced in the interest of that "social prosperity" which depends upon "the collective force of the citizens," not "the authority of the government."[49] "What political power," Tocqueville asked,

> could ever carry on the vast multitude of lesser undertakings which associations daily enable American citizens to control? . . . The more government takes the place of associations, the more will individuals lose the idea of form-

---

[45] Even under the most consistent of the "real socialism" regimes, that in East Germany, provision of kindergartens and elderly residences was to some extent left to church groups, and under several other Communist regimes church and other groups that posed no threat to the regime were allowed to provide a variety of carefully regulated services—though not education (except for the training of their clergy). See Glenn, *Educational Freedom*.

[46] Wolfe, *Whose Keeper?* 86–87.

[47] Humboldt, *Limits of State Action*, 92.

[48] Tocqueville, *Democracy in America*, 15.

[49] Ibid., 90.

ing associations and need the government to come to their help. That is a vicious circle of cause and effect. . . . The morals and intelligence of a democratic people would be in as much danger as its commerce and industry if ever a government wholly usurped the place of private associations. Feelings and ideas are renewed, the heart enlarged, and the understanding developed only by the reciprocal action of men one upon another. . . . If men are to remain civilized or to become civilized, the art of association must develop and improve among them at the same speed as equality of conditions spreads.[50]

It is quite in the spirit of Humboldt and of Tocqueville that Wolfe asks in turn, "When government is relied on to furnish rules of moral obligation, will it weaken the very social ties that make government possible in the first place? . . . if the assumption by government of moral responsibility is seen as subtracting from a sense of personal responsibility for the fate of others once associated with the intimate realm of society, the problems of the political approach to moral obligation begin to seem more serious."[51]

Wolfe makes a distinction between ensuring that benefits, services, and protections are provided and actually providing them directly. "Whether government can act as a giver of care, especially those forms of care we associate with families and communities, is another matter entirely."[52]

Although Wolfe believes that the "third sector" institutions of the civil society are essential, he has grave concerns about their ability to stand up to the all-invasive market, and the individualistic, self-gratifying mentality that it encourages. "Future trends will not be so positive if the market continues to grow as a moral code for individual decision-making."[53] Reliance upon either the state or the market to define and to meet our moral obligations has the effect of further incapacitating us "as moral agents capable of finding our own ways to resolve the paradoxes of modernity. We need civil society—families, communities, friendship networks, solidaristic workplace ties, voluntarism, spontaneous groups and movements—not to reject, but to complete the project of modernity."[54]

Others, while taking a rather less pessimistic view of the status of voluntary associations in the United States, share Wolfe's conviction that they play an essential role in a healthy society. "Social structures," political scientist Stephen Monsma writes, "give the sense of purpose and meaning all persons crave. Typically, it is within families, religious congregations, and neighborhoods that persons find meaning and purpose in life. . . . persons

---

[50] Ibid., 515–17.
[51] Wolfe, *Whose Keeper?* 109.
[52] Ibid., 129.
[53] Ibid., 94.
[54] Ibid., 20.

find a basic sense of morality in the groups within which they live."[55] This is why schools that have a religious character are likely to be more effective at creating the sort of community that can support learning than are schools whose basis for attendance is the happenstance of geography. This led sociologist James Coleman to suggest that "policies which would bring about expansion of choice should contain provisions that encourage the growth of social structures that can provide the social capital important to a school. Policies . . . that would facilitate the creation of schools by institutions in which parents of prospective students are already involved [such as their churches] exemplify this."[56] Similarly, David Hargreaves has argued that Muslim or Evangelical schools in Britain—not presently included in the public funding received by more established denominational schools—"enhance social cohesion within a sub-community (e.g., of a shared religion or culture) and in a pluralistic society there can be no national cohesion that fails to foster and build upon more local and specific forms of social cohesion."[57] Burke's "little platoons," in short.

Ethicist Helmut Thielicke takes a similar position, arguing that under some circumstances that arise in social welfare the essential "service can be rendered only in a way which the state as such does not have at its command. There are inner aspects to such complete helplessness which require the kind of aid which the state, with its impersonal machinery and its lack of message, is simply unable to give. The state . . . should delegate as many tasks as possible, leaving as much initiative as possible to independent agencies and institutions, and providing as little direct aid as possible."[58]

Nor is this a view held only by political thinkers; survey research shows that Americans in general support policies that rely upon nonprofit organizations. One careful study found that "46 percent of respondents said they had a great deal of confidence in 'charities providing health or social services,' compared with only 21 percent who said the same for business, 28 percent who said this about the United States Congress, and 22 percent who felt as much confidence in organized labor." In other research, "only one person in five (21 percent) thought that 'spending more money on government welfare programs' would help a lot, while 42 percent of the public thought it would not help at all. Faced directly with the comparison between voluntary organizations and government programs, moreover, 72 percent of the public said they agreed with the statement 'Private charities are generally more effective than government programs.' "[59]

[55] Monsma, *When Sacred and Secular Mix*, 17–18.
[56] Coleman and Hoffer, *Public and Private*, 243. For a discussion of the policy implications of this suggestion, see Glenn, "Free Schools."
[57] Hargreaves, "Diversity, Choice, and Excellence," 20.
[58] Thielicke, *Theological Ethics*, 308–9.
[59] Wuthnow, "Tocqueville's Question Reconsidered," 301.

It is for this reason, presumably, that in all of the countries studied by Salamon and Anheier, nonprofit organizations were not simply used to provide public services when government provision was inadequate, but were deliberately favored as a matter of policy. As we will see in the discussion of "neocorporatism," Germany and the Netherlands go so far as to forbid government from providing certain services if a suitable nonprofit is available to do so.[60]

Voluntary Associations under Pressure

It is true, however, that powerful changes have been reshaping nonprofit organizations providing services to the public. The role of volunteers has become marginalized by the growing importance of professional norms and training, as we will see in chapter 5. Hiring professional staff increases costs exponentially, while also introducing norms of service that may be in conflict with the founding principles of the agency. Nongovernment schools feel constant pressure to expand their programs and resources to match those of local public schools. Most cannot hope to match the salaries paid to public school teachers. In 1993–94, the average teacher salary in nonpublic schools was $21,898, compared with $34,189 in public schools; in "conservative Christian" schools, the average teacher salary was only $15,823.[61]

Government funding has become essential to the operations of many nonprofit social agencies. It takes many different forms, including

> direct payments for a specified use; project grants such as training or research funds; high-risk loans, low-interest loans, and guarantees of loans from private lenders; insurance at favorable premiums; in-kind donations of goods such as used furniture or surplus food; free use of government property, facilities, or equipment; free assistance by government personnel to perform certain tasks; free instruction, consultation, or training by government personnel; reduced postal rates; low-interest bonds for capital improvements; educational vouchers and child-care certificates; student scholarships, grants, and fellowships; and tax credits, deductions, and I.R.C. § 501(c)(3) exempt status enabling receipt of tax-deductible contributions. [In addition] several governmental programs confer aid to individuals . . . child-care certificates for low-income parents, federal tax credits for the child-care expenses of working parents, special-education services for handicapped students, the G.I. Bill and federal guaranteed loans for post-secondary education students, and state income-tax

---

[60] Salamon and Anheier, *The Emerging Nonprofit Sector.*
[61] National Center for Education Statistics, *Private Schools,* 93.

deductions for parents paying tuition to primary and secondary schools. These indirect forms of aid can carry with them financial assistance regulation of religious institutions.[62]

Chapter 4 discusses the effect upon institutional autonomy of the "strings" that come attached to government support.

The Religious Factor

Although Wolfe refers in general terms to institutions of the civil society, the reality is that a high proportion of those that provide social services or education are religious.[63] Of the 26,091 nonpublic schools in the United States in 1993–94, only 5,563 were "nonsectarian," and 1,290 of the latter were special education schools supported largely with public funds.[64] In other countries as well, "almost universally, the major founders of NPOs [nonprofit organizations] are organized religions or other ideological groups rather than individual entrepreneurs." Their primary objectives are religious—"to maximize faith or adherents rather than monetary profits"— and an emphasis upon education, family services, and health care provide opportunities to "foster taste formation, socialization, and group identification." Subsidized with funding and volunteer or near-volunteer staffing by their sponsoring churches or other religious organizations, "they have a cost advantage over for-profit firms and can even compete effectively with government."[65]

It is thus by no means a matter of historical accident that a high proportion of the nongovernmental schools and social agencies in most countries are religious in nature, even if sometimes only residually. Their religious character in fact provides them with certain real advantages, in addition to the motivation to provide services that are not financially rewarding. "For many that is what binds constituencies to them in support of their programs, serves as a motivating and inspiring force for their staffs, and forms an integral part of their frequent successes with clients or students."[66]

The growing interest in a partnership between government and faith-based social service organizations is based upon a sense that they can reach their clients at a level and with an effectiveness that secular "treatment-

[62] Esbeck, "Constitutional Case."
[63] Wolfe is not alone in minimizing the role of faith-based institutions. One of the best surveys of the role and potential of nonprofit organizations in the United States, Smith and Lipsky, *Nonprofits for Hire*, scarcely mentions the religious factor.
[64] National Center for Education Statistics, *Private Schools*, 57.
[65] James, *Nonprofit Sector*, 4–6.
[66] Monsma, *When Sacred and Secular Mix*, 192.

oriented" programs cannot match. After all, "no bureaucracy, and no amount of money, can buy the reformation of morals that is desperately needed"[67] by many of those served by social service agencies. Religiously motivated organizations can press the demand for such reformation in ways that governmental agencies and those nonprofits that model themselves on bureaucratic impersonality cannot. The "third sector" of private, nonprofit organizations "tends to be best at performing tasks that generate little or no profit, demand compassion and commitment to individuals, require extensive trust on the part of customers or clients, need hands-on, personal attention . . . and involve the enforcement of moral codes and individual responsibility for behavior."[68]

The public policy advantages of making use of religious organizations to deliver social (and educational services) have been well described by Monsma, whose work will be cited frequently in the chapters that follow. He notes that "government can make use of and build on the sense of dedication, empathy, and closeness to the people being served that tends to mark the workers in religiously based programs." In addition, "religious associations have a basis on which to build a bond or sense of trust and to motivate persons with whom they are working that governmental and other secularly based agencies lack."[69]

Some of the most forceful advocacy for giving religious institutions a larger public role has been by African-American social thinkers like Stephen Carter and Glenn Loury. Loury is critical of the positions of both Right and Left on the appropriate policy response to urban poverty and social disintegration. "Both points of view," Loury argues,

> suggest that behavioral problems in the ghetto, or anywhere else for that matter, can be cured from without by changing government policy, by getting the incentives right. Both smack of a mechanistic determinism wherein the mysteries of human motivation are susceptible to calculated intervention. Both have difficulty explaining why some poor minority communities show a much lower incidence of these behavioral problems than others, and are apparently less influenced by the same objective economic forces. . . . They fail to engage questions of personal morality, of character and values, and of moral leadership in the public sphere. Politicians and social scientists have had little to say in public about what is wrong with the ways people in a particular community are living, and what ways of life are better for them and their children.

Perhaps, indeed, politicians and social scientists would not do much good if they tried to give advice to poor people. Loury suggests that "we

---

[67] Olasky, *Renewing American Compassion*, 24.
[68] Osborne and Gaebler, *Reinventing Government*, 46.
[69] Monsma, *Positive Neutrality*, 257–58.

are going to have to look to the nongovernmental agencies of moral and cultural development in particular communities to take on some of the burden of promoting positive behavioral change. In every community there are agencies of moral and cultural development that seek to shape the ways in which individuals conceive of their duties to themselves, their obligations to each other, and their responsibilities before God. The family and the church are primary among these. These are the natural sources of legitimate moral teaching—indeed, the only sources. If these institutions are not restored, the behavioral problems of the ghetto will not be overcome." Loury contends that "reports of successful efforts at reconstruction in ghetto communities invariably reveal a religious institution, or set of devout believers, at the center of the effort."[70]

Similarly, the pressure for some means of public funding of faith-based schools is based not only upon a desire to respect the rights of parents but also upon growing research evidence that these schools do an especially good job with pupils who are at some risk of failure. One important study found, for example, that "the achievement of students in Catholic high schools was less dependent on family background and personal circumstances than was true in the public sector."[71] Another reported, "The achievement growth benefits of Catholic school attendance are especially strong for students who are in one way or another disadvantaged: lower socioeconomic status, black, or Hispanic. . . . The dropout rates from Catholic schools are strikingly lower than those from public schools or other private schools. This reduced dropout rate holds both for those who show no signs of problems as sophomores and for those who as sophomores are academically or disciplinarily at risk of dropping out."[72]

The effectiveness of these schools cannot be explained simply by structural and other factors; it derives directly, in part, from their religious character. "The belief system of the Catholic high school infuses the basic organization of the school and is regularly acted out in its daily life. . . . organizational coherence results. The structure and the activities that occur in such places can be interpreted and understood within the context of the prevailing belief system. Life within such a school makes sense to its members," and that makes the school effective in teaching academics and in developing character.[73]

It is more difficult to document comparisons of agencies than of schools, but Amy Sherman has described a number of urban social ministries of an Evangelical inspiration that seek to render these services that are beyond

---

[70] Loury, "Professors and the Poor," 210–13.
[71] Bryk, Lee, and Holland, *Catholic Schools*, 57.
[72] Coleman and Hoffer, *Public and Private*, 213.
[73] Bryk, Lee, and Holland, *Catholic Schools*, 145.

the competency of government, calling them by the biblical term *restorers*.[74] She contends that these programs, "unlike most government agencies, many secular programs, and even some well-intentioned but misguided churches, treat needy people personally, flexibly, and creatively. RESTORERS build friendships with the disadvantaged while addressing people's physical, emotional, intellectual, and spiritual needs. They challenge "can't-do-it" attitudes; they counteract cultural messages of hedonism, promiscuity, and moral relativism; and they build self-esteem, wield moral authority, and care for people in ways that encourage self-sufficiency rather than prolonged dependency. What they do *works*."[75]

The ministries described by Sherman are mostly based in local congregations and place a strong emphasis upon volunteers who form helping relationships with individuals and families in need. "To overcome the challenges of the street, [they] reinforce decent families in distressed neighborhoods."[76] The emphasis is not upon material assistance so much as upon advice and emotional support, support that does not hesitate to call for fundamental changes in attitude and behavior. "This demand that clients recognize their personal responsibility and repent of their mistakes distinguishes [these groups'] 'tough love' from the therapeutic social work of other organizations," argues Sherman, noting that the volunteers "also encourage clients to get beyond a victim mentality."[77]

Remarkably, several state governments have welcomed these church-based volunteer efforts and have facilitated their work with families receiving public assistance or in crisis. These governments have done so because of a growing recognition that something was lost through the professionalization of caretaking earlier in this century, as we will see in chapter 5. Sherman claims that a "new consensus" is emerging that "doubts whether any welfare program that neglects moral and spiritual issues can offer long-term hope and argues that private organizations, particularly churches and faith-based ministries, must play a greater role in social welfare while the government must reduce its expectations of what it can reasonably achieve through its impersonal and bureaucratic public aid programs."[78]

There is nothing new about government contracting with or otherwise funding nonprofits—including many with a religious character—to carry out public services or to provide education. This is more the norm than the exception in Germany, the Netherlands, and other Western democra-

---

[74] From Isaiah 61:4 NIV: "They will rebuild the ancient ruins and restore the places long devastated; they will renew the ruined cities that have been devastated for generations," and other texts.

[75] Sherman, *Restorers of Hope*, 17.

[76] Ibid., 37.

[77] Ibid., 60.

[78] Ibid., 20–21.

cies. In the United States, the Salvation Army, Catholic Charities, and other organizations receive hundreds of millions of dollars from government each year to provide a wide range of services. What *is* new, at least in this country, is a recognition that it is precisely the religious character that makes these organizations desirable partners with government in the public interest. This belief is reflected in recent policy initiatives in Texas and other states, the Charitable Choice provision of the new federal welfare law, and proposals for "charity tax credits" and other measures to encourage direct citizen involvement in meeting human needs.

Dangers Ahead?

There is support across the political spectrum in this and other countries for a greater reliance upon nonprofit organizations to provide the social services associated with the welfare state. Public funding for nongovernment (including faith-based) schools has become almost a nonissue in most Western democracies, though it continues to be strongly resisted by the education establishment in the United States. Even among the supporters, however, a variety of concerns are expressed. Some are identified briefly here and discussed more extensively in the chapters that follow.

INEQUITY

"In the distribution of social policy benefits," Smith and Lipsky point out, "government is overwhelmingly driven by concerns of equity." That is, government programs must seek to provide equivalent benefits or services to those whose circumstances are similar. Difficulty arises from the fact that no two clients have precisely the same needs and resources, nor do two children in the same class have precisely the same strengths and weaknesses. "To achieve responsiveness within the strictures of equity, public welfare agencies have developed policies that recognize differences but are articulated in incredibly elaborate formal rules."[79] It is this overelaboration of procedures—treatment protocols, eligibility standards, procedural safeguards—that, according to many observers, make public schools and public agencies ineffective in dealing with the subtle stuff of human nature.

Voluntary organizations, nonprofit agencies, and independent schools, informed as they commonly are by a sense of mission to serve particular clients in distinctive ways that reflect an ethos that is often essentially religious, may be highly effective with some and not at all with others. Their fundamental value is not equity—serving everyone who comes to them alike—but responsiveness. "The very strength of the private organizations

[79] Smith and Lipsky, *Nonprofits for Hire*, 122–23.

lies in their workers' interest in claimants as individuals"; their staff, often poorly paid in comparison with those in public schools and agencies, "find gratification in providing aid to people one at a time."[80] Smith and Lipsky point out that this results in a tension with the norms by which government social welfare (and education) programs function: "In contrast to government, nonprofit agencies are more tolerant of client selection procedures that are not based upon rigid standards of equity—both in client selection by staff and client self-selection. Nonprofit organizations are more willing to say that they can help some people and not others."[81] But the premise of government programs is that everyone in similar need must be treated in similar ways.

This difference in approach has often led to concern that reliance upon nongovernment providers would open the door to arbitrary treatment of those in need, for example by excluding potential clients who will not subscribe to the religious orientation of an agency, or pupils who have handicaps or troubled school records, or that clients would be subjected to indoctrination by "religious fanatics." These charges have not in general been confirmed in practice, and the policies under which public funds are provided to nonprofit agencies forbid discrimination. For example, the new Charitable Choice provisions of federal welfare law protect freedom of conscience and ensure that clients will have access to nonreligious social services.

Unleashing "The Uncontrollable Forces of Religion"

By no means all those who reflect about educational and social policy are enthusiastic about a greater role for faith-based agencies and schools. Most are deeply secularistic in their assumptions and profess themselves worried about the potential for social strife and intolerance that could result from allowing religion out of the strictly private sphere within which they would confine it. Religious conflict in Northern Ireland, Bosnia, or India is often mentioned as warning that "it could happen here" if we allow public funding for religious schools. Less often noted is the fact that such funding is the norm in most other industrialized democracies, and no religious conflict has resulted . . . though it raged, precisely around schooling, in France and Germany, Belgium and the Netherlands, *before* public support was extended to the schools chosen by parents.[82]

The assumption that religion is a dangerous force is strongly reflected in Supreme Court decisions under the First Amendment, for example. Ge-

---

[80] Ibid., 124–25.
[81] Ibid., 127.
[82] See Glenn, *Choice of Schools*.

rard Bradley traces what he calls the "divisiveness doctrine" to an influential article by legal scholar Paul Freund, in which he wrote that "political division on religious lines is one of the principal evils that [the] first amendment sought to forestall."[83]

Although—as we will see in chapters 3 and 4—American governments at all levels seem not to hesitate to contract with or provide grants to faith-based social service agencies, the United States is unique among the Western democracies in refusing, as a matter of principle, to fund faith-based schools. Monsma notes the irony that "it is in this area of K-12 education that the evidence documenting the excellent job being done by religious nonprofits is most complete. . . . [But] it is in this very area the Supreme Court has largely foreclosed the normal public-nonprofit partnership as a public policy option."[84] He and Soper suggest that "the fact that Enlightenment liberal thinking did not place as great an importance on the services these agencies offered as it did on public education, which involved issues of national unity and the inculcation of democratic values, no doubt made it easier to adopt public policies that included religious associations."[85]

Controlling Faith-Based Institutions to Death

If the secular establishment has deep reservations about enlisting faith-based schools and agencies in carrying out welfare state activities, there is by no means unanimity in the religious communities that it would be a good idea to allow their institutions to be enlisted to serve the purposes of government. Hesitation is strongest among Evangelicals, for some of whom the state is perceived as an agent of deeply inimical values. Schools and agencies and volunteer efforts would be co-opted and lose their religious character.

Estelle James has shown how something along these lines in fact took place during the War on Poverty in the United States, and also in postwar Japan and Britain.

> In the face of strong ideological resistance to state welfare, Great Society reformers in the United States in the 1960s built an elaborate system of "third-party government" in which the national government financed a sizable array of welfare services but turned to other institutions, among them private, non-profit organizations, to deliver the resulting services. . . . The upshot is to convert nonprofit organizations into mere "agents" of the state, rather than true "partners" with it. Thus, for example, Japan's social welfare corporations (sha-

[83] Freund, "Public Aid."
[84] Monsma, *When Sacred and Secular Mix*, 167.
[85] Monsma and Soper, *The Challenge of Pluralism*, 208.

kaifukushi hojin) are so restricted to performing tasks assigned to them by central and local governments that they think of themselves more as quasi-governmental organizations than private nonprofit organizations, even though this is their legal form. Few issues are as crucial to the future of the nonprofit sector, in fact, as this one of determining how to fashion cooperation with the state in a way that protects the nonprofit sector from surrendering its basic autonomy and thus allows it to function as a true partner with the state and not simply as an "agent" or "vendor." This issue has become a vital one in the U.K., where a shift from outright grant aid to purchase-of-service contracting has occasioned complaints that government is undermining the independence of nonprofit providers and threatening the sector's advocacy function.[86]

As the United States Supreme Court has suggested again and again, the provision of public funding is likely to increase the scope and intensity of government oversight. It is for this reason that many evangelical schools do not participate in federal programs that provide surplus food and milk for school meals; they fear the effects of the slightest "entanglement" of their religious mission with government as much as some civil libertarians do the slightest entanglement of government with religion.

A serious threat is posed by the policy (enacted into law as the Civil Rights Restoration Act) that if any part of an institution's program receives federal funding support, every other aspect can be reviewed by government investigators for compliance with federal laws and regulations.

If faith-based schools and agencies become conformed to government expectations and ways of doing things, they may lose much that is valuable about their distinctive approach, as we will see in chapter 7.

Self-Betrayal on the Part of Voluntary Organizations

A fourth danger, not so often recognized by those secularists who see religion as a raging fire that must be contained, nor by those believers who see it as an ever-cheerful flame, is that the religious distinctiveness of schools or agencies may simply die down and at last go out. As a British observer has noted, "the search for alternative methods of welfare provision will intensify. The role of the churches, and indeed the whole voluntary sector, will become increasingly important. However, if the sector has become so compromised by its involvement with the state as to have lost its distinctive character, then it will not be able to make an effective contribution to the debate."[87]

What if these faith-based organizations surrender to the educational and social work models prevalent in their secular counterparts, through the

---

[86] Salamon and Anheier, *The Emerging Nonprofit Sector,* 120–21.
[87] Whelan, *The Corrosion of Charity,* 98.

professionalization of their staff or through coming to accept the dominant understanding of good practice? Then Olasky's question becomes pertinent: "How were these programs really different from governmental programs? Were they based on a different worldview, a different sense of the nature of man? Did they see spiritual change as the key to material change, or had they adopted the belief that the sum of man is what he eats and where he lives? The general sense was that many religious programs had effectively been secularized, and with it the excitement of sacrificing to keep them going was gone."[88] The "ambiguous embrace," in these cases, has become a fatal embrace.

In this and other ways, developments within the civil society and within the faith-based organizations themselves can force the latter into the arms of government. If their staff—and boards—come to lack conviction about the necessity of maintaining a distinctive approach and if they also lack financial and volunteer—yes, and moral—support from fellow believers, they are unlikely to remain independent in a way that has any meaning or value. This would be a pity.

> What is perhaps as distinctive about the United States as the actual services provided by the voluntary sector is the ideology that surrounds voluntarism in American society. We not only give time and money to voluntary associations as a way of supplementing the work of government and business; we believe strongly that voluntarism is the best way of doing things. We cherish the traditions and values it stands for. We want it to be an autonomous sector. And we view it as an alternative to the other main sectors of our society. In contrast with France, for example, where voluntarism is often described as a second-best way of doing things that the state should really be taking care of, Americans are likely to champion the voluntary sector as a way of keeping government in its place. Unlike Sweden, where it is simply expected that voluntary associations will be orchestrated by the government, we feel nervous about too close an alliance between the nonprofit realm and government.[89]

[88] Olasky, *Tragedy of American Compassion*, 149.
[89] Wuthnow, "Tocqueville's Question Reconsidered," 300–301.

2

STRINGS WITHOUT MONEY

I T WOULD BE too simple to equate public funding with government interference. Oversight occurs in a variety of ways without funding, and funding is sometimes provided with a minimum of oversight. The necessary context for discussing the possible effects of government support upon faith-based organizations is the government supervision and interference that occur *absent* public funding. We may find that the real issue is not the "strings" that come with funding but rather how government exercises a general oversight over the civil society. After all, "the courts have held that states already have the authority to regulate social-welfare ministries as a matter of police power. Thus, as a matter of juridical realism, participating in financial-assistance programs does not increase government's net power to regulate religious social-welfare ministries."[1]

Similarly, states have exercised jurisdiction over nonpublic schools in many ways, even though many do not receive or seek public funds.

> The state can mandate that the instructional language be English *(Meyer)*. The state can require private schools to provide an education that is "basic," "equivalent [to public education]" *(Yoder,* 406 U.S. at 213), or an "adequate education" *(Wolman v. Walter,* 433 U.S. 229, 240 [1977]) that meets "minimal educational standards" *(Yoder,* 406 U.S. at 239). The state can regulate the "quality and nature" *(Board of Education v. Allen,* 392 U.S. 236, 245 [1968]) of the curriculum consisting of "elemental skills" *(Wolman v. Essex,* 342 F.Supp. 399, 411, aff'd, 409 U.S. 808 [1972]) and "prescribed subjects of instruction" *(Allen,* 392 U.S. at 246 [1968]) "necessary for a productive and valuable life" *(Wolman,* 342 F.Supp. at 411). The state may also set the standards requiring "minimum" hours of instruction *(Allen,* 392 U.S. at 246). Teachers may also be examined to ensure that they have received "specified training" *(Allen,* 392 U.S. at 246). The state may also inspect schools to ensure that they are in compliance with "fire inspections. Building and zoning regulations" *(Lemon v. Kurtzman,* 403 U.S. 602. 614 [1971]) and "safety standards" *(Wolman).*[2]

This is not to say, of course, that funding may not vastly increase the real influence of government upon civil society institutions, including

---

[1] Esbeck, "Constitutional Case."
[2] Randall, *Private Schools and Public Power,* 75.

schools and social agencies. No doubt it does, but we will first consider government oversight and regulation of faith-based organizations absent public funding. It may be that government funding represents a threat, not so much because of new forms of enforcement authority, as because civil society institutions are prone to be seduced by it. This may, as we will see, result from the professionalization of staff that public funding both permits and (often) requires. In the following chapters we will review constitutional and other legal issues surrounding such funding, and then discuss the primary modes of accountability that can accompany the more direct forms of government support.

The Stakes in Government Oversight

Many aspects of the civil society that are not government-funded are nevertheless subject to the supervision of public officials, to legislative action, and to court intervention. Restaurants, for example, may not discriminate unlawfully in whom they serve or employ, are subject to health inspection, must meet various working and pay conditions, and often must collect taxes on behalf of the city or state. Similarly, nonpublic schools and social agencies are subject to regulation, quite apart from their source of funding: they may not discriminate in employment (subject to an exception discussed in chapter 6), for example, and they must protect the health and safety of those whom they serve. Courts have held repeatedly that the application of reporting requirements and other oversight measures to faith-based schools, even those that are operated as ministries of churches, is not unconstitutional as such, provided that it is rationally related to ensuring that school-age children receive an education equivalent to that provided by the public education available locally.[3]

While government has a general right to regulate in the public interest, there are limits, in any free society, upon how extensive this regulation may be; "the regulatory scheme [for schools] must not be so comprehensive, intrusive, and detailed as to eliminate the possibility of private schools offering a program of instruction that is indistinguishable in important respects from the public school program."[4] There seems, however, to be a natural tendency for government's oversight to become increasingly comprehensive, intrusive, and detailed. Loconte was told by one cynical nongovernment agency director in Massachusetts that the reason regulation tends to expand is that "these people, their whole lives, their whole careers

[3] *Attorney General v. Bailey*, 386 Mass. 367.
[4] Van Geel, *Courts and American Education Law*, 23.

are based on regulating, on finding things wrong."[5] Nor is the problem merely one of bureaucratic encroachment; over the past several decades a wide range of groups in society have managed to have their agendas written into laws and regulations in ways that—in many instances—affect organizations that do not accept public funding. Perhaps the leading example is the now-ubiquitous requirement that facilities open to the public provide access for the handicapped, even when there is very little likelihood that handicapped individuals will seek admission.

But there are limits to the reach of government in seeking to promote its social agenda through regulating civil society institutions. "Courts essentially have said that states may not destroy the nonpublic educational sector by incremental regulation."[6] In an important case, the Ohio Supreme Court ruled that the state-mandated "standards are so pervasive and all-encompassing that total compliance with each and every standard by a nonpublic school would effectively eradicate the distinction between public and nonpublic education, and thereby deprive these appellants of their traditional interest as parents to direct the upbringing and education of their children."[7] Nor may government, under the American Constitution, seek to make nonpublic schools or social agencies its instruments in imposing particular viewpoints. This could occur in many different ways, some not immediately obvious even to those affected by them:

> in 1987, Iowa modified its income-tax code to permit taxpayers enrolling dependents in nongovernmental primary or secondary schools to claim a deduction for the cost of tuition and textbooks. To qualify, the independent school must be accredited by the state. . . . The requirements for state accreditation that implicate the religious liberty of independent schools are as follows: "Educational programs shall be taught from a multicultural, nonsexist approach. . . . Global perspectives shall be incorporated into all levels of the educational program." If the state were to aggressively impose a doctrinaire perspective on faith-based schools through these ambiguous and controversial concepts, costly litigation would be necessary to resist the government's overreaching into a matter of curricular freedom.[8]

It could be hard for the leadership of a faith-based school to oppose such "politically correct" sentiments, and thereby to deny financial benefits that would follow to parents struggling with school expenses, but the consequence of vigorous enforcement of such a curriculum requirement by

---

[5] Loconte, *Seducing the Samaritan*, 5, 16.

[6] Sacken, "Regulating Nonpublic Education," 399.

[7] *The State of Ohio v. Whisner*, Supreme Court of Ohio, July 28, 1976, 351 N.E.2d 750, at 768.

[8] Esbeck, "Constitutional Case," 19–20.

true believers in office might be serious damage to the integrity of the school's mission.

The courts have in general been sensitive to the danger of overreaching by government seeking to advance political or ideological agendas through the schools, even those it operates itself. In a case decided during World War II, brought on behalf of Jehovah's Witness pupils who were expelled or threatened with expulsion from public school for refusing to join in the Pledge of Allegiance as a patriotic ceremony, the Supreme Court held that

> [p]robably no deeper division of our people could proceed from any provocation than from finding it necessary to choose what doctrines and whose program public educational officials shall compel youth to unite in embracing. . . . freedom to differ is not limited to things that do not matter much. That would be a mere shadow of freedom. The test of its substance is the right to differ as to things that touch the heart of the existing order. If there is any fixed star in our constitutional constellation, it is that no official, high or petty, can prescribe what shall be orthodox in politics, nationalism, religion, or other matters of opinion.[9]

If this is true of what occurs in public schools, it should be all the more true with respect to schools that are established as an alternative to the public system. The significance of their autonomy depends in many cases upon their ability to articulate an alternative understanding of the world, one that may well be offensive to the majority. This should not exempt them from all public oversight—there is a public interest that the rising generation be well informed and skilled—but it implies that government should exercise extreme restraint with respect to matters of values and worldview.

> The states may require privately educated students to be taught certain subjects such as English, arithmetic, and American history. And states may not prevent private education from including religious instruction. But whether states may, for example, require all private schools to attempt to produce patriotic and loyal citizens, or bar private schools from instructing children in communism or Marxism, is not so easily answered. . . . the Constitution and relevant cases strongly suggest that the formation of opinions, attitudes, values and beliefs should largely be in private hands and not governmentally controlled. . . . it is unlikely that courts would sustain any regulations but those reasonably designed to assure the private education was minimally adequate.[10]

---

[9] *West Virginia State Board of Education v. Barnette*, 319 U.S. 624 (1943).
[10] Van Geel, *Authority to Control*, 19.

Oversight of Faith-Based Schools

State regulation is an especially delicate affair when the nonpublic schools or social agencies being regulated have a religious basis. Government must not inhibit the free exercise of religion without a compelling public interest in doing so; on the other hand, "if the state exempts church-affiliated facilities from regulations [that apply to other organizations], e.g., minimum space per child requirements, that cannot be shown clearly to raise free exercise violations, then the state becomes so accommodating that it flirts with a violation of the establishment clause."[11]

Typically, state approval of nonpublic schools in the United States is entrusted to local school departments (the direct rivals of those schools, of course) and is based upon their providing an educational program generally equivalent to that of the public schools. This is a free-floating criterion, given the enormous range in quality and resources of public schools, and leads commonly to situations in which public school staff are sitting in judgment upon nonpublic school staff.

In most cases, it is important to add, approval of nonpublic schools occurs routinely and without difficulties on either side. The unproblematic character of much of this oversight has led some school choice advocates to propose it be adopted as the model of accountability for nonpublic schools that receive vouchers. States should be prevented from "enlarging controls upon curriculum, facilities, and school employment policies beyond the modest regulations that have traditionally applied to private schools." After all, this light regulation has worked to the benefit of the affluent children who attend elite independent schools.[12]

Other supporters of school choice are less sanguine about limiting government interference if funding is provided, pointing to recent developments in Milwaukee where the Wisconsin Department of Public Instruction is attempting to regulate nonpublic schools that receive vouchers as though they were public schools. Some see this as a sign that "voucher opponents will wage a relentless campaign either to regulate religious schools or frighten them out of the programs altogether."[13]

Faith-Based Schools That Resist Oversight

A minor case in the federal court in Massachusetts, *Braintree Baptist Temple et al. v. Holbrook Public Schools et al.* (1984), provides a good example of the conflicts that can arise when faith-based schools fear that their integrity is

[11] Van Geel, *Courts and American Education Law*, 25.
[12] Coons and Sugarman, *Scholarships for Children*, 32.
[13] Loconte, "Paying the Piper," 31.

under threat. A small-town public school superintendent had written to the pastor of a local church that operated a school, requiring that he submit various information in order to obtain approval so that pupils attending the church school could meet the state's compulsory attendance law. In addition to information about safety, supervision, and transportation, he asked for evidence that the school's teachers were certified (though this is not a Massachusetts requirement for nonpublic schools) and asked to be provided with the school's curriculum for all grade levels, "to be approved by appropriate Holbrook principals, department heads, and/or supervisors for recommendation to the School Committee." He also informed the pastor that "various personnel involved, i.e., principals, department heads" would visit the school in order to verify the information submitted, and that perhaps the School Committee would visit as well.

Refusal to cooperate with public school authorities would come at a heavy cost. The father of two of the children in the school reported that he was informed by an attendance officer that he must place his children in an approved school or face prosecution.

This faith-based school and another similarly situated sued the local school systems, claiming that "their religious beliefs preclude them from seeking approval" for carrying out a ministry of their churches"; the defendants countered disingenuously that the approval process did not "prevent the operation of the schools; it merely bars those schools from serving to fulfill the compulsory education requirements if they do not obtain approval." But of course it is fruitless to seek to operate a school if the parents of the pupils will be prosecuted for enrolling them. The court found that the guidelines that the school systems had sought to impose, "including determinations as to adequacy of textbooks, and inquiry as to educational philosophy and evidence of adequate financial support, . . . exhibit the potential for excessive government entanglement." Quoting a 1979 First Circuit decision in *Surinach v. Pesquera de Busquets*,[14] the judge noted that "in the sensitive area of First Amendment religious freedoms, the burden is upon the state to show that implementation of a regulatory scheme will not ultimately infringe upon and entangle it in the affairs of a religion to an extent which the Constitution will not countenance."[15]

In another Massachusetts case involving a faith-based school, the plaintiffs stated that as a matter of conscience they could not acknowledge that their educational ministry—which was distinctly and sincerely religious—was subject to state approval.

> Grace Bible Church . . . has adopted a totally Christian curriculum which is a
> Bible-based course of study used in all fifty states and which is permeated with

---

[14] 604 F.2d 73.
[15] 616 F.Supp. 81, passim.

Bible verses and truths. All subjects are taught from a Christian perspective. To provide members' children with a non-Christian education is believed to be a sin against the dictates of their faith. The congregation of Grace Bible Church view [the school] just as they do their Sunday School ministry or Bible study classes. For them it is a ministry of Grace Bible Church permeated entirely with religious doctrine. As a matter of religious conviction, Grace Bible Church could not nor did it ever seek approval from any government agency as a pre-condition to its operation.

Since the school was not government approved, the requirement that they provide the local school system with the names of the pupils enrolled would expose the parents of those children—who were sending them to the school as a matter of conscience—to persecution for violating the compulsory attendance law. This reporting requirement was not as inconsequential as it first appeared. While the court was accurate in holding that "the State does not seek to regulate or in any way become involved with the religious activities of the school or church,"[16] it was nevertheless true that the state's actions—through enforcement of attendance at a *government-approved* school—threatened to deprive the school of its pupils and the parents of their right to the form of schooling they had chosen for religious reasons.

There may be a natural inclination of public school officials to want to see their nonpublic rivals subjected to as many paperwork requirements as they must themselves suffer, and without a doubt state officials can always find additional matters about which to collect information. The resistance to this continual expansion of government oversight was evident in a better-known case involving a number of Christian schools in Maine. The state claimed the right to close those that refused to seek approval from local public school officials, who were responsible for determining whether children were receiving an education comparable to that provided in their own schools. In addition to health, sanitation, and safety provisions—over which there was no controversy—the state's regulations required that nonpublic schools follow the basic state curriculum and employ only certified teachers. The school that took the lead in this case had in fact been approved in the past, but its leadership came to the conclusion in 1977 that they should not submit the required five-year plan as the basis for reapproval. While the schools had always complied with government requirements, "in order to qualify as a safe, healthful, bona fide school," the leaders objected to "the increasing involvement of government" and feared that this new measure would eventually lead to state "control [of] religious instruction." Contrasting the "humanistic and secular approach of the public education system" with the "integrated Christian approach" at his schools,

---

[16] 386 Mass. 367 at 379.

he asked that they be allowed to control their own educational planning and direction.[17] Over the next several years, this developed into a refusal by a number of new Christian schools to seek state approval, "because acquiescence to state approval might imply a state right-of-control, and because acquiescence might later be used in court to demonstrate that their professed religious beliefs regarding state control were based on nonreligious preferences, rather than religious conviction." They expressed the fear that the state would seek to impose "its 'child-centered' teaching methodology . . . a secular humanist philosophy . . . sex education courses and other programs and approaches offensive to Christian values."[18]

In this case, the federal judge found—on the basis of state law—that the state could prosecute the parents for the "truancy" of their children (though noting that the state commissioner of education had denied any intention of doing so) but could not prosecute those operating the schools the children attended since there were "no statutes forbidding the operation of unapproved private schools." He also noted that closing such schools would "burden the First Amendment rights of . . . those teaching and preaching at, and those supporting and attending, the institution."[19]

A clearer signal about the right of faith-based schools to remain free of excessive entanglement in their affairs by government was provided by a case cited above, *Surinach v. Pesquera de Busquets*, involving an attempt by the government of Puerto Rico to require the Catholic school system to provide detailed financial data. The federal judge pointed out that compliance with the government's demand would "permit it to intrude upon decisions of religious authorities as to how much money should be expended and how funds should best be allotted to serve the religious goals of the schools. Either form of involvement strikes us as 'a relationship pregnant with dangers of excessive government direction of church schools and hence of churches.' "[20]

The Scope of Government Regulation of Nonpublic Schools

The United States

Our discussion of American practice will necessarily be somewhat general since "in some states, private education is virtually deregulated, while other states impose a wide variety of curricular and teacher qualification stan-

---

[17] *Bangor Baptist Church et al. v. State of Maine, Department of Educational and Cultural Services*, 576 F.Supp.1299 at 1311, 1302.

[18] *Bangor Baptist Church*, 1304, 1306.

[19] Ibid., 1307, 1327.

[20] 604 F.2d 73 at 79.

dards."[21] States may, for example, require that the language of instruction in private schools be English, or that these schools develop a love of this country through instruction in patriotism. Private schools in Michigan must select textbooks that give a positive message about the achievements and accomplishments of different ethnic and racial groups.[22] The recent wave of accountability requirements through standardized testing extends to nonpublic schools in some states, and not in others.

In no case, however, does the range of decisions made by public officials about nonpublic schools in the United States come anywhere close to those they make about public schools, unlike in the Netherlands and other countries where government funds the full cost of nonpublic schooling and regulates all schools to essentially the same standards. A study published by the Organisation for Economic Cooperation and Development in 1991 sought to estimate the proportion of decisions that were made at the school level in a number of member nations. OECD found that, while public schools in the United States had less autonomy than did those in other nations studied—because of the intrusive decision-making role of local educational authorities—American nonpublic schools had far more autonomy than did any schools in the other nations. For example, both public and nonpublic schools in the Netherlands reportedly made 22 percent of the decisions about personnel and programs completely autonomously. In France, public schools made 10 percent of the decisions autonomously, while nonpublic schools made 44 percent. In the United States, public schools made only 6 percent of the decisions autonomously, while nonpublic schools did so for 78 percent of their decisions.[23]

Nongovernmental organizations are more free than are government agencies to determine whom they will serve as pupils or clients, but whether they receive public funding or not makes a significant difference in whether they are subject to antidiscrimination requirements. Schools and other organizations that do not accept public funds have fairly wide latitude to discriminate in ways directly related to their mission, to the extent that they are intimate associations engaged in transmitting shared ideals and beliefs and in providing individuals with a community of thoughts, experiences, and beliefs.[24] In the case of a nonreligious "white academy" that had advertised widely, however, the Supreme Court decided

[21] Sacken, "Regulating Nonpublic Education," 396.

[22] Van Geel, *Authority to Control*, 157; for a comprehensive recent summary of laws affecting private schools, see, for example, Valente with Valente, *Law in the Schools*, 326–71; for a more thoughtful discussion, see Randall, *Private Schools and Public Power*.

[23] From Centre for Educational Research and Innovation, *Education at a Glance*, table P21, p. 93; the authors point out that this is an experimental measure based upon questionnaires directed to the participating nations.

[24] Van Geel, *Courts and American Education Law*, 26.

that it had forfeited its right to be considered a strictly private enterprise. The Court explicitly did not decide whether faith-based schools would be prohibited from practicing racial discrimination for religious reasons and noted that American law would not permit government to forbid a non-public school from teaching a racist philosophy.[25] This is in contrast with the law in most European countries, which require nonpublic as well as public schools to confirm their teaching to broad principles of human rights.

Esbeck points out that the implications for faith-based organizations of being required to comply with federal antidiscrimination laws (not to mention those that states and even some cities enact) can go far beyond simply not discriminating. "The 'price' to a religious organization of coverage under these four civil-rights acts[26] is not merely compliance with nondiscrimination requirements. Often the heavier costs are in the regulations that accompany the nondiscrimination mandates. These include the following obligations: undertake a self-evaluation study, publicize the ministry's obligations to protected classes, file annual compliance reports, submit to compliance reviews, keep extensive records, submit to federal investigations looking into complaints, waive rights of confidentiality, and keep abreast of new regulations."[27]

Government may also mandate norms for the type and quality of service provided, in some cases norms that directly conflict with the manner in which a faith-based organization seeks to work. Drug treatment programs, for example, based upon an explicit call for religious conversion do not comply with the medical/psychological model of treatment required for state licensure. Norms developed by organized professions are enforced through their alliance with government upon organizations that are seeking to maintain conflicting norms based upon religious convictions (see chapter 5).

Perhaps the most significant form of government intervention into the activities of faith-based organizations that do not seek public funding involves their licensing or accreditation. Whether or not a particular activity requires licensing is a decision that government itself makes, and the range

[25] *Runyon v. McCrary,* 427 U.S. 160 (1976).

[26] "Title VI of the Civil Rights Act of 1964, as amended, which prohibits discrimination on the bases of race, color, and national origin; the Age Discrimination Act of 1975, as amended, which prohibits discrimination on the basis of age; Section 504 of the Rehabilitation Act of 1973, as amended, which prohibits discrimination against otherwise qualified handicapped individuals, including individuals with a contagious disease or infection such as HIV; and finally, Title IX of the Educational Amendments of 1972, as amended, which prohibits discrimination on the bases of sex and visual impairment in educational institutions" (Esbeck, "Constitutional Case," 28–29).

[27] Ibid., 33.

of activities regulated in this way seems to expand constantly. "Virtually all residential facilities, day-care centers, drug-treatment centers, and a myriad of other service providers require government licensing. And the licensing tool, with its staffing and program demands, sets a rock-like mold for providers."[28]

As we have seen, bitter controversies have arisen over state insistence upon approval of nonpublic schools as a condition for meeting the requirements of mandatory school attendance laws. Such laws were adopted by most American state governments and by national governments in other countries beginning in the mid–nineteenth century, and they are now virtually universal in the developed nations. Schooling is compulsory to age eighteen in Belgium and Germany, to age fourteen in Korea, Portugal, and Italy, and to somewhere in between in many industrialized nations and in states of this country. Though we take them for granted, these laws were in fact highly controversial when first proposed; Horace Mann, for example, did not support compulsory school attendance laws in the 1840s, "finding them out of harmony with the American idea of democracy."[29] Half a century later, there were still many who feared that compulsory school attendance placed the state in direct conflict with the rights of parents to decide how their children would be educated. Even today some—on the left as well as the right—argue that compulsory *education* is appropriate, compulsory *schooling* not.

The states are generally strict about school attendance and make it difficult to obtain approval for alternatives to formal schooling, whether in public or nonpublic schools. The idea of "home schooling," except in cases of medical necessity, seems strange to most Europeans; in the Netherlands, for example, there is the greatest freedom to start and obtain public funding for alternative schools and to choose such schools for one's children, but little provision for excusal from formal schooling altogether. The fact that hundreds of thousands of American children do not go to school at all—and by all accounts suffer no harmful consequences—is cause for astonishment abroad.[30]

[28] Loconte, *Seducing the Samaritan*, 111.

[29] Ensign, *Compulsory School Attendance*, 48–50; see Chevallier, Grosperrin, and Maillet, *L'Enseignement français*, for an account of the resonance of this question in another republic.

[30] Postma points out that, in the unlikely event that other means of ensuring educational freedom ("bringing the school to the child" through establishing a school or "bringing the child to the school" through free transportation) are inadequate, there is provision under Dutch law for excusing a child from the mandatory attendance law (*Handboek*, 117). According to Professor Hermann Avenarius (personal communication, December 29, 1997), "In all German Länder the parents are obligated not only to educate their children but to send them to school for education. It was Art. 145 of the *Weimarer Reichsgrundschulgesetz* of 28 April 1920 which prescribed compulsory school education. . . . Children who are 'schulun-

To meet a typical state compulsory schooling requirement, parents must send their children to an approved school or obtain approval from public education officials to educate them at home. But what should be the standard by which government determines whether a nonpublic school or a home-schooling arrangement should be approved? If the educational provision is required to resemble that in local public schools, isn't the purpose of allowing a choice defeated? And, to the extent that many of the characteristics of public schools are the result of historical accident or political compromise rather than deliberate design, isn't it irrational to require those seeking to offer an alternative education to conform to their model? After all, "many private school regulations, such as teacher certification, class size, and specific textbooks, have not been empirically substantiated as essential and closely linked with explicit state educational goals, or proven capable of achieving their intended objective."[31]

The question of criteria for *approval* of schools should be distinguished from that of criteria for *funding* them, even if in most industrialized nations—but not the United States—the latter ordinarily follows the former. In France, for example, a school must have operated with government approval for five years before it is eligible to enter into a contract under which its teachers will be paid with public funds; this is one of the reasons why Muslim schools have not sprung up in France as they have in the Netherlands, where public funding (and reimbursement of set-up costs) is provided after a school has survived for one year on its own.

Must government approve *any* alternatives to its own schools, or can it maintain a monopoly of schooling? In Communist Poland, for example, the education regulations adopted in 1965 provided for the approval of nonstate schools, but the government simply never acted on applications. This silent veto continued until 1989, when approval of independent schools was a sign of the totalitarian ice breaking up, and Solidarity joining the government with the education portfolio.[32]

The right to operate and to choose nongovernment schools has come to be recognized, though not without decades of struggle in France, Germany, Belgium, the Netherlands, and the United States. According to the International Covenant on Economic, Social and Cultural Rights:

> the States Parties to the present Covenant undertake to have respect for the liberty of parents . . . to choose for their children schools, other than those established by public authorities, which conform to such minimum educational

---

fähig' (not able to be educated) are not obliged to attend school." Similar provisions exist in other European countries.

[31] Randall, *Private Schools and Public Power*, 91.

[32] See Glenn, *Educational Freedom*, 133ff.

standards as may be laid down or approved by the State and to ensure the religious and moral education of their children in conformity with their own convictions.[33]

This question was resolved, for the United States, by the Supreme Court in its 1925 decision in *Pierce v. Society of Sisters;* the court struck down an Oregon law requiring all children to attend public schools until completion of the eighth grade, finding that this unjustly threatened the rights of private corporations (schools) to carry out their business and that it interfered with the right of parents to direct the education of their children.

The fundamental theory of liberty upon which all governments in this Union repose excludes any general power of the state to standardize its children by forcing them to accept instruction from public teachers only. The child is not the mere creature of the state; those who nurture him and direct his destiny have the right, coupled with the high duty, to recognize and prepare him for additional obligations.[34]

The Court, it should be noted, also stressed

the power of the state reasonably to regulate all schools, to inspect, supervise, and examine them, their teachers and pupils; to require that all children of proper age attend some school, that teachers shall be of good moral character and patriotic disposition, that certain studies plainly essential to good citizenship must be taught, and that nothing be taught which is manifestly inimical to the public welfare.

Subsequent decisions about state regulation of faith-based schools have weighed this broad language against First Amendment rights of parents, teachers, and school sponsors.

If the states are the "laboratories of democracy" under the American system, free to try out many different approaches, this is nowhere more evident than in how they oversee the education of children who are not attending public schools.

Some states have consciously deregulated their private schools. These states expressly limit state administrative authority to promulgate regulations. Tennessee, for example, provides: "The state board of education and local boards of education are prohibited from regulating the selection of faculty or textbooks or the establishment of a curriculum in church related schools." Private schools in Tennessee still have the option of seeking state approval. North Carolina presents a somewhat similar option, with two 1979 laws that deregu-

[33] Article 13, 3, in Fernandez and Jenkner, *International Declarations and Conventions.*
[34] 268 U.S. 510.

late all private schools. Prior to passage of the law, the state board had gradually expanded its regulatory framework for private schools until teachers, courses of study and textbooks had to be substantially the same as in the public schools. Under the new law, North Carolina has minimal requirements for recordkeeping (pupil attendance and disease immunization) and requires that the schools select and administer a nationally standardized test to students each year. The schools keep the tests on file and make them available to state inspectors. Eighth graders must be given a competency test.[35]

Other states are far more prescriptive, requiring that private school teachers hold state certification and follow state curriculum guidelines. "There has been very little public dialogue about what would constitute proper controls. The assumption seems to be that proper controls are whatever the state declares them to be." As Randall points out, "This great diversity in state regulations of private schools is symptomatic of the often ambiguous and vague nature of education. The wide variety of approaches in state supervision suggests that any number of regulatory arrangements are perceived to provide quality controls for private education."[36]

To the extent that those making the approval decisions focus upon such inputs as teacher qualifications and computers and other teaching materials, they may make it prohibitively expensive for many nonpublic schools to demonstrate their equivalence to local public schools. The tremendous increase in per-pupil spending in American public schools in recent decades is one of the reasons that the Catholic system has been under such pressure.[37] A more equitable approach would be to focus upon specific measures of quality as reflected in student outcomes compared with public schools serving similar student populations. This is the approach taken by the Ohio Supreme Court in 1976, holding that government could impose educational standards that would ensure the civic, social, and economic self-sufficiency of graduates of nonpublic schools, but could not require that these schools have resources, programs, and goals equivalent to those of public schools.[38]

After all, it is somewhat ironical that "the same government and educational officials who presided over this dramatic decline in the quality of American education still insist on being qualified to tell private schools

---

[35] Lines, "Private Education Alternatives," 196.

[36] Randall, *Private Schools and Public Power*, 4–5.

[37] In the Netherlands in the nineteenth century it was the increased expenditure on public schools that forced the Protestant and Catholic schools to increase their own costs, leading to the long and ultimately successful drive to obtain public funding for them. See Glenn, *Myth of Common School*, 248–49.

[38] *The State of Ohio v. Whisner*, 351 N.E. 2d 750.

what is required for a good education and enforcing such opinions through regulations."[39] Requiring evidence of results protects the public interest adequately and makes more sense than telling private schools how to achieve those results.

Western Europe

This is in fact essentially how the approval process works in countries that have strong outcome standards for schools in the form of high-consequence examinations tied to a national curriculum. Regulating inputs is much less important in such cases. An individual or group wishing to start a nonpublic school in France, for example, must provide notice of that intention to local and national government, together with information about the proposed facility and documentary evidence of the good character and the educational qualifications of the founders; absent well-founded objections, the school can open after a month. Local officials may not block the establishment of a nonpublic school because there are more than enough places available in the local public school, or because they have political or pedagogical disagreements with the founders.[40]

Once the school is in operation, the municipality has the right and duty to inspect the facilities periodically, and national education officials may intervene in cases involving misconduct by a nonpublic school teacher. "State control does not extend over the pedagogical freedom of the establishment, but is limited to monitoring its conditions of operation."[41]

The question arises, in France, whether the concept of teacher "misconduct" could be extended to teaching views considered subversive of the political and social order. The state inspectors who visit nonpublic schools have the right to demand to see textbooks and pupil notebooks, since the minister of education has a general right under French law to oversee all materials used in schools, public or not. That the state must not allow itself to be menaced by the ideas taught in private schools has been an accepted principle in France for more than a hundred years.[42] In the United States, as well, but with considerably less success, "states have . . . sought to regulate private schools to insure that these schools would not become an incubus of culturally and politically divisive ideas and practices." As Van Geel notes, "the more the states attempt to regulate private schools the greater the likelihood they will stamp out the diversity these schools represent, and

---

[39] Randall, *Private Schools and Public Power*, 112.
[40] Monchambert, *La liberté de l'enseignement*, 75–76.
[41] Ibid., 80.
[42] Ibid., 82–83.

the promotion of diversity, the offering of alternative concepts and forms of education, is a central function served by private schools today."[43]

The really effective state control in France is indirect, however: under a monopoly enacted into law in 1880 (and building upon that established by Napoleon I), only the Ministry of Education is authorized to issue diplomas, based upon passing national examinations. Nonpublic schools have no choice but to follow the curriculum that prepares pupils for these examinations.[44] The same model of quality control is employed in other European countries. It has been suggested recently that this emphasis upon the outcomes rather than the process of schooling, and the "signals" that it gives to teachers and pupils alike, is a major factor in the superior achievement of Western European adolescents compared with Americans.[45]

In Germany there is a constitutional right to establish private schools, but if they are to serve as a substitute *(Ersatz)* for public schools for meeting mandatory attendance requirements, they must be approved for that purpose by the state. "Such approval must be given if private schools are not inferior to the state or municipal schools in their educational aims, their facilities and the professional training of their teaching staff, and if segregation of pupils according to the [financial] means of their parents is not promoted thereby" (article 7, paragraph 4). On the other hand, the German constitution goes on to limit this right:

> A private elementary school shall be permitted only if the education authority finds that it serves a special pedagogical interest, or if, on the application of persons entitled to bring up children, it is to be established as an inter-denominational or denominational or ideological school and a state or municipal elementary school of this type does not exist in the community.[46]

In other words, a superior right to establish a school is recognized when the motivation for doing so is related to exercise of the right to freedom of belief. If the organizers are interested in a different pedagogical approach that has no religious or ideological basis, their right to approval is subject to a judgment on the part of public education officials. This provision, by leaving it up to public education authorities to decide whether a particular form of schooling "serves a special pedagogical interest," has had the effect, according to Jach, of reducing significantly the diversity of German education. For example, an independent alternative school might be turned down on the grounds that there was no experimental justification

---

[43] Van Geel, *Authority to Control*, 153.
[44] Georgel and Thorel, *L'enseignement privé en France*, 145–52.
[45] Bishop, "Signaling, Incentives."
[46] Jenkner, *Das Recht auf Bildung und die Freiheit der Erziehung*, 119.

for it because similar schools already exist elsewhere, even if inaccessible to some parents wishing such a school.[47]

While the right to operate independent schools is guaranteed under German law, the process of administrative approval of such schools has created growing pressure upon them to conform to the model of state schools.[48] The very detailed requirements spelled out in the education statutes of the various *Länder* provide many occasions for officials to make it difficult to start and operate nongovernment schools. The requirement of close conformity to the standards set by state schools is a heavy price to pay; "accordingly a state-approved [substitute] school will take care not to risk its privileges by deviating too greatly in its syllabus and method."[49] Nongovernment schools in general follow the state curriculum guidelines in order to ensure the comparability of their certificates, though they are required only to correspond to public schools in structure and goals, in teacher qualifications and the holding of examinations, not in learning objectives and content.[50] There are some exceptions, including Montessori and Waldorf schools, which have very distinct goals and programs and may therefore be "recognized" but not "state-approved"; their pupils must transfer for a final year of secondary school to a public or state-approved school in order to prepare for and take the *Abitur* at the conclusion of their schooling.

Jach charges that "educational diversity in the sense of different forms of schooling that coexist on an equal basis" doesn't exist in the state educational systems of Germany, and that independent schools are in an unequal position because of overregulation and an elaborate approval process. The approval process itself is based upon judgments about the purposes of schooling that may conflict with the educational priorities shared by teachers and parents who have created a particular school, and thus with the constitutional guarantee of the free development of personality. The state is required to be neutral, Jach points out, and educational freedom must mean the right of those who operate each school to shape its goals as well as its perspective on the world and its teaching methods. This is not to say that "educational freedom" applies only to teachers, however, since it would be naive to assume that their goals will always accord with those of parents. No, there must be freedom to educate and also freedom to choose schools.[51]

---

[47] Jach, *Schulvielfalt als Verfassungsgebot*, 51.
[48] Jenkner, "Das Recht auf Bildung als Menschenrecht," 237.
[49] Vogel (1979), quoted by Weiss and Mattern, "Situation and Development," 55.
[50] Commission of the European Communities, *Structures of Education*, 44.
[51] Jach, *Schulvielfalt als Verfassungsgebot*, 25–26, 49, 80.

The state's ideological neutrality, some argue, should forbid the definition of a single set of goals for education and model of personal development or of a single model of schooling, even for the public system. Significant groups within the society—perhaps even the majority—who think otherwise are forced either to subject themselves to demands with which they do not agree or to leave the public system to which they are entitled and use private schools.[52]

In the Netherlands, a government monopoly on the right to provide or to authorize schools was ended as long ago as 1857, and freedom to establish schools is guaranteed by the constitution. This guarantee, however, is "without prejudice to the authorities' right of supervision and, with regard to the forms of education designated by law, its right to examine the competence and moral integrity of teachers" (article 23, paragraph 2).[53] Over recent decades the Dutch Parliament and Ministry of Education have elaborated an enormous body of regulations and guidelines. The expanded role of government in education is reflected in the growth of the staff of the Ministry of Education and Science from 1,547 in 1966 to 3,804 twenty years later; between November 1982 and May 1985 the Ministry issued forty-one laws, 123 general regulations, 287 decrees, and 811 ministerial circulars, not counting those of other agencies that applied to schools.[54] In general, these requirements weigh as heavily upon nonpublic as upon public schools, though they must in every instance respect the right of nonpublic schools to retain and express their distinctive religious or philosophical character (richting). The issue has arisen frequently in recent years, whether the rights of school sponsors and of parents associated with recognition of a richting is limited to those defined by religious viewpoint or extends to distinctiveness on the basis of pedagogical methods or organization.[55] This goes to the question of intention: does the constitution seek to protect only freedom of conscience (clearly the original intention), or does it protect consumer preferences as well?

Although the Dutch constitution gives the government authority to supervise nonpublic education whether or not this is publicly funded, in fact there is little provision in law for supervising any that are not government supported, and they can even—for example, in the case of international schools—serve to meet the requirements of the mandatory school attendance law.[56]

[52] Hennecke, *Staat und Unterricht* (Berlin, 1972), quoted by Jach, *Schulvielfalt als Verfassungsgebot*, 79.

[53] Jenkner, *Das Recht auf Bildung und die Freiheit der Erziehung*, 138.

[54] Braster, *De inspecteur en de school*, 26–27.

[55] Postma, *Handboek*, 120.

[56] Ibid., 115.

The national government in Spain and the governments of its "autonomous communities" like Catalonia set standards for pupil/teacher ratios, teacher qualifications, and facilities. These standards apply to all schools, including nonstate schools that receive no public funding. Additional requirements having to do with the process of appointing school boards and directors apply to public schools and also to nonstate schools "with economic agreements with the State," mostly Catholic schools supported by public funds. Publicly funded schools are also subject to controls on the selection of pupils and the removal of unsatisfactory teachers, and they may not charge supplemental tuition to make up for the inadequacy of their state funding. As a result of these restrictions, many nonstate schools prefer not to enter into agreements under which they would receive public funding, though they continue to be subject to the requirements noted above.

Overregulation of how schools and social agencies go about their business, including the qualifications of their staff and the procedures that they follow, is a reflection in part of the difficulty of specifying the results that they are expected to achieve. Even though "there may be no demonstrable relationship between the imposition of a requirement and the objective in whose name it is imposed,"[57] officials may feel obligated to show their zeal by insisting upon performance standards or resource standards that have little bearing on outcomes. Chapter 4 will consider this common scenario at more length.

Summary

It is generally conceded that government has a right and even a duty to oversee to some extent the activities of nongovernment organizations that provide human services, including education, and especially those that serve children. This oversight is exercised in the name of protection of those unable to protect themselves, and also the public interest in promoting a generally high level of education and training.

There is a somewhat less extensive agreement that this government oversight should not take such intrusive forms that it infringes upon the rights of those who provide nonpublic human services including schools; especially is this the case when their motivations are religious. The liveliest controversy has surrounded state regulation of faith-based schools, since government, parents, and churches all have a major stake in what children are taught to value and to believe.

For the sake of both effectiveness of oversight and care not to intrude upon protected rights, there is a growing—though by no means universal—

---

[57] Smith and Lipsky, *Nonprofits for Hire*, 131.

conviction that it is more desirable for government to hold nonpublic schools accountable for results than for the process by which they reach those results. The same principle applies to other human services, but setting clear outcome standards is controversial and difficult.

The discussion so far has left aside what is perhaps the most difficult question of all: who has a right to decide which persons are qualified to provide counseling, to teach, or to engage in other sensitive activities? Who should decide the norms of good practice, and how does this affect the nature of the services that may or may not be provided? We return to these issues in chapters 5 and 6.

When government undertakes to *fund* organizations that it does not directly control to provide services, the situation grows even more complicated. The provision of public support for private choices lifts the issue out of the context of what could be called consumer protection. A higher degree of oversight seems to be warranted when government funding seems to place a seal of approval upon the provider of education or counseling or other human services.

Most of the independent organizations that are willing and able to provide such services are or have been religious. In the American context, this raises legal questions that do not trouble our European counterparts, for whom (apart from the French) the separation of church and state has not taken the form of an article of faith.

To these distinctively American questions we must now turn.

INTERLUDE

TEEN CHALLENGE

TEEN CHALLENGE developed out of a Protestant Pentecostal "street ministry," seeking to reach inner-city youth gangs with a message of conversion and new life. As its work with drug addiction has become institutionalized and recognized as one of the most successful programs for substance-abusing youth and adults, Teen Challenge has retained its explicitly religious character. What is more, this character is expressed in every detail of its work. As the organization itself insists, "Leaders in Teen Challenge credit the spiritual component of the program as the key to the high success rate of Teen Challenge graduates."[1]

The treatment strategy of Teen Challenge is based upon a belief that "drugs are not the root problem of the addict, but a symptom of a deeper internal problem." That root problem, the organization does not hesitate to say, "is the sin[ful] nature of people which causes them to focus on self-centered attempts to find personal meaning and fulfillment in life." Such efforts at self-therapy—as in much New Age practice—are sure to fail. "When one does not have a personal relationship with Jesus Christ, that person has a great emptiness inside. Drugs are only one of many things a person may turn to in search of true happiness. But these efforts are futile and only lead to addictions."[2]

Evaluations by independent researchers of this privately funded program—which as of 1995 was operating some 130 programs in forty-three states and Puerto Rico with a staff of over fifteen hundred—have found that its long-term success rate is considerably higher than that of government-funded alternatives.[3]

Despite a record of success over three decades—and despite not seeking public funding—Teen Challenge has run into difficulties with government. Most notably, in 1995 the Texas Commission on Alcohol and Drug Abuse threatened to revoke Teen Challenge's license to operate if it did not provide certified chemical dependency counselors and other professional staff.

---

[1] Teen Challenge National Training and Resource Center, *Research on the Effectiveness.*

[2] Batty, *Philosophy of Teen Challenge,* 2.

[3] "According to these studies, between eighty and ninety percent of Teen Challenge graduates were abstaining from illegal drugs seven years after exiting the program, and between ten and twenty-six percent of publicly-funded secular program graduates were drug-abstinent six years after exiting their programs" (Bicknese, "Teen Challenge Drug Treatment in Comparative Perspective: A Crossroads Monograph Proposal," citing three scholarly reports).

Teen Challenge insisted, however, that addiction was primarily a moral and spiritual rather than a medical problem and refused to change its approach, which employed no psychiatrists, social workers, or certified counselors or other professionals. "The methodology or expertise such people would apply would be fundamentally at odds with our faith-based approach," the director of the center in San Antonio told a congressional hearing. "It would drastically reduce our level of success."[4]

Amid a storm of publicity, Texas governor George W. Bush publicly backed Teen Challenge and appointed a statewide task force "to examine the benefits of faith-based self-help programs." As his spokeswoman told the press, "Governor Bush believes that religious faith tends to make people more responsible." Under this pressure, the state agency backed down.[5]

Even in this case, and with such powerful support, the victory for Teen Challenge was an ambiguous one. The organization had been given a drug-rehabilitation license a few years earlier, with the benefit that its clients could qualify for federal aid while in the program; this was taken away in 1995 by state officials who, according to newspaper accounts, "told Teen Challenge and its 25 clients that treatment centers must be staffed not with preachers but with trained professionals. They said the addicts should be treated through detoxification," and that addiction was a disease that should be treated as such and not with moral exhortation.

This negative attitude toward Teen Challenge and other alternative addiction-treatment programs reflects that of the National Institute on Drug Abuse (NIDA), which provides 90 percent of all drug-abuse funding nationwide. "NIDA refers to drug addiction as 'a complex disease that can be successfully addressed by scientific research.' . . . Government-approved treatment usually includes medication (methadone detoxification clinics, for example, intended to ease addicts off of more serious drugs) and therapy (a fixed number of counseling sessions with a clinical psychologist). . . . Only agencies licensed by the state to offer rehabilitation services are eligible for contract money in the first place. Securing a state license means 1) tailoring programs to suit government (secular) models of treatment and 2) hiring a staff of psychologists and medical professionals trained in the state's clinical approach to treatment."[6]

The insistence that only the medical model of addiction-treatment has credibility persists despite a study funded by NIDA itself, and now more than two decades old, which found strong positive benefits from the Teen Challenge program. The former medical director for the New York Hospital Methadone Clinic interviewed program participants who had entered

---

[4] Haase, "Coats Hears from Religious Groups," E10.
[5] Herrick, "Christian Drug-Abuse Group Wins," 42.
[6] Loconte, *Seducing the Samaritan,* 88–89.

Teen Challenge through the Brooklyn center in 1968, to determine how many of them were drug-free, not in trouble with the law, employed or in school, married, active in a church, and in good physical and mental health. Urine samples were collected to confirm claims about drug use.

Three groups of participants were distinguished: those who had entered the program in Brooklyn but then dropped out, after an average of thirteen days (P1); those who completed the Brooklyn program but dropped out of the residential phase on a farm in rural Pennsylvania, after a mean length of stay of three months (P2); and those who graduated from the residential program, after a mean length of stay of 7.6 months (P3). Altogether 186 participants were interviewed, 90 percent of whom had been arrested (a total of 1,020 times) before entering Teen Challenge, and all of whom had been involved in substance abuse: 87 percent were heroin users, 83 percent on a daily basis, and 31 percent reported they had been hospitalized for an overdose. Those who completed the program were more likely to have been heavy users of heroin (three or more times a day) than were those who dropped out of the program.

The study found that 67 percent of the graduates (P3) were drug-free (which, by Teen Challenge standards, means not using narcotics, marijuana, alcohol, or cigarettes!) as indicated by the urinalysis test, and nearly nine out of ten had not required additional drug treatment programs after Teen Challenge. 87.5 percent of former addicts were abstaining from the use of marijuana seven years after completing the program, and 95.3 percent were abstaining from the use of heroin.

By comparison, "of a sample of 1970s graduates from Public Health Service hospitals, [only] 26% were using no illegal drugs, with the exception of less-than-weekly use of marijuana, six years after completion of the program. . . . [This] rate would include those addicted to *legal* drugs such as methadone."[7] The NIDA study concluded that there was "a striking drop in reported opiate use and arrest status consequent to treatment" by Teen Challenge, especially for those who completed the program, together with a "lesser tendency to make use of illicit means of support" and to use alcohol. "It appears reasonable to conclude that involvement with Teen Challenge is associated with dramatic changes in behavior for a substantial number of heroin users."

The study found also that 72 percent had continued their education, that 75 percent were employed (more than half of those at their present job for

---

[7] Bicknese, "Teen Challenge Drug Treatment in Comparative Perspective: A Crossroads Monograph Proposal." The usual standard for "drug free" under the medical rehabilitation model is that the graduate consumes no more than a six-pack of beer, a bottle of wine, or seven ounces of hard liquor a week; Teen Challenge calls for total abstinence.

more than a year), and that 67 percent were regularly attending church. Fourteen of the sixty-four graduates interviewed in the NIDA study had become ministers, and twenty-two had attended Bible colleges, though as a group they were less likely than the program dropouts to report that they had been religious before entering the program. Forty of the graduates were married at the time of the survey. Puerto Rican youth appeared to benefit significantly more than did black youth from Teen Challenge.[8]

Dr. Catherine Hess, who directed the NIDA-funded study, told a journalist some years later, "It was probably the most effective rehabilitation program I have seen anywhere—and it still is."[9]

A more recent (1992–94) study, conducted by a professor of criminal justice at the University of Tennessee, interviewed a random sample of fifty graduates of the Teen Challenge program in Chattanooga. Of this group, 67 percent were abstaining from illegal drugs or alcohol, and 88 percent had not required additional drug treatment programs. Although 60 percent had been in embroiled with the law before entering the program, this was true of only 24 percent of the graduates; 72 percent were employed (half of them at the present job for more than a year), and 8 percent were students. Seventy-six percent reported that they attended church regularly.

To counter the possible suggestion that participants in Teen Challenge were an unrepresentative group because of the religious nature of the program, the report points out that "over 70% of the respondents [came] to Teen Challenge of Chattanooga after unsuccessful results with several drug treatment programs," in many cases three and in some four or more. "It must be emphasized that many had been around the track a few laps before entering this drug treatment program. The data suggest a major change in lifestyle following their experience with Teen Challenge of Chattanooga. . . . A change in lifestyle is apparent, significant, and long-lasting. A dramatic change in attitude and behavior cannot be denied."[10]

A third study of the results of Teen Challenge was conducted by Aaron Bicknese for his dissertation at Northwestern University, based upon telephone interviews with fifty-nine Teen Challenge graduates six, twelve, eighteen, and twenty-four months after their completions of the program, and a control group consisting of clients of publicly funded programs whose current rates of drug abstinence at the same intervals has been compared to those of Teen Challenge graduates.

---

[8] National Institute on Drug Abuse, *Evaluation of Teen Challenge*; Hess, "Research Summation."

[9] Manuel, "Teen Challenge."

[10] Thompson, *Teen Challenge of Chattanooga*; Teen Challenge National Training and Resource Center, *Research on Effectiveness*.

Bicknese suggests that the success of Teen Challenge can be explained through Viktor Frankl's conceptual framework of logotherapy as well as through standard sociological reference group theory. "According to logotherapy, . . . man is principally motivated neither by a will-to-pleasure as the Freudians would assert nor principally by a will to-power as posited by Adlerian psychology, but rather, man's chief motivation in life is a will-to-meaning, that is, 'his deep-seated striving and struggling for a higher and ultimate meaning to his existence.' When this will-to-meaning goes unfulfilled, an 'existential vacuum' results, and it is precisely this, asserts Frankl, which drives the unfulfilled to proxy attempts at escaping from meaninglessness. One such attempt is drug abuse."

If drug and alcohol abuse stem, at least in part, from a sense of meaninglessness, is it possible that faith-based programs like Teen Challenge are more effective than the medical model of treatment because they place the assertion of meaning at the very center of the client's experience? According to Bicknese, "Teen Challenge may provide the recovering drug abuser with meaning in life to a greater extent than secular programs can." He stresses the contrast between *the disease-controlling model* of addiction treatment (. . . where clients are called *'patients'*) and *the character-building model* on the other (embodied in Teen Challenge, where addiction is understood as a matter of values or morality and clients are called *'students'*). Notice that in the student model, where the ex-addict is responsible for building his own character and deciding himself to overcome a destructive habit, he is the agent. In the medical model, however, the drug, not the user, is the agent, and the user is but a passive host."

This interpretation of the Teen Challenge approach as concerned above all with *meaning* is consistent with the program's insistence, "When man becomes Christ-centered, his symptoms of meaninglessness and compulsive deviant behavior are replaced by a meaningful life that enables him to realize his fullest potential."[11] Bicknese's respondents (former addicts who had successfully completed the Teen Challenge residential program) placed this religious dimension first in their explanations of the success of their own experience: "the clearly model response (34) was Jesus Christ or God. . . . The second highest number of citations (11) went to responses having to do with maturation . . . followed by attributions to Teen Challenge (7) and to families (4). . . . Several mentioned a 'void' or an 'emptiness' in their lives that they were attempting to fill with drugs or alcohol: 'It was an attempt to satisfy an area in my life that couldn't be satisfied until that emptiness was filled with Christ.' "[12] Such responses are consistent with the explicit philosophy and strategy of Teen Challenge. In con-

---

[11] Wever, *Teen Challenge Therapeutic Model*, 5.
[12] Bicknese, "Teen Challenge Drug Treatment Program" (1999), 178–79.

trast with the emphasis in many secular medical-model programs on helping the patient to understand his past experiences as holding the clue to
his pattern of drug abuse, Teen Challenge tells participants,

> If you have failed to shake the drug habit, God will give you the strength to
> do it, if you allow Him to come into your life. Individual problem areas do not
> need to be specifically identified or individually handled. There is no need to
> spend time looking for the multiple questionable causes of why he is an addict
> and then proceed to turn his life around. The basic approach of Teen Chal-
> lenge to those abusing drugs is:
>
> 1. There is hope.
> 2. Drugs are not the major root problem.
> 3. Sin is the major root problem.
> a. Drugs are not sin; they are a symptom of the problem.
> b. The only cure for sin is Jesus Christ.
> c. Jesus Christ died on the cross to save a man from his sin.
> d. Through faith in Jesus Christ you can be forgiven and cleansed from the
> power of sin.
> e. The knowledge that your sins have been forgiven and you no longer have
> to be controlled by them becomes the motivation to change your lifestyle.
> Christ within you gives you the power to overcome the loneliness and the
> nothingness that has filled your life. You take sin out of your life and put Christ
> in. When sin is taken out, you take the symptoms out: drugs, alcohol, hate,
> jealousy pride, selfishness, etc.[13]

This spiritual challenge appears to be an important aspect of what the program is able to accomplish. The outside evaluation found that "the main
focus of Teen Challenge of Chattanooga, Inc. is that of being a spiritual
growth center where biblical principles are taught. 80% of the respondents
credited developing a personal relationship with Jesus Christ as a major
influence in helping them stay off drugs."[14]

Teen Challenge insists that it is not in the first instance a substance-
abuse program; it "starts with discipleship training which battles man's
sinful nature and has the side-effect of eradicating drug and alcohol
abuse. . . . The purpose of the program is not to 'rehabilitate' in the usual
sense of returning the individual to a previous state. The goal is to create a
new person from the old—a person who does not need addictive substances
because he has found contentment in a personal relationship with Jesus
Christ."[15]

---

[13] Hess, "Research Summation," 9.

[14] Teen Challenge National Training and Resource Center, *Research on Effectiveness;* see
Thompson, *Teen Challenge of Chattanooga,* 15.

[15] Mellor, "Teen Challenge," 1.

In addition to this simple (skeptics would say simplistic) message about the decisions that the client must and *can* make in order to obtain healing, and that this does not depend upon his own power alone, the Teen Challenge program also provides a community within which recovery is strongly valued and indeed insisted upon as the condition of continued participation. The reference group made up of staff and fellow participants in the intensive setting of a rural retreat makes it possible for the change to take place; the relatively high level of continuing participation in a church no doubt sustains the change as it becomes a habitual mode of life. "Drug abuse . . . is but a symptom of the deeper problem 'loneliness,' which can only be addressed adequately at the spiritual level by a 'personal relationship with God,' and at the social level by a close-knit Christian community for material and morale-building needs which the new believer may face."[16] Both program and church are part of that "third sector" which is neither government nor market, and which may be more effective than either in "the enforcement of moral codes and individual responsibility for behavior."[17]

There are a number of different medical and psychological approaches that work reasonably well to wean an addict from the use of drugs for a few weeks or months; what they seem to lack is the ability to help the addict to find a substitute purpose in life. By stressing Christian discipleship and life-skills, and connecting former addicts with local churches, Teen Challenge seems to have a much greater "holding power" over the long term. As one of its core documents explains, the "primary goal of this counseling is not simply to stop the addiction and related deviant behavior, but to develop a whole new way of living—one free from compulsive destructive behavior. It is the premise of Teen Challenge that this new way of living can only be achieved and maintained for life when built on a personal relationship with Jesus Christ."[18]

If the outside evaluators and the Teen Challenge staff and leadership— and graduates—are correct in believing that it is the life-changing power of religious conviction that makes possible a high success rate among those who persist and complete the program, it would surely be bad public policy to require Teen Challenge to abandon that aspect of its "reeducation" as the price of receiving public funding. It would also be bad public policy to persist in relying exclusively on responses to drug addiction whose long-term results have been decidedly mixed simply because of discomfort with the religious nature of Teen Challenge.

[16] Bicknese, "Teen Challenge Drug Treatment Program" (1999), 24.
[17] Osborne and Gaebler, *Reinventing Government*, 46.
[18] Batty, "Philosophy of Teen Challenge," 3.

Government should not *require* that anyone undergo a program of treatment based upon a particular worldview, whether religious or secular (the "medical model," after all, is scarcely neutral in its understanding of the goals and meaning of human life!), but there should be no objection to offering a program like Teen Challenge as a freely chosen alternative for those who are entitled to public support as they seek to overcome their addiction. To deem it ineligible because of its religious character would not be the neutrality on the part of government mandated by the First Amendment, but antireligious bias.

The decision by the Texas Commission on Alcohol and Drug Abuse in 1995 was that Teen Challenge of San Antonio—in operation since 1977—would have to be licensed and, in order to meet licensing requirements, would have to adopt a rehabilitation approach consistent with the secular methods and assumptions that represent the professional norm. The decision was not directly against the religious character of Teen Challenge (if the organization had been seeking public funds, that would presumably have been an issue as well), but by requiring substitution of a nonreligious understanding of the causes and cure of addictions it would have made it impossible for the Teen Challenge emphasis upon conversion and discipling to work.

Another successful program that was targeted by Texas officials was Victory Fellowship, founded by Teen Challenge graduate Freddie Garcia. Garcia told a congressional hearing that his Victory Home for addicts in San Antonio

> achieves a 70 percent success rate at a cost of $25 to $30 per person a day. In contrast, government programs cure less than 10 percent of their clients and cost hundreds of dollars a day, he said. Victory Home's approach to dealing with addicts differs fundamentally from that of the government. "We believe that sin is the reason why people take drugs," he said. "We believe that the drug addict is a slave to sin, not to drugs. We believe that drug addiction is a spiritual problem, and that Jesus Christ is the solution."[19]

A reporter who looked into Garcia's program told readers,

> In 1966, strung out on the streets of Los Angeles, Garcia accepted a friend's invitation to seek help at a Christian home called Teen Challenge. Several months later, Garcia says, he stumbled to the altar during a revival and, tears filling his eyes, asked Jesus to *"pasame quebrada,"* or "give me a break." He then set out to convert others. After graduating from the Latin American Bible Institute in La Puente, Calif., Garcia returned to San Antonio and opened a home for "barrio" drug addicts. Today, there are five San Antonio homes under

[19] Haase, "Coats Hears from Religious Groups," E10.

the Victory Fellowship umbrella. "We teach Jesus in the morning, Jesus at noon, Jesus at night," says Garcia. "You leave Jesus out, man, you're like every other treatment program in the United States." In Garcia's world, there is no room for social and economic analysis, psychiatry and psychology. Man sins, or he repents. He is lost, or he is saved. Such a view of drug abuse makes state officials uneasy. Rehabilitation, they say, is not an exercise in black and white. "I'm not one to say God's not in the miracle business," says John Cook, a spokesman for the Texas Commission on Alcohol and Drug Abuse. "But addiction is not a moral issue. It's a disease," he claims. Garcia, however, insists he gets results: Nearly two out of three of the people who study the Bible at Victory Fellowship for three to six months overcome their addiction to drugs or alcohol, he says.[20]

Garcia wanted to advertise Victory Fellowship as a "rehabilitation center," but state officials told him he would have to either apply for a state license or advertise as a church. But getting a license to treat drug addiction would mean meeting state health and safety codes. "Even Garcia admits that would be tough, since his shelters seldom turn away the desperate no matter how full. It would also mean having licensed counselors, which would mean hiring staff with college degrees. Garcia says he does fine with dropouts from the 'barrio.' 'My people have educations you can't get at Yale University,' he says."

Victory Fellowship and Teen Challenge understand themselves as Christian ministries. "Like the Church," an official Teen Challenge statement insists, "TC is a healing community. And, like the church, TC exists to evangelize and disciple." Like any evangelistic crusade, but with an emphasis upon a gradual process of change rather than "one-time experiences for complete eradication of life-controlling problems," Teen Challenge is fond of citing conversion statistics: over twelve thousand recorded in 1991![21] But neither is precisely a church, and both count themselves successful if their graduates become active members of local churches that include others who are not former addicts.

Teen Challenge official documents are careful to distinguish it from addiction-oriented programs, in order to shield it from state interventions as well as to help participants to keep their focus. Government insistence upon treating the program as analogous to secular drug and alcohol treatment programs based upon the medical/psychological model has often led to "a clashing of philosophies of treatment. Resultingly TC centers have been forced to stray from their mission statement. A clear statement to agencies especially regulatory, regarding what TC is should legitimately

---

[20] Herrick, "Welfare from the Streets," A1.
[21] Wever, *Teen Challenge Therapeutic Model*, 11, 12.

move TC away from being considered part of what drug and alcohol efforts are doing."[22]

Perhaps the distinctiveness of Teen Challenge—and other programs like Victory Fellowship—is brought out most clearly in the fact that it does not speak of *clients* or of *rehabilitation*, but of *students* and of *discipling*. The goal is not to return participants to their former condition, before they became addicted to drugs or alcohol, but to lead them to become "a new creation" in Christ. Teen Challenge describes itself as a "discipleship training environment."[23]

Like other successful approaches to fundamental change of lives, Teen Challenge understands itself as providing a growth environment rather than a therapeutic environment. It is a characteristic of growth-oriented programs that they tend to threaten professional norms and to escape from bureaucratic constraints.[24] They can be judged only by their results, and those results are frequently such that wise public policy would not ignore the contributions that they can make or place unnecessary barriers in their way.

Another difference is that these programs assert that drug addiction *is* a moral issue, indeed an evidence of moral failure. So is willful evasion of responsibility for one's life and that of one's family. So is a life of crime or of prostitution. And so are other forms of behavior that—together with factors beyond the individual's control—bring people to the point that they need the agency's help in getting their lives back together. Teen Challenge and similar organizations (they might prefer to call themselves "ministries") offer the opportunity for repentance and newness of life, based upon unapologetic condemnation of the old life that has entrapped those whom they serve.

Although direct public funding, through grants or contracts, was not at issue in the Texas controversy, we can anticipate increased debate over eligibility of alternative therapies for Medicaid and other forms of reimbursement. This is in contrast, ironically enough, with the practice in the more highly secularized societies of Western Europe. Monsma and Soper describe a group of Christian nonprofits in England that operate drug and alcohol rehabilitation residential programs and receive nearly a third of their budget from the government. These programs insist that there is an intimate link between the social and therapeutic work that they do and a set of explicit religious convictions. They believe that "the best means of achieving true freedom for the drug dependent person is by rehabilitation through discipleship to Jesus Christ as Savior and Lord." However,

[22] Ibid., 10.
[23] Ibid., 8.
[24] Glenn, "Treatment-Oriented Agencies."

"we do not insist upon, or force, such a commitment upon anyone." The
staff must sign a "Bible believing" statement of faith as a condition of employment, and the center residents, who volunteer for this form of treatment, are required to participate in Bible studies twice a week as well as
church services.[25]

Similarly, "*De Hoop* (The Hope) is a drug treatment residential program
in Dordrecht [in the Netherlands]. . . . All their workers are required to
be Christian believers and there are prayers before meals, devotions and
prayers every evening, and twice a week Bible studies. All these religious
activities are voluntary in nature, but clients are invited to take part in
them." There is no controversy about the public funding supporting this
organization.

> In the dominant Dutch mindset public funding of social service organizations
> does not violate church-state separation or governmental religious neutrality,
> as long as such funding goes to the organizations of all religious traditions
> and to those of nonreligious secular groups as well. In fact, to do otherwise is
> seen as discriminating against religion. Undergirding this mindset is the
> rejection of an assumption often made in the United States. Namely, that reli-
> gious organizations have a bias or a distinctive ax to grind, while nonreligious
> secular organizations are neutral. In the Netherlands secular and religious or-
> ganizations alike are seen as operating out of certain distinctive philosophies
> or beliefs.[26]

Programs that seek to change deeply rooted addictions must put something equally powerful in place of the addiction, and this, whether secular
or religious, can hardly be neutral toward fundamental issues of human
life and meaning. Teen Challenge makes no pretense of philosophical
neutrality, and that is surely one of the reasons for its effectiveness. It is
also a reason why it might have difficulty qualifying for public funding.
"Christian drug treatment centers presumably could not unequivocally
condemn drug use as an offense before God and attempts to integrate help
and support for the addict with spiritual assurances of God's love and his
presence would risk legal action. As a result, the most promising path for
dealing with drug addiction and its accompanying social horrors remains
unexplored."[27]

Teen Challenge is addressing, with apparent success, one of the most
serious problems facing American society. Should it be receiving public
funding to extend this work? And if it did, would it be forced or influenced
to adopt the "professional" model of treatment of addictions that has been

[25] Monsma and Soper, *The Challenge of Pluralism*, 145–46.
[26] Ibid., 76, 78.
[27] Monsma, *Positive Neutrality*, 261.

notably less successful? Would it no longer to able to tell the addicted person that his real problem is sin—rebellion against God? Would it be able to offer the recovering addict a faith and a relationship to build a new life around? Bicknese warns that public funding might reduce the sense of commitment and of "living by faith" that enables Teen Challenge to elicit such deep involvement on the part of its staff, and would challenge its ability to require participation in the religious activities which are an essential part of its program.[28]

[28] Bicknese, "Teen Challenge Drug Treatment Program" (1999), 211–19.

3

HOW CLOSE AN EMBRACE?

J UDICIAL INTERPRETATIONS of the religion clauses of the First Amendment to the American Constitution, though often seen as unrelievedly hostile to faith-based organizations, in fact allow public funds to go to many that serve children and youth . . . so long as they are not schools. This chapter will describe this illogical—and uniquely American—prohibition on funding religious schools, and recent developments that could affect future policies.

Three Ways of Understanding Government's Relationship to Religion

While it would not be useful to venture too far into the tangled thicket of church-and-state jurisprudence, some fundamental distinctions are necessary. Three positions that may be distinguished are *strict separation*, *strict neutrality*, and *positive neutrality*. All three are mingled together confusingly in the policies of our federal and state governments, and in state and federal court jurisprudence, but will be presented here as "ideal types."

Strict separation seeks to exclude religious themes, motivations, and organizations from everything that government touches upon. Since government has extended its helping hand (or its grasp, if the reader prefers) into more and more spheres of social and cultural life over recent decades, the logic of strict separation is to drive religion into the corner of aspects of private life that have no public consequences.[1] Underlying this objective, as reflected in the reasons advanced by many of its advocates, is a belief that religion is a dangerous and divisive force. Militant secular humanist Paul Blanshard wrote, for example, "Our schools may not teach Johnny to read properly, but the fact that Johnny is in school until he is sixteen tends toward the elimination of religious superstition."[2] While other strict-separationists may not be so outspoken in their mistrust of the disruptive power of religion—may indeed see themselves as friends of religion—there is wisdom in Reichley's conclusion that "a society that excludes religion totally

---

[1] Neuhaus, *The Naked Public Square*.
[2] Paul Blanshard, "Three Cheers for Our Secular State," *Humanist*, March–April 1976, 17–25, quoted by Monsma, *Positive Neutrality*, 42.

from its public life, that seems to regard religion as something against which public life must be protected, is bound to foster the impression that religion is either irrelevant or harmful."[3]

For at least some, the solution is not so much a "naked public square" as one in which an alternative belief-system is established, one that we will call "secularism." A characteristic articulation of this goal is John Dewey's little book *A Common Faith* (1934) or, more recently, Louis Legrand's *L'école unique: À quelles conditions?* (1981) and Paul Kurtz's *Living without Religion: Eupraxophy* (1994). In contrast with Dewey, Kurtz takes pains to insist that humanism is not religious; the changing legal situation since Dewey's proposal that schools teach a nonsupernatural religion has given secularism the upper hand. Whereas for Dewey there were rhetorical and tactical advantages to claiming that his educational objectives were in some sense religious, there is now much more to be gained by claiming to be resolutely secular. Nevertheless, as Monsma and Soper point out, "secular perspectives and belief structures represent a point of view, a worldview as much as various religious perspectives and beliefs do." Given the force and coherence of the secularist perspective, government policies that accord it a privileged position through funding institutions and programs that promote this perspective while handicapping faith-based perspectives by excluding them from the ever-enlarging sphere of government activity are scarcely neutral.[4]

While it seeks to appear under the guise of neutrality, the strict separationist position is hostile to revealed religion, either intentionally or through lack of reflection. For example, it supports freedom of speech in public settings like schools, so long as the content of that speech is not religious. Government officials like school principals are placed in the position of censoring what teachers say to ensure that it remains safely secular.

John Peloza, a biology teacher in a public high school in California, contended that the school district's requirement that he teach the evolutionary account of human origins as an established fact violated his constitutional rights because evolution is a religious theory, making him "an unwilling agent of the school district in the establishment of the religion of secular humanism, in violation of the First Amendment" (*Peloza v. Capistrano Unified School District*, 782 F.Supp. 1412 [1992]). The federal district court held, however, that "there is a compelling state interest for secondary school teachers to adhere to the curriculum set forth by the appropriate school district." Peloza also asserted "that even if he is not permitted to teach his theory of creationism in the classroom, he should be permitted to privately discuss religion and his theory of creationism in conversa-

---

[3] Reichley, *Religion in American Public Life*, 165.
[4] Monsma and Soper, *The Challenge of Pluralism*, 46.

tions with students during private, non-instructional time on the campus, during lunch, class breaks, and before and after school hours." The court found that "the plaintiff's right to free speech must be balanced 'against his student's right to be free of religious influence or indoctrination in the classroom.' "

But exclusion of religious speech and motivations, of religious organizations and programs from equal participation in the "public square" and in public funding is not neutral in its effects. As Monsma argues convincingly, "If, to receive the normal benefits of public policies that similar, secularly-based organizations are receiving, a religious nonprofit organization must downplay or give up certain of its religious practices, public policy is interfering with its free exercise of religion."[5] When New York State offered funding for nonpublic colleges only if they were not sectarian, many Catholic colleges quickly abandoned aspects of their self-expression that could make them seem too Catholic. "One university rewrote its brochure to delete references to it as a Catholic university, took down the crucifixes from the classroom walls, and removed its entry from the annual Catholic Directory."[6]

As Justice Stewart pointed out in his dissent from the Supreme Court's 1963 ruling banning the use of the Bible in the opening exercises for the public school day, doing so did not result in a religiously neutral school environment. It should not be seen "as the realization of state neutrality, but rather as the establishment of a religion of secularism, or at least as government support for the beliefs of those who think that religious exercises should be conducted only in private."[7]

Strict neutrality, by contrast, insists that government should not be in the business of making distinctions between religious and secular speech and other activities, and should confine itself to ensuring that neutral rules are enforced upon each. Strict neutrality seeks not to influence either positively or negatively the choices that people make "for or against any particular religious or secular system of belief. It should neither advantage nor burden religion."[8] A government committed to strict neutrality would fund equally qualified day care providers or youth programs without regard to their religious character and would be concerned to be strictly fair by favoring neither religion nor secular ideologies nor the lack of all convictions. We could call this position "secularity," in distinction from the secularism that lurks behind the strict separationist position. While secularism is an ideology that seeks to make converts, secularity is a posture of evenhandedness.

---

[5] Monsma, *When Sacred and Secular Mix*, 126.
[6] Burtchaell, " Alienation of Christian Higher Education," 173.
[7] *Abington Township School District v. Schempp*, 374 U.S. 222 at 313.
[8] Monsma and Soper, *The Challenge of Pluralism*, 10.

An example of strict government neutrality in practice is the right of student groups to gather on their own initiative for religious activities if school policies allow student-initiated groups for secular activities. This "equal access" will be discussed below.

Applying this principle consistently to education would require, in Stephen Carter's words, that "if neutrality means that the government cannot take steps to treat religious schools better than other schools, it surely means as well that the government cannot take steps to treat religious schools worse."[9]

Positive neutrality takes the position that government should under some circumstances give its support to religious activities and motivations, when they serve a purpose whose benefits are primarily social rather than religious in nature and can do so especially well or in a way that responds to the desires and respects the consciences of those involved. There are, Monsma points out, a variety of public policy advantages to government partnership with faith-based organizations. "The first is that the government can make use of and build on the sense of dedication, empathy, and closeness to the people being served that tends to mark the workers in religiously based programs. . . . A second advantage . . . is that religious associations have a basis on which to build a bond or sense of trust and to motivate persons with whom they are working that governmental and other secularly based agencies lack. . . . A third advantage . . . is the flexibility thereby given public policy."[10]

In Germany the contribution of religion—or at least of the recognized Protestant and Catholic churches—is so highly valued that the government collects church taxes and gives preference to church-sponsored social welfare activities over its own (as is described in the interlude on neocorporatism). The understanding behind such policies is that "the state must . . . have a holistic view of human beings. People are religious, ideological beings. The state should not favor any one religion or ideology, but it must make room for the religious, ideological nature of humankind" in the provisions that it makes for social welfare and education.[11]

It seems to have been the intention of the framers of the Bill of Rights to establish such a positive neutrality toward religion, requiring government to act in such a way that it does not influence individuals or organizations to be or not to be religious. Reichley points out that "the First Amendment is no more neutral on the general value of religion than it is on the general value of the free exchange of ideas or an independent press."[12]

[9] Carter, *The Culture of Disbelief*, 200.
[10] Monsma, *Positive Neutrality*, 257–58.
[11] Monsma and Soper, *The Challenge of Pluralism*, 190.
[12] Reichley, *Religion in American Public Life*, 166.

In fact, "the Free Exercise Clause, on its face, prefers religion, favoring it as no other activity is favored. There is no parallel constitutional protection for free exercise of tourism, boating, hiking, beer drinking, or environmentalism. . . . the Establishment Clause [as applied in a strict-separationist manner] may be seen as a discrimination against religion and a burden upon religion, and therefore, arguably, a Free Exercise Clause violation. There are no parallel clauses preventing the establishment of science, philosophy or speech."[13]

This constitutional mandate to treat religion with special deference has—as we saw in chapter 2—frequently been invoked by faith-based schools in their resistance of excessive government interference. It has less often been the occasion for approving any form of government support of and partnership with such schools. One of the rare recognitions, by the United States Supreme Court, of what is taken for granted in most of Europe, in Canada, and in Australia and New Zealand, was Justice White's opinion for the majority in a 1967 case. In approving the loan of secular textbooks to religious schools, the Court acknowledged "that private education has played and is playing a significant and valuable role in raising national levels of knowledge, competence, and experience."[14] In other words, *government does not and should not have a monopoly on serving the public good*.

Positive neutrality rests upon a pluralist understanding of the political and social order that recognizes the important role of faith communities and associations alongside other forms of voluntary organization in maintaining society and in transmitting the habits and values that sustain it. A pluralist political order integrated such communities and associations "into the life of the body politic." Neutrality is not, from this perspective, an end in itself but a means to ensure fair play among individuals and groups, whatever their views, so long as they abide by the ground rules that make society possible.[15]

The interlude on neocorporatism in Europe will discuss how such pluralistic thinking plays out in Germany and the Netherlands.

Monsma provides an interesting example of positive neutrality in his discussion of military cemeteries. Government, he points out, "is neutral in that neither Christian nor Jewish religious symbols are uniformly placed onto the graves of all those who were killed in action. . . . neutrality is not gained by stripping the governmentally owned and operated cemetery of

[13] Stephen L. Pepper, "The Conundrum of the Free Exercise Clause—Some Reflections on Recent Cases," *Northern Kentucky Law Review* 9 (1982): 293–94, quoted by Monsma, *Positive Neutrality*, 52.

[14] *Board of Education v. Allen*, 392 U.S. 236, at 247.

[15] Monsma, *Positive Neutrality*, 176, 200.

all religious symbols, but by the active, positive use of religious symbols corresponding to the religious faiths of the fallen men and women. Religion is recognized and given its due.... structural pluralism accepts and even celebrates pluralism over uniformity and diversity over conformity, even when things appear a bit messy as a result."[16]

The income tax code gives favorable treatment to religious organizations, for example in authorizing tax-free housing allowances for clergy, and legislatures, prisons, and the armed forces do so in appointing and salarying chaplains. The provision for conscientious objector status because of sincerely held religious beliefs is yet another example. Church exemption from property and income taxes represents positive neutrality, as does the individual right to observe religious holidays and to seek exemption from military service on the basis of religious conviction. "The aim," Esbeck writes, "is to minimize the effects of governmental action on individual or group choices.... a state cannot adopt a program of aid that funds all providers of welfare services public and private, but explicitly disqualifies participation by religious providers." In an example of positive neutrality, "a recent case in the Sixth Circuit... held that the U. S. Army violated the free exercise clause when it excluded religious but not secular child-care providers from operating on its bases and receiving various direct benefits. *Bartman v. Stone*, 68 F.3d 953 (6th Cir. 1995)."[17]

There are those who object, on First Amendment grounds, to the exemption of churches from various forms of taxation; others point out that this demonstrates that government policies can legitimately "advance religion, albeit in a pluralist and non-preferential way."[18]

Outside the Wall of Separation

But there are other respects in which the judicial interpretation of the First Amendment cuts against equal participation by religious organizations. Faith-based schools, in particular, have fallen under the ban, and their treatment is in contrast with the relatively greater accommodation of religious social agencies like the Salvation Army and Catholic Charities.

Unlike the abortion decision, this is not simply a case of the courts overturning what state legislatures had decided. Many states had already adopted restrictions in their laws or constitutions against public funding of religious schools or organizations, usually out of anti-Catholic and anti-

[16] Ibid., 174.
[17] Esbeck, "Constitutional Case."
[18] Viteritti, "Choosing Equality," 133.

Mormon sentiment. By 1875, nineteen states had adopted constitutional provisions prohibiting the use of public funds for religious schools, and sixteen more did so by 1900; only a handful now lack such constitutional prohibitions. Contrary to a widely held impression, judicial interpretation of the First Amendment is not the only barrier to public funding of faith-based schools and agencies; indeed, the language of the state constitutions are in some cases a greater barrier.[19] The Massachusetts Constitution, for example, provides that "[n]o such grant, appropriation or use of public money or property . . . shall be made or authorized for the purpose of founding, maintaining or aiding any church, religious denomination or society."[20]

Since, as we will see in what follows, faith-based organization can use public funds to deal with adolescents in sensitive areas of value-formation and life-direction, it is difficult to see why faith-based schools should not also receive support. There is, however, a string of Supreme Court decisions striking down efforts by state or local policymakers to extend public funding or services to K-12 schools that have a religious identity. Religiously identifiable schools, even those that are not owned by a church, have been held to be invariably "pervasively sectarian" in a way that makes them ineligible for government support of any of their educational activities. In fact, no faith-based institutions other than schools have ever been found by the Supreme Court to be categorically "pervasively sectarian," without an examination of particular cases. The Court has been willing to recognize, in the case of every other sort of faith-based institution, that it is capable of providing secular social or educational services without unlawful indoctrination or promotion of religion with public funds.

Occasionally, dissenting voices on the Supreme Court, like that of Justice White in the landmark case *Lemon v. Kurtzman*, argue, "Where a state program seeks to ensure the proper education of its young, in private as well as public schools, free exercise considerations at least counsel against refusing support for students attending parochial schools simply because in that setting they are also being instructed in the tenets of the faith they are constitutionally free to practice." He would have upheld programs in Rhode Island and Pennsylvania that—in Pennsylvania—allowed state education officials to "purchase . . . secular educational services" from nonpublic schools or—in Rhode Island—provided 15 percent salary supplements for nonpublic school teachers teaching subjects offered in the public

[19] Viteritti (ibid.), discusses this extensively.
[20] Article 46, section 2; for a compilation, state by state, of constitutional and statutory language prohibiting public funds for religious schools, see appendix A in Bryson and Houston, *Supreme Court and Public Funds*, 143–319.

schools. After all, White pointed out, there was "nothing in this record indicating that any participating teacher had inserted religion into his secular teaching or had had any difficulty in avoiding doing so."[21]

Justice Burger's majority opinion in that case conceded that "in the abstract" it was certainly possible to separate secular and religious education. He found "no basis for a conclusion that the legislative intent was to advance religion" and agreed that "a state always has a legitimate concern for maintaining minimum standards in all schools it allows to operate." He conceded also that "the line of separation, far from being a 'wall,' is a blurred, indistinct, and variable barrier depending on all the circumstances of a particular relationship." Nonetheless, he concluded, the programs could not be allowed because the close supervision by state officials required to ensure that teachers in religious schools remain "religiously neutral" would result in a "kind of state inspection and evaluation of the religious content of a religious organization ... fraught with the sort of entanglement that the Constitution forbids."[22] Thus it was in part for the sake of the religious schools themselves that the state aid should be forbidden: "the history of government grants of a continuing cash subsidy indicates that such programs have almost always been accompanied by varying measures of control and surveillance. In particular the government's post-audit power to inspect and evaluate a church-related school's financial records and to determine which expenditures are religious and which are secular creates an intimate and continuing relationship between church and state."[23]

In effect, the Court was saying, we're cutting faith-based schools off from public support for their own good, protecting them from the fatal embrace of government. No inquiry seems to have been made into whether government oversight of religious schools in other countries, where it is routine, has done serious damage to their mission.

Anticipating a distinction the Court has returned to again and again, Justice Burger stressed that "inculcating religious doctrine is, of course, enhanced by the impressionable age of the pupils, in primary schools particularly."[24] This distinction on the basis of the age of those subject to influence has often been used, by the federal courts, as the basis for treating religious activities at the college level more indulgently than those in K-12 schools; it does not explain why public funding for faith-based child care programs does not raise the same objections.

---

[21] 403 U.S. 602 at 665, 666 (White, J., dissenting).
[22] Ibid., 613, 618, 620.
[23] Ibid., 621–22.
[24] Ibid., 616.

In a concurring opinion, Justice Douglas stressed the theme of entanglement by describing the two state programs as placing "the state astride a sectarian school and giv[ing] it power to dictate what is or is not secular, what is or is not religious."[25] That is, as we will see, just what the Ninth Circuit would later do in *Kamehameha*. Justice Brennan added that "the picture of state inspectors prowling the halls of parochial schools and auditing classroom instruction surely raises more than an imagined specter of governmental 'secularization of a creed.' . . . Policing the content of courses, the specific textbooks used, and indeed the words of teachers is far different from the legitimate policing carried on under state compulsory attendance laws or laws regulating minimum levels of educational achievement."[26]

What does the phrase "pervasively sectarian" mean? We should first note that the term *sectarian* itself is a put-down; the term is seldom used by religious groups to describe themselves, or other groups toward which they are well disposed. "Throughout American history," writes ethicist Richard Baer, " 'sectarian' has been used to exclude and to ostracize. It is a term used to disparage and marginalize particular groups of Americans and particular kinds of thinking." Why is the term disparaging? Because it "always implies that there exists a contrasting mainstream, a right way of thinking, a common position that deserves to be accepted by everyone." Baer argues that the Supreme Court's use of *sectarian* is by no means neutral. "Thus the Court refers to 'sectarian exclusivity,' 'narrower sectarian purpose,' 'sectarian division,' 'sectarian controversies,' 'political fragmentation on sectarian lines,' and 'sectarian bickering and strife.' Terms such as 'bitter controversies,' 'proselytizing function,' and 'bias' are closely conjoined with the term 'sectarian.' . . . Conversely, the Court uses more neutral or even positive language in conjunction with the terms 'secular' and 'nonsectarian.' "[27]

It was Thomas Jefferson who started the fashion of referring to Christians who held to traditional teachings about the divinity of Christ as "sectarian," in contrast with his own unitarian beliefs. Jefferson believed that the inevitable movement of history was toward general acceptance of a rational and moralistic version of Protestantism freed from "superstition," and that those who continued to hold to "narrow sectarian" doctrines were standing in the way of progress. Like Horace Mann and others who shaped public education before the Civil War, Jefferson insisted that his position represented true religion, and he applied the term *sectarian* only to "*the wrong kind of religion.* Rather than sticking to the simple teachings of Jesus that constituted the true 'non-sectarian' essence of Christianity that all

---

[25] Ibid., 637 (Douglas, J., concurring).
[26] Ibid., 650–51 (Brennan, J., concurring).
[27] Baer, " Supreme Court's Discriminatory Use," 449–53.

Christians held in common, the 'sectarians' insisted on adding to this common heritage the dogmas and superstitions of ignorant men."[28] This negative connotation has continued to be attached to the term *sectarian*, and this helps to explain several decades of Supreme Court decisions against public support for religious schooling.

How has the term been applied? As defined in one case, in order to be considered "pervasively sectarian" a school must not only be run directly by a church, but have "attributes such as integration of secular and religious education, mandatory religious instruction, religious based admission policies [and have] as a central purpose the inculcation of religious values [or the preparation of] students for a religious career."[29]

In *Hunt v. McNair*, a case from 1973 involving state construction aid to colleges, the Court defined "pervasively sectarian" as indicating that the secular activities of an institution cannot be distinguished from its sectarian (i.e., religious) ones. Public funding could be provided only to those secular activities of faith-based colleges that could be separated out in that way. In 1976 the Court found, in *Roemer v. Board of Public Works*, that a group of Roman Catholic colleges were not pervasively sectarian, even though they "employed chaplains who held worship services on campus, taught mandatory religious classes, and started some classes with prayer."[30] The colleges were not barred from receiving public funds because they had a high degree of autonomy from the Roman Catholic Church, religious criteria were not used in hiring faculty and they had complete academic freedom except in religious classes, and students were chosen without regard to their religion. It is easy to see how applying such criteria could tend to detach colleges from their religious identities, or from any overt expression thereof: government action, whether intentionally or not, is objectively hostile to religion under those circumstances.

Nonpublic elementary and secondary schools in New York State, by contrast, were judged to be pervasively sectarian because they "placed religious restrictions on student admissions and faculty appointments, they enforced obedience to religious dogma [whatever that means, in the late twentieth century!], they required attendance at religious services, they required religious or doctrinal study, the schools were an integral part of the mission of the sponsoring church, they had religious indoctrination as a primary purpose, and they imposed religious restrictions on how and what the faculty could teach."[31]

---

[28] Ibid., 459; drawing, for Mann and other school reformers, on Glenn, *Myth of Common School*.

[29] *Cuesnongle v. Ramos*, 713 F.2d 881, at 883.

[30] *Roemer v. Maryland Board of Public Works*, 426 U.S. 736 (1976); Esbeck, *Regulation of Religious Organizations*, 12n.

[31] Esbeck, *Regulation of Religious Organizations*, 13n.

Parochial schools were distinguishable from a Catholic university, the First Circuit found in another case, because they had "attributes such as integration of secular and religious education, mandatory religious instruction, religion based admissions policies, ha[d] as a central purpose the inculcation of religious values, [and] prepare[d] students for a religious career, with other similar features. These sorts of schools are deemed pervasively sectarian."[32]

Of course, this conflicts with the ample evidence that Catholic schools and mainline Protestant schools are, if anything, hotbeds of tolerance and that the latter are seldom owned by or subordinated to a religious denomination. The Supreme Court has been reluctant, for reasons already mentioned, to permit the lower courts to examine the practices of faith-based schools in detail to determine whether or not they are "pervasively religious." They have been judged ineligible for public support sight unseen.

Faith-Based Social Services: Where the Wall Is Not So High

By contrast with its treatment of schools, the United States Supreme Court has held that religiously affiliated colleges and social agencies can separate their "secular" activities from their religious mission in such a way that the former are legally eligible for public funding. Public funds may be and are being used for day care centers operated by churches, and for church-related programs for school-age adolescent girls, though not for schools for children of the same ages. Government in fact funds a wide range of social services provided through faith-based organizations. Esbeck points out that "government assistance to faith-based charities and colleges has never been disallowed by the Supreme Court" and goes on to provide examples of faith-based services that are sometimes publicly funded:

> A nonexhaustive list includes preschools and child day-care centers; temporary shelters for abused children; foster homes and adoption placement agencies; residential-care or group-care homes for abused or neglected children and adjudicated juvenile offenders; adolescent or teen counseling centers; crisis-pregnancy counseling centers; maternity homes for women with crisis pregnancies: temporary shelters for battered women: rehabilitation centers for alcoholics, drug abusers, and the unemployed; AIDS hospices; prison ministries, police and prison chaplaincies: halfway houses for adults convicted of crimes: storehouses of free (or reduced-price) food, used clothing, and household items: centers for free meals (soup kitchens) and temporary shelters for the

---

[32] *Hunt v. McNair*, 413 U.S. 734 (1973).

homeless (rescue missions): low-income housing renovation programs: refugee aid and resettlement: disaster relief: clearinghouses for volunteers rendering home-based care to the disabled: long-term care facilities for the disabled, retarded, and mentally ill: long-term care facilities for the elderly (retirement, nursing, and invalid homes): elderly day-care centers: centers for vocational training or employment of the disabled; literacy and English-as-a-second-language programs; hospitals and community-health clinics: dispute resolution and legal-aid centers: draft counseling centers: financial counseling centers: marital and family-counseling centers: recreational programs, summer camps and retreat centers for youth and adults: and support groups of every stripe for persons suffering from life's many vicissitudes.[33]

Our concern here will be with services provided to school-age children, and especially those that have some educational elements, since it is in these cases that the most relevant precedents for funding of religious schools will be found. The most significant case is *Bowen v. Kendrick* (1988), in which the Supreme Court upheld the constitutionality "on its face" (that is, subject to subsequent challenge of specific arrangements that might violate the Establishment Clause) of the federal Adolescent Family Life Act (AFLA) of 1981. This law was enacted by Congress in response to the "severe adverse health, social, and economic consequences" that often follow pregnancy and childbirth among unmarried adolescents. As Chief Justice Rehnquist pointed out in his majority opinion,

> Congress expressly recognized that legislative or governmental action alone would be insufficient: "[S]uch problems are best approached through a variety of integrated and essential services provided to adolescents and their families by other family members, religious and charitable organizations, voluntary associations, and other groups in the private sector as well as services provided by publicly sponsored initiatives." The AFLA implements this goal by providing in § 300z-2 that demonstration projects funded by the government "shall use such methods as will strengthen the capacity of families to deal with the sexual behavior, pregnancy, or parenthood of adolescents and to make use of support systems such as other family members, friends, religious and charitable organizations, and voluntary associations"[34]

Under this act the federal government had funded "state and local health agencies, private hospitals, community health associations, privately operated health care centers, and community and charitable organizations. It is undisputed that a number of grantees or subgrantees were organizations with institutional ties to religious denominations."[35]

---

[33] Esbeck, *Regulation of Religious Organizations*, 8n.
[34] *Bowen v. Kendrick*, 87 U.S. 589 (1988) at 596.
[35] Ibid., 597.

While a wide range of research and pilot programs have been funded under AFLA, the most interesting for our purposes are those, under section 300z-1(a)(4)(G), that provide "educational services relating to family life and problems associated with adolescent premarital sexual relations, including (i) information about adoption; (ii) education on the responsibilities of sexuality and parenting; (iii) the development of material to support the role of parents as the provider of sex education; and (iv) assistance to parents, schools, youth agencies, and health providers to educate adolescents and preadolescents concerning self-discipline and responsibility in human sexuality." Such activities are very much parallel with some high school programs and indeed confront questions of morality and worldview much more directly than most of what goes on in schools.

Schools: The Unhappy Exception

The majority opinion in *Bowen v. Kendrick* seems judicious and nuanced in contrast with the confused decisions about aid to faith-based K-12 schools. Some programs might be "pervasively sectarian" (and thus ineligible for public funding), Rehnquist conceded, but that was up to government officials or the lower courts to determine on a case-by-case basis; there should be no presumption that this was true of all faith-based organizations. "This Court," he wrote, "has never held that religious institutions are disabled by the First Amendment from participating in publicly sponsored social welfare programs."[36]

The applicable precedent was the cases allowing public funding to go to denominational colleges, on the grounds that "[r]eligious institutions need not be quarantined from public benefits that are neutrally available to all."[37] The colleges, the Court had decided without examining actual practices, were only superficially religious, and government was funding their nonsectarian educational mission. K-12 parochial and other denominational schools, by contrast, were inescapably religious and thus under no circumstances could they receive public funds for instructional purposes, even in subjects with no ostensible religious content.

In fact, however, "the record showed that the five church-affiliated [colleges] that received funds had mandatory religion courses, had some classes that were begun with prayer, employed some instructors who wore religious garb to class, and that the great majority of the students were Roman Catholic. Nevertheless, the Court concluded that religion did

[36] Ibid., 609.
[37] *Roemer*, 736.

not permeate these institutions."[38] As against the presumption that faith-based colleges are only marginally or separably "sectarian," the leading organization of evangelical colleges requires that members meet the following conditions:

1. A commitment to an educational setting that accepts precepts of a religious faith as operating principles for the institution.

2. A commitment to hiring only faculty, staff, and administrative personnel who actively reflect the acceptance of the religious faith in their own personal lives.

3. The imposition of lifestyle guidelines on students who attend the college that are consistent with the sponsoring denomination's interpretation of a lifestyle of faith.

4. The governance of the college by a board of trustees who must, as a condition of election, be members of the religious faith.

5. Close ties to the overall mission of a denomination's desire to educate its students in the context of religious values.[39]

Sandin identified seventy-three liberal arts colleges, nineteen comprehensive universities, and twenty-five two-year colleges as "pervasively religious"; of these, thirty-four were Catholic and the others Protestant.[40] Many—perhaps most—of these institutions receive various forms of public funding support, if only through the Pell Grants and government-backed loans that their students use to pay tuition; some receive funding for facilities and for research as well. There is necessarily a degree of unspoken collusion between college officials and the government officials who oversee these programs. As David Winter points out,

At Westmont for example, the college motto is "In all things Christ preeminent," taken from Colossians 1:18. The college generally presents itself in that light, indicating that every campus program expresses its commitment to Jesus Christ. . . . Yet when the officials from the state or federal government visit Westmont's campus they hear a different emphasis. College officials, in order to dispel any charges of being narrowly or harmfully sectarian, speak of the genuine academic freedom that exists, the diversity-within-limits that is represented among students and faculty, the lack of discrimination in race and sex, and the generous spirit Westmont seeks to foster in its students toward people of different convictions.[41]

---

[38] Van Geel, *Courts and American Education Law*, 44.

[39] Christian College Coalition, *Resource Guide*, 9.

[40] Sandin, *The Search for Excellence*, 130–32; I owe this reference to Cliff Hersey's (as yet) unpublished dissertation, "Professed Out Loud and Honestly," on the subject.

[41] Winter, "Rendering unto Caesar," 248–49, quoted from Hersey, "Professed Out Loud."

This need not indicate any form of deceit; an institution as complex as a college can be described accurately from several different angles. Strong religious conviction is often combined with genuine acceptance of others. Some would define the difference between Protestant Fundamentalists and Evangelicals by the openness of the latter to viewpoints with which they disagree.[42] Many faith-based K-12 schools that, to the federal courts, are assumed to be "pervasively sectarian" without further inquiry are in fact open to the world in this sense and do not deserve to be caricatured as authoritarian and repressive, concerned single-mindedly with religious indoctrination.[43]

Nor are they necessarily subordinated to denominational authorities. Stephen Monsma informs us that "an official of a national association of conservative Protestant schools made the explicit point that almost all of their member schools have no formal church ties. Instead, they all are independently established as nonprofit bodies. . . . roughly 14 percent of the children in the New York City Catholic schools and 13 percent in the Brooklyn Catholic schools are non-Catholics. . . . The pervasively sectarian standard simply does not distinguish between religious secondary and elementary schools and other religious nonprofit organizations."[44]

In fact, as Monsma found in his study of nongovernmental relief agencies, child service agencies, and colleges, most religious nonprofits receiving public money are not pervasively sectarian, as this term is used by the Supreme Court.[45] Yet it is indisputable that much of what occurs in evangelical colleges could not readily be distinguished from the activities that government funds in their entirety in public colleges. Esbeck points out that "it is a myth that religious welfare and educational ministries take place within discrete and clearly defined boundaries easily segregated (like corporate subsidiaries) between the social and the sectarian."[46]

Faith-based organizations providing adolescent services have been treated, by the courts, like colleges and unlike schools. The effect of *Bowen v. Kendrick* was that they could receive public funds unless it was shown that a particular program stepped over the line into "religious indoctrination. . . . The facially neutral projects authorized by the AFLA . . . are not themselves 'specifically religious activities,' and they are not converted into

---

[42] "The difference is strategic: evangelicalism's core task of evangelizing and influencing the secular world encourages the movement to curb absolutism, conformity, and fanaticism, in a way that fundamentalism's core tasks of defending the theological fundamentals against liberalism and remaining pure from the world do not" (Smith, *American Evangelicalism*, 85).

[43] A recent example of this caricature is provided by Dwyer, *Religious Schools*.

[44] Monsma, *When Sacred and Secular Mix*, 125.

[45] Ibid., 124.

[46] Esbeck, *Regulation of Religious Organizations*, 49.

such activities by the fact that they are carried out by organizations with religious affiliations."[47]

The dissenting minority in the case actually saw more clearly on this point, arguing that "on a continuum of 'sectarianism' running from parochial schools at one end to the colleges funded by the statutes upheld in *Tilton, Hunt,* and *Roemer* at the other, the AFLA grantees described by the District Court clearly are much closer to the former than to the latter."[48] After all, "There is a very real and important difference between running a soup kitchen or a hospital, and counseling pregnant teenagers on how to make the difficult decisions facing them."[49] Justice O'Connor, though voting with the majority, echoed this distinction in her concurring opinion: "Using religious organizations to advance the secular goals of the AFLA, without thereby permitting religious indoctrination, is inevitably more difficult than in other projects, such as ministering to the poor and the sick."[50]

Counseling pregnant teenagers, and especially with the "moralistic" end in view of encouraging them to behave responsibly about sex and about parenthood, is indeed about as sensitive and value-laden as anything that society can undertake; that's why, in something like desperation, Congress was reaching out to faith-based organizations for help. Government agencies do not do it very well, but the nongovernmental, nonmarket "third sector tends to be best at performing tasks that generate little or no profit, demand compassion and commitment to individuals, require extensive trust on the part of customers or clients, need hands-on, personal attention . . . and involve the enforcement of moral codes and individual responsibility for behavior."[51] Churches and other religious institutions have been doing this unapologetically and with some measure of success for thousands of years; it is for that reason, surely, that Congress decided to include them in the provisions of the AFLA. As Rehnquist pointed out in the majority opinion, "it seems quite sensible for Congress to recognize that religious organizations can influence values and can have some influence on family life, including parents' relations with their adolescent children."[52] The Senate committee that heard the bill recognized "the limitations of Government in dealing with a problem that has complex moral and social dimensions" and stated its belief "that promoting the involvement of religious organizations in the solution to these problems is neither inappropriate or illegal."[53] Positive neutrality, in brief.

[47] *Bowen v. Kendrick,* 613.
[48] Ibid., 632 (Blackmun, J., dissenting).
[49] Ibid., 641 (Blackmun, J., dissenting).
[50] Ibid., 622 (O'Connor, J., concurring).
[51] Osborne and Gaebler, *Reinventing Government,* 46.
[52] *Bowen v. Kendrick,* 607.
[53] *Senate Report on the Adolescent Family Life Act,* 15–16.

But if it is appropriate for government to meet the social and educational needs of at-risk adolescents through faith-based programs, it is hard to see why it would not be equally appropriate for government to fund schools for them that operate on the basis of the same orientation.

Nor would this necessarily mean that such schools would have to abandon their distinctive character. "No statutory language [in AFLA] specifically barred the use of grant monies for worship, prayer, or other intrinsically religious activities. . . . After describing the broad outlines of AFLA, the majority spoke of the establishment clause and public aid in sweeping terms as permitting an equality-based rule. It said that 'religious institutions need not be quarantined from public benefits that are neutrally available to all,' and that 'this Court has never held that religious institutions are disabled by the First Amendment from participating in publicly sponsored social welfare programs.' "[54] This seems to be a recognition of the sort of positive neutrality that Esbeck, Monsma, and others have urged as an alternative to "strict separation."

If a faith-based organization invokes its understanding of the nature and basis of responsibility while counseling youth, it is because that is what it knows how to do with some effect; to require that it refrain from doing so would be to require it to fight with one hand tied behind its back. Surely it would be foolish, as a matter of public policy, to summon a powerful ally into the fray and then cripple its ability to do what it knows how to do best. The minority dissenting opinion stressed (more candidly than did the majority) that successful counseling by a religious organization will inevitably have religious overtones. Where the minority went astray was in asserting that this constitutes "advancing religion at public expense" in an unconstitutional manner. What such an organization is in fact doing is advancing the cause of responsible behavior by teenagers. To imply that this is somehow a cover for engaging in self-aggrandizing indoctrination is to fundamentally misunderstand the motivations that lead faith-based organizations to engage in such ministries. "When the religious organization is directly engaged in pedagogy, with the express intent of shaping belief and changing behavior," as the minority puts it, it seems clear that this serves a legitimate secular purpose that few other institutions of our society can perform as well.

The Double Bind Created by "Pervasively Sectarian" Analysis

There is a good reason why courts might avoid close inquiry into whether and to what extent the activities of an educational institution have religious significance, as we can see from the way the Ninth Circuit Court of Appeals

---

[54] Esbeck, *Regulation of Religious Organizations*, 16.

treated a case involving nonpublic schools. The question was not whether they were too religious but whether they were religious enough to qualify for an exemption from the federal law forbidding discrimination in hiring on the basis of religion. The Kamehameha Schools—one for boys, the other for girls—were set up and are maintained under a charitable trust established in 1854 by Bernice Pauahi Bishop, a member of the Hawaiian royal family; public funding was not at issue. Among the provisions of her will was "that the teachers of said schools shall forever be persons of the Protestant religion, but I do not intend that the choice be restricted to persons of any particular sect of Protestants."[55]

Was this requirement simply an expression of anti-Catholic sentiment? More likely in the context of the time (and given the strong influence of New England), it expressed *also* a concern that a set of commonly held Christian beliefs, free of denominational particularities, shape all aspects of the schools' life and instruction. If so, it would not be inconsistent with that understanding for the present leadership of the schools to "disavow any effort to instill particular religious beliefs in their students" while providing required "courses about religion and a general effort to teach good values," and to do so out of a conviction that this was the "religious" way to proceed. Indeed, many Catholic schools—especially those serving high proportions of non-Catholic pupils—would, like the Kamehameha Schools, disclaim any intention of converting their pupils. On trial for discrimination in hiring, the schools' leadership conceded that there was nothing about their instruction in academic subjects that would require a Protestant viewpoint, but the district court accepted the argument that their requirement of a course in "Protestant" religion and of prayers qualified the schools as religious.[56]

The Kamehameha Schools lost on appeal, however, when the court held that, in enacting Title VII, "Congress did not anticipate schools that disavow any effort to instill particular religious beliefs in their students would come within the exemption" and that

> the curriculum of the Schools has little to do with propagating Protestantism, especially in grades 7–12. Seventh and eighth grade students study the nature of religious belief and the tenets of major faiths, and high school students take a one quarter course exploring the interrelationship of western religions and Hawaiian culture, but efforts to propagate Protestantism are not evident in this or any other coursework or in required activities of the Schools. Courses about religion and a general effort to teach good values do not constitute a curriculum that propagates religion, especially in view of the Schools' express

[55] *Equal Employment Opportunity Commission v. Kamehameha Schools/Bishop Estate*, 990 F.2d 458 (9th Cir. 1992).
[56] Ibid., 780 F.Supp. 1317.

disclaimer of any effort to convert their non-Protestant students. The Schools' publications demonstrate religion is more a part of the general tradition of the Schools than a part of their mission, and serves primarily as a means for advancing moral values in the context of a general education.[57]

Can K-12 schools have a religious association and yet not be "pervasively religious" in the sense that, according to the Court, disqualifies them from receiving public support for their educational mission? In its *Kamehameha* decision in 1993, in order to conclude that curriculum of the schools was not "directed toward the propagation of a particular religion," the Ninth Circuit examined "all significant religious and secular characteristics . . . to determine whether the [schools'] purpose and character are primarily religious." It would not be enough, the court reasoned, if an educational institution was "merely 'affiliated' with a religious organization."[58] In the case of the Kamehameha Schools, the Court found that only three of the faculty had "specific religious teaching duties." The schools were not religious enough to meet the qualifications to be allowed to hire on the basis of religion, even though "some official school activities have religious overtones. Teachers in kindergarten through eighth grade lead their classes in a daily prayer, and all boarders say grace before dinner. Athletic teams pray before games, and the School's daily bulletin usually reprints a Bible verse. The Bishop Memorial Church holds services every Sunday during the school year which all boarding students must attend."

The Court was convinced by the fact that no effort was made in the "secular" courses to instruct in Protestant doctrines, "and the Schools have explicitly disavowed any effort to convert non-Protestant students." Although students were required to take each year a religious education class, designed, according to the teacher, "to teach the basic truths about how God and through his son Jesus Christ teaches us how to live a joyous and fulfilling life," this was not enough to make the schools pervasively religious. The Court concluded that "the religious characteristics of the Schools consist of minimal, largely comparative religious studies, scheduled prayers and services, quotation of Bible verses in a school publication, and the employment of nominally Protestant teachers for secular subjects. . . . We conclude the Schools are an essentially secular institution operating within an historical tradition that includes Protestantism, and that the Schools' purpose and character is primarily secular, not primarily religious."

---

[57] *Equal Employment Opportunity Commission v. Kamehameha Schools/Bishop Estate*, 990 F.2d 458 (9th Cir. 1993).

[58] *EEOC v. Townley Eng. & Mfg. Co.*, 859 F.2d 610, 613, 617 (9th Cir. 1988).

The decisive consideration, for the Ninth Circuit, appeared to be that these schools did not attempt to convert their students, which the Court took to distinguish them from "pervasively sectarian" parochial schools. "Courses about religion and a general effort to teach good values do not constitute a curriculum that propagates religion, especially in view of the Schools' express disclaimer of any effort to convert their non-Protestant students. The Schools' publications demonstrate religion is more a part of the general tradition of the Schools than a part of their mission, and serves primarily as a means for advancing moral values in the context of a general education."

Such a detailed examination of a school's relationship to its religious tradition, if applied in the cases concerned with public funding, would no doubt find that many Catholic and other schools with a religious identity are no more committed to "indoctrination" than are the Kamehameha Schools. The Ninth Circuit was willing to make such an examination as the basis for denying a school the right to make hiring decisions on religious grounds, but no court has done so in order to permit funding of the secular activities of teaching mathematics or geography or chemistry. As the Supreme Court "explained" in 1975, in *Meek v. Pittenger*, "it would simply ignore reality to attempt to separate secular educational functions from the predominantly religious role performed by many of Pennsylvania's church-related elementary and secondary schools."[59] In *Grand Rapids v. Ball*, indeed, the Supreme Court concluded that it was not possible to make a distinction between the secular and the sacred; in the case of faith-based schools, from the Court's point of view, everything was sacred.

Kamehameha is not a First Amendment case, of course, but it suggests that *the "pervasively sectarian" label is imposed only when it disqualifies a religious school for public funds, not when it protects the autonomy of such a school from government intervention in its hiring decisions.*

The logic of *Kamehameha*, such as it is, is consistent with that of the majority in *Bowen v. Kendrick*; both point to the instrumental character of religious teaching (seeking to shape "moral values") as exonerating the activity from the charge of being indoctrination. By contrast, it has been simply assumed that everything done by parochial schools is "sectarian."

It seems unwise for a court—or a government agency—to be making judgments about whether a school's religious mission is sufficiently pervasive and central to its purpose to justify selecting staff on the basis of their agreement with that mission. In view of the difficulty and sensitivity of making such distinctions, however, it is understandable that the Supreme

[59] *Meek v. Pittenger*, 421 U.S. 349 (1975) at 365.

Court has chosen to consider all faith-based K-12 schools as pervasively sectarian and all faith-based agencies and colleges as not. Understandable, but unjust.

New Cracks in the Wall of Separation

How can we explain the Court's position, that faith-based programs that teach and counsel adolescent girls are presumed not to be sectarian until shown on a case-by-case basis to have overstepped some poorly defined line, while faith-based schools are presumed without examination to be engaged in indoctrination? It does seem anomalous that schools should be subjected to much tougher standards than other organizations serving essentially the same population. Coughlin notes that "when the Court considers challenges to other First Amendment guarantees such as the free exercise of religion and the freedom of press and association, it generally prefers to balance competing interests rather than to develop absolute rules." In considering the constitutionality of AFLA, for example, the Court took into account legitimate social goals that argued for the appropriateness of an alliance with faith-based organizations that might be especially capable of changing the behavior of teenaged girls. Why has the Court been unwilling to perform the same balancing act with respect to faith-based school, despite their unquestionable contributions to the education of poor and vulnerable children? In fact, "the Court refuses to consider the possibility that a program's secular effect might, on balance, outweigh its failure to satisfy the entanglement prong" of the *Lemon* standard. "No secular purpose and effect, no matter how compelling, have been deemed worthy to assure judicial deference to a program of parochial school aid"[60] . . . at least until very recently.

The majority opinion in *Bowen v. Kendrick* argued that AFLA was " 'religion-blind' . . . the law did not violate the establishment clause merely because religious beliefs and the moral values urged by AFLA overlap." As a result, "after *Kendrick*, a violation of the establishment clause must now be buttressed by palpable evidence that religion is being unconstitutionally advanced."[61] But K-12 schools with a religious character continued to be considered, by the Supreme Court, as presumptively "sectarian" and ineligible for public funding for anything related to their educational mission. The Court's logic (spelled out in *Grand Rapids School District v. Ball* in 1985) is that every aspect of the teaching of such schools involves "indoctrination into the beliefs of a particular religious faith" and a "substantial risk that, overtly or subtly, the religious message . . . will infuse the supposedly secu-

---

[60] Coughlin, "Common Sense in Formation," 310, 312.
[61] Esbeck, *Regulation of Religious Organizations*, 17, 19.

lar classes." They are thus "pervasively religious," a term that is bandied about by the Court as though it were self-explanatory.[62]

The explanation must lie in the unique significance that public schools hold in the Whig orthodoxy (if we may so characterize the historical understanding reflected in the Court's decisions in this area), and the long-entrenched belief that Catholic schools in particular are somehow un-American and threatening to our entire system. It is striking how often in American history the question of public funding for or even tolerance of parochial schools has been presented as a danger to the public school and to society itself. Nor is this attitude uniquely American; for much of the nineteenth century educational policy struggles in Western Europe were dominated by the question whether nonpublic Catholic and Protestant schools would create deep social divisions, *deux jeunesses*.[63]

This is an attitude that finds particularly direct expression in Justice Black's dissent in *Board of Education v. Allen*, a case authorizing loan of textbooks in secular subjects to nonpublic school:

> The same powerful sectarian religious propagandists who have succeeded in securing passage of the present law to help religious schools carry on their sectarian religious purposes can and doubtless will continue their propaganda, looking toward complete domination and supremacy of their particular brand of religion. And it nearly always is by insidious approaches that the citadels of liberty are most successfully attacked. . . . The First Amendment's prohibition against governmental establishment of religion was written on the assumption that state aid to religion and religious schools generates discord, disharmony, hatred, and strife among our people, and that any government that supplies such aids is to that extent a tyranny. And I still believe that the only way to protect minority religious groups from majority groups in this country is to keep the wall of separation between church and state high and impregnable as the First and Fourteenth Amendments provide. The Court's affirmance here bodes nothing but evil to religious peace in this country.[64]

It is startling to find such intemperate remarks eight years after the election of Kennedy seemed to lay to rest—at least in polite discussion—the idea of a Catholic conspiracy to achieve "complete domination and supremacy" over American society and political life.

The majority opinion in *Allen*, in fact, took a reasonable position that seems to anticipate recent treatment of faith-based social agencies, when

---

[62] *Grand Rapids School District v. Ball*, 473 U.S. 373 (1985); *Hunt v. McNair*, 743, one of the cases allowing public funding to denominational colleges, distinguished these from "an institution in which religion is so pervasive that a substantial portion of its functions are subsumed in the religious mission."

[63] I have traced this history at length in *Myth of Common School*.

[64] *Board of Education v. Allen* (Black, J., dissenting), 253–54.

it observed that "we cannot agree with appellants either that all teaching in a sectarian school is religious or that the processes of secular and religious training are so intertwined that secular textbooks furnished to students by the public are in fact instrumental in the teaching of religion."

The Court appears to be returning to this more practical stance in its decision in *Agostini v. Felton*, decided on June 23, 1997. Two decisions in 1985—*Aguilar v. Felton* and *Grand Rapids School District v. Ball*—had been a devastating setback for the view that the state had a legitimate interest in providing strictly secular services within the context of faith-based schooling. Grand Rapids struck down a school district program that provided supplementary courses such as arts and crafts, home economics, Spanish, gymnastics, chess, and model building during and after the regular school day in classrooms leased from nonpublic schools to pupils in those schools; the classrooms were leased by the school system, had to be free of religious symbols, and displayed a sign "public school classroom"! The Court decided that the teachers might be influenced by the "pervasively sectarian" atmosphere of the schools in which they worked (forty out of forty-one participating nonpublic schools were faith-based) to indoctrinate the children in particular religious beliefs, that the program created the appearance of state endorsement of religion, and that the religious functions of the schools were subsidized indirectly through relieving them of other costs they might have borne.[65] *Aguilar v. Felton* struck down a federally funded program under which employees of the New York City school system provided remedial instruction to poor children attending faith-based schools, on the basis that supervising those employees closely to ensure that they did not further the religious mission of the schools would necessarily create an "excessive entanglement" of public officials with religion.[66]

Reversing in large part these earlier decisions, Justice O'Connor announced for the *Agostini* majority "that the Court has abandoned *Ball*'s presumption that public employees placed on parochial school grounds will inevitably inculcate religion or that their presence constitutes a symbolic union between government and religion." Articulating something like a doctrine of "positive neutrality," she found that no impermissible state incentive to religious practice existed when "the aid is allocated on the basis of neutral, secular criteria that neither favor nor disfavor religion, and is made available to both religious and secular beneficiaries on a nondiscriminatory basis."

The prohibition against government entanglement in the affairs of religious bodies was modified as well. Justice O'Connor pointed out that "not all entanglements . . . have the effect of advancing or inhibiting religion.

---

[65] *Grand Rapids School District v. Ball*, 373.
[66] *Aguilar v. Felton*, 473 U.S. 402 (1985).

Interaction between church and state is inevitable, . . . and we have always tolerated some level of involvement between the two. Entanglement must be 'excessive' before it runs afoul of the Establishment Clause. See, e.g., *Bowen v. Kendrick*, 487 U. S., at 615–17 (no excessive entanglement where government reviews the adolescent counseling program set up by the religious institutions that are grantees, reviews the materials used by such grantees, and monitors the program by periodic visits); *Roemer v. Board of Public Works of Md.*, 426 U.S. 736, 764–765 (1976) (no excessive entanglement where state conducts annual audits to ensure colleges are not used to teach religion)."

There may, therefore, be a certain softening in the Court's assumption that everything that a faith-oriented school does involves indoctrination. An apparently strong indication of such a change was the Court's decision in November 1998, on an eight to one vote, not to review the constitutionality of the state program in Wisconsin that provides vouchers for low-income children in Milwaukee to attend faith-based (as well as secular) nonpublic schools (*Jackson v. Benson* [Case No. 98–376]). The Supreme Court thus left intact a ruling by the Wisconsin Supreme Court, in June 1998, that the state voucher program's inclusion of religious schools did not violate the prohibition against government establishment of religion. Since no opinion was issued in this case, we cannot be sure how far the precedent extends.

In the wake of its 1997 *Agostini* decision and its decision, in 1998, not to review the Wisconsin voucher program, can we expect to see the flexible and pragmatic approach taken by the Supreme Court toward faith-based programs for adolescents applied to faith-based schools? Should only pregnancy entitle young people to be exposed—by a voluntary decision on their part or that of their parents—to religiously based ways of understanding the moral order and the nature of a good life? Is the "wall of separation" beginning to crumble in education, as it has in other human services? And, if it does, will this create new dangers for faith-based schools?

Summary

The position of the federal courts toward public funding of faith-based social services and higher education has recognized that they may provide valuable public services that draw strength from their religious character without unlawfully advancing religion; this could be described as "positive neutrality" toward religion, recognizing the contributions that it can uniquely make to society.

The Ninth Circuit decision in *Kamehameha* shows that a close examination of the actual program of a school with a religious character may demonstrate that it seeks to educate rather than to indoctrinate, while respecting the consciences of its students. Ironically, this was held against the school's freedom to select staff on the basis of religious criteria.

In cases involving public funding for faith-based schools, however, the courts have adopted a "strict neutrality" doctrine that treats them as so pervasively sectarian that their legitimate secular purposes cannot be publicly funded without an unlawful advancement of religion and/or entanglement of government with religion.

The recent decision in *Agostini*, building on *Rosenberger* and several decisions that have allowed aid when the benefit could be understood to go directly to the student, holds out the possibility that the Supreme Court will move toward "positive neutrality." This would support policy decisions seeking not to influence individual decisions for or against religion. Positive neutrality would offer assistance equally to religious and nonreligious institutions on the same terms. The Court's decision not to review the constitutionality of the Wisconsin voucher program points in the same direction.

4

FUNDING WITH GOVERNMENT

OVERSIGHT

AS WE HAVE SEEN, there are deep ambiguities in the American jurisprudence that determines what activities with a religious character government may and may not fund. Services for small children and for adolescents, and college-level education, receive public funding without discrimination based on the religious character of the institutions that provide them, but faith-based schools have been denied such assistance. This distinction is a peculiarly American phenomenon; other Western democracies do not to share this reluctance to provide public funds for faith-based schools.[1]

As a result, American parents who want schooling for their children based upon a secular worldview receive it free, while those who want a religious schooling must provide it at their own expense, if indeed they can do so. While with respect to daycare and to higher education government operates on the basis of strict neutrality, "evenhandedness among people of all faiths and of none,"[2] this is far from being the case when it comes to K-12 schooling.

Several recent court decisions discussed in the last chapter could expand the scope for K-12 schools to be treated with a greater measure of "positive neutrality." The *Kamehameha* decision—though it may have been wrongly decided—seems to signal a willingness to recognize that schools with a religious character may not seek to "indoctrinate" but may treat diversity of viewpoints with as much respect as do the colleges that the courts have found not to be pervasively sectarian. Ironically, a decision by the liberal Ninth Circuit that has been read as unfriendly to religion could serve as the basis for reconsideration of assumptions about schools with a religious identity.

The *Agostini* decision suggests that some amount of "entanglement" necessarily associated with any system of accountability for the use of public funds need not be a barrier to supporting nonreligious educational activities in religious schools, provided that the services themselves are "secular, neutral, and nonideological."

---

[1] See Glenn, *Choice of Schools.*
[2] Monsma and Soper, *The Challenge of Pluralism*, 10.

The decision of the Wisconsin Supreme Court, that a state voucher program's inclusion of faith-based schools does not violate the U.S. Constitution's prohibition against government establishment of religion, and the decision of the U. S. Supreme Court not to review that decision, could prove a major breakthrough toward allowing parents to choose between secular and religious schooling for their children without paying a financial penalty, and toward putting new energies behind the reform of public education, through no longer equating it with schooling provided by government.[3]

How Much Oversight?

These developments in the interpretation and application of the religion clauses of the First Amendment combine—probably not by accident—with the growing interest in policy circles in finding ways of "putting the civil society to work." Government assumption of civil society functions has proved more expensive and less effective than hoped by generations of elite reformers, and it has proved to be loaded with unanticipated negative consequences. On the other hand, few policy specialists believe that Western societies can or should return to the laissez-faire nineteenth century. The public expects that government will continue to guarantee a variety of services and protections at the same time that it complains—especially in the United States—that government has become too large and its services insufficiently responsive and effective. Provision of services by nongovernmental institutions with government support and oversight seems a happy way out of this dilemma.[4]

This makes all the more acute the question of *how* government can make use of the institutions of the civil society without fatally distorting their nature. Must the effect of public funding be to make nongovernmental organizations as bureaucratic and rule-bound as the public agencies whose inadequacies they are intended to remedy? Two Dutch sociologists have concluded that this may be inevitable:

> Government guarantees with respect to welfare in the areas of income, education, housing, nursing, etc., have called to life an apparatus that can only be managed through bureaucratic means. Even where the government has entrusted the delivery of aspects of welfare into the hands of apparently autonomous foundations and associations (as is especially the case in the Netherlands ...), this "private initiative" is almost entirely financially dependent [on

---

[3] See the discussion of the "educational finance monopoly" by Quade, *Financing Education*.
[4] Perhaps the most influential presentation of this position in the United States has been Osborne and Gaebler, *Reinventing Government*.

government and must develop] organizational structures able to deal with administrative regulations. Without becoming bureaucratically organized, the institutions would in the most literal sense lose contact with government.[5]

As a result of such considerations some observers, while conceding the desirability of giving a larger role to faith-based and other independent organizations, yet have deep doubts about whether this can be achieved at an acceptable cost to the civil society itself. Even as voucher supporters in Milwaukee celebrated their legal victories, they were faced with what one observer called "a barrage of private school regulations the [Wisconsin] Department of Public Instruction threatened to impose," despite a governor favorable to the voucher program.

These dangers are the subject of a recent study of government contracting with social service agencies in Massachusetts by Joe Loconte, associate editor of *Policy Review*. Loconte details the way in which "more and more regulations are being developed that implement a certain value that bureaucrats have, or certain interest groups have," with a profoundly distorting effect on the mission of nongovernmental organizations dependent upon public funding.[6]

Some faith-based organizations appear to coexist with government and to derive a substantial proportion of their funding from government without as a consequence selling their souls. Much depends upon safeguards in the laws or programs from which they receive support. It is not enough that faith-based organizations be eligible for funding unless they are also protected from interference with how they approach the work for which they are funded. Loconte found that most agency directors he interviewed agreed "that the state—through statutes, regulations, and the fine print in contract language—exerts a powerful influence over caregiving decisions."[7] The "Charitable Choice" provision of the new federal welfare legislation (described below) seems to promise a greater respect for institutional integrity.

The Dutch constitution protects the right of nonpublic schools that receive full public funding to do so "with due regard . . . to the freedom to provide education according to religious or other belief," and there is a high-level council (the Onderwijsraad) one of whose responsibilities is to ensure that this freedom is respected in all government decisions. The right to maintain a distinctive character has direct implications for the decisions that must be left up to each school, including "counseling of pupils, choice of materials, organization of community events, division of tasks among staff, refresher courses and in-service training, working-out of pupil sup-

---

[5] Adriaansens and Zijderveld, *Vrijwillig initiatief en de verzorgingsstaat.*
[6] Loconte, *Seducing the Samaritan*, 72.
[7] Ibid., 55.

port functions within the school. . . . in short, the organization of education cannot be separated from the goals, the distinctiveness, and the character of schools."[8] While we will see that there are definite limits on this freedom, the problem is at least out on the table and hotly debated in the Netherlands (see the interlude on neocorporatism).

Whether the "strings" attached to public funding pose a serious threat to the autonomy and mission of faith-based schools and other organizations depends to some extent upon the mechanisms by which government regulates and funds; that will be the theme of this chapter. It depends also, however, upon the integrity with which the organization itself maintains its character and focus. Just as government officials are tempted to expand their reach into virgin territories of regulation, so agency officials are tempted to respond to every inducement to expand their services . . . even if that takes their organizations in quite new directions. Loconte notes that "the hungry response of the social service industry to government funding is decisive."[9] We will return to that crucial temptation in chapter 7.

The question of government regulation as a condition of funding inevitably overlaps to some extent with that of government regulation in the public interest. As we saw in chapter 2, such regulation is imposed upon agencies and schools even in the absence of funding. We will need to consider the possibility that each of the ways in which public funding may be provided would increase the burden of government oversight to the point that a nonpublic institution became functionally indistinguishable from its public counterparts. At some point, the combination of funding and regulation could have the effect of making it in the eyes of the law a "state actor," subject to all the constitutional and other obligations imposed upon government itself.

> If public dollars flowing to private institutions under a voucher system are accompanied by excessive governmental regulations, there is cause for concern. This is clear from the Section 8 low income rental certificate program decisions in which federal courts have found statutory and regulatory restrictions so encompassing that the tenants have secured a constitutionally protected properly right in their leases. In a most instructive 1986 decision, the federal district court for Northern California . . . noted that the flow of money alone to the private landlords was insufficient to constitute governmental action. "When, however, the relevant statute and regulations are viewed in their entirety this court concludes that 'state action' exists."[10]

---

[8] Wetenschappelijk Instituut voor het CDA, *Ruimte voor kwaliteit*, 63.

[9] Loconte, *Seducing the Samaritan*, 40.

[10] Kemerer, Hairston, and Lauerman, "Vouchers and Private School Autonomy," 601–28, 612.

What this means is that a private landlord can under some circumstances be regulated by government in the same way that it regulates its contractors, and be held to the same requirements.

There are thus two sorts of "strings" that may come attached to public funding. The first are the specific requirements attached to a funding program, the second (potentially) the necessity of behaving like a public institution in ways that go beyond funding requirements. Private schools that exist to serve pupils with special educational needs tuitioned-in by local or state education authorities, for example, are required under the federal Individuals with Disabilities Act to operate in most respects as if they were public schools. The law requires that "in all such instances, the State educational agency shall determine whether such [private] schools and facilities meet standards that apply to State and local educational agencies and that children so served have all the rights they would have if served by such agencies."[11]

There are many nongovernmental agencies that came into existence in order to provide human services under government contracts. For them, the burden of regulation is part of the necessary cost of doing business; having started out to do work for government, they may experience little strain as a result.[12] For a faith-based school or agency, however, the problem goes much deeper, since to the extent that it becomes like a public school or agency, it may lose its very reason to exist. This danger was recognized by the Ohio Supreme Court in its *Whisner* decision, in which public funding was not at issue (the Tabernacle Christian School did "not receive any form of state or federal aid, and would not accept it if offered, because '[a]nything they give to you they control' "). The court found that the state's "minimum standards" for approval of nonpublic schools "are so pervasive and all-encompassing that total compliance with each and every standard by a nonpublic school would effectively eradicate the distinction between public and nonpublic education, and thereby deprive these appellants of their traditional interest as parents to direct the upbringing and education of their children."[13]

The issue at stake is not *whether* states may regulate, but *how intrusive* that regulation may be before the nongovernmental school or agency loses its distinctive character and becomes in effect part of the state apparatus, subject to all of the constraints that have made the human service bureaucracy and the public education system so unwieldy and so ineffective.

---

[11] 20 *U.S. Code*, sec. 1413(a)(4)(B)(ii) (1988), quoted by Kemerer, Hairston, and Lauerman, "Vouchers and Private School Autonomy," 607.

[12] Smith and Lipsky, *Nonprofits for Hire*, 40.

[13] *The State of Ohio v. Whisner*, Supreme Court of Ohio. July 28, 1976. 351 N.E.2d 750, at 768.

Protecting the ability of faith-based agencies and schools to be *unlike* those operated by government is essential both to their own integrity and also to the contribution that they can make to a diverse society. That depends in part (as we will see later) upon their own efforts, but it depends also upon the mechanisms by which public support is provided to them, and what forms of accountability are required. As one cross-national study found, "executive leadership of the agencies reported few instances of unacceptable governmental requirements imposed on their service programs, governance, or administration. Nor did governmental funding seem to inhibit advocacy. This is not to say that there were no complaints about red tape or about the burdens of complying with an excessive number of regulations. These were, however, found almost exclusively *in the United States, where there is a much greater emphasis on reporting and accountability, as well as more concern with the preservation of independence than in the other countries.*"[14] That is the central concern of this chapter.

Modes of Funding

Government has a number of ways of supporting nongovernment organizations (NGOs) that provide human services or education;[15] perhaps the most significant are

Model	*Government*
Contracting	Enters into a formal agreement for the specific services to be provided by an NGO
Vouchers	Issues vouchers to those entitled to services, allowing them to purchase the services from any approved NGO
Grants/subsidies	Gives general support to enable NGOs to provide services, or to increase the level of services
Shared space	Provides or funds services within the context of, but distinct from, an NGO's program
Franchise	Designates an NGO as sole provider of a publicly funded service in an area
Asset sale	Sells its assets to an NGO in the expectation that it will continue to provide the services previously provided by government directly

[14] Kramer, "Use of Government Funds," 227, emphasis added.
[15] The following schema is adapted from Wubbenhorst, "POS Reform in Massachusetts."

Contracting

"Purchase of service" (POS) contracts between government and private nonprofit organizations have become very common in recent decades, as a result initially of the deinstitutionalization of the mentally ill and retarded and a shift toward community-based treatment of juvenile delinquents. A further impetus in some states was the assumption by state government—which lacked delivery systems reaching into every community—of a variety of social welfare services that had previously been provided by municipal government.

The mentally ill and retarded in Massachusetts had been cared for in large state institutions for 150 years; this was a focus of Horace Mann's efforts as a politician before he turned to promoting the state's role in education. The combination of unfavorable publicity—including lawsuits—about the quality of care and of life in such "asylums" with the availability of new drug and behavior modification techniques convinced state policymakers to turn to community-based programs through contracting with private nonprofit groups. Soon the state was using this method for providing day care and foster care, as well as case management services by social workers employed by nonprofits. More and more public school pupils with special educational needs were served by private schools specializing in such children, under contracts with local school systems. "Demand for community programs consistently outstripped supply in the 1970s. As a result, state purchasing agents often had to lobby advocates to establish programs with which the department could then contract."[16] "In fiscal year 1989," Smith and Lipsky tell us, "14 Massachusetts state agencies spent over $800 million, about 8.5 percent of the state budget, to purchase from over 1,150 contractors such services as alcoholism rehabilitation, family crisis intervention, instruction in English-as-a-second language, and daycare."[17]

It is important to note that, while state and local government had long made grants to nonprofit organizations that seemed worthy of public support, this "contract regime" involved very different levels of accountability. In effect, nonprofits were being asked to function as agents of government, often making decisions with profound effects upon vulnerable clients (children in foster care, for example). This was a fundamental shift. As recently as 1965 "public funds accounted for only eight percent of [family service] agencies' income. For the same year, a survey of health and welfare agencies in 13 urban areas found that public funding in all fields only accounted for

---

[16] Ibid.
[17] Smith and Lipsky, *Nonprofits for Hire*, 4.

six percent of revenues. . . . a study of over 800 service organizations found that 80 percent did not receive public funds." But within a decade "non-profit agencies [had] became agents of government in the expansion of the American welfare state."[18]

In addition to the presumed advantages of arranging to have services provided by community-based agencies, the contracting (or purchase of service) system also allowed state managers to evade the hiring freezes imposed periodically on their agencies, as well as bureaucratic and union contract rigidities in the state hiring—and firing—process.[19] And despite the complaints of nonprofits about red tape connected with state contracts, they tend to be much less constrained than are the government agencies themselves. "No other group of Americans must deal day in, day out with the kind of rule-bound workplace civil servants confront. Overregulation saps their morale and efficiency, in the end making self-fulfilling prophecies of the invidious judgments commonly made about appointive officials' lack of energy and imagination."[20] By comparison—at least in theory—nonprofits can respond to client needs and changing situations more flexibly.

Contracting can take different forms but by its nature involves detailed requirements before, during, and after the period of the contract.

> There are two principal types of social service contracts used by state agencies to support social programs. One is the cost-reimbursement approach. Under this scheme, a nonprofit group provides services to a target population and is reimbursed for expenses—overhead, staff time, and supplies—by the state. The state determines what is reimbursable and at what rate of payment. The service provider, of course, must submit receipts, time sheets, and other evidence of all of its relevant costs. The other approach is known as a unit-rate contract. . . . state agencies translate direct assistance into quantifiable, billable units of service. The Bureau of Substance Abuse, for example, wants to fund a detoxification program and buys a "bed-day" of service—a precise estimate of everything it costs to serve a client for a day, including counseling sessions, direct care, and staff salaries.[21]

Cost reimbursement requires elaborate administrative controls to keep track of costs and allocate them properly; many faith-based organizations are not equipped to provide these, or see them as a restraint and a diversion

---

[18] Ibid., 54, 71.

[19] As a Massachusetts state government manager for twenty-one years, I can attest to how eagerly we "out-sourced" much of our work rather than seeking to appoint regular state employees. It should be noted, however, that the public employees' unions have resisted this practice with considerable success, forcing abandonment of various initiatives (see Kirby et al., *Income Support*, 53).

[20] Garvey and DiIulio, "Sources of Overregulation," 12.

[21] Loconte, *Seducing the Samaritan*, 23.

from serving immediate needs. In effect, they are forced into becoming at least somewhat like the government agencies whose inefficiencies they are intended to replace. Sometimes this results from interpretations of the law that fail to recognize the distinctive nature of civil society institutions, as when "a New Jersey appellate court refused to set aside the state's stringent bookkeeping and accounting practices for private schools serving students with disabilities, stating that 'Private schools that choose to receive handicapped public school pupils under [state law] must therefore relinquish some of the privacy and control over their affairs that they otherwise would have under the general provisions' " of the state law pertaining to private schools.[22]

Some faith-based agencies, founded and staffed by volunteers or low-paid staff whose primary motivations are religious and charitable, choose not to seek public funding because of the distorting effect of such requirements. Others find that they must themselves become bureaucratic in order to comply with bureaucratic demands. "If a nonprofit group secures state contracts from several different state agencies, it must file bundles of reports—with overlapping or identical information—with each agency."[23]

The other approach—the unit-rate contract—is simpler to keep track of but poses significant risks to a small organization unable to absorb the losses connected with miscalculation of costs or unexpected increases in expenses. A single client with extremely expensive needs could drive such an organization into bankruptcy.

If a purchase-of-service contract is used as the vehicle for providing public funding for services provided by a faith-based organization, the organization is likely to be required to abide by very specific requirements spelling out not only how the services are to be provided but also how selection of clients and staff is to be carried out. For example, faith-based organizations are often required to surrender the right to use religious criteria in making employment decisions as a condition of being given a government contract. This is one of the concerns addressed by the Charitable Choice provision of the welfare reform law (Personal Responsibility and Work Opportunity Reconciliation Act of 1996), designed to protect the integrity of such organizations.

Charitable Choice

Briefly stated, "if a state chooses to use federal welfare funds to contract with, or to provide vouchers redeemable by, any nongovernmental social-service provider, then the state must comply with the Charitable Choice

---

[22] Kemerer, Hairston, and Lauerman, "Vouchers and Private School Autonomy," 609.
[23] Loconte, *Seducing the Samaritan*, 11.

requirement not to discriminate against faith-based providers." This applies to the Temporary Assistance for Needy Families program that has replaced AFDC, and also to the Supplementary Security Income (SSI) program and the food stamps and Medicaid programs, "to the extent [which is considerable] that states administer these programs using contracts or vouchers with nongovernmental providers."[24] Faith-based organizations will be able to compete for any contracts or to offer to provide services in exchange for vouchers on the same basis as secular organizations; their religious character is to be neither an advantage nor a disadvantage. If funded, faith-based organizations "have the right to maintain a religious environment by displaying religious art, scripture, religions apparel, and other symbols. They retain their right to use religious criteria in hiring, firing, and disciplining employees, while remaining subject to other anti-discrimination laws. They can limit the scope of fiscal audits by segregating federal funds into a separate account."

On the other hand, "a faith-based provider may not discriminate against a beneficiary on the basis of religion, a religious belief, or the beneficiary's refusal to actively participate in a religions practice," and "faith-based providers may not use contract funds to pay for worship services, sectarian instruction, or proselytization, so as to avoid the appearance of governmental promotion of the provider's religious doctrines. No such restriction is necessary in the case of vouchers."

> In counseling beneficiaries concerning the need for changes in behavior or attitudes, some organizations use principles originating in a religious tradition. Such principles may not be prohibited simply due to their religious roots. . . . So long as a public purpose is served by the principles being taught, such as instilling the virtues of responsibility, self-control, care for dependents, and work, a faith-based organization may use principles rooted in its belief system.
>
> Religious organizations may not compel beneficiaries to actively participate in a religious practice. However, beneficiaries may be expected not to disrupt or disturb such practices, as such behavior may interfere with the faith-based provider's autonomy or its control of its mission. Beneficiaries have access to an alternative provider and may be deemed to have consented to the religious characteristics and practices from whom they accept service.

Though resembling in many respects the German and Dutch "positive neutrality," providing schooling through a variety of faith-based organizations (described in the interlude on neocorporatism), Charitable Choice does not go so far to protect freedom of choice on the part of clients. It does not guarantee to each human service client "the right to receive ser-

---

[24] These and the following quotations are from Center for Public Justice, *Guide to Charitable Choice*.

vices from a faith-based provider that reflects his or her own religious beliefs. Charitable Choice intends to expand the participation of faith-based providers in government-funded welfare to fulfill the public purpose of more effectively serving the poor and needy. It is not a program to ensure that religions groups will receive government funds nor that beneficiaries will receive services guided by some particular religious faith." If extended to cover the provision of education, Charitable Choice would be preferable to the present prohibition of support to faith-based schools, but it would not satisfy the need to guarantee real educational freedom for those who cannot pay for private schooling. In the terms described in chapter 3, it brings the American welfare system into line with a "strict neutrality" standard, but not as far as "positive neutrality."

Federal antidiscrimination law, as we will see in chapter 6, provides an exception for faith-based organizations, but states and cities may attach their own, more restrictive strings to their contracts for services. In Massachusetts, for example, "once state funds flow to a nonprofit, the Commonwealth prohibits discrimination based on religious or sexual orientation, no matter how sectarian the group or agency." In 1994, the state advisory Commission on Gay and Lesbian Youth "recommended that all foster parents and halfway-house workers—many of them church-based—undergo 'sensitivity training' in working with troubled gay youth," and insisted, though with limited success to date, that those state-funded providers of services refusing to do so lose their contracts.[25]

Government contracting for educational services provided by faith-based child care centers and programs for adolescents is, as these examples attest, always under the shadow of requirements that conflict with their mission or with their faith. It can be very hard to surrender contracts that make it possible to do much more than could be done with voluntary contributions alone. As we will see in chapter 6, the Salvation Army (with other organizations) took a stand on hiring policies in New York City in 1984 that was exceptional, but its hasty retreat in San Francisco a decade later shows how difficult it can be to maintain such principled position.

The issue does not, as yet, arise for faith-based schools since, as we saw in chapter 3, a string of federal court decisions since 1971 have warned that the close state supervision required to prevent religion from somehow creeping into the publicly funded instruction or services would result in an excessive and unconstitutional entanglement of state and church. Curiously, for government to supervise the Salvation Army's policies toward homosexual employees does not raise the same red flag for the courts, though as an organization it is far more committed to evangelization than are many parochial schools. The "entanglement" standard

---

[25] Loconte, *Seducing the Samaritan*, 77, 84.

seems to be applied selectively, to the consistent disadvantage of faith-based organizations.

Despite the problems and potential problems mentioned above, their effect should not be exaggerated. As so often, the saving grace of government is its inefficiency!

> Perhaps the most noteworthy condition mitigating any substantial challenge to the freedom of the voluntary agency is the low level of accountability demanded by government. . . . Although extensive record keeping and burdensome reporting requirements were the most frequent complaints among voluntary agencies receiving public funds in the United States—in addition to the perennial objections to inadequate rates of reimbursement—they are not perceived as necessarily or even significantly impairing agencies' freedom. In several instances, United Way requirements in the United States were regarded as more unacceptable. . . . [Government] monitoring was insufficient to ensure compliance.[26]

France

The practice of contracting for educational services provided by Catholic schools is very widespread in France, America's only rival in strictness of church-state separation. Under the *loi Debré*, enacted in 1959, the French government enters into contracts with more than 98 percent of the country's nonpublic schools; their teachers are salaried in full, and other educational costs are paid as well. Fifteen percent of elementary pupils and 20 percent of secondary pupils attend nonpublic schools, the great majority of them Catholic. Careful research has demonstrated that more than one-third of all pupils in France obtain at least part of their schooling in nonpublic schools, since these have become an important resource for families (many not practicing Catholics) when their children are experiencing difficulties in the public schools. Sociologist Robert Ballion describes middle-class parents as consumers of education for their children.[27]

Those who sponsor schools can choose whether to accept government requirements as to curriculum and testing in exchange for staff salaries *(contrat simple)*, or to accept, in addition, some government control over pedagogy and the selection of teachers, in exchange for operating expenses as well as salaries *(contrat d'association)*. To receive support under the *contrat d'association*, a school must demonstrate that it meets an educational need. "The question remains open," Piveteau comments, "whether this official government recognition of an educational need lies in the hands of

---

[26] Kramer, "Use of Government Funds," 230.
[27] Langouet and Leger, *Public ou privé*, 48; Ballion, *Les consommateurs d'école*.

the government or of the population."[28] In other words, is the fact that parents desire a particular form of education different from that provided by public schools sufficient basis for determining that a need exists for the alternative?

Schools under either form of contract are required to teach the regular public school curriculum leading up to the state examinations (which they would do in any case, since there is no other way for their pupils to obtain university admission or vocational qualifications), but are explicitly protected in maintaining their distinctive religious character and may require that the state-salaried teachers respect that character. Although the teachers in Catholic schools under contract are paid by the national government on terms that are parallel to those of public school teachers, they are required to respect Catholic moral expectations: in a 1978 case, for example, the firing of a divorced-and-remarried teacher was upheld.[29]

Suspicion has persisted that government funding of nonstate education would lead to increasing government control, with private schools carried irresistibly by a sort of escalator effect into the public system. This intention of doing so was expressed by anticlerical forces in 1959: "If the private sector is destined to receive State aid, it is appropriate that it be subjected to the financial, administrative and pedagogical control" of the national Ministry of Education.[30] This expectation is the background of the major political crisis over education in the early 1980s that led to the fall of a Socialist government. The government had declared its intention of forcing private schools under contract to conform more closely to the practices of the public system, especially with respect to employment of staff, and a massive mobilization of parents rallied successfully to defend the right to maintain the distinctive character of these schools.

The French arrangement for funding nonpublic schools, though it is referred to as a "contract," in fact has much in common with grant programs and with what we will refer to as "shared space" programs. The *contrat* under which Catholic and other schools are funded is in a sense a form of renewable grant. This suggests that, even in a society strongly opposed to mixing of church and state, a reasonable accommodation can be reached by putting aside rhetoric and focusing upon the practical goal of ensuring the adequacy of the schools that all children attend. American policymaking, by contrast, seems determined to turn its back on the nonpublic schools—many of them drastically underfunded—attended by millions of children, by no means all of them from financially secure families.

[28] Piveteau, "Catholic Education in France."
[29] Madiot, "Le juge et la laïcité," 76.
[30] Leclerc, *La bataille de l'école*, 72–73.

Vouchers

Some state and federal programs provide the agencies administering them the option of doing so through vouchers rather than through contracts with providers. If government funds the services provided by a faith-based organization through issuing certificates or vouchers to clients, allowing them to choose freely among providers, the strings of government supervision are likely to be much looser than in the case of direct contracting. In this case, it is not a government official who is the "customer," but a parent or other person in need of services. In a well-functioning market of services with adequate information about a variety of qualified providers, the customer is able to decide which services are most satisfactory, and so a natural discipline is imposed upon the provider that does not require detailed specifications or close government supervision.

Of course, no such "market" will ever function perfectly, since information available about the quality of services is inevitably imperfect and those who receive publicly funded services are often poor and characteristically inexperienced at making decisions about such complex matters. This is why, for example, successful school choice programs must make a concerted effort not only to reach parents with information but also to provide support and counseling so that parents can make good use of it.[31]

Child Care Vouchers

Much discussed as a possible mechanism for enabling government to support faith-based schooling through the private choices of parents, vouchers have in fact already been introduced with little controversy to enable low-income persons to purchase food, housing, and child care. The last-mentioned is most relevant to the discussion of schooling, since the federal courts have frequently pointed to the tender age of impressionable schoolchildren as the reason not to extend to faith-based schools the forms of subsidy already provided to faith-based colleges.

Government support for child care in the United States is very large-scale and very chaotic. According to a General Accounting Office study, in 1992 and 1993 there were more than 90 early childhood programs funded and administered by eleven federal agencies.[32] States have their programs as well, and many school systems and municipalities provide day care and other early childhood programs, as do hundreds of private employers. In Massachusetts, there are three state agencies that administer various pro-

---

[31] Glenn, McLaughlin, and Salganik, *Parent Information.*
[32] Olsen, "The Advancing Nanny State."

grams; to give some idea of the scale, state-administered vouchers provide for about 16,500 children, while 10,000 are in programs for which the state contracts. A recent report notes, "The absence of shared goals among these state-level departments has inhibited coordination and provided the justification for separate administrative structures. While some formal discussions have taken place regarding increased coordination . . . , it appears that there is more competition for control than collaboration occurring between them. . . . Families will have various degrees of success in obtaining child care subsidies. . . . the working poor, however, are faced with a confusing system."[33]

The Child Care and Development Block Grant Act of 1990 (amended in 1996) permits public funds to be used for educational activities carried out by faith-based organizations. Low-income working parents, especially those coming off of welfare, are eligible for these services, which may be provided by family members as well as by secular or religious organizations. Authorized funding is $21 billion over seven years; in addition, states are allowed to transfer up to 30 percent of their federal welfare funds for this purpose, to support women entering the workforce.

States may choose to administer the funds either through issuing child care certificates (i.e., vouchers) for low-income parents or by entering into contracts with eligible centers for direct payment. In either case, the state or local agency administering the program must ensure that those who provide child care comply with the health and safety and health requirements of state and local law. When the certificate mechanism is used (and thus the public funds flow as a result of the individual decision of a parent), the child care center is more free to express its religious character. To quote the language of the federal regulations, the certificate "may be used for child care services provided by a sectarian organization or agency, including those that engage in religious activities, if those services are chosen by the parent; it may be used by providers for any sectarian purpose or activity that is part of the child care services, including sectarian worship or instruction." How is that possible, given the famous "Wall of Separation"? It is because "funds received via certificates are not considered grants or contracts . . . but are assistance to the parent."[34] Even if state constitutions have stricter provisions against funding faith-based organizations than those of the First Amendment,[35] the state handling federal day care funds must use them according to the federal rules. On the other hand, if the state chooses

[33] Kirby et al., *Income Support*, 39.

[34] "Final Rule," sec. 98.30(c) and explanatory preamble to the "Final Rule" for the Child Care and Development Block Grant Act of the Department of Health and Human Services, in Tobin, *A Summary and Analysis*, sec. A, pp. ii–iii.

[35] Viteritti, "Choosing Equality."

to contract directly with centers, this is considered "assistance to the provider" and may lead to a greater degree of governmental oversight. In such cases, the funds may not be used for "sectarian purposes."

Administration of these federal funds by state and local officials is monitored to ensure that they have not done so in a way that unduly limits parent choice among different types of providers . . . and that eligible parents are informed of the range of these choices rather than being counseled in a single direction. The regulations specify that "to ensure broad parental choice, Grantees [that is, public agencies administering for federal funds] must issue certificates for child care services directly to the parents. For the purpose of purchasing child care services, Grantees must implement programs which allow certificates to be used as flexibly as cash between the parent and eligible providers. . . . it is essential that the certificate program provide parents with the maximum choice possible and give them the discretion to choose from a wide range of child care arrangements."[36] This provision is necessary because of the bias of many human service bureaucrats in favor of secular agencies, included those operated by government itself; on the other hand, those doing the monitoring are likely themselves to share that bias, and there is reason to doubt that this requirement is being met conscientiously in all cases.

Even when there is an effective system to provide information to clients, government is likely to insist upon deciding which organizations are qualified to receive public funds via vouchers in exchange for services. While in theory that decision might best be left up to parents and other clients, there seems little chance that such unconstrained choice will become public policy. As a private agency director told Joe Loconte, "In the regulatory agencies the mindset is, if it isn't regulated, it's a deadly peril. They don't think that anybody in society can take care of themselves unless there's a government agency overseeing them."[37]

The current push, at both the federal and the state level, to increase not only the amount of subsidized day care but also the proportion of it that is in government-regulated centers reflects an mistrust of the care now provided in so-called family day care settings. A study conducted for the Department of Health and Human Services, however, "found no indication that unregulated family day care was either harmful or dangerous to children; in fact, it caters successfully to the needs of the children in care."[38]

---

[36] Explanatory preamble to the "Final Rule" for the Child Care and Development Block Grant Act of the Department of Health and Human Services, in Tobin, *A Summary and Analysis*, sec. A, p. iii.

[37] Loconte, *Seducing the Samaritan*, 5.

[38] Olsen, "The Advancing Nanny State," 9.

School Vouchers in Milwaukee

Is there any reason why the government oversight under a voucher program should be more extensive than that which already exists in the case of organizations that provide the same services without public funding? Experience seems to show that the legitimate societal concern with protecting children from being abused or badly educated in nonpublic schools can be met by a nonintrusive approval process or by peer accreditation. Certainly there is no evidence that children attending such schools are worse treated or worse educated than those attending public schools; the system seems to be working. Why, then, should assistance with public funds to parents who enroll their children in schools that have so far been lightly regulated require that those schools suddenly become heavily regulated? The implication is that we care more about the money than we do about the children: it was all right for *them* to be at risk, so long as no public funds were at risk!

This question of what strings to attach to a publicly funded voucher scheme surfaced in Wisconsin, where since the 1990–91 school year low-income parents have had the opportunity to receive a voucher for the schooling of their children; the Milwaukee Public Schools (MPS) must, under state law, provide a voucher—at a level much less than its own per-pupil expenditures—for each pupil who leaves its schools for a participating nonreligious private school. The legislature subsequently widened the program to include faith-based schools, and this unprecedented step has been sustained by the Wisconsin Supreme Court, whose decision has been allowed to stand by the United States Supreme Court.

Having failed to block this program—to which it strongly objected—the public education establishment sought to choke it to death with regulation. The state department of education and other opponents of vouchers took the position that "[t]he supposedly 'private' schools participating in the Choice Program provide . . . public education at public expense, to the tune of $2,500 per student taken directly from the MPS appropriations. Accordingly, they are subject to the requirements of the uniformity clause" requiring that "district schools . . . shall be as nearly uniform as practicable." In short, they argued, receipt of vouchers (even though no more than 49 percent of the pupils in each school could be funded in that way) turned these nonpublic schools into regular public schools, subject to all the requirements associated with that status.[39]

Voucher supporters disagreed; they "argued that the statutory requirements upon private schools constitute sufficient regulation and pointedly

[39] Kemerer, Hairston, and Lauerman, "Vouchers and Private School Autonomy," 616.

added, 'For the state to turn to private schools to educate disadvantaged inner-city youngsters, and then to subject those schools to stifling controls, would be to defeat the entire enterprise.' " Fortunately for the program, the judge who considered the opposing arguments (that the program was unconstitutional but implemented properly by the state, or that the program was constitutional but implemented improperly), supported their position, writing, "I am not persuaded that this program turns private into public schools; and if they are not public schools, they are not subject to the Uniformity Clause. . . . Here it seems more accurate to characterize participating schools as private schools that accept public school students."[40]

The Wisconsin voucher law itself did not prescribe detailed requirements beyond nondiscrimination and compliance with health and safety standards; its emphasis was upon outcomes. The Milwaukee superintendent was required to "submit an annual report to the legislature and each participating private school comparing the academic achievement, daily attendance record, percentage of dropouts, percentage of pupils suspended and expelled, and parental involvement activities of pupils attending private schools under the Program with the same information about pupils attending MPS schools."[41] Rather than setting up an abstract standard, the legislation wisely required that the nonpublic schools be compared with comparable public schools, and information on that comparison provided to parents as a basis for deciding whether to participate in the program or not.

The Voucher Debate

Voucher has become a code word in educational policy debates, capable without further explanation of rousing into fury the defenders of the present system under which each local school system enjoys a monopoly on the right to provide publicly funded schooling within its geographical boundaries.

There are three arguments commonly made for vouchers as a way of providing public funding for schooling. The first is that they place the decision about which school will best serve the interests of a particular child in the hands of that child's parents, who are in the best position to know their own child and how a school is meeting or not meeting their hopes for that child. This argument may be based on the efficiency of dispersed decision-making through a market, but it may also be based on

---

[40] Ibid., 616–18.
[41] Ibid., 614.

the conviction that human rights require that parents possess that freedom. As legal scholar John Coons points out,

> The right to form families and to determine the scope of their children's practical liberty is for most men and women the primary occasion for choice and responsibility. One does not have to be rich or well placed to experience the family. The opportunity over a span of fifteen or twenty years to attempt the transmission of one's deepest values to a beloved child provides a unique arena for the creative impulse. Here is the communication of ideas in its most elemental mode. Parental expression, for all its invisibility to the media, is an activity with profound First Amendment implications.[42]

It is for this reason that the various international covenants defining human rights specify that parents have a right to decide about the schooling of their children.[43]

A second line of argument for vouchers (in contrast with other means of funding nongovernmental organizations) is that such a mechanism keeps government at arm's length: because parents or clients are making the decisions about which provider of services to use, the need is reduced for detailed supervision of providers by government officials.

This is an argument that has also been used *against* vouchers, since opponents argue that they would be subject to abuse by those able to mislead ignorant or naive parents. The massive antivoucher advertising campaign in California in 1993, funded by the teachers' unions and other elements of the educational establishment, claimed "that the dearth of government regulations will lead to the proliferation of secretive, fraudulently operated voucher schools."[44] Television was saturated with antivoucher ads, including one showing the holocaust in Waco, with a voiceover suggesting that David Koresh could have used vouchers to run a school. This campaign of vilification was successful in convincing the voters, despite the general support for parent choice expressed in opinion surveys, that insufficient provisions for government regulation made Proposition 174 a dangerous experiment.

The concern was shared among elite elements of the private school world in California, who generally opposed the voucher initiative. Reporters found that "at schools that have labored for accreditation from the respected Western Association of Schools and Colleges, for example, there is the sense that a host of new 'diploma mills' might open with little regulation and low standards. 'There's no doubt that a lot of them would form,'

[42] Coons, "Intellectual Liberty," 511.
[43] Fernandez and Jenkner, *International Declarations and Conventions.*
[44] Chavez and Wilgoren, "Private Schools Polarized," A1.

said one administrator at an expensive private school in San Francisco. 'There would be no financial oversight.' "[45]

As a result of such concerns, although study after study has found broad support—especially among minority and low-income respondents—for some form of voucher that would enable parents to choose schools, popular opinion also insists upon substantial government oversight.[46] The major challenge for voucher proponents in the future will be to convince the voters that it is possible to have accountability and protections with something less than the full weight of the California Education Code—the twelve hundred pages of state laws applying to public schools.

The California example demonstrates how important it is that voucher programs be designed with as much attention to detail—and to ensuring that the role of government is clear and forceful where it should be and restrained where it should not—as any of the alternative mechanisms for government use of nongovernmental organizations. Coons and Sugarman suggest that government regulations should be modeled upon those already applying to private schools; as we have seen, these are quite limited. Their own proposal specified that "[i]n order to assure scholarship schools that they will be able to operate in distinctive ways, the legislature (and other organs of government) are specifically disabled from enlarging controls upon curriculum, facilities, and school employment policies beyond the modest regulations that have traditionally applied to private schools (although we acknowledge that those controls vary from state to state). It is a practical motto of choice supporters that, whatever state laws have proved benign for the children of the rich should be adequate for us all."[47]

The third argument for vouchers is that First Amendment restrictions upon public funding of faith-based schools would not apply, because the choice among schools is placed in the hands of parents and not of government officials. This reasoning has not yet been accepted by the federal courts, though the decisions in *Mueller v. Allen* (1983) and *Witters v. Washington Department of Services for the Blind* (1986) have encouraged some to believe that the door is open to voucher programs that are appropriately constructed. "Opinions in U.S. Supreme Court cases in recent years strongly suggest that subsidies to individuals may be properly spendable in religious schools so long as the system of finance overall is reasonably neutral as between secular and religious institutions and as between public and private sectors. Locating the authority to choose in the parent and provid-

---

[45] Asimov, "Many Private Schools Wary," A19.

[46] The most in-depth study to date—not yet published—demonstrates both points; data were provided by Professor Terry Moe of Stanford at the conference "Rethinking School Governance," Kennedy School of Government, Harvard University, June 1997.

[47] Coons and Sugarman, *Scholarships for Children*, 32.

ing a wide array of similarly treated public, secular, and religious schools avoids the problem raised by financial aids directed to institutions."[48] This confidence was confirmed by the recent decision of the Wisconsin Supreme Court (mentioned above and in chapter 3), upholding the constitutionality of a state voucher program under which thousands of pupils attend religious schools, and the decision of the U. S. Supreme Court not to review this decision.

The distinction described above in the administration of federal child care funds between contracting—with restrictions on religious activities—and providing certificates to parents—without such restrictions—illustrates the advantages that a voucher system could provide.

Grants and Other Subsidies

Grants and other forms of subsidy are by their nature less prescriptive than are contracts—the penalty for failing to comply with the terms of a grant is ordinarily no more drastic than not receiving another grant, or receiving one only after expressions of contrition—but subsidies may nevertheless come with strings attached. In one case involving the Salvation Army, the fact that an employee was paid under a government grant was sufficient to convince the judge that the exemption of faith-based organizations from the requirement not to discriminate on the basis of religion should not apply. The employee had been dismissed when her supervisors discovered she was a member of the Wiccan religion and was making unauthorized use of the office photocopy machine to reproduce materials for witchcraft ceremonies.[49]

Government grants are a common way of supporting social services that only religiously motivated groups are prepared to offer at a limited cost because of their own ability to call upon volunteer assistance, such as hospice care and shelter for the homeless. The cynical might point out that policymakers often do not care much about the quality of services provided to these clienteles and thus are willing to use the uncomplicated mechanism of a grant to ensure that minimal needs are met.

Grants offer the advantage, from a legal point of view, that the supervision and accountability that accompany them are typically much less elaborated than those that go with contracts. The government agency making a grant to a faith-based organization need not engage in excessive "entanglement" with religion of the sort frowned upon by the Supreme Court, and

---

[48] Ibid., 35.

[49] *Dodge v. Salvation Army*, 48 Emply. Prac. Dec. ICCH par. 38619 ISD Miss. 1989, cited by Esbeck, *Regulation of Religious Organizations*, 33n.

the grant may be specified for an activity that minimizes the risk of endorsement or support of specifically religious activities. For example, the construction assistance to denominational colleges by state and federal governments is provided on terms that forbid conducting worship services in those facilities until after a certain number of years, when the government interest is considered to have lapsed.

Grants to Nonpublic Schools in Europe

In France, local government makes grants to Catholic and other nonpublic schools for operating expenses like cleaning, heating, and furniture: little "entanglement" is necessary, since the amount is calculated based upon the costs of equivalent public schools.[50]

Almost the entire cost of education in the Netherlands, both public and private, is borne by the government, and nonpublic schools are guaranteed a level of funding equal to that of equivalent public schools. This can therefore be considered a grant, since the amount provided to a nonpublic school is determined automatically, without a need for line-by-line justification; an approved school has a right to this funding. Article 23, section 7 of the constitution specifies that "private comprehensive elementary education that meets the requirements that are to be set by law is to be funded from the public treasury by the same standard as public education," and makes similar provision for secondary and higher education.[51]

Ordinary salary costs, including teacher salaries, are paid in most cases directly by the national government, but some municipalities provide extra staffing for their own public schools, and in that case must do so equally for local nonpublic schools.[52] Local government pays for elementary school facilities and equipment and for operating expenses, but receives a per-pupil and per-classroom reimbursement from the national government; the national government pays these expenses for secondary schools.[53] While nonpublic schools are funded for operating expenses at the same level as public schools and may not charge tuition (though many raise modest amounts from parents for supplementary activities), the amount of funding that private schools have actually available for programs is often higher. The difference is accounted for by a lower burden for bureaucratic school system costs—for example, having repairs done by private contractors

---

[50] Monchambert, *La liberté de l'enseignement*, 104–7; this should be distinguished from the educational costs paid by the national government, and discussed elsewhere.

[51] Postma, *Handboek*, 52.

[52] Leune, "Besluitvorming in het onderwijsbestel," 369.

[53] Van Kemenade, "Het onderwijsbestel in hoofdlijnen," and Ritzen, "Onderwijs en economie," 47, 293–97.

rather than by the municipal public works department—and the flexibility with which private schools may manage their budgets.[54]

With these generous financial arrangements come significant strings. Nonpublic schools must meet a quality *(deugdelijkheid)* standard to receive public funds, though not to operate without such funds. The quality of publicly funded nonpublic schools must be as high as that of public schools, though it can be expressed in different ways: the fifth section of article 23 provides that "the requirements of quality . . . are to be set by law, with due regard to the freedom of *richting* [literally "direction," in the sense of religion or worldview] of private schools." This provision was included because, as one of those who crafted the constitutional language in 1917 pointed out, "if you put the same demands [of quality] on public and on private education, freedom of *richting* will be in danger." The compromise has been described as "not the same demands of quality, but demands of the same quality."[55]

Postma suggests that the attention of those concerned with educational freedom has been directed too exclusively toward protecting the right to establish schools *(oprichting)* and not enough toward that of determining what happens in the school *(inrichting)* once established: "a free school needs a great deal of freedom to actually remain a free school." Perhaps the gravest threat from government to the identity of faith-based schools has to do with employment practices, which we will discuss in chapter 6, but issues arise in relation to program as well. The government prescribes the subjects that must be covered each year, and the time to be allocated to each, but the content and materials to be used are determined by the board (whether municipal or private) sponsoring each school and by school staff. Despite rumblings about requiring heterogeneous grouping of pupils in place of ability-grouping, it seems clear that government does not have the authority to prescribe how nonpublic schools choose to teach.[56]

In summary, the Dutch system of grants to nonpublic schools provides reasonably good protection for the autonomy to shape education along religious or other lines, though, as we will see, the vulnerable point has to do with employment decisions. As in France, the primary government control is an indirect one, through the examination system for which schools must perforce prepare their pupils. In August 1995, there was a brief but intense flare-up over how these examinations might infringe upon the freedom of schools to teach based upon religious convictions. The government had decided several years before that the biology examinations would not

---

[54] Van Gendt, *Educational Financing.*

[55] Postma, *Handboek,* 140.

[56] Ibid., 149.

include Darwin's theory of evolution; schools would be required to teach about it but could then assess student knowledge by their own tests. This decision was based upon advice by the board responsible for interpreting constitutional guarantees of educational freedom. Evolution, it concluded, was a sensitive matter (comparable to abortion and euthanasia) that each school should be allowed to handle in its own way, to protect its distinctive identity.

Members of the left-of-center coalition sought in 1995 to require that the theory of evolution be required on the nationwide examinations. Much press commentary, typically, presented this as a choice between science and obscurantism, referring often to the more backward sections of the United States. "Should we allow innocent children to be taught lies in the framework of misplaced Christian propaganda?" asked those who insisted that evolution was no theory but the essential foundation for all of biology. Theologians should conform their teaching to the discoveries of science. "It would be better," a sociologist wrote, "to hit a child on the head every day with a wooden mallet than to leave him ignorant of evolution!"

Those on the other side argued that the question was whether there was a divine purpose for human life or whether it was a meaningless accident, and that public policy should respect the convictions of that part of the population who chose schools where this purpose was considered central. Supporters of educational freedom rallied, and the effort to require the Darwinian version of evolution in the examinations failed.

In the Dutch case, restrictions upon nonpublic schools are almost entirely based upon their receipt of government funding, since the constitution permits the imposition of quality standards only in connection with public support. These restrictions are part of the price that has been paid for a system under which the freedom to establish and to select a nongovernment schools has been elaborately protected and subsidized. It seems a reasonable generalization that grants—because of their greater stability and simplicity—are a better way than contracts for government to support faith-based organizations that are carrying out tasks recognized to be in the public interest. It seems also to be likely that they will come with their own, perhaps less elaborated, strings attached.

Like nonpublic schools, nonprofit social service agencies in the Netherlands "do not really have a contracting system. Instead, nonprofit agencies have almost monopoly status within their service jurisdiction. These agencies are reimbursed for their costs in accordance with prevailing laws which respect their autonomy."[57]

---

[57] Smith and Lipsky, *Nonprofits for Hire*, 110.

Shared Space

Provision by government, under its own control, of social or educational services within the facilities and even as part of the program of a nongovernment agency or school might be called "shared space."[58] It is, for example, very common for inner-city and rural churches to rent or loan their facilities for government programs like Head Start and health screening. A simple and uncontroversial example of what we are calling "shared space" is the surplus food provided to low-income children or elderly persons participating in programs run by churches and other faith-based organizations, including parochial schools. Another form of shared activity—upheld by the Supreme Court in *Everson v. Board of Education of Ewing Township*, 330 U.S. 1 (1947)—is the transportation provided or reimbursed by some states for pupils attending nonpublic schools.[59] Similarly, textbook loan programs, diagnostic tests, health services, and other educational services to such pupils have been upheld by the Supreme Court. In each case, the rationale is that the aid is to the pupil and does not support the religious mission of the school.

Another common form of shared space is the renting or borrowing of public facilities by religious groups. The guiding principle here is that government should not distinguish between qualified users of, say, an auditorium on the basis of the message that they plan to offer, unless public safety considerations arise. This can cause difficulties when the use of a public facility might create the impression in the public mind that government is promoting or endorsing the religious message, and schools in particular have been cautious about such impressions.

Students in public high schools that allow student-initiated groups during nonacademic time may form organizations to study the Bible together or take part in other religious activities, provided that they do so at their own initiative and comply with the requirements for student groups in general. As a result of complaints that many schools were not allowing pupils to meet for religious purposes during time set aside for extracurricular activities, Congress passed the Equal Access Act of 1984 (P.L. 98–377), making it unlawful, if any student-initiated groups were allowed, to deny recognition on the basis of the religious, political, or philosophical content of discussions or activities.

---

[58] This use of the term should not be confused with the "shared time" programs under which pupils in some localities leave public schools for voluntary off-campus religious instruction.

[59] See the essays marking the fiftieth anniversary of *Everson*, in Formicola and Morken, *Everson Revisited*.

The constitutionality of this law was upheld in 1990 by the Supreme Court, which found student religious groups legal "if the school uniformly provides that the meetings are voluntary and student-initiated; are not sponsored by the school, the government, or its agents or employees [such as teachers]; do not materially and substantially interfere with the orderly conduct of educational activities within the school; and are not directed, controlled, conducted, or regularly attended by nonschool persons" such as adult religious leaders.[60] Properly conducted so that there could be no question of official endorsement by school authorities, these religious activities do not taint the secular purity of the public school.

The recent *Agostini* decision, discussed in chapter 3, opens the door to the mirror image of religious activities in secular schools: secular activities that are conducted within the context of a religious school without being tainted by religion. This distinction has long been the justification for public funding to religious colleges and social agencies. The possibility of making such a distinction had been denied, for K-12 education, by *Ball* and *Aguilar* and other decisions that attached the label "pervasively sectarian" to everything done within a faith-based school. Now perhaps we can begin to think about how government can realize some of its secular purposes for K-12 schooling through religious schools.

The arrangement that supports Catholic schools in France, although called a "contract," might better be described as a form of "shared space." Government in theory contracts only for the secular educational services provided by these schools; this "saves" the French insistence that the state is secular. Under a *contrat d'association*, "the private school is associated with public education; the State takes on the cost of expenditures for all or part of the classes in which the instruction is in conformity with the programs and rules of public education. . . it is thus public education that is provided at the heart of a private school, but the latter keeps its specific character, its uniqueness, its distinctive atmosphere, because it remains free to provide teaching and scholastic activities not included in the contract and to ask families to pay the related cost."[61] Religious teaching, retreats, and other devotional activities are paid for by supplemental fees.

The French example is perhaps more useful as we think about possibilities for American policy changes than are those of the Netherlands, Britain, or Germany, because the French resistance to mixing of church and state is at least as strong and of much longer standing than that in the United States. There is no "In God We Trust" on French coins, and for many decades the prohibition on any sort of aid to nonpublic schools was even

---

[60] *Board of Education v. Mergens*, 496 U.S. 226 (1990).
[61] Lelièvre, "Considerations historiques," 157.

stronger than that in the United States.[62] The fact that an accommodation has been reached in the area of education, fought over for the whole of the nineteenth century,[63] suggests that we might learn from France something that could be applied to our own evolving situation.

As might be expected, the arrangement is not without its tensions. The Constitutional Court (Conseil constitutionnel) has ruled that protecting the distinctive character of nonpublic schools is essential to educational freedom. The character of the school, however, must be expressed and protected in a way that also protects freedom of conscience of the pupil.[64] How this is to be done, and whether it requires that the instruction provided be secular, has been much debated.

In the eyes of the law, the "distinctive character" of nonpublic schools that is to be protected refers to the school itself but not to the instruction that it provides; public funding is provided to the (secular) instruction and not to the (religious) school. In fact, it is difficult to see how the character of the school could fail—or *should* fail—to mark that of its instruction. How real would be the right to entrust one's children to an alternative, nonstate school if the instruction was required to model itself slavishly on "the stereotype dreamed up by a secular state"? The education in "free schools" should have a distinctive *orientation*, though it should not be militant *(un enseignement de combat)*. It is not sufficient, supporters of Catholic schools argue, to put side by side an academic program modeled on that in state schools and an hour or two of catechism a week. "Catholic education proposes essentially a single interpretation of the world; that's what distinguishes it in a radical manner from secular education."[65] Government has prudently refrained from seeking to purge the instruction carried out "under contract" in nonpublic schools of all religious overtones.

The shared-time arrangements appear to work smoothly in France and have come to be largely accepted even by the Socialists now in power. The parallel with what American law has permitted under AFLA is obvious: the secular services provided are not sanitized from religious influence as thoroughly as in both French and American legal theory they should be, because it is recognized that this would not be in the interest of providing effective services in a time of diversity and individual choice.

This suggests a further reflection: that the answer to the concern about the pervasively religious character of faith-based schools is not to seek to insulate their "secular" activities from the overall climate of the school by

---

[62] Monchambert, *La liberté de l'enseignement*, 104.
[63] See Glenn, *Myth of Common School*, chaps. 1, 9, and 10.
[64] Monchambert, *La liberté de l'enseignement*, 172–73.
[65] Georgel and Thorel, *L'enseignement privé en France*, 202–5.

the sort of fiction that has been employed in funding religious colleges. It would be far better to recognize that a religious dimension—provided in a context of freedom of choice—is entirely consistent with accomplishing the secular educational mission of a school and that "positive neutrality" demands that such a dimension not be held against the eligibility of a school for public support.

Franchise

Granting a monopoly upon a particular form of publicly funded services to a nongovernmental organization makes sense in those cases when, for example, a low-incidence need can be met efficiently only by concentrating all services under the auspices of a single provider. In principle, there is no reason why this provider should not be a faith-based organization. In general, however, the presumption must be against such monopolies, especially when the service to be provided rests upon or expresses an understanding of the world and of the nature of the Good. Education and counseling, for example, are value-laden activities, and one would hesitate to see an effective monopoly of their provision entrusted to a religious organization. By the same token, giving such a monopoly to government—which is a routine practice—should be equally objectionable to those who care about freedom of conscience.[66]

Under the Charitable Choice provision of the new federal welfare law, discussed above, it is the responsibility of the state agency administering the federal funds to "ensure that potential beneficiaries are aware of the religious or nonreligious character of each provider, of the choices available to them, and of their right to an alternative should they object to the religious character of a provider." No client will be required to receive services from a religious organization, which means that states will not be able to grant exclusive "franchise" areas.[67]

Asset Sale

When government chooses to stop providing a service and instead to turn over the facilities through which they have been provided to a nongovernmental organization, significant improvements in efficiency or cost may be achieved. It has been common (and much appreciated by their patrons) for government cafeterias to be turned over to private management, and there

---

[66] Arons, *Compelling Belief*.
[67] Center for Public Justice, *Guide to Charitable Choice*, 8.

have been well-publicized experiments with doing so with public buses and even prisons. The same approach can be taken to devolving social or educational services to private providers. In so doing, management tasks might become simpler, especially in replacing work-rules for government employees with simpler standards. In addition, this would permit a rapid expansion of the number of nongovernment providers, who would not face the heavy facilities and start-up costs that Coons and Sugarman see as a limitation on the capacity of most voucher initiatives to make a significant difference in educational opportunities.

Although not strictly a switch to private management, the policies under which several hundred public schools in England were allowed, by the last Conservative government, to "opt out" of their local systems and function under their own boards have been a form of "asset sale," as have those state policies in the United States that allow existing public schools to become charter schools. In both cases, the result continues to be legally a public school, but one that is intended to function as much like a private school as possible.

What is the potential for public schools to become faith-based schools? There is no problem in England, where about a third of the publicly funded schools are owned by the churches; indeed, the problem lies in the other direction, since some church-sponsored schools that "opt out" may seek to sever their church as well as their local government ties. In the United States the situation is much more complex, though it seems likely that the charter school movement will see some developments in that direction. For example, in a move that has been described as "likely to push the limits of what has been defined as public education in America," several prominent black ministers in New York State have announced that they plan to take advantage of the state's new charter school law—the thirty-fifth in the nation—to seek public funds for schools using their church facilities. Former congressman Floyd Flake proposed taking over several "failing" public schools near his Methodist church. Baptist minister Wyatt Tee Walker— formerly a top aide to Dr. King—explained that the school that his church would house "would be nonsectarian and would admit children by lottery, as required by law. But he said religious instruction would be available to those who wanted it before or after school. 'We are not apologetic about being under the umbrella of religious institutions.' "[68]

Here's how such charter schools could evolve a distinctively religious character. The fundamental premise of charter schools is that the staff and parents of individual schools should be encouraged to find their own distinctive ways to educate, that there is no single valid model of a public school. If, over time, the board and teachers and parents of a charter school

[68] Hartocollis, "Religious Leaders Map Plans," A17.

began to develop a curriculum and a manner of teaching that was clearly based upon a particular religious tradition, would that be valid grounds for the state to cancel its charter? Not so fast: that would be a form of "viewpoint discrimination" in violation of the First Amendment, placing government in the position of inquiring into and forming a judgment about the opinions held and expressed by the participants in this particular school. If every publicly funded school were required to teach the same curriculum and from the same viewpoint, presumably, our imaginary school could be required to conform, but how could the state say that it will encourage dozens of different approaches to education, so long as none of them have religious elements? Would it not be the responsibility of the state to remain neutral among these alternative viewpoints?[69]

This may seem a far-fetched scenario, but once government moves away from uniformity in education it is difficult to see why only religious worldviews should be forbidden. That would seem to be the implication of a decision in 1996 that spoke of "the requirement of viewpoint neutrality in the Government's provision of financial benefits." The Supreme Court agreed to review the case to decide whether "the Establishment Clause compels a state university to exclude an otherwise eligible student publication from participation in the student activities fund, solely on the basis of its religious viewpoint, where such exclusion would violate the Speech and Press Clauses if the viewpoint of the publication were nonreligious." The opinion of the majority was that the First Amendment did not require—nor did it justify—such discrimination against a publication simply because it was religious.[70] One can imagine that the Court could hold that a state that had approved a variety of curriculum approaches based upon various philosophies of education should not disapprove another because of, say, its biblical basis. Positive neutrality, neither favoring nor discouraging any expression of an understanding of life, would seem to require as much.

In the growing number of states that allow existing public schools to "opt out" of local education agency control to become charter schools—in effect, independent public schools—the concept of an "asset sale" may be the most applicable framework for thinking about the consequences. The implication is not that government is somehow abandoning the concern that led it to provide a particular services, but that it can ensure that this service is provided more effectively by creating the conditions for a "third sector" institution to do so. In their influential book *Reinventing Government*, Osborne and Gaebler describe this as government returning to its proper and essential role of governing: steering rather than rowing the boat. "Governments that focus on steering actively shape their commu-

---

[69] For a fuller discussion, see Glenn, "What Would Equal Treatment Mean."
[70] *Rosenberger v. University of Virginia*, 515 U.S. 819 (1995).

nities, states, and nations. They make more policy decisions. They put more social and economic institutions into motion. Some even do more regulating. Rather than hiring more public employees, they make sure other institutions are delivering services and meeting the community's needs."[71]

Summary

Public funding of nonpublic agencies and schools can take many different forms; much depends upon how wisely the mechanism is chosen and with what provisions for and limitations on accountability it is designed. The combination of public funding with detailed government supervision could cause an organization to be considered a "state actor" required to abide by all of the constraints upon government itself.

Contracting for services—probably the most common mechanism—lends itself to government interference with how the work is done and to close specification of what its goals should be, as well as requiring the recipients of contracts to develop elaborate administrative systems for reporting their activities and expenditures.

Vouchers put the decision about which provider to use in the hands of clients rather than government, thus reducing legal as well as administrative entanglements. Public support for educational vouchers is accompanied by the expectation that there will be enough government oversight to protect the children participating.

Grants and subsidies, illustrated from the Dutch experience, ensure more autonomy and stability than does contracting, but may be accompanied by the expectation that nonpublic organizations receiving them model themselves on their public counterparts. Because they are a form of general support, however, grants and subsidies may raise more "red flags" about government support of religion than contracts and other mechanisms that specify the services to be provided.

"Shared space," provision of public services within the context of a faith-based organization, is likely to be explored vigorously in the wake of the 1997 *Agostini* decision. The French experience with funding nonpublic schools suggests that it will not be easy—nor would it be desirable—to insulate these "secular" services completely from the overall mission of the host school or agency.

"Franchising" public services is not described in any detail here because any sort of territorial service arrangement would create particular difficulties in the case of faith-based organizations. The Charitable Choice leg-

[71] Osborne and Gaebler, *Reinventing Government*, 32.

islation illustrates how individual freedom of conscience might be protected in situations in which such an organization provides services on behalf of government.

"Asset sales," illustrated by American charter schools and British "grant-maintained" schools that have opted out of local government control, could be a way to expand the availability of nonpublic service providers rapidly. In some cases this could permit them, in response to staff and client wishes, to adopt a religious understanding of their mission in a way that the courts could accept as consistent with evolving First Amendment jurisprudence.

Whatever method of providing public support is used, it is likely to bring with it pressures for professional management and service-delivery that may change profoundly the nature of a faith-based agency or school. We turn now to considering "professional norms."

INTERLUDE

NEOCORPORATISM IN EUROPE

A GERMAN CATHOLIC LEADER in 1969 said, "The ultimate basis for the church's legal status vis-a-vis the state rests on the fact that the pluralistic state has to turn to social groups that establish and preserve values, and this the churches are better able to do than other social groups."[1]

In the Netherlands and Germany, the relationship between government and faith-based nonprofits has taken a different form than it has in the United States. The elaborated welfare state in these countries relies heavily upon institutions with a religious character to provide public services. "In the Netherlands, about 70 percent of GNP is allocated by government in some way, but only 10 percent of GNP is directly controlled by core government: the other 60 percent is accounted for by" nonprofit schools and agencies.[2] Public funding from local, regional, and national government supports nonprofit organizations and agencies with an explicit church connection; in Germany, the government even collects a special tax for the two dominant churches. "The churches bear responsibility for much of what would otherwise be left to the state and which in most other countries does in fact fall to state or voluntary charitable agencies. Their activities extend from maintaining homes for the blind, training places for school drop-outs, and insane asylums to travelers' aid offices in railroad stations, seamen's homes, and emigrant advisory bureaus."[3]

But this description, which could be applied to the United States as well (think of Catholic Charities or the Salvation Army), does not do justice to the "established" nature of the Dutch and German models. American governments contract with or provide grants to nonprofit organizations, some of which are religious, because of efficiencies that can be achieved thereby, and often on a competitive basis, but in Germany governments are expected to give preference to nongovernmental providers of day care and other services and only to provide those services themselves if private provision is inadequate. In the Netherlands, most schooling is provided by nongovernment organizations and networks of schools, and most social services are provided by nonprofit agencies; government routinely consults with these entities as it formulates policy. In both, more than efficiency

---

[1] Spotts, *Churches and Politics in Germany*, 284.
[2] Aquina, "PGOs in the Netherlands," 94.
[3] Spotts, *Churches and Politics in Germany*, 201.

and effectiveness is at stake. There is an assumption that it is preferable to rely upon the churches to provide "human care of human beings." And, perhaps more significantly, in neither case is it a matter of open competition with new providers entering the "market" all the time, but of long-established agreements with a few very large associations that occupy a near-monopoly position in certain areas of public welfare.

While there are historical reasons for this pattern,[4] it is more significant for our purposes to note that the arrangements in place in Germany and the Netherlands, contrasted with those in the United States, reflect different ways of thinking about the nature of society and of citizenship. The difference is captured by Belgian legal scholar Jan De Groof:

> Basic rights are not limited to the rights of individuals in relation to the state. People exercise their rights through their participation in the activities of *collective bodies*, often in the context of a philosophy which has been provided with an institutionalised setting. Because of their activities, these collective bodies may be considered to be working in *the public interest*, because they assume a role that would otherwise have to be filled by the state and its various services. . . . In this respect, the time-honoured borderline between the public and private fields of competence seems to have become blurred. The rights of these collective groups and the "socialisation of fundamental rights" have been described in a legal context as the "third-generation" of human rights, subsequent to the principles of *freedom* and *equality*.[5]

Such collective rights have not been given the same attention or status in the United States or, for example, in France, countries that have a history of inventing their political cultures and institutions on the basis of individual rights.[6]

Of course, voluntary associations have always played a very important role in American life, as noted by Tocqueville, in contrast with a France swept clean of associations by the Jacobin desire to subordinate all loyalties to the unitary Republic. It was not, after all, until 1901 that France adopted a law recognizing and regulating associations—and then it was immediately directed against Catholic orders perceived to be a threat to the Republic.[7] Compared with the French reserve toward organized groups, perceived as potentially making claims upon their members inconsistent with their participation as individuals and free citizens in French society, the Ameri-

---

[4] A brief account of the historical background may be found in Glenn, *Choice of Schools.*
[5] De Groof, "Overall Shape," 33.
[6] This is not to take sides in the argument among historians and political scientists about whether the original impulse in the United States was toward an individualistic or a "republican" understanding of society; see Shain, *Myth of American Individualism*, 3–18, for an overview of the scholarly debate.
[7] Partin, *Waldeck-Rousseau.*

can position is a sort of benevolent neutrality that values all sorts of organizations but gives them little official status.

To illustrate the spectrum of official posture toward associations in democratic societies, ethnic organizations of all sorts are permitted and largely ignored in the United States, while it is only within the past decade that noncitizens have been allowed to form associations in France. At the other extreme, Sweden and the Netherlands provide subsidies to immigrant associations and consult them formally and often in the formulation of policies that will affect those they claim to represent. In 1990, there were 125 Yugoslavian and 166 Finnish organizations (among others) recognized by the Swedish government as "dialogue partners" in the formulation of policy, and publicly funded to publish newspapers and carry out youth and cultural activities designed to perpetuate ethnic identity and group cohesion.[8]

Whether or not it is true, as Otto von Gierke (1841–1921) claimed, that "the Germanic people have a gift other peoples lack, by means of which they have given the idea of freedom a special substance and the idea of unity a more secure foundation—they have the gift of forming fellowships *[Genossenschaften]*,"[9] there is an enormous proliferation of associations in Germany and in the Netherlands that are legally recognized, as De Groof suggests, as "working in the public interest, because they assume a role that would otherwise have to be filled by the state and its various services." Nongovernmental organizations in Germany

> run 60,517 institutions in the areas of health care and youth and family services, as well as services for the handicapped, elderly, and poor. They provide 70 percent of all family services, 60 percent of all services for the elderly, 40 percent of all hospital beds, and 90 percent of all employment for the handicapped. The free-welfare associations employ nearly 500,000 full-time and about 175,000 part-time staff members. Operating independently but organizationally linked to its 60,517 institutions are 22,120 self-help groups, clubs, and local voluntary associations. *Caritas* alone employs more people than the industrial conglomerate Siemens.[10]

The term *neocorporatism* has sometimes been applied to these arrangements, though there is actually nothing "neo" about them and they predate the "corporatism" that is usually associated with fascist regimes of the 1920s and 1930s. "The concept of corporatism has been rehabilitated within political theory in the last ten years," writes the author of *Corporatism and Political Theory*, "and is now widely applied in studies of organized interests in democratic as well as authoritarian settings." Cawson defines

---

[8] Koekebakker, *Immigrant in Europa*, 59.
[9] In Skillen and McCarthy, *Political Order*, 92.
[10] Anheier, "West Germany," 84–85.

corporatism as "a specific socio-political process in which a limited number of monopolistic organizations representing functional interests engage in bargaining with state agencies over public policy outputs. In exchange for favourable policies, the leaders of the interest organizations agree to undertake the implementation of policy through delivering the co-operation of their members."[11] Thus these groups are given an officially recognized role both in formulating public policy and in carrying it out, and their activities are funded in large part by government.

While these organizations enjoy a privileged position with respect to access to policy decisions and public funding, they are also more closely drawn into the "ambiguous embrace" of government than is the case with publicly funded NPOs (nonprofit organizations) in the United States. Over time, government is likely to dominate in setting the agenda rather than responding to demands that emerge from the civil society. "Whereas in pluralist theory interests are seen as existing before organization and political mobilization, in corporatist theory the state is identified as a crucial agent in shaping interests and affecting the outcome of group processes."[12] The arrangements in the Netherlands under which government provides full funding for nonpublic schools on the basis of their choice by parents are by no means identical with the voucher proposals advanced by market enthusiasts for the reform of American education. Thus, "corporatism may be contrasted with legal-bureaucratic and market forms of regulation which involve a markedly different form of relationship between the state and interest organizations."[13]

Austria is often considered the contemporary democracy with the strongest corporatist polity,[14] and the United States—with its emphasis on individual rights and participation mediated largely by the political system, and with a militantly secularist legal orthodoxy that is baffling to most Europeans (except in France)—one of the weakest, despite the highly visible political role of interest groups in American policy formulation. The relationship of nongovernmental organizations to the formulation of policy under the Dutch system is significantly different from the lobbying and pressures exerted by interest groups under the American system. Cawson distinguishes between American style "pluralism" and corporatism: "Whereas in a pluralist system a large number of voluntary interest associations compete with each other for members, resources and access to government in order to influence the direction of public policy, in a corporatist system there is a limited number of noncompetitive organizations with

[11] Cawson, "Corporatism," 104.
[12] Ibid., 104.
[13] Ibid., 105.
[14] See, for example, Bischof and Pelinka, *Austro-Corporatism*.

compulsory or semicompulsory membership. These organizations have a privileged status with respect to government in that they co-determine public policy and are responsible for its implementation by disciplining their members to accept bargained agreements.[15]

Compare the German practice of registering each birth by the religion of the child with the prohibition on including even voluntary questions about religion on the United States census.[16]

Although it seems more likely that the corporatist structure of welfare and education provision owe more to historical developments and balance of political forces than to the working out of a theory, it is often justified in the name of "subsidiarity," which has more recently become one of the founding principles of the European Union.[17] The classic articulation of this principle is that of Pope Pius XI in 1931: "just as it is gravely wrong to take from individuals what they can accomplish by their own initiative and industry and give it to the community, so also it is an injustice and at the same time a grave evil and disturbance of right order to assign to a greater and higher association what lesser and subordinate organizations can do. . . . those in command should be sure that the more perfectly a graduated order is preserved among the various associations, in observance of the principle of 'subsidiary function,' the stronger social authority and effectiveness will be, and the happier and more prosperous the condition of the State."[18] Or, expressed as a program of institutional reform in the words of Catholic philosopher Jacques Maritain (1882–1972), "in order both to maintain and make fruitful the movement for social improvement supported by the State, and to bring the State back to its true nature, it is necessary that many functions now exercised by the State should be distributed among the various autonomous organs of a pluralistically structured body politic."[19]

Dutch Protestant political thinking has developed the more radical concept of "sphere sovereignty" (*souvereiniteit in eigen kring*), usually associated with statesman-theologian Abraham Kuyper (1837–1920). The associations and institutions that make up the civil society, Kuyper insisted, should not be considered subordinate divisions of the state, enjoying only those rights and that scope which the state chooses to entrust to them, but possess their own fundamental rights that derive from the purposes for which they exist. The role of the state is to mediate among these "spheres," ensuring

[15] Cawson, "Corporatism," 104.

[16] Spotts, *Churches and Politics in Germany*, 198; Kosmin and Lachman, *One Nation under God*, 2.

[17] See Lenaerts, "Subsidiarity and Community Competence," 33.

[18] *Quadragesimo Anno* (On Reconstructing the Social Order), excerpted in Skillen and McCarthy, *Political Order*, 166–67.

[19] From *Man and the State* (1951), excerpted in Skillen and McCarthy, *Political Order*, 195.

that justice is done, the rights of individuals are protected, and tasks that can only be undertaken by the whole society are carried out. The state must not, however, seek to take over the functions of the family, to define the canons of art or of science, to prescribe the teachings or practices of religious organizations, to tell business where to invest or how to produce, or to interfere in what occurs between teacher and pupils. Government touches upon all of those spheres of activity, of course, as it carries out its own mission, but it does so, as it were, from the outside, preventing abuses. The relationship between government and the other spheres of social life is thus of an entirely different nature than the relationship among levels of government.

> Autonomy of parts of a whole and sphere sovereignty of radically distinct societal relationships are principally different matters. In a differentiated society the degree of autonomy depends upon the requirements of the whole of which the autonomous community remains a part. Sphere sovereignty, however, is rooted in the constant, inherent character of the life sphere itself. Because of their intrinsic natures, differentiated spheres like the family, the school, economic enterprise, science, and art can never be part of the state.[20]

The concept of sphere sovereignty thus goes beyond that of subsidiarity or decision making as near as possible to where the decision must be implemented. "A truly pluralist social order seems to require recognition of the fundamental and not merely the relative independence of different spheres and institutions in a differentiated society. To achieve this recognition, the ontological status of institutions must be grasped and upheld. In our opinion, the subsidiarity-autonomy framework does not do this."[21] Sphere sovereignty insists upon the right of the school—for example—to function by its own rationality and in accordance with its own purposes, not those of government or of any other sphere (including the family or a religious institution).

The Netherlands

In the Dutch educational system, government negotiates with the umbrella organizations *(koepels)* of Catholic and Protestant and municipal schooling, each of which represents thousands of schools serving about a third of all elementary pupils in the country. Decisions about standards, funding, and the goals of education are made through a process of negotiation that has

---

[20] Herman Dooyeweerd, *Roots of Western Culture* (1979), excerpted in Skillen and McCarthy, *Political Order*, 289–90.
[21] Skillen and McCarthy, *Political Order*, 385.

been described as "the politics of accommodation."[22] A recent example is the Scheveningen Consultations (July 1993) in which the minister of education worked out with representatives of the organizations a series of wide-ranging agreements on decentralization, lump-sum funding of schools, coordination of efforts to address urban underachievement, and other matters.[23] When the government resolved to adopt a broad and coordinated assault on social problems, it would have been un-Dutch to lay out the strategies without an extensive consultative process, including negotiating the ways in which local government and private schooling would collaborate.[24]

"Collective expenditures"—what is spent by government and by nonprofit organizations on such services as health, education, and social security—are one measure of how extensive the welfare state is in different countries. According to OECD, these expenditures represented 33.3 percent of gross domestic product in the United States in 1996; the proportion in the Netherlands, by contrast, was 50 percent, just ahead of Germany at 49.6 percent.[25] In the Dutch case, the high level of collective expenditure, especially for education and social services, occurs primarily through nongovernment schools and agencies, most of which have at least a residual religious character. The tradition of organizing society through denominational associations is so well established that, when social services of all sorts were greatly expanded—subsidies for all social services increased a thousandfold between 1952 and 1977—it was natural to do so through funding nongovernmental organizations to provide services.[26]

In a country of about 15 million people, there are approximately one hundred thousand associations and a similar number of nonmembership institutions addressing every imaginable need and interest within the society. Many are gathered under the denominational umbrella organizations that are a relic of the "pillarization" (*verzuiling*) of Dutch society growing out of nineteenth-century struggles over the control and character of elementary schooling. The settlement, in 1917–20, of the "school struggle" was the basis for tremendous growth of the portion of Dutch life divided along denominational lines on the model of proportional representation and support first developed for schooling. Emancipation of the "little people" for whom their Roman Catholic or Calvinist beliefs were central, their emergence into public life bringing their convictions with them, required organization. The passions and the habits of organization developed dur-

---

[22] Lijphart, *The Politics of Accommodation.*
[23] Hoefnagel, "Developments in Dutch Education Policy."
[24] Van der Wouden et al., *Evaluatie sociale vernieuwing,* 117.
[25] Sociaal en Cultureel Planbureau, *Sociale en Culturele Verkenningen 1997,* 115.
[26] Kramer, "Use of Government Funds," 218; Aquina, "PGOs in the Netherlands," 103.

ing the struggle for confessional schooling found expression across the whole range of social life. One Dutch legal scholar notes that "*verzuiling* is inexplicable apart from the 'school struggle.' "[27]

As the issue of confessional education had led the way to the development of power blocs in the political arena, so the implementation of such education played a leading role in the institutionalization of confessional differences. Whereas in 1920 55.3 percent of elementary students attended public schools, the proportion had dropped to 37.7 percent by 1930 and to 26.8 percent by 1960, rising again to 31.7 percent in 1980. Of more than one million students attending nonpublic elementary schools in 1960, 37 percent attended Protestant and 60.4 percent Catholic schools; by 1980 these proportions had shifted to 43 percent Protestant, 57 percent Catholic.[28]

The role of religiously identifiable institutions continues to be very significant in the Netherlands despite widespread secularization, which has proceeded much further than in the United States. In 1995, 94 percent of those surveyed in the United States said that they believed in God; the comparable response for the Netherlands was 55 percent. In the United States, 93 percent reported that they belonged to a church, though only 34 percent had attended church in the previous week; comparable figures for the Netherlands were 44 percent and 16 percent.[29] The major denominations—Roman Catholic, Dutch Reformed (Hervormde) and Evangelical (Gereformeerde) have all suffered major losses in recent decades, while there is a growing number of smaller religious groups.[30]

Despite this extensive secularization, however, there continues to be support for institutions with a religious identity. Approximately 35 percent of all respondents prefer a faith-based school for their own children, and 6 percent want denominational sports clubs for youth. The support is much stronger among the Gereformeerden; 95 percent of those who attend church regularly want denominational schools, and 80 percent want denominational sports clubs. More significant, perhaps is that even among the "marginal" members of this group, 87 percent want schools and 47 percent want sports clubs that have a denominational character, and 36 percent of those who have definitely left the Evangelical churches still want denominational schools. On the other hand, support for separate schools

[27] Akkermans, *Onderwijs als Constitutioneel Probleem*, 159.

[28] Glenn, *Myth of Common School*, 271.

[29] Becker and Vink, *Secularisatie in Nederland*, p. 27, table 2.1, and p. 30, table 2.4.

[30] It is interesting in connection with our overall theme to note that the Salvation Army enjoys much more approval among the Dutch than do any of the other smaller groups; in 1994, 50 percent of respondents reported favorable feelings, with the nearest competitors, humanism and the anthroposophy of Rudolf Steiner, enjoying 32 percent and 11 percent favorable ratings (Sociaal en Cultureel Planbureau, *Sociaal en Cultureel Rapport 1996*, 477).

(54 percent) and sports clubs (14 percent) is now lower among marginal Catholics, who a generation or two ago would have lived in an almost entirely Catholic social and institutional world.[31]

It should perhaps be noted here that the continuing attachment to some forms of confessional structuring of life—especially that affecting youth—has been accompanied by massive changes in attitudes about a variety of issues. For example, surveys have found that there is very little animosity or suspicion between Catholics and Protestants, and that both are as positive toward the rights of Muslims to say and do what they will as are the unchurched (Catholics 68 percent, Evangelicals 69 percent, unchurched 67 percent positive).[32]

Although many social agencies and more than two-thirds of schools continue to claim a religious identity, there is considerable evidence that this has been "hollowed out" by decades of dependence upon the government as well as growing secularization. Since World War II shook up all aspects of Dutch society, "the non governmental organizations that delivered services for the public benefit became more professionalised. The professionals cared less about the identity of the organization than about professional codes. . . . This central planning and subsidizing had as consequence that non governmental organizations who wanted subsidy made their policies according to the policy of the government. By these trends and by the decentralization, since 1977, many of the private organizations are merged and have loosened (lost) their ties with their constituency. Simultaneously new organizations are established."[33]

Research on social services in the Netherlands found that the professionalization of staff coincided with a weakening of the zeal with which the religious communities protected the distinctive character of the institutions operating in their name. This has occurred even though the Dutch government must respect their distinctive approaches to social and educational ministries. "One of the developments which has contributed to the process described above is secularization. The nongovernmental organizations were after 1950 more and more losing the financial and moral support of their rank and file. The consequence of this: more financial dependency on governmental financial support."[34]

But as organizations become more oriented toward government, they become even more estranged from the religious rank and file. Another study confirmed that "the connection of many Netherlanders with worldview institutions of volunteer work has strongly declined, and the

---

[31] Becker and Vink, *Secularisatie in Nederland*, 147–48 and table 5.13.
[32] Ibid., 149, table 5.15.
[33] Van der Ploeg, "Introduction to the Dutch Model," 19.
[34] Doek, "Relations in Child Protection," 85.

entire collective provision [for those in need] is set up in such a professional
and perfectionist way that the impulse to lend a hand is removed."[35] As a
result, there has been a perceptible decline in what has been a strong tradition of volunteering, or rather a diversion of the volunteering impulse toward groups seeking to promote causes—often in the Third World—and
raise funds rather than provide direct help. "As the societal middle ground
continues to lose its independence," Adriaansens and Zijderveld point out,
"volunteering changes its character and loses significance." The irony is
that the new forms of volunteering directed toward affecting public policies
themselves contribute to an ever-expanding state role and further weakening of the civil society.[36]

Alongside professionalization and the devaluing of volunteer help, the
growing secularization and weakening of the denominational "pillars" has
also changed the nature of the nonprofit organizations that provide social
services and education. Organizations that had provided an all-encompassing religious sense of meaning within Catholic or Protestant subsocie-
ties lost their taken-for-grantedness and became at best lifestyle choices
and at worse shells stripped of all meaning.[37]

Concern continues to be expressed about the "loss of the social middle"
as a result of the incursions of bureaucracy on the one hand and markets
on the other.[38] There has been a gradual handing-over of functions that
were performed by families and the local community to organizations of
the civil society, and these in turn have been taken over to a large extent
by government, while remaining formally independent. This in turn
has led to institutionalization and professionalization of the function of
human care of human beings, whether children in school, the handicapped, the elderly, or any other group for whom a government program
can be devised.

We are fortunate in having an account of this process from the inside,
by a social worker who served a succession of neighborhood houses over
the period of decisive change between 1956 and 1982. The influence of
churches on the youth programs set up under their auspices declined dramatically, and by the end of the eighties they had become a political instrument in the hands of local authorities, which financed the work and determined policies, scope, and goals.[39] Simonse takes the reader step-by-step
through his experience of settlement-house work in different settings and
in relation to a variety of challenges.

[35] Adriaansens and Zijderveld, *Vrijwillig initiatief en de verzorgingsstaat*, 54.
[36] Ibid., 10, 74.
[37] Ibid., 124.
[38] Sociaal en Cultureel Planbureau, *Sociaal en Cultureel Rapport 1996*, 537.
[39] Simonse, *De teloorgang van het kerkelijk*, 29.

After the war, there was a general sense in the Netherlands that government was not competent to implement work with youth and other groups, but should make that possible by subsidizing the work of private organizations, most of which were religious. These subsidies began in 1949, but without clear specifications for the work or its goals. Significant freedom was thus left to the local groups carrying out the work to decide how it would be done. The youth clubs were led by volunteers, with a few paid staff for coordination and program development.[40]

Those who pioneered evangelical youth work in the Netherlands saw it as a process of re-Christianizing working-class youth who had no connection with any church, as missionary work. This should be accomplished, they thought, by showing love and understanding and acceptance, but always relating that explicitly to the Christian message. Youth work would take place outside of church structures, but oriented toward the goal that youth would become part of the church fellowship. As one wrote, "The question is, how we can announce Christ to men and women who have no words [about such matters] available to them. And the answer is: the Church must become visible to them. The wordless must see her in her acts of service and usefulness."[41]

Simonse began his own work along these lines in a small town in Friesland in the 1950s. Soon there were tensions between the youth club and the sponsoring church, whose lay leaders came to feel that the presentation of the Gospel should be made more explicit and were frustrated to be told that the youth workers were not trained to do so and that the government subsidies were not for that purpose.[42] Simonse himself moved on to work in a Protestant neighborhood house in a working-class area of Rotterdam, where tension again arose with the sponsoring church groups. The youth workers argued that the encounter with Jesus was implicit in everything that they did, and that "when youth in a group are helped to accept each other, to get along together and to work together, there something of salvation is apparent, there is proclamation." "As workers," Simonse tells us, "we had again and again to detach our understandings of faith from the middle-class packaging that it had in our lives. . . . Proclamation must not take the form of proclamation of middle-class norms, or bourgeois morality." Against this view, he quotes the minutes of a meeting with the oversight board, in which one of the women is reported as complaining, "We've thrown proclamation [of the Gospel] overboard. We try it with all sorts of methods, psychological and sociological, but we lack the boldness to speak the Word. . . . And as a result we don't see any spiritual

[40] Ibid., 35–36.
[41] Ibid., 40, 44, 49.
[42] Ibid., 68.

results." She gave the staff, no doubt ironically, credit for "an outstanding report. It's the objective recounting of a fiasco, the fiasco of our work without faith, of our work depending on methods, the fiasco of the expectation that our work will produce results." The response, from "Dr. H.," was that it required a long preparation before direct proclamation was possible, only to be reminded by another member of the board that "if you wait until children 'get it,' you never get to the proclamation. An orderly presentation has to come first, then forming of habits, then understanding will develop by itself."

Simonse, not at all abashed when reporting this discussion, suggests in his retrospective account that the secularization of youth work in fact began with the conclusion on the part of youth workers that not only norms and values but also the very way in which faith was understood were largely determined by sociocultural factors, that "bourgeois" religion could not be made relevant for the working class.[43] In other words, well before government began to place its detailed requirements on programs that it funded through religious organizations, the staff of these programs, in their theological oversophistication, in effect lost the conviction that the faith in which they had been brought up could have any meaning for working-class youth.

The situation could only get worse, from the point of view of the churches, when the original staff with their confused theology began to be replaced by staff with no interest at all in religion. Government requirements played a part in this change, since only "secular" functions of the denominational programs were subsidized. Staff who saw their work as essentially pastoral or concerned with spiritual matters gradually were pushed aside, and the gap between neighborhood house and church widened. Gradually there was no more discussion of the relationship of social and educational development to spiritual nurturing, which in the early years of evangelical youth-work had seemed self-explanatory.[44]

The relationship between the evangelical churches and neighborhood house work was influenced, Simonse concluded, by four factors. The first two went together: changes in the goals and thus in the character of the work, and professionalization of the work. He reports that in the large evangelical youth-serving agency where he worked in 1969, a study found that nearly half of the professional staff but only 5 percent of the volunteers and board members were critical of its religious character, and that as often as not the agency's distinctive mission had not been discussed during the hiring and orientation process.[45] In other words, the staff were prepared

[43] Ibid., 98–102.
[44] Ibid., 121–22, 126.
[45] Ibid., 167–68.

to throw overboard a religious identity that was still important to the un-
paid participants.

This is consistent with research around the same time by sociologist
J. A. van Kemenade, who would later serve as minister of education. He
found that 57 percent of the parents with children in Catholic schools
thought that the religious character of a school was important, but only 30
percent of Catholic school teachers agreed![46] In effect, then, there was a
sort of betrayal from within resulting from changing conceptions of the
nature of professional work, and loss of conviction about the possibility of
reconciling religion with professional norms. This has been a matter of
deep concern in recent years for leaders in the confessional-school sector,
as we will see below.

The second two factors identified by Simonse also went together: the
increasing government share in the funding of the work, and the question
of working together with other, nonevangelical, organizations. Beginning
in the late 1960s, the government more and more made such collaboration
a condition of funding.[47] While the government is not allowed, under the
Dutch constitution, to interfere with the religious character of the organizations that it funds, this was an indirect way of encouraging conformity
with a common approach and has continued to be a theme of central and
local government initiatives. Under the Scheveningen agreement mentioned above, for example, inner-city schools could receive extra funding
only on the basis of a multischool strategy.[48] This could force Protestant
and Catholic schools to collaborate with secular schools on a lowest-com-
mon-denominator basis.

The Identity of Denominational Schools

One might expect that the Netherlands, where two-thirds of the schools
have a religious identity, would be a utopia for religiously distinctive education, but many Protestant and Catholic schools and agencies are only
residually religious. Some policy analysts argue that they have thereby lost
their raison d'être and should simply be taken over by the state.[49] In a
period of declining enrollments and school closings, determining in practice the meaning of school distinctiveness acquires considerable importance. The availability of a nearby Catholic school, for example, would
permit the closing of another that is underenrolled, even though the staff
of the two schools might approach Catholic teaching from very different

[46] Van Kemenade, *De Katholieken en hun onderwijs*.
[47] Simonse, *De teloorgang van het kerkelijk*, 144, 156.
[48] Van der Wouden et al., *Evaluatie sociale vernieuwing*, 116.
[49] Van Schoten and Wansink, *De nieuwe schoolstrijd*.

perspectives, with one stressing liberation theology and another the traditional catechism. Such situations are by no means unheard of, and indeed as long ago as 1933 the Dutch government decided that a group of more conservative Protestant schools deserved to be treated as a separate category from the more liberal Protestant schools, thus creating a right on the part of a group of parents with a sufficient number of children to have the establishment of one sort of Protestant school funded even if the other sort was available locally.[50]

More recently the question has arisen whether a "neutral" private school, one that reflects no single belief or worldview but is distinctive only in terms of pedagogy, may be considered equivalent to a public school offering the same program and (by law) committed to the same religious neutrality. Is there, in other words, a right to such a private school distinct from any issue of conscience? An advisory opinion of the Education Council in May 1985 found that there *is* such a right, since even the deliberate lack of common convictions can be seen as a "philosophical foundation."[51]

Such discussions grow directly out of the perceived need to consolidate schools for budgetary purposes, but they also reflect developments in Dutch society in recent decades. First of these is a growing secularization, in which the weakening of traditional religious loyalties has reduced not only church attendance but also commitment to institutions based upon religious identification. This secularization has led to questions about the continuing need for confessional schooling, at least on the present scale.

The second development, related in a complex fashion to the first, is a certain loss of nerve among those upon whom confessional schooling depends to confirm its purpose, from church hierarchies to teachers. If schools are no longer distinctively Catholic or Protestant beyond their labels, public school advocates ask, how does their maintenance with public funds guarantee liberty of conscience? Given the growing ethnic diversity of Dutch society, would it not be better to abandon confessional schooling in favor of a common school that would bridge not only confessional and class differences, but ethnic ones as well?

Education, as a collective provision, provides for the constantly changing needs of the community, according to some public school advocates. That is why society pays for it; authorities expect schools to make a contribution to the removal of social inequalities and cultural apartheid as the precondition for the full participation of everyone in the life of the society. Because private (and especially confessional) schooling was established to perpetuate rather than to remove group loyalties, it cannot—these critics charge—contribute to cultural integration. "Whenever a private school seeks to

---

[50] Koppejan, "Ontstaan en groei van het reformatorisch onderwijs," 96.
[51] Struik, "Openbare school."

contribute to cultural integration, it is faced with a dilemma: give preference to its testimony or to dialogue with those who think otherwise."[52]

Such a dialogue would require treating those views as of equal value, say opponents of private schooling, and expressing this equality concretely by the appointment of teachers, parent council, and governing board members who hold these views. It would require, indeed, placing the ethos, the *richting*, of the school up for discussion. A private school that refused to make such fundamental changes in its nature and direction could not, by this definition, be of equal quality with a public school in terms of the expectations placed upon schools to contribute to state-directed social change. Thus the authorities would be justified, even compelled, to withdraw financial support. A private school that did accept such conditions might as well be a public school in any case; having lost its distinctive *richting*, it would have lost its claim upon support as an educational alternative.

In brief, this assault on confessional and other private schooling—in the Netherlands as in the United States—calls into question the value of school distinctiveness, in the name of the socializing function of education in a society of growing diversity and need for integration.[53] While this angle of attack has not yet resulted in changes in the legal status of nonstate schools in either country, or in the right of Dutch nonpublic schools to full funding equivalent to that received by state schools, it has put many teachers and school boards on the defensive about any distinctive aspects of their curriculum or school practices that could be perceived as socially divisive, including the assertion that a particular religious tradition possesses essential truth.

From another perspective, however, the evolution of Dutch society has actually increased the importance of school distinctiveness. Whereas formerly schools were able to serve a sector of society and in effect were guaranteed pupils whose parents were part of that sector, whether it be Protestant or Catholic or secular, now schools are much more left on their own to convince parents, many of whom are quite open to choosing schools from among all of the sectors. The increased diversity in the Dutch population may also tend in the same direction: in the past there were three large sectors of society and thus of schooling, but within each people tended to resemble one another in their attitudes. Now there's a far wider range of individual differentiation and thus choice.[54]

The question of school distinctiveness leads inevitably to the reciprocal question of common goals for all schooling in Dutch society. Is it possible

[52] Van Schoten and Wansink, *De nieuwe schoolstrijd*, 93–94.
[53] For a recent American parallel, see Dwyer, *Religious Schools*.
[54] Nuis, "Onderwijs als maatschappelijk goed," 7.

to reconcile goals defined on a national level with the autonomy of schools to shape their educational mission in accordance with the convictions of those directly involved with the school, including parents? Educators in nonpublic schools express concern and reserve about centrally established goals, which they say treat with insufficient respect the distinction between public schools, which government can regulate in detail, and nonpublic schools, which constitutionally are free to organize their own internal lives. It is possible that differentiated concrete goals may be quite appropriate, but they object to globally stated but vaguely defined goals that could provide excuses for government to interfere in all aspects of the way that a school does its business.

Insofar as the goals established for Dutch education in general allow different schools to provide their own interpretations and attach their own content and meaning to these goals, they can serve a useful purpose, ensuring that there are elements that are held in common by all Dutch schools and are part of the experience in common of all Dutch children.

A threat to school distinctiveness arises, according to some Dutch educators, from the recent tendency to emphasize dimensions of school quality that they take to be too narrow. As parents make choices among schools, they should be encouraged not to do so exclusively on the basis of the measurable qualities of a school such as resources or test scores. They need help to recognize that distinctiveness and clarity of focus, the ability to educate as well as to instruct, are critical aspects of a good education. Educators and parents should not accept the fact/value distinction in the sense of two spheres of knowledge, one of the factual world, and the other of values. To accept Max Weber's separation between spheres of facts-without-values and values-without-facts, Dutch Protestants argue, is fatal to creating the kinds of schools that are needed, because it suggests the possibility of adding on elements of moral teaching or character development as a supplement to the fundamental instructional mission of the school. Schools should rather integrate their entire program of instruction in subject matter and also development of character and the habits that sustain it into a single value-impregnated vision of what the school is about. A Christian school should not seek to express its religious character simply by a prayer at the beginning of the school day, or a period each week of religious instruction, or by reading from the Bible now and again. A serious engagement with what it means to be a Christian school would require that every aspect of the school be examined from that perspective.

This does not mean, they take care to point out, that a little flavoring, a little sauce of Christianity should be poured over every subject, but rather that in the entire teaching enterprise of the school there should be a fundamental seriousness about raising the important questions and addressing them from the perspective of a consistent framework of values and convictions. Specifically when issues of worldview are being discussed, they should be discussed in relation to the competencies that pupils are developing in the school and not as a separate and otherworldly set of concerns. By the same token, when competencies are being developed and discussed, there should also be consideration of how and why they are being developed and for what purposes they will be used. As schools express their distinctiveness within the framework of general educational goals, this needs to be worked through in all the details of how the schools operate, of their *distinctive character*.

Education policy is, in a sense, becoming school based: increasingly, the significant point where education policy is discussed and determined is at the level of the individual school, and people in schools have to learn new ways of thinking, new habits, new skills in order to be able to take advantage of that. This is similar to the situation in France, where "in recent years the State has disengaged itself from educational affairs. More and more it relies upon the grassroots [*la base*] to solve educational problems and acts as though their resolution could only be through local arrangements. The policymaker gives way to the civil society."[55]

Dutch schools are required to create their own individual plans within the framework of law and regulations and then are responsible for carrying out these plans in ways that ensure the quality of instruction and of the educational experience in general. This arrangement has similarities to current initiatives in a number of countries under which schools develop some form of charter or statement of their mission and how they propose to carry it out as the basis for an enhanced degree of autonomy. This is then reviewed by responsible authorities and, having been approved, becomes the guidelines by which a school lives day to day without ongoing intervention from government.

Have these decentralization measures led to more real autonomy by schools? Education law expert Andres Postma cautions that "central government is withdrawing so that it is better and more effectively able to guide schools in the direction it wants them to go where the main issues are concerned. The educational institutions cannot develop in the way they want to, but are obliged to strive for the goals that central government has set them. When this is compared to the principle of subsidiarity the inevitable conclusion is that although the schools have been given more power over the means, central government is still pulling the strings when it comes to the aims."[56]

Establishment by government of educational goals can represent a threat to the effective implementation of school autonomy. If the goals come to

---

[55] Ballion, *La bonne école*.
[56] Postma, "Principle of Subsidiarity," 286.

represent all that is expected of a school, if what government prescribes becomes the way we understand quality in education, the scope for school autonomy will become drastically limited. On the other hand, if government seeks to include in its goals every aspect of education, there will be a potential for intolerable interference by government in the ability of schools to shape their own distinctive mission. Parents will also be limited in their opportunity to choose among schools based upon their own preferences, unless these reflect the views of the government rule-makers. It has thus been suggested by some that it is not what is common to all schools that should be the criterion for quality, but rather primarily the unique goals of each individual school.

The common standards of quality should be a nonnegotiable foundation, but schools should be encouraged to differentiate themselves, and parents to choose among schools, by other aspects of education, such as approaches to the development of character, or of creativity, or of religious conviction, that are not appropriately subject to common standards. This would be a good description, be it noted, of how elite independent schools in the United States have always marketed themselves to prospective parents, taking for granted a strong college preparation.

Social organization and daily interactions are primary in shaping not only the climate but also the very character of a school, the explicit way in which the life and mission of the school are presented both externally and internally. This is not to say that we should minimize the importance of either the curriculum of the school or its pedagogical and organizational dimensions. In a coherent school, a shared worldview informs the curriculum and is expressed in the relationships of adults and children and of adults with one another.

There is thus no such thing as a single model of what a Protestant, Catholic, Muslim, Jewish, or humanist school should be like. Each must find its own specific way of combining these elements in a form that reflects the understandings and commitments of those participating. What is essential is that the realization of the elements not be inconsistent one with another, or in conflict. It is, unfortunately, by no means always the case that schools consciously and effectively work to develop a unity of these components of their life and mission. The identity of a school therefore should not be seen as simply an add-on, but as a fundamental vision working its way through all that the school does. It is very easy for a school to add a label or statement of purpose that does not emerge out of the sort of process that clearly marks how a school lives day by day.

On the other hand, a school cannot be completely autonomous, particularly when the society as a whole recognizes the qualifications certified by the school, allows the school to meet mandatory school attendance requirements, and even provides it with public funding. The autonomy of the school is exercised within the general framework of democratic decision-making on behalf of society as a whole. To the extent that national educational goals and strategies to ensure accountability for meeting those goals in measurable ways dominate, there's a real danger that the effect will be a distortion of the educational mission of a school exclusively toward those things that can be measured. The close connection between knowing and doing is therefore broken. In fact, as Dutch Protestant educators point out, this reveals a deep misunderstanding of the nature of human existence, one that suggests that knowing and doing can in fact be separated, and that it is possible to talk of value-neutral understanding and action. Knowledge that has not been thoroughly integrated into the basis of action and decision is generally very quickly lost and has little significance.

Any nationwide or broad-based evaluation system that seeks to judge the quality of schools cannot, by any means we are aware of, take into account the ways in which different schools approach their broadly educational function. It can't readily capture the education that is occurring in schools. It can only capture the learning of specific skills and information. It therefore is appropriate that Dutch policy has emphasized the responsibility of individual schools to set goals for quality, and to evaluate themselves against those goals. Only in this way and to the extent that schools take seriously their broad educational function is there some assurance that teachers and others engaged in the work of the school will be getting continuous feedback that addresses their mission in the broadest possible sense, rather than simply feedback from standardized tests that address only what are arguably relatively marginal aspects of their mission.

The character of a school in the Netherlands is often sufficiently distinctive that it becomes an important factor in the process of enrolling new children. "If the beliefs of parents are not consistent with the confessional basis of the school, they would be asked explicitly to respect that basis. In the few cases when they are not prepared to do so, they are encouraged to choose another school. If it appears that a parent enrolling a child is not completely clear that the school is Protestant, that is stressed. One principal does this by giving a hint to the parents: 'Keep in mind that your child could start singing a hymn loudly at the check-out in the supermarket.' For some parents, this warning is sufficient reason to choose another school. . . . the enrollment of pupils is a negotiation process through which school and parents sound each other out. The categorical refusal of a pupil seldom occurs."[57]

It should be noted that the debates over parental choice in the Netherlands do not center around arguments about the contribution of market forces to the effectiveness of schools as measured by standardized tests,

---

[57] Van Esch, Laemers, and Vrieze, "Vooral professionele eisen," 8.

though there is some evidence that the more highly profiled schools do in fact produce better results.[58] Dutch educators, parents, and policymakers are fairly unanimous about the educational desirability of diversity, though there are those who strongly oppose the predominance of religious as contrasted with pedagogical differences among schools.

Summing Up

The Dutch discussions illustrate the high seriousness with which the question of the identity and purpose of school—or social agency—deserves to be considered if it is to be coherent and also if it is to give clients and prospective clients an honest account of what values will inform its work. Joop Simonse's account reminds us, however, that identity and purpose can be undermined by the professionalization of staff and the imposition of bureaucratic and professional norms that leave little scope for the definition of a distinctive mission.

Professionalization tends to chase out volunteerism, or to relegate volunteers to subordinate roles, and thus to undermine two aspects of a good school or social agency whose importance has recently been rediscovered: the ability to convey moral judgments in a convincing way, and the personal relationships that—often scorned as "paternalistic"—can make a decisive difference for the most vulnerable pupils and clients.[59]

The Dutch continue to volunteer more than do some of their neighbors; in 1994, 29 percent reported that they volunteered at least once a month, and 37 percent in the past year, compared with 13 percent and 15 percent in Germany. Church members (57 percent) were more than twice as likely as nonmembers (23 percent) to do volunteer work, and a substantial discrepancy remained even when only their nonchurch volunteering was counted: 40 percent of the church members did volunteer work unrelated to a religious organization.[60] But this volunteer participation is increasingly directed into channels that limit its vitality as an expression of a healthy civil society. The increasing scale of the tasks that the welfare state has taken on, even when it entrusts many of those tasks to nongovernmental organizations, exacts a heavy cost of bureaucratic routinization and control.

> Government guarantees of caretaking in the areas of income, education, housing, nursing, and so forth have called into existence an apparatus that can only be kept under control by bureaucratic means. Even when government has turned the implementation of caretaking over to apparently autonomous institutions and organizations (as is still to a great extent the case in the Nether-

[58] Van Marwijk Kooy-von Baumhauer, *Scholen verschillen.*
[59] Adriaansens and Zijderveld, *Vrijwillig initiatief en de verzorgingsstaat*, 18.
[60] Sociaal en Cultureel Planbureau, *Sociaal en Cultureel Rapport 1996*, 546.

lands as a relic of *verzuiling*), such "private initiative" is in almost complete financial dependence, . . . [requiring] an organizational structure on the part of the various institutions that can play the game of [funding] agency regulation. Without being bureaucratically organized, the institutions would in the most literal sense lose contact with government.[61]

This isn't what they intended, some within Dutch Protestant and Catholic circles are saying, despite the great success of their organizations in maintaining a share of public funding for education and social services that far exceeds the proportion of active church members in the society. "The hope is that this indulgence of Social Democratic neo-corporatism will stop. It is necessary to move to new conceptions that approximate the Protestant idea of 'sovereignty in its own sphere' "[62] What form that could take, however, is much less clear, given the continuing expectation that government will fund and give direction to many aspects of Dutch society that have not traditionally been considered part of the "sphere" of the state.

As we have seen, the expanding government role in setting common educational standards, a process that is gathering speed in most Western democracies, need not be inimical to the distinctive character of faith-based schools, provided that they manage to persuade parents to choose on the basis of the unmeasurable characteristics that are essential to providing a good education.

Germany

Germany, like the Netherlands, relies heavily upon nongovernmental organizations to carry out what are recognized to be public functions, and to do so, not by their own initiative and voluntary support alone, but as an integral part of the implementation of public policy with public funding. While this pattern has roots long in the past—in the "corporations" and guilds of pre-Napoleonic German states, and in the state churches of Protestant regions—it became especially marked after World War II. The Catholic Church and the Protestant state churches came out of the war "organizationally intact and generally prestigious as the only institutions not to have been 'coordinated' into the Nazi state[;] they stood as something solid and reputable amid the boundless moral and material rubble of Germany in 1945. . . . Until a German government was reestablished in 1949, the churches constituted the most powerful and articulate voice of the German people."[63]

---

[61] Adriaansens and Zijderveld, *Vrijwillig initiatief en de verzorgingsstaat*, 78.
[62] Sap, "From Opponents to Responsible Partners," 169.
[63] Spotts, *Churches and Politics in Germany*, 47, 51.

In part because of horrendous experience with totalitarianism, German policymakers in the 1950s were prepared to entrust many functions that involved the shaping or expression of values to nongovernmental institutions. Those that stood most ready organizationally as well as morally to assume such functions were the churches.

> By the mid-1960s there was a steady shift from the ideal of the church as a political power and a privileged institution in the state to the concept of the church as an institution with certain unique qualifications to carry out certain public functions in service to the state. This new approach coincided with an unprecedented readiness of the Social Democrats no less than the Christian Democrats to work with the churches in the public sphere. The approach on both sides is no longer, as it was in the 1950s, one of paying off favors, but one of joint partnership for broad social objectives without regard for narrow church interests. The sum result has been an intensification of the partnership between church and state despite the deepening secularization of German society.[64]

The two primary players in the nongovernmental social welfare field are the Catholic Caritas and the Protestant Diakonie, both of which function nationwide to provide coordination and advocacy on behalf of regional church organizations. Other coordinating associations have a secular character.

> The *Diakonisches Werk* (Protestant), founded as the *Innere Mission* (Inner Mission) in 1848–1849, developed outside the official Protestant church structures. It began as a welfare-oriented evangelical movement, often in conflict with the secular political world. In contrast, *Caritas*, ideologically grounded in Catholic social ethics and the principle of subsidiarity, developed within the Catholic church and is integrated into the religious hierarchy. The *Arbeiterwohlfahrt* (Workers' Welfare, secular), founded in 1919, has historically been linked to the Social Democratic Party. . . . The *Deutscher Paritätischer Wohlfahrtsverband*, founded in 1920, is a consortium of nondenominational, nonpartisan private welfare organizations.[65]

The role of the faith-based associations in providing public services has remained predominant despite the advance of secularization. In the early 1990s, 67 percent of those surveyed in Germany professed belief in God, contrasted with 94 percent in the United States. The proportion of those reporting that they belonged to a church was nearly as high as in the United States, 89 percent to 93 percent, no doubt because of the government policy of so identifying children at birth, but only 15 percent (contrasted with

[64] Ibid., 207.
[65] Anheier, "West Germany," 84–85.

34 percent in the United States) reported that they had attended church during the preceding week.[66] It is not clear, however, that this pattern of low church attendance represents a new phenomenon; "at the height of the Wilhelmine period," before World War I, "according to one church historian's estimate, only about three percent of the Protestant population was attending religious services."[67] As in the Netherlands, the support for faith-based institutions may extend to many who do not themselves participate in the core activities of religion.

Our focus here will be upon kindergartens, in the provision of which the churches play a major role; nationally, about 536,000 pupils are in kindergartens under Catholic, and about 400,000 under Protestant sponsorship, representing more than 70 percent of all kindergarten slots. Even under the former Communist regime of East Germany, despite the insistence of its education law of 1946 that "education of youth in schools is exclusively an affair of the state," many kindergartens remained under church sponsorship.[68]

The contrast between a near monopoly by the state in providing schools[69] and its relatively modest role in providing kindergartens reflects, in part, the German understanding that a kindergarten should be largely free of an instructional agenda. Meyer and his coauthors comment on "the remarkably 'low tech' approach German pre-schools still take to child care and education. No TVs, no computers, no 'report cards' for three-year-olds, no all-pervasive anxiety to get children 'school ready'. Instead, old fashioned play, wooden toys, a comparatively slow and quiet pace, even cooking lunch on-site with children involved . . . this is likely to be at least partially due to the strong presence of church-affiliated pre-schooling."[70] It seems equally likely, however, that there has been little impetus for the state to take over kindergartens because they are not seen as an integral part of schooling and thus may safely be left to the civil society; it has been suggested that a sort of implicit bargain exists, that the churches will not challenge the near monopoly of the state with respect to schooling (including schooling with a confessional character and religious instruction), in exchange for public funding of their efforts in other domains of the formation and expression of values.

The discussion that follows draws heavily upon research about the distinctive character of Catholic and Protestant kindergartens in several German states conducted under the direction of sociologist Heinz-Dieter

---

[66] Becker and Vink, *Secularisatie in Nederland*, p. 27, table 2.1, and p. 30, table 2.4.
[67] Spotts, *Churches and Politics in Germany*, 6.
[68] See Glenn, *Educational Freedom*, 274.
[69] For a discussion, see "Parental Choice in German Education," in Glenn, *Choice of Schools*.
[70] Meyer et al., "Welfare between Charity *(Nächstenliebe)* and Bureaucracy," 65.

Meyer on behalf of the Ambiguous Embrace project; his full report and conclusions will appear in the forthcoming article in the *ZENS Jahrbuch*. Meyer and his associates visited thirteen kindergartens (five Catholic, five Protestant, and three public) in predominantly Protestant Lower Saxony and twenty-eight (eight Catholic, eight Protestant, and twelve public) in predominantly Catholic Bavaria, conducting interviews with the head teacher in each case and administering written questionnaires, as well as observing facilities and activities. They also conducted telephone interviews with the directors of three Catholic and one public kindergarten in North Rhine-Westphalia and interviewed directors and students of a public and a Catholic institution for training preschool teachers. Finally, Meyer interviewed officials of Diakonie and Caritas.[71]

Preschool programs in Germany must be approved by the municipal Youth Office (*Jugendamt*), and this approval may be withdrawn if authorities find that a program is not functioning in the interest of the children. Public funding support varies from state to state (*Land*); Lower Saxony, for example, pays 25 percent of salary costs for nonpublic preschools, with extra funding for those that integrate handicapped children or that have an unusually high proportion of immigrant minority or disadvantaged background. Parents pay tuition on a sliding scale based upon income (roughly $150 to $440 per month for all-day kindergarten, and less for half-day). The municipality pays a portion of the operating budget of those preschools that pass their three-year safety inspection. This portion covers 66 percent of the operating budget of public preschools and 36.5 percent of that of nonpublic or "free" preschools.[72] The sponsoring church or association has to make up the difference; German churches enjoy significant revenues from church taxes collected for them by the state.

While our focus here is upon kindergartens, serving children aged four and five, it should be noted that the same provisions of law and regulation apply to day care centers for younger children and after-school centers (*Horte*) for schoolchildren up to age fourteen. All three are required, for example, to "promote the equality of rights of boys and girls through education" and to integrate handicapped pupils and those of different backgrounds such as the children of immigrants. The law requires that institutions caring for children admit them without regard to their "religion, worldview, nationality, or language."[73]

---

[71] Participants in the research under Dr. Meyer's direction: Silke Tollmien (Hannover and Göttingen), Andreas Flegel (three cities in Bavaria), Oliver Schwarz (teacher-training institutions), and Suzanne Moeller (legal and financial context). The documents that they prepared are referenced individually.

[72] Suzanne Moeller, "Rahmenbedingungen und Kontrollinstanzen."

[73] Silke Tollmien, "Ergebnisse der Feldbesuche" (in Göttingen), 27.

The focus of this by Meyer and his associates was to determine "whether the governmental and nongovernmental carriers of welfare provide *recognizably different life-worlds for their inhabitants*."

Distinctiveness of Staff

"Employees in nonprofit organizations," including kindergartens in Germany, "essentially function like civil servants and receive comparable training and compensation."[74] Whether such quasi civil servants have a vision for providing a kindergarten program based upon a distinctively religious understanding of child development and the purposes of education is especially important because the sponsoring organizations (both local churches and the more distant Diakonie and Caritas) exert little direct influence over what occurs in the kindergartens associated with them. The head teacher and staff of each kindergarten are in large measure free to shape what they do with the children, how they discuss religion and incorporate religious observances within their program, and how they interpret their objectives to parents.[75] The right of the sponsoring church or organization to have a say in the program and to be kept informed[76] seems in most cases to have little practical effect; the contacts between church and kindergarten staff, though reportedly cordial, are largely informal.

In order to ensure a supply of staff who understand the mission of kindergartens from their confessional perspective, both Catholic and Protestant churches maintain teacher-training institutions with the help of public funding, which pays 80 percent of the costs.[77] In reality, however, graduates of the three types of teacher-training institutions are well represented in all three types of kindergartens.[78]

The motivation behind the establishment, about a hundred years ago, of the first confessional institutions to train preschool educators included convictions about the importance of developing the future teacher's personality, faith, and commitment as well as technical competence and efficiency,[79] and this has continued to be a distinguishing characteristic of their mission, despite growing dependence on state funding and corresponding standardizing pressures. For example, one Catholic institution, in a statement of goals in 1985, stressed professional training on the basis of the life-orientation of the Gospel, with attention to developing personal moti-

[74] Salamon and Anheier, *The Emerging Nonprofit Sector*, 127.

[75] Tollmien, "Ergebnisse der Feldbesuche," 25.

[76] Moeller, "Rahmenbedingungen und Kontrollinstanzen," 14.

[77] Heinz-Dieter Meyer, "Interviewtranscript Diakonie."

[78] Oliver Schwarz, "Zur Ausbildung von Erzieher/innen in Deutschland: Vergleich einer öffentlichen und einer katholischen Erzieher/innenschule," 52.

[79] Dietrich von Derschau (1987), quoted by Schwarz, "Zur Ausbildung," 53.

vation and social and religious commitments. This required that staff be not only competent but endorse the institution's goals, and that prospective students be interviewed to ensure their openness to the demands of personal development during their training.[80]

Schwarz found significant differences between a Catholic and a municipal institution training preschool teachers, with a lower level of motivation and emphasis on educational goals in the broad sense in the public institution, which tended to stress factual knowledge and narrower developmental goals. Students in the Catholic training institution gave significantly more positive responses to a recent survey by the Institut Frau und Gesellschaft than did those in the municipal institution. Interviews by Schwarz with students at both confirmed a lower level of expectations (*Anforderungen*) and motivation and greater frustration at the municipal institution. He suggested, however, that the latter was seeking to evolve in the direction of the richer understanding of the goals of education characteristic of the Catholic institution.[81]

The distinctiveness of the Catholic institution is maintained, in part, by its insistence upon interviewing student applicants, which is not possible for its municipal counterpart; previous academic achievement is less important in the admission process than personal qualities, though being Catholic is not a criterion. Religious instruction is a regular part of the curriculum of both institutions, not (contrary to American expectations) a characteristic distinguishing between them, since all schools and preschools in most German *Länder* are required to provide religious instruction.[82] While this was simply a (not considered very interesting) subject at the municipal institution, it was—in a broadly ecumenical form—central to the self-understanding of students and faculty at the Catholic institution, expressed most commonly in terms of ideals such as "caring for others," rather than in explicitly creedal terms.[83]

Nor are such ideals without consequences. In Göttingen, municipal authorities tend to send problem children to the confessional kindergartens rather than to their own, counting on the staff of the former to make the extra efforts—based upon their values—that could not be demanded of public employees.[84]

The study found that staff of all three types of kindergartens were drawn from both public and confessional training institutions, and only rarely were all of the staff of an establishment Catholic or Protestant or un-

---

[80] Fachakademie für Sozialpädagogik in Würzburg, "Für die Jugend, für den Glauben, für das Leben," quoted by Schwarz, "Zur Ausbildung," 54.

[81] Schwarz, "Zur Ausbildung," 54–55.

[82] Lambert, "School Legislation in Germany," 260.

[83] Schwarz, "Zur Ausbildung," 60–61.

[84] Tollmien, "Ergebnisse der Feldbesuche," 26.

churched. There was a suggestion that sponsors were more concerned with the sincerity of religious convictions (whether Catholic or Protestant) more than with official membership or training, and there were examples of Protestant kindergartens with Catholic directors and vice versa. A Protestant kindergarten in Hannover interpreted the hiring expectation of "Christian conviction and church membership" as satisfied by "a readiness to engage with Christian values" [Bereitschaft zur Auseinandersetzung mit christlichen Werten].[85] A Catholic kindergarten in Göttingen makes sure that at least one of the two staff responsible for each group is a sincere Christian. While preference was often expressed for staff who had been trained in a confessional institution, in the Protestant kindergarten in Göttingen (the most markedly Christian in its program of the three studied) all three of the staff had been trained in a public institution.[86]

In heavily Catholic Bavaria, the Protestant kindergartens visited make membership in a Christian church a criterion for employment, while Catholic kindergartens, more strictly, expect that their staff will be Catholic; in fact, however, some had Protestant and even unchurched staff.[87]

Despite the Christian religious identity of many kindergartens, very few report tensions with Muslim families, who not uncommonly represent a substantial proportion of the children enrolled. In one Protestant kindergarten, for example, the staff have voluntarily taken a course about Islam in their free time and make an effort to incorporate appropriate foods and symbols into their program, as well as inviting parents in to talk about Islam.[88]

The director of one Protestant kindergarten suggested that municipal establishments tended to hire less-qualified child care workers (Kinderpflegerinnen) in lieu of the more expensive early childhood educators (Erzieherinnen) sought by the confessional kindergartens, and a small-scale sample seemed to confirm this judgment: 20 percent of the staff of the municipal kindergartens visited, but only 7 percent of their Protestant equivalents, were child care workers.[89]

Distinctiveness of Program

The regulations under which kindergartens operate—and receive public support—are quite explicit (in the German fashion) as to requirements, but they include provisions to maintain the autonomy of nongovernment

---

[85] Tollmien, "Forschungsbericht: Vier Kindergärten in Hannover" (1997), 3.
[86] Tollmien, "Ergebnisse der Feldbesuche," 23, 29.
[87] Andreas Flegel, "Religiöse Erziehung im Kindergarten," 3.
[88] Tollmien, "Ergebnisse der Feldbesuche," 48.
[89] Ibid., 22.

institutions. Diversity of "contents, methods, and approaches to work" must be respected by public authorities, to such an extent that they should abstain from providing services themselves in competition with recognized "free" youth-serving organizations *(anerkannte Träger der freien Jugend-hilfe).*[90] Thus the recognized associations like Caritas and Diakonie "occupy a quasi-monopolistic position: for example, since 1961 municipalities or other potential suppliers are barred from establishing child-care and youth institutions if the free-welfare associations are planning to do so. Alternative suppliers need the consent of the free-welfare associations."[91]

Kindergartens are required to spell out the distinctive character *(Konzeption)* of their work, though within limits defined by the government; for example, promoting gender equality and integrating handicapped children are nonnegotiable requirements. In the case of kindergartens operated by churches, the statement of goals is generally developed in consultation with the sponsors and reflects the guidelines of Caritas or Diakonie, though these may be rather loosely interpreted. Catholic church leaders have more authority in relation to the programs of Caritas than do Protestant leaders in relation to Diakonie, which places less emphasis on structure and more on cooperative spirit. In fact, in both cases local sponsors and staff are free to decide to what extent they will follow denominational guidelines with respect to program content. These denominational guidelines are, in any case, quite general.[92]

> Evangelical [Lutheran] day care centers for children are based upon a Christian understanding of human beings. Three core proclamations characterize this understanding: Each person is created unique by God. People are accepted by God in all their strengths and weaknesses. God invites people to trust him. . . . the experiences of children are discussed on the basis of the biblical revelation. . . . periodic child-centered liturgical observances can help in experiencing Christian fellowship. It's also important to put daily life in relationship with God. . . . children can also experience central aspects of faith in the common life [of the center].

Similarly, the Reformed [Calvinist] kindergarten in Göttingen declares that "the fundamentals of the Christian faith that we want to pass on are Love, Security, Trust, Forgiveness and Hope." One of the Catholic kindergartens stresses that religion is taught about through daily activities, through pictures and books, prayers and songs, all of them made understandable to children. Another describes its goal of leading children to faith

---

[90] Moeller, "Rahmenbedingungen und Kontrollinstanzen," 12.
[91] Anheier, "West Germany," 85.
[92] Moeller, "Rahmenbedingungen und Kontrollinstanzen," 13–14.

not only through the festivals of the Christian year but also by daily interactions through which the center seeks to develop their sociability.[93] Christian faith is often in effect equated with social dispositions.

The researchers found that the explicit religious content of the Catholic kindergartens was greater than that of their Protestant counterparts, where less stress (as might be expected) was placed on religious symbols and other reminders of the character of the center. There seems to be a tendency in the Protestant centers to stress religion as individually experienced in daily life and relationships rather than as encountered through traditional and universally accessible symbols. According to the mission statement of one Protestant kindergarten, "religious education is not a separable 'special task' but a foundational element of the entire work of the kindergarten, addressing all of the learning and developmental stages of the children, especially in their attitudes and relationships." In the Catholic kindergartens, more time was devoted to role-playing stories from the Bible, and prayers were a routine aspect of the day at meals and other times. Imposition of ashes at the beginning of Lent and a bread-and-water breakfast on Fridays in Lent helped to make preparation for Easter vivid for the children.[94] Nor were Protestant kindergartens uniformly devoid of evangelistic effects; in one visited in Hannover, the discussion of baptism attracted so much interest on the part of parents that a number of children and even parents were baptized. Both Catholic and Protestant kindergartens organized special services for children to which parents were encouraged to come. The fact that the Protestant kindergartens were more inclined to stress the implications of Christianity for daily life rather than the symbolic elements that played a larger part in the Catholic kindergartens made it easier for the former to work with Muslim children, and indeed *Diakonie* has for years provided guidelines in this sensitive area.[95]

By contrast, the kindergartens operated by municipalities are more consistently secular, even though there is no legal requirement in Germany (unlike in the United States) that they avoid anything that could appear to promote religion. Despite the training they have received in teaching about religion, the teachers in the public kindergartens in Göttingen shy away from mentioning the religious significance of Christmas and other public holidays and instead use these as occasions to inveigh against "the consumer mentality of our society" and the role of the electronic media. Socialization is the dominant motif of the public centers. "We are unpoliti-

[93] Ibid., 18–19.
[94] Tollmien, "Ergebnisse der Feldbesuche."
[95] Tollmien, "Forschungsbericht," 3, 8.

cal—we have no program," one public kindergarten director said (rather bizarrely) in explanation of why Christmas songs with religious content were avoided in her center.[96]

The situation is rather different in culturally Catholic Bavaria, where public kindergartens are more likely to incorporate explicitly Christian and even Catholic elements, and the Protestant kindergartens—perhaps because, in Meyer's phrase, they are in a "diaspora" situation—are more explicit about religious content. Teachers in municipal kindergartens tell Bible stories to explain the Christian holy days that mark the year in municipal as well as confessional kindergartens and commonly display crucifixes and other religious symbols, though they are less likely than are staff of confessional kindergartens to say grace out loud before meals, escort the children to church services, or emphasize the religious meaning of the holy days.[97]

The themes that arise in a kindergarten are of course not entirely under the control of its staff, and much can be learned from how they respond to issues raised by the children in circle discussions and in other ways. The researchers found that, in responding to the questions that arise when a child's grandparent or other relative has died, staff in the church-sponsored kindergartens were able to reinforce quite naturally the assurances that the children were being given a home that "Grandpa is in heaven now," while in the public kindergarten they tended to feel the need to relativize the belief by saying, "Yes, there are some people who believe that someone who dies goes to heaven." Similarly, public kindergarten staff were very reluctant to talk in terms of "Good and Bad," since these categories did not correspond to their pedagogical views; by contrast, teachers in the church-sponsored kindergartens were more likely to discuss such distinctions as good and bad or rich and poor.[98]

The religion of parents and their children is not—and may not be—a factor in admission to the church-sponsored kindergartens; indeed, little selection is exercised. The sponsors expect that parents will accept the religious character of the program, though both Protestant and Catholic centers make various accommodations for Muslim and other non-Christian children when asked to do so by parents—like holding festivals in the parish hall rather than the church—though tensions remain over aspects of the curriculum that deal with sexuality. One of the municipal kindergartens visited in Bavaria failed to make an effort to help Muslim children to refrain from eating pork, but none of the confessional ones did so.[99]

---

[96] Tollmien, "Ergebnisse der Feldbesuche," 36–37.
[97] Flegel, "Religiöse Erziehung im Kindergarten."
[98] Tollmien, "Ergebnisse der Feldbesuche."
[99] Flegel, "Religiöse Erziehung im Kindergarten," appendix 3, p. 2.

Efforts are made by the church-sponsored centers to involve parents actively not only in kindergarten but also in church activities; on parent evenings, presentations are made about the religious instruction that is provided to the children so that the parents can answer questions and reinforce it at home.

Summing Up

Confessional kindergartens in Germany vary widely in the extent to which they stress the doctrinal positions and the devotional practices of their sponsoring churches; the variation seems to be explained more by the way that staff understand how religious beliefs and values can best be communicated to young children than by any limits that come with government funding and regulation. It is clear from interviews and observations that in general religious elements are taken quite naturally as regular aspects of early childhood education, even in a rather secularized society, and that most municipal kindergartens by no means exclude religious activities and themes; the difference between confessional and public kindergartens is in general more a matter of degree than of an absolute contrast, as it would be in the United States.

Few of the staff of Protestant and Catholic kindergartens rated religious objectives as the most important for their centers; much more emphasis was placed on the social, physical, and emotional development of the children. On the other hand, there appeared to be a tendency for the religious character of some kindergartens to find expression in a warmer tone, an emphasis on concern for others (*Nächstenliebe*) that was frequently mentioned by staff.

Meyer interviewed representatives of Caritas and Diakonie in an attempt to explore the ability of kindergartens and other programs sponsored by these associations to maintain their distinctive character. "While they incorporate," he concluded, "by their very nature, a permanent conflict between pragmatists and religious orthodoxy, . . . it is by no means clear that the pragmatists are bound to win." The fact that there are now "increasing competition with private for-profit suppliers of social services . . after certain recent legal changes have opened the door for privatization [and] a shrinking tax base due to a decline in active members is forcing the [church-sponsored associations] to reconsider their priorities, often with the result that [their] original Christian mission is emphasized more, not less strongly."[100]

Under this scenario, the semiestablished Catholic and Protestant churches of Germany might break out of their "mainline" complacency

---

[100] Heinz-Dieter Meyer, email to the author, January 26, 1998.

and begin to behave more like the competitive American churches.[101] In particular, their kindergartens and other agencies serving the public might seek to distinguish themselves in an increasingly competitive market by emphasizing their distinctiveness, to ensure a loyal market share by making a virtue of ways in which they differ from the lowest common denominator of cultural assumptions.

That's one scenario; others less favorable to religious distinctiveness are not difficult to imagine. Robert Whelan has described the leaching away of religious distinctiveness from denominational social agencies in Britain, and the resulting impoverishment of their contribution to a diversified civil society:

> it is this sense of "otherness" which seems to be missing, this spiritual perspective on material needs which should separate church-based from statutory programmes of assistance. In short, the churches no longer present an alternative. They seem to be content to provide services in much the same way as the state, taking taxpayers' money and reporting to local authorities and government departments. . . . the search for alternative methods of welfare provision will intensify. The role of the churches, and indeed the whole voluntary sector, will become increasingly important. However, if the sector has become so compromised by its involvement with the state as to have lost its distinctive character, then it will not be able to make an effective contribution to the debate.[102]

This does not yet seem to have occurred with the confessional kindergartens in Germany. Meyer and his associates found distinctive practices and staff attitudes in most of those they visited, and what seemed to be a tendency to become more explicitly religious when that represented a contrast with the surrounding environment: thus Protestant kindergartens in culturally Catholic Bavaria were more up front with their religious character than were those in Lower Saxony.

Government pressures do not seem to threaten the confessional elements in kindergarten programs, nor, in general, do parents appear to object to these elements. It may well be that the most crucial question is how professional staff and those who train them think about what is appropriate in a kindergarten program. If professional norms come to disparage religious themes and activities—perhaps in the name of tolerance or of what is "developmentally appropriate"—the likelihood is that teachers will gradually abandon them.

The approach used by Catholic kindergartens—emphasis on symbols and rituals—has the advantage of being dramatically appealing to young children and possible to implement without extended discussion. Even staff

---

[101] Smith, *American Evangelicalism*, 86f. and passim.
[102] Whelan, *The Corrosion of Charity*, 98.

who attach no deeper meaning to these practices or who have given them no particular thought can continue them through the succession of seasons and holy days of the church calendar. The vulnerability of this approach is the pressure to drop this or that practice that any parents—unchurched or Muslim, for example—may object to, until gradually little is left. It seems possible that the approach used by Protestant kindergartens, stressing Christian living and engagement with the demand of showing love for the (unattractive or immigrant or handicapped) neighbor in ways that go beyond the common morality, may have more staying power. (Of course, this theme is by no means absent from Catholic kindergartens.) The threat to this approach is that it demands a great deal of the teacher, and a team of teachers who share the same understanding of their work. Only through focused attention to the selection of staff and to ongoing staff development and discussion—hard work!—is this likely to prevail over the contrary pressures exerted by a secularized society and culture.

Conclusions

The relationship between government and faith-based organizations that provide social and educational services takes a very different form in Germany and the Netherlands than it does in the United States. It is based upon an unembarrassed (by American standards) assumption that religious institutions are especially well situated to provide human care of human beings, and that for government to fund these activities—provided that clients have a choice of providers—does not violate any civic freedoms or the ideological neutrality of the state. And it is also based upon explicit protections of the distinctive character of institutions receiving public funds.

Common standards to ensure that social goals are met are not such an issue for kindergartens as they are for the later stages of schooling. Testing and the reporting of results to parents and the public is an important form of accountability, but it can have a distorting effect upon schools that are pursuing—as all schools should—a vision of education that goes beyond what can be measured on a test. The explicitly religious (or philosophical) character of a school can help its staff to keep "on task" in this broader sense and to interpret the school's mission to parents. This may help to explain the reportedly greater effectiveness of faith-based schools.

The Dutch examples—neighborhood houses and schools—remind us, however, that it can be a constant battle for a school or agency to maintain a distinctive religious character when professional norms have become highly secular. Catholic and Protestant kindergartens in Germany appear to be doing so, though the wide variety of approaches and the low priority given by staff to this aspect of their work suggest that their religious identity may be fragile.

How staff in faith-based schools and agencies think about the religious dimension of their work is decisive, more so than policies or organizational arrangements. Those who train staff and articulate professional norms will ultimately make all the difference. If they do so in ways that validate faith-commitments and theologically informed ways of understanding professional practice, it seems likely that confessional schools and agencies will be capable of resisting the pressures of secular uniformity. If they do not, the battle will be lost.

5

PROFESSIONAL NORMS

GOVERNMENT REGULATION, criteria for funding, and accountability requirements can threaten the distinctive character of faith-based organizations in many ways. As we have seen, however, the power of government in a free society is limited, and nongovernmental organizations are by no means without legal and political ways of resisting undue interference with their mission, whether or not they receive public funding.

Monsma and Soper, in their study of faith-based agencies in five Western democracies, conclude that the threat to their autonomy comes less from regulation by government than from what they call "changing norms of religious schools and agencies."[1] In this chapter we will discuss the nature of professional norms in social work and in education, how they developed, and the difficulties that they can pose—as alternate and conflicting systems of meaning—for faith-based organizations. In chapter 6 we will discuss the employment policies and practices of faith-based organizations, and how antidiscrimination statutes and professional norms can threaten their ability to maintain their distinctive character.

Professional Norms and Government

Assumption of responsibility, by government, for many of the functions previously carried out by families and voluntary organizations is commonly described as the emergence of the welfare state. This reality of life in contemporary societies is often criticized for overreaching into aspects of life that should remain the responsibility of civil society institutions, and especially the family. Defenders of active state intervention counter that those institutions, and especially the family, have been so profoundly damaged by recent social and cultural developments that they are incapable of fulfilling their traditional role. It takes a whole village, they insist, to raise a child, and, since few of us live in traditional villages, it takes the active intervention of human service professionals. Critics counter that the welfare state has itself contributed to the pathologies that it claims to address. As usual in such questions, the truth may lie to some extent on both sides.

---

[1] Monsma and Soper, *The Challenge of Pluralism*, 108.

The public policy challenge is to find ways to retain the unquestionable benefits of the welfare state while restraining and even rolling back its distorting interventions in the society.

We have no phrase comparable to *welfare state* for describing the assumption by the state of responsibility for schooling, which occurred some decades before the corresponding developments in social welfare. Unpopular as some of the effects of government control of schooling may be, it is seldom directly challenged.[2] It may be that the gradual extension of state control over schooling had less visible effects, since it mostly occurred in the relationship between the professional staff in schools and government officials at local and state levels; parents continued to send their children to the same schools where the same rituals of education occurred that they themselves had known as children. The result is that the few voices from the Libertarian Right or Left calling for state disengagement from schooling are accorded far less attention than are those who urge that the welfare state be dismantled.

Providing one form or another of "the human care of human beings" increasingly occurs within government agencies, or in settings for which the terms are set—and the bills are paid—by government. This has long been the case for those who teach in schools. Even in Belgium and the Netherlands, where the majority of pupils attend private schools, these schools dance to government's tune in many ways.

Social workers, teachers, and other professionals are prone to complain about bureaucracy and to present the norms of their profession as a bulwark against its effects upon those they serve. Doctors and nurses, for example, complain about managed health care systems, and teachers about school system bureaucracy. It is not often noticed that most professions, and especially the emerging ones like teaching and social work, have developed in close company with the development of the welfare state and the "One Best System"[3] of public education. Government employment, rather than the competition of a market for services, accounts for the particular form that these professions have taken.

Indeed, as we will see, the taken-for-granted predominance of professional staff in social service work is in part the result of government assumption of responsibility for paying for such work through its own agen-

---

[2] An exception is the quirky but interesting book by Samuel L. Blumenfeld, *Is Public Education Necessary?* Myron Lieberman in *Privatization and Educational Choice* and Douglas Dewey have published proposals to abolish mandatory school attendance and government funding of schools. The latter wrote, in *Policy Review* (November–December 1996), that "the state funding of education . . . is not a benign concern for the cultivation of citizenship, but a hostile assumption of ownership." It is safe to say that this is a minority opinion, even among conservatives.

[3] Tyack, *The One Best System.*

cies and through purchase-of-service contracts and other mechanisms. Not only does government funding make it possible to provide more adequate and stable salaries, but the necessity of focused accountability under such arrangements requires more extensive management skills and clear (though often deceptively so) specification of the work to be done. "An effective executive now must identify measurable stages of client progress, design improved recordkeeping systems, and insist that staff keep better records, track client success, and summarize client outcomes in ways that satisfy sponsors."[4] Professional managers require professional staff to supervise and keep their records, and so volunteers are ever more marginalized. Thus "government funding of nonprofit agencies produces a separation of direct and support service roles and tends to shift volunteers out of direct service and into support roles."[5] This in turn changes the nature of the service provided, making it in many ways more skilled but in other ways less personal and potentially engaging. We are reminded of Berger and Neuhaus's warning that "there is a real danger that such [mediating] structures might be 'co-opted' by the government in a too eager embrace that would destroy the very distinctiveness of their function."[6]

Government officials must have a way to specify the quality of whatever it is they are purchasing, often in far more detail than with comparable goods and services produced by government itself. Since quality is extremely difficult to define in education and the human services, there is a strong inclination to set standards in terms of the formal qualifications of staff. Bureaucrats try above all to avoid situations for which they could be blamed. Alternative forms of treatment (or education) do not fit readily within this framework of accountability; the official responsible for approval or for funding is unlikely to want to take a chance on an approach that has not been preapproved and accepted as normative.

The growing professionalization of social work since the early twentieth century reflects its status as one of the preeminent occupations for women as they aspired to satisfying employment with scope for influence broader than could be obtained in a classroom or at the bedside of a patient. Jane Addams, Frances Perkins (New Deal secretary of labor), and many others pursued careers through social work and social reform that would not then have been possible for them in law, politics, or other rewarding and influential fields. As middle-class women moved into the workforce, "the ranks of professional social workers rose from 40,000 in the 1930s to over 250,000 in 1978."[7]

[4] Smith and Lipsky, *Nonprofits for Hire*, 81.
[5] Ibid., 111.
[6] Berger and Neuhaus, *To Empower People*, 163.
[7] Smith and Lipsky, *Nonprofits for Hire*, 102.

Alongside the professional social workers with MSW degrees and rising status, the welfare state has continued to employ an army of welfare case-workers and others who work in large organizations under highly regulated conditions and with little discretion, though protected in their job status by militant unions.

> Social workers, viewed as an occupational category, exhibit an extraordinary amount of diversity. They range from the proverbial little old lady in tennis shoes, armed with good intentions and a high school diploma, ministering to the needs, as she interprets them, of her caseload, to the young man with a Ph.D. degree from a graduate school of social welfare engaged in a program of evaluative research on the merits of a new casework technique. Matching the variety of training undergone and tasks performed by workers is the diversity of settings in which they operate, some few functioning as solo practitioners, most typically as family counselors, others working for special-ized private agencies, and the majority serving as employees in a variety of public settings—schools, hospitals, correction facilities, and public assistance agencies.[8]

The situation of public school teachers is more parallel to that of welfare caseworkers than to that of graduate social workers engaged in counseling or research. They work for local government in a capacity generally parallel to that of civil servants. Despite the efforts of their unions, teachers have continued to be treated as essentially interchangeable parts in a great ma-chine; indeed, the union insistence on uniform salaries, on job security without regard to merit, and on seniority as the primarily criterion for particular positions has encouraged this belief and has held back the emer-gence of real professional status.

Social work and education both emerged as occupations within local church life, and it is only in quite recent times that both became secularized (in the original sense of that term) and associated with the state. The order of development of professional status was different in the two cases: in education, the state assumed responsibility first, and then school adminis-tration and finally teaching took on many of the characteristics of a profes-sion, but always within the context of bureaucratic subordination.[9] Even in England, where government was late in taking responsibility for popular schooling, "[a]s the State assumed financial responsibility for the elemen-tary schools, it laid down conditions regarding their conduct. Among other matters it set out requirements which must be fulfilled by those who taught in them."[10]

---

[8] Scott, "Professional Employees," 83.

[9] For an account of the professionalization of school administration, see Tyack and Hansot, *Managers of Virtue*; see also Lieberman, *Education as a Profession*.

[10] Carr-Saunders and Wilson, *The Professions*, 251.

In social work, by contrast, professionalization preceded and to a considerable extent stimulated government assumption of responsibility, as social workers took the lead in advocating social welfare policies. Lubove points out that "the values and institutions associated with the professionalization of social work were generated primarily in the private sphere. Individuals connected with public welfare lent their support, but the organized system played a subordinate role in defining the professional norms and creating the supporting institutions."[11]

This is no doubt one of the reasons why social work is more "advanced" as a profession than is schoolteaching, which has been carried out within government-defined settings and bureaucratic control for several generations longer. Americans who advocated effectively for universal systems of free schooling were generally not teachers but lawyers (like Horace Mann) and clergymen (like Calvin Stowe). This was true in Europe as well; it was scientists (Cuvier), philosophers (Cousin), theologians (Schleiermacher, Hofstede de Groot), historians (Guizot), clergymen (Van der Palm), political theorists (Humboldt, Diesterweg), journalists, lawyers, anything but teachers who shaped the agenda for state schooling. The professional norms of teachers have in consequence largely been defined to apply in bureaucratic contexts. The idea sometimes advanced of "teachers in private practice" has an exotic flavor, while private practice is a real career choice for social workers.

Invisible as these changes may have been to most parents, they were profound in their effects on the nature of the teaching profession, in ways that paralleled the effect of the development of the welfare state on the nature of social work. As Dutch scholars have noted, the right to social services "is not only (and perhaps not even primarily) of benefit to the citizens who receive the services, but also (and perhaps even especially) to the experts in caregiving, the often highly specialized professionals." In place of the personal dependency and inequality that characterized the older caretaking, undertaken as a personal favor or on the basis of social solidarity, "the new caretaking as a right was characterized by formal (bureaucratic) dependency and thus by formal inequality."[12]

It is of the essence of a profession that its members define for themselves the norms of practice and of qualifications to practice, and the established professions have made government their ally and agent in enforcing the norms that they have defined. The reference group for professional staff in a nonprofit agency is no longer the nonprofessional board and volunteers, but their professional peers in other agencies (perhaps founded on

---

[11] Lubove, *The Professional Altruist*, 53.
[12] Adriaansens and Zijderveld, *Vrijwillig initiatief en de verzorgingsstaat*, 18.

entirely different principles of service) and in government.[13] This is of a piece with their preference—despite their complaints about bureaucracy—for working within the secure framework provided by government. "From the standpoint of the service professional, funding by the public sector is the much more desirable option. . . . the immediate economic discipline endemic to the market sector is missing."[14] But becoming dependent upon government is not without its costs.

Government agencies, in this country and in other countries as well, have traditionally relied upon the means of control characterized by Max Weber as bureaucratic rationality: detailed prescription by rules of what lower-level staff should do in all circumstances, and detailed allocation of resources with little discretion on the part of those using the resources. Routines and required procedures, with periodic supervision, are a quite effective means to ensure against corruption and a fairly effective means to ensure against abuse of the power that government places in the hands of those who deal in its name with the public.

But bureaucratic rationality is a very ineffective way to control the work of teachers, social workers, and others engaged in "the human care of human beings," activities that require exercise of a large measure of discretion by those lower down in the organization. "No body of rules can be complex or subtle enough correctly to regulate contacts with clients."[15] What works reasonably well for issuing driver's licenses does not work at all well for educating children or helping an addict to put his life back together. As Weber put it, bureaucratic control is characterized by "the dominance of a spirit of formalistic impersonality, '*Sine ira et studio*,' without hatred or passion, and hence without affection or enthusiasm."[16] Affection and enthusiasm would be out of place in issuing driver's licenses or collecting taxes, but they are essential ingredients of an effective school, and they may make the crucial difference in the counseling given to a pregnant teenager.

Some things government does very well through routine procedures, others it does adequately, but caring for human beings it does quite badly under most circumstances; what is most needed by particular developing children or particular adults in crisis does not lend itself well to detailed specification. Most of us, in deciding to entrust our young child to a day care center or our elderly parent to a long-term care facility, care less about the detailed procedures that will be followed than about the character and attitudes of those who will be providing the care. Church-sponsored pro-

[13] Gerrichhauzen and van Mierlo, "Het particuliere bestuursstelsel," 13.
[14] Kellner and Berger, "Life-Style Engineering," 15.
[15] Scott, "Professional Employees," 132.
[16] Weber, *Theory of Social and Economic Organization*, 340.

grams for children and for the elderly tend to be popular even with those who do not share the faith upon which they are based; the religious connection seems to offer assurances about the motivations of the caretakers and about how they will make decisions. This is no doubt why Muslim parents in England and the Netherlands are reported often to prefer Christian schools over secular public schools.

The current discussion, in the United States, about "national child care standards" is a good example of the way in which professional norms are often translated into requirements for licensing or public funding. Advocates "generally argue that (1) parents are unable to distinguish between low- and high-quality care, (2) the government has the information to determine what constitutes high-quality care, and therefore (3) the government should set standards to guarantee high-quality care for all children. That line of reasoning assumes that parents are ignorant of the quality of care their children receive. It further assumes that there is one universal definition of 'high-quality care.' "[17]

But in fact there is not such a universal definition and probably never will be, because children differ and the circumstances and values of their parents differ. The National Research Council concluded in 1996 that, in Olsen's paraphrase, "we do not even know what constitutes the 'basic ingredients' of quality care, let alone understand the long-term effects of different types of child care arrangements." As a result, "there is no consensus, scientific or political, on what is best for every child. That makes sense to parents who know firsthand that every family and every child have unique needs."[18]

The standards actually proposed, in fact, have more to do with staffing, training, accreditation, and salary levels than they do with how children are treated and to what ends. They are thus a typical example of a profession seeking to have its own interests defined as quality norms. "With the quality of social services difficult to measure and available performance indicators open to multiple interpretations, public officials fall back on process measures such as the number of professionals who actually deliver services."[19]

I would not be misunderstood on this point. There is much to be said for ensuring that there are enough adults to give careful and sustained attention to a group of children, and that those who work with young children have their best interests at heart and have the skills to use the time entrusted to them productively. Those who provide child care can benefit enormously from good training and ongoing access to resources and ad-

[17] Olsen, "The Advancing Nanny State," 5.
[18] Ibid., 10.
[19] Smith and Lipsky, *Nonprofits for Hire*, 107.

vice. But there is no reason to believe that good child care can be provided only in professionally run centers (rather than in family-style child care), or that parents are incapable of judging when their children are being well served. When children end up with inadequate caretakers, it is generally because their parents cannot afford better alternatives. Providing resources (child care vouchers) and information to parents will enable them to seek out good situations for their children and make them effective advocates for the interests of those children.[20]

It is of the nature of a profession that those who have invested years in acquiring that status seek to prevent competition from others who have not, and who are therefore willing or forced to work for less pay or under less attractive conditions. The simplest way to ensure a monopoly on providing certain services is to persuade government to make professional credentialing a requirement to practice. Thus, for example, "in many states professional social workers and counselors have tried to win legislative approval of regulations that would require a professional license to be a counselor in an alcohol or drug abuse program. This effort has been resisted, sometimes quite vigorously, by lay people including recovering alcoholics and recovering addicts, who argue that lay people can be better counselors than professionals,"[21] as we have seen in discussing Teen Challenge and similar programs.

Additional requirements may be set in relation to public funding. For example, a government agency may require particular staffing levels and arrangements for supervision.[22] "Numerous state contracts for counseling, therapy, rehabilitation, and education," Loconte found, "sustain layers of requirements for caregivers. 'Every staff member is independently licensed, either as a psychologist, psychiatrist, or as an independent clinical social worker,' says James Gorman, director of planning and evaluation for Catholic Charities in Boston. . . . According to one government report 'staff credentials may be required which bear no relation to actual job responsibility or to client need.' "[23] Indeed, government seems at times the junior partner, according to a Dutch study; the professions are as prepared to defend their prerogatives, in the name of "necessary quality standards," over against government as over against their clients and the general public.[24]

In public school teaching, state certification based upon completion of required courses and practice teaching (rather than professional control of

[20] Glenn, "Letting Poor Parents Act Responsibly," 1–18.
[21] Smith and Lipsky, *Nonprofits for Hire*, 108.
[22] Ibid., 105.
[23] Loconte, *Seducing the Samaritan*, 62–63.
[24] Adriaansens and Zijderveld, *Vrijwillig initiatief en de verzorgingsstaat*, 40.

credentials to practice) is the norm, and the various loopholes that have been created are much resented. Recent interest, in many states, in alternative routes to certification[25] are seen as weakening even further the ability of the profession to pass on the sorts of attitudinal norms that may be—though increasingly are not—developed in teacher-training institutions.

The primary response to growing state control and consolidation of school districts into larger and larger units has been aggressive and now almost universal unionization. It is as though teachers had said to local and state administrators, "if you're going to treat us in a routinized and rule-driven fashion, we'll press to elaborate additional rules in our favor!" During the tight budget times of the late 1970s, in particular, elected school boards—responsive to well-organized teachers—often bargained away administrative authority in lieu of pay increases. There has come to be a cultural expectation among big-city teachers that they will "work to rule," and there is little incentive to assume responsibility for setting objectives for which they could then be held accountable. The result is that educational mission plays a role distinctly secondary to compliance with procedures. This has in turn impeded the development of professional status, which is based upon the presumption of internalized norms rather than external regulation.

It seems paradoxical, then, to speak of teaching as dominated by professional norms, but there are in fact a number that are acquired through training or through the peer culture. Some are positive though general, speaking of a high calling to shape the future and to cultivate learning and character. "The leaders of an emerging profession take pains to construct and publish a code of ethics. Unfortunately, because the knowledge on which their occupational performance is based is not highly developed, the codes they construct are full of vague generalities."[26] Others norms are negative and more concrete, discouraging inappropriate touching of children or siding with a parent in conflict with a fellow teacher. Yet others have to do with an understanding of the goals of education as liberating children from the "dead hand of traditional beliefs," and here is where (as we will see below) conflict with faith-based schools may arise.

Semiprofessionalism

If the expanding role of government has stimulated the professionalization of social work in some ways that may distance social agencies from the clients they serve, it has also produced effects that "deprofessionalize"

---

[25] See the state-by-state review in Education Commission of the States, *Alternative Routes*.
[26] Barber, "Sociology of the Professions," 677.

many staff by routinizing their work and eliminating the exercise of professional judgment that is the essence of a profession. This has been even more true of teachers who work in large school systems.

There is reason to believe that the ineffectiveness of large school systems and large welfare bureaucracies derives in part from a mismatch between the routinized and rule-driven manner in which they are controlled and the infinitely varied and unpredictable work that they are called upon to perform. It is for this reason that most recent proposals for school reform have called for allowing teachers control over their own work through some form of school-based management. Whether such "professionalization" of teaching can be reconciled with a contract-driven labor-union culture seems doubtful, and this is why even more recent reform proposals call for autonomous charter schools that are free of centrally bargained contract restraints.

Nor is this problem to be solved simply by moving from direct provision of services by government to reliance upon nonprofit agencies, if the terms under which government relates to those agencies force them to bureaucratize their mode of functioning. Competition, touted by some as the solution to the stagnation of large school systems, could have the effect of further deprofessionalizing teachers if schools were forced to compete on the basis of cost-effectiveness to receive funding. "There is some reason to think," Smith and Lipsky observe, "that deprofessionalization is a product of the contracting regime rather than of government funding of nonprofit agencies as such. Over time, contracting may reward agencies that offer low costs when quality of service remains difficult to judge,"[27] as it is in social work and in education, because both involve clients who are infinitely variable.

The problem has grown more acute in recent decades. Rather than understanding their work as a high calling—more sacred, Horace Mann insisted, than that of the minister in his pulpit—public school teachers rely instead upon a vaguer concept of "professionalism." But this is a professionalism distorted by administrative constraints and the lack of an adequately defined body of expertise rooted in theory. As a result, it lacks the characteristics that sociologists use to define a profession: autonomy, self-regulation, high status, demonstrated skill. The public school itself is no longer seen as the high temple of democracy and of Americanism (except, in suitably secularized form, in the rhetoric of the teacher unions), but as a troubled and often ineffective institution on a par with public housing.

In the absence of an inspiriting sense of belonging to a calling with a noble mission, those who supervise government-employed teachers must rely upon detailed prescriptions that can never reach to the most important

[27] Smith and Lipsky, *Nonprofits for Hire*, 110.

aspects of what a teacher does in relation to children. It seemed for a time that this had reached its logical culmination in the development of "teacher-proof curriculum," but this in turn has been surpassed by some forms of computer-assisted instruction in which the teacher almost vanishes from the picture. Teaching and social work have been numbered among the "heteronomous semi-professions."

> Semi-professionalism denotes that the profession does not rest on a firm theoretical knowledge base; the period of training involved is relatively short; members cannot claim monopoly of exclusive skills; and the special area of their competence, i.e., their function, is less well-defined as compared with the full-fledged established professions. Heteronomy, on the other hand, means that members of the profession are guided and controlled not only from within—that is, by internalized professional norms, expert knowledge, and the professional community—but also by administrative rules and by superiors in the organizational hierarchy.[28]

The situation of social workers is somewhat more varied than that of teachers, since they work in more diverse roles and institutional settings and have more clearly distinguished levels of qualifications than do teachers. Caseworkers who handle public assistance or child protection, for example, work to even more detailed prescriptions than do teachers, with little discretion in how they assess and respond to their clients' practical needs; at the other extreme are graduate social workers—often with middle-class clients—who see themselves as engaged in a form of psychotherapy, complete with fifty-minute sessions in their offices. The latter function on the basis of professional norms alone, often with little or nothing in the way of bureaucratic accountability.

In general, however, social workers no longer understand themselves as uplifting humanity, but as attempting—with scant success—to patch up the victims of an unjust social order, or to help them to adjust more successfully to their circumstances.

As the "ideal interests" that played such an important part in the evolution of social work and—to some extent—in the development of teaching have faded in their power to motivate and to guide, the role of material interests has become more significant. This leads to a concern to limit access to the right to practice, and in particular eligibility to receive public funds for doing so. Perhaps the most dramatic form that this has taken in recent years has been the ferocious opposition of the teachers' unions to any form of public support for nonpublic schools, which typically are not required to employ certified teachers or, if they do, are free from the constraints of centrally bargained union contracts.

---

[28] Toren, "Semi-professionalism and Social Work," 153.

How Professional Norms Developed

Which comes first: a profession or the norms that define it? In most cases, the former. Changes in the society, new needs and new modes of meeting them, encourage the emergence of the consciousness of common interests among those who make a lifelong career out of doing so. Some of these interests are material: for example, protecting salary levels through raising the qualifications for entry and thus limiting the number of persons qualified for employment. Other interests, however, are "ideal" and require articulating norms that assure insiders and convince outsiders that professionals can be trusted always to act in the best interests of the client or pupil or patient. Professionals, by [self-]definition, are never "just doing a job." They possess a superior insight into what is in the interest of others, and, while what they do may hurt at times, it is always for the best. "[T]he professional dictates what is good or evil for the client, who has no choice but to accede to the professional judgment."[29]

Although in theory these norms of professional practice are based upon both scientific evidence and the accumulated experience of the profession, in practice many of them can be understood to respond to practical exigencies or to have emerged through the evolution of the occupational group that has come to define itself as a profession. As Lubove observes about the development of social work, "even if professionalization was not associated necessarily with substantial scientific achievement and control, it was unquestionably associated with changes in the definition of social work functions, the organization of social work services, and the values and institutions of American society. The professionalization of social work is perhaps better understood in relation to these changes, especially the development of a professional subculture, bureaucratization, and specialization, than to any unique social work knowledge base rooted in science."[30]

Having convinced themselves (and perhaps others) that they have a privileged insight into what is needed in some sphere of human life, it is by a natural progression that leaders in most professions come to believe themselves entitled to prescribe for the society in general. Educators are especially prone to believe that they possess the key to human progress and are entitled to determine the purposes as well as the means of education. Let us reshape the rising generation, Horace Mann and his allies promised, and crime and misery will be no more.[31] But the children must be entrusted to them entirely, with no interference from parents: " 'When they come

---

[29] Greenwood, "Attributes of a Profession," 12.
[30] Lubove, *The Professional Altruist*, 21.
[31] See Glenn, *Myth of Common School*, chap. 3.

through that door,' said an education despot in the seat of government, 'they're mine.' "[32]

John Dewey, though ordinarily rather cautious and oblique in articulating his agenda for education, was stimulated by the crisis of the depression to insist that educators could not be neutral; they *would* shape society for good or ill and should see themselves not as the servants of society, but as its guides. After all, he wrote,

> the schools will surely, as a matter of fact and not of ideal, share in the building of the social order of the future according as they ally themselves with this or that movement of existing social forces. This fact is inevitable. . . . according as teachers and administrators align themselves with the older so-called "individualistic" ideals—which in fact are fatal to individuality for the many—or with the newer forces making for social control of economic forces. . . the teacher will . . . not be content with generalities about the desired future order. The task is to translate the desired ideal over into the conduct of the detail of the school in administration, instruction, and subject-matter.[33]

A similar development in self-understanding occurred in social work. What had been a role of coordinating volunteers in local efforts to relieve misery and put individuals on the right track, one by one, came to seem an opportunity to remake the entire society on just and humanistic principles.

> National Conference of Social Work president Owen Lovejoy announced in 1920 that social workers would have a new kind of task. While volunteers had endeavored "to ameliorate evil social conditions, to lighten the burdens of poverty, to reduce the volume of ignorance, combat the ravages of disease and otherwise labor diligently to assuage the flood of human sorrow and wretchedness," social workers and their allies would be "social engineers" capable of creating "a divine order on earth as it is in heaven."[34]

Professionalization thus initiated and was itself the occasion of a fundamental shift in thinking about the nature of social services. As Lubove points out, "The motto of the Boston Associated Charities had been 'Not Alms But a Friend.' In the early twentieth century a different concept evolved: neither alms nor a friend, but a professional service. . . . Social workers could not so readily reconcile scientific philanthropy with presumptions of moral superiority in a period when the poor were considered the victims of a hostile environment."[35]

[32] Budziszewski, "Politics of Virtues," 38–44, 44.
[33] Dewey, "Can Education Share?" 207–8.
[34] Olasky, *Renewing American Compassion*, 67.
[35] Lubove, *The Professional Altruist*, 23.

In striking contrast with this "professional" understanding of the nature of reform, the heart of nineteenth-century efforts to improve the lot of the poor—from which many faith-based organizations are directly or indirectly descended—was a conviction that people in need could and must undergo fundamental and positive change through the assistance and example of volunteers, assistance that was "friendly" but at the same time demanding. The conviction was articulated notably by William Booth in his call to arms, *In Darkest England and the Way Out* (1890): "To get a man soundly saved it is not enough to put on him a pair of new breeches, to give him regular work, or even to give him a University education. These things are all outside a man, and if the inside remains unchanged you have wasted your labour . . . All material help from without is useful only in so far as it develops moral strength within. . . . My only hope for the permanent deliverance of mankind from misery, either in this world or the next, is the regeneration or remaking of the individual by the power of the Holy Ghost through Jesus Christ."[36] The stress upon internal change was shared by many less colorful than Booth; it was widely believed at the time that most of the problems that social workers were called upon to relieve originated as a result of intemperance, improvidence, indolence, ignorance, and other personal shortcomings. "Not technical training or scientific understanding of human behavior but moral insight" was needed by those who would help. Professional staff lacked "the spontaneity and zeal of volunteers,"[37] the willingness to enter into a life-changing personal relationship with someone in need.

The role of the paid staff of charity organizations was to coordinate but not to replace the work of volunteers. In Britain "in the mid-1880s . . . half a million women worked as full-time volunteers in charities, assisted by another 20,000 who were paid."[38] It was assumed that volunteers could provide what the paid staff could not, something like the natural social relationships and influence of the socially superior toward the socially inferior of a traditional rural community. This has been described as an attempt "to reestablish the patterns of social interaction of the small town or village, where the primary group exercised powerful social controls," and this "to restore the 'natural relations' which the city had destroyed."[39]

Although we tend to recoil from what seems to us the condescension of such a relationship *de haut en bas*, there is ample testimony that real kindness was involved. Those who were prepared to undergo its influence—the "deserving poor" mocked by Shaw—were not infrequently enabled to

---

[36] Quoted by Whelan, *The Corrosion of Charity*, 40.
[37] Lubove, *The Professional Altruist*, 13.
[38] Whelan, *The Corrosion of Charity*, 15.
[39] Lubove, *The Professional Altruist*, 14.

change their circumstances for the better through timely assistance given in the expectation that amendment of life would follow. Was this really more patronizing than the current assumption that the destitute can do very little to affect their own circumstances? As Gertrude Himmelfarb has noted in another connection,

> Today, when the very idea of preaching is suspect, the word itself pejorative, Methodist sermons evoke the familiar charges of paternalism and social control, the imposition upon the poor of alien values designed to domesticate and manipulate them. In earlier times, when church-going (or chapel-going) was a natural activity and the sermon a familiar part of the service, there was nothing invidious in being preached to. What was invidious was not being preached to, not having access to the kinds of moral, religious, and communal experiences that were a normal part of life for those not so poor as to be deprived of them. For Wesley no one was so poor.[40]

Moral judgment that carries with it an expectation that a person not only should but *can* change is more likely to be found, today, in programs that involve poor people helping other poor people.[41] For the best part of a century, the profession of social work has evolved through rejecting such judgments. There has been a congruence and mutual reinforcement between this stance of amoralism—understanding behavior as "functional" or "dysfunctional" rather than right or wrong—and the bureaucratic impersonality, emptied of all normative themes, characteristic of government-provided services.

The change in the nature of social services away from the charity organization and "friendly visitor" model was based upon (or justified by?) a growing conviction, among social workers, that amateur efforts were inadequate if not downright harmful. As T. H. Marshall pointed out in a classic essay about the developments in Britain, "the centre of gravity moves from the voluntary supporters to the professional employees of the society."[42] Similarly, in the United States the development of the social sciences, with their powerful explanatory models for human behavior, tended in effect (though not always in intention) to reduce the role of individual choice in explaining why people's lives turn out the way they do and thus to devalue the sort of moral appeals that volunteers were qualified to make. Professional expertise, developed and certified by new professional schools and associations, was exercised within formal organizations with little for enthusiastic amateurs to do besides raise funds.[43] As a result, individuals moti-

[40] Himmelfarb, *The Idea of Poverty*, 32–33.
[41] See the extraordinary account by Colarelli and Siegel, *Ward H;* also Brager, "The Indigenous Worker."
[42] "Voluntary Action" (1949), in Marshall, *Class, Citizenship*, 350.
[43] Lubove, *The Professional Altruist*, 18.

vated primarily by a desire to do good that was based in their religious
convictions no longer played an important role even in agencies with a
religious identity; "the whole collective provision [of services] became so
professional and perfectionist that it removed the motivation to make a
personal contribution to it."[44]

It is only in very recent years that we have realized that something
valuable was lost as a consequence of turning away from upon volunteer
efforts and moral challenges in social services . . . and in education as well.
Education in the nineteenth century was unabashedly moralistic, from the
copybook lessons with which children learned to read and write to the
required course in "moral science" with which higher education concluded
and that was, as Marsden points out, the "integrating feature" of the college
curriculum.[45]

The shift to a nonjudgmental posture (which is actually highly—though
selectively—judgmental, of course) is a very recent feature of American
schooling, compared with social work, where it has flourished much longer,
and indeed may owe something to the growing presence of psychologists
and social workers in schools. Dewey and other influential contemporaries
of the social work pioneers were by no means advocates of value-free
schooling. It was the values of parents and of contemporary society to
which Dewey objected, not the proposition that schooling must be value-
laden.

Social science—what Dewey and others liked to call "trained intelligence"—claimed to provide a sound basis for reconstructing society, ethics,
and the educational system, and an explanation of the causes, in economic,
social, and psychological conditions, of the distressed state in which the
clients of agencies found themselves. It seemed more appropriate to address those conditions than to exhort clients to rise above them through
their personal efforts. "Personality flaws," the new science insisted, "had
social origins, and in any event 'social justice' required an end to scrutiny
of behavior, since 'the origin of economic or social need is far less important than the fact of its existence.' . . . They saw *no* valid reason for
categorizing individuals as 'deserving' or 'not deserving' "[46]

The emerging social work profession—"professional altruists," in Lubove's phrase—"argued that challenge was not necessary because individuals who needed to change would do so as soon as they were placed in a
pleasant environment so that their true, benevolent natures could come
out. . . . A good environment would save all. Compassion meant accepting
wrongful activity and postponing any pressure to change until the person

[44] Adriaansens and Zijderveld, *Vrijwillig initiatief en de verzorgingsstaat*, 54.
[45] Marsden, *Soul of American University*.
[46] Olasky, *Tragedy of American Compassion*, 169.

was in a good environment."[47] Although the profession of social work was developed largely within private nonprofit agencies, the dynamic that it helped to create was in the direction of government responsibility for social welfare. "Private charity," the Progressive Era reformers believed, "was inconsistent, unreliable, and parochial; thus, the state needed to assume the responsibility for the distribution of services through a state bureaucracy of professional workers who would distribute social welfare services as an entitlement rather than a gift."[48] This was a period of unlimited faith in what could be accomplished by trained intelligence, as reflected in "academic credentials, more rigorous intellectual and professional standards, and an emphasis on the ethos of a discipline as well as on its technical lore."[49]

Professional Training

It is in the nature of government programs to function by impartial rules that must be written in terms broad enough to cover many different situations with relatively little discretion exercised by those on the firing line. Administrators seek ways to subject to such impersonal rules the cop on the beat, the teacher in the classroom, the social worker face-to-face with a client, each of whom must make decisions that cannot be specified unambiguously in rules. Careful recruitment is recommended (but this is subject to often-conflicting criteria), training is required (but this can rarely provide a realistic anticipation of the ambiguity of experience), close supervision is proposed (but this is expensive . . . and often resented). Ultimately, the human care of human beings cannot be regulated in detail; "one can hold a social worker accountable for making a visit to a family, following up with phone calls, and performing other appropriate tasks. But one cannot know if her judgment was sound and her intervention ultimately effective."[50]

The most effective way to ensure that "street-level" staff behave appropriately is through making sure that they have a settled disposition to do so, based upon convictions held and habits developed.[51] The first "normal schools" for secular teachers were modeled upon the Catholic and Lutheran Pietist seminaries where teachers had been trained as much through spiritual exercises and community life as through academic work. Accounts

---

[47] Ibid., 121, 137.
[48] Smith and Lipsky, *Nonprofits for Hire*, 15.
[49] Randall, *Private Schools and Public Power*, 16.
[50] Smith and Lipsky, *Nonprofits for Hire*, 199.
[51] See Delattre, *Character and Cops*.

of the student experience in the normal schools set up by Horace Mann in Massachusetts around 1840 (several headed by Unitarian ministers) and of those that played such an important role in spreading "republican" values in France later in the century invariably stress intense, even claustrophobic, community and the deep seriousness with which the directors lectured about the ideals and character of a teacher.

Over the past hundred years, however, there has been a shift from focusing on the character of professionals to focusing on their expertise. Professions are said to differ from other occupations because "the skills that characterize a profession flow from, and are supported by a fund of knowledge that has been organized into an internally consistent system, called a *body of theory*." While other occupations may require a high order of skill and the mastery of complex information, "no books appear on the theory of punch-pressing or pipefitting or bricklaying."[52] It is partly for this reason that it is more difficult to be a Christian psychologist or social worker than a Christian bricklayer: the theories about human nature and about good and evil that have been elaborated as the basis for those professions are at important points in conflict with the biblical understanding of humanity's created purpose.

Professions "on the make" use the development of university-based training as a crucial means of distinguishing themselves from occupations that do not require such training, and this in turn requires the definition of a body of expertise that they and no others may be said to possess. The "semiprofessions" like social work and teaching have found this difficult to achieve, in part because their knowledge base is uncertain and subject to faddish instability. The professionalization of social work was based on "changing aspirations and organization of services rather than objective scientific achievement. Social workers undoubtedly acquired a proficiency and dexterity in certain operations, such as the preparation of case records, and this, combined with a terminology drawn from psychiatry and psychology may have obscured a largely subjective performance."[53]

The difficulty that social workers and teachers have had in defining themselves as "professionals" arises in part from their lack of unique professional competencies. Arguably, at least, both simply do what all the rest of us do, though more skillfully. Their practice rests upon "knowledge which is at once too broad and too vague"[54] to warrant fully professional status. The tacit knowledge that is so important to both social work and teaching is acquired at least as much through practice and experience as it is through study, and this makes it particularly difficult to distinguish the

[52] Greenwood, "Attributes of a Profession," 11.
[53] Lubove, *The Professional Altruist*, 105.
[54] Wilensky, "The Professionalization of Everyone?" 149.

claims that the "professional" can make from those of the "amateur" who has successfully engaged in the same form of work for some years.

This blurring of boundaries has been acknowledged in K-12 education by provisions for alternative teacher certification that does not require formal study in a university-based teacher-training program. Widespread acceptance—except by the teacher unions—of this alternative cuts at the very basis of the claim to a distinguishing professional expertise. So does allowing nonpublic schools and publicly funded charter schools to employ teachers who have not met state certification requirements based upon professional training, a practice not generally allowed in Europe. After all, as Tyack and Hansot noted, "educators justify their control of educational processes by their expertise. Permitting nonstandard education would interfere with educators' professionalizing efforts, in effect delegitimating pedagogues' claims of special knowledge."[55]

The need to meet norms for how they go about their work—norms set by professional bodies that define good practice in ways that exclude religious considerations, rather than simply failing to take religion into account—in order to be eligible for public funding is one of the sources of difficulty for faith-based organization seeking to provide social services (of course, it does not presently affect faith-based schools in the United States, since they are not eligible for public funding). Another has to do with the criteria that they may employ in determining whom they will employ to carry out that work.

On one level, this is a question of professional qualifications, and of the training that most professions have entrusted to institutions of higher education with which they are in close alliance. Professional training is one of the means by which secular ways of understanding the purposes—or lack of purpose—of human life are introduced into the practice of faith-based institutions. "This forced standardization of teacher training is exactly what many private school leaders fear when they oppose teacher certification requirements. They do not want their teachers trained exactly as public school teachers are trained."[56] After all, one of the major purposes of professional training is to shape an individual's "own attitudes and values . . . in accordance with the accepted norms and values of the profession," and these are expected to become personal traits, " 'a constellation of sacred and secular objects and attitudes.' The profession was not only a career but a way of life that shaped personality by offering it a medium of expression."[57] On another level, as we will see in the next chapter, it involves the

[55] Sacken, "Regulating Nonpublic Education," 404, paraphrasing Tyack and Hansot, *Managers of Virtue*.

[56] Erickson, "Bad Fences," 232.

[57] Lubove, *The Professional Altruist*, 137, 118.

issue whether a criterion that would not usually be thought of as a professional qualification—religious belief or adherence—may be used in making employment decisions.

Undoubtedly a great deal has been gained through raising standards of training and supervision for those who work with children and with those in need. No doubt well-trained social workers are more discerning about what is really going on in a person's life, and what may be preventing her from doing whatever is necessary to get her life back on track. But something has been lost, as well, in surrendering the capacity for moral indignation:

> The persistent efforts of caseworkers to establish a scientific knowledge base and methodology, to limit the area of intuition, moralism, and empirical insight ... showed the extent to which the goal of rationality permeated the subculture. "Universalism" demanded an "affective neutrality," obliging the professional to provide skilled service to the maximum of his ability despite any personal reaction to the client. . . . They were the professional representatives of a social institution rather than agents delegated the responsibility of reforming the character of the deserving poor. Antisocial behavior became a challenge to the worker's professional skill, instead of a cause for moral indignation and condemnation.[58]

Those who developed the norms for training future social workers, early in this century, were convinced that trainees "who were easily shocked and found it difficult to withhold moral judgment had not achieved the objectivity which the 'professional obligations of social work demand.' "[59] But isn't the capacity to be shocked by someone's behavior a measure of respect, of high expectations? We are not shocked by the most degraded actions of those we despise or consider hopelessly far below our own standards. Perhaps the willingness to exercise moral judgment in relation to other persons is essential to recognizing their full humanity, that they are fundamentally "like us" and should be held to the same standards to which we hold ourselves. The willingness to assert and to accept moral judgments can be the basis of a relationship that, while paternalistic and unequal, is nevertheless more personal than that developed within a bureaucratically defined context.[60]

The professionalization of social work has led to tensions with the non-profit agencies where many of them work. "Professionals bring norms and values that often conflict with the orientation of the community. . . . The professional social work orientation may contradict the orientation of some

---

[58] Ibid., 121.
[59] Ibid., 156.
[60] Adriaansens and Zijderveld, *Vrijwillig initiatief en de verzorgingsstaat*, 18.

community organizations such as battered women shelters and programs for the poor and hungry, which are founded on philosophies of self-help, political action, and lay control of services." The founding purpose of a nonprofit agency, whether religious or secular, is put aside.[61] The mode of service that it provides may be changed profoundly. "Informal care tends to give way to formal care when government funding flows into an organization previously structured predominantly along volunteer, informal lines. This is not simply an inevitable turn in the course of organizational maturation. Many organizations that are part of the informal care network, such as Alcoholic Anonymous chapters and other self-help groups which do not accept government funds, have been able to exist for decades without significant professionalization or formalization."[62] If they sought public funding, would this have been possible?

Although, as we will see, this poses special problems for faith-based organizations and agencies, they are not alone in experiencing pressures to abandon their original purposes as government funding leads to increased professionalization of their staff. "Supporters of women's organizations such as rape crisis centers and battered women shelters believe that the hiring of more professional staff and the displacement of volunteers leads to a more conventional social service approach than the one with which these organizations started," and thus decreases their effectiveness.[63] Similarly, the federally funded antipoverty programs of the late sixties and the seventies "had a profound effect on the character of Puerto Rican nonprofit organizations. They provided funds for much-needed social services and helped agencies to become firmly established. But at the same time, the funds fostered the bureaucratization of these institutions. Voluntary work was replaced by paid work,"[64] and the organizations grew away from their community.

In some respects, indeed, faith-based organizations may be better able to protect their distinctive character than are their secular counterparts, precisely to the extent that the character rests upon a coherent and articulated set of beliefs about human nature and destiny. Monsma surveyed both religious and secular agencies about the impact of government funding and found that "the heavily negative effect of making the agencies less flexible and more 'bureaucratic' was cited more often by the secular than the religious agencies, and more often by the agencies that were low rather than high" on the religious-practices scale that he devised.[65]

[61] Smith and Lipsky, *Nonprofits for Hire*, 84.

[62] Ibid., 113.

[63] Ibid., 100.

[64] Rodríguez-Fraticelli, Sanabria, and Tirado, "Puerto Rican Nonprofit Organizations," 44.

[65] Monsma, *When Sacred and Secular Mix*, 93.

Professional Norms and Faith-Based Organizations

It is evident from the success of Teen Challenge and other programs that manage to change lives that an element of judgment cannot be avoided when the behavior or attitude of the person being helped has contributed to the difficulty in which he or she is caught. Professional training intended to ensure that the social worker takes an impersonal and nonjudgmental position toward the client may deprive the latter of both the insight and the impulse required to experience a real change of heart . . . and of life. There is, in policy circles, a growing realization that helping people to change behaviors that keep them poor or unhappy requires changing their habits and perhaps even their values, as well as their skills. Simply exposing them to new opportunities will not change their circumstances without the attitudes and self-discipline required to profit from those opportunities.

Willingness to engage at a personal level and to call insistently for "repentance and amendment of life" characterized nineteenth-century programs to help the poor and has continued to mark the "gospel missions" of our own time. Sometimes the continuity is made explicit from paradigmatic figures like Jerry McAuley, the reformed "bully, drunkard, and convict" who founded New York's Water Street Mission in the 1870s. McAuley's work was "with the unworthy poor, the drunkards, prostitutes, convicts and thieves. For Jerry had been one, and he knew God changed him and could change them, too."[66] He and other "wounded healers" are heroes to the 250 "rescue missions" that shelter all comers today, serving 30 million meals a year and giving shelter to more than twenty-seven thousand people each night. Olasky quotes a leader in an inner-city church-based ministry as saying that the goal was not to deal with poverty alone, but with "impoverishment—long-term hopelessness, humiliation, and degradation, a culture unto itself. It takes more than money to redeem the lives of those who have become spiritually destitute."[67]

The extent of faith-based social service—almost always strongly local in its management and orientation—in the nineteenth century is astonishing. Olasky reports, "One analysis of activity among 112 Protestant churches in Manhattan and the Bronx alone showed that 397 social agencies were run by the churches, including 48 industrial schools, 45 libraries or reading rooms, 44 sewing schools, 40 kindergartens, 29 small-sum savings banks and loan associations, 21 employment offices, 20 gymnasia and swimming pools, 8 medical dispensaries, 7 full-day nurseries, and 4 lodging houses."[68]

---

[66] Burger, "125 Years," 9.
[67] Olasky, *Renewing American Compassion*, 122.
[68] Olasky, *Tragedy of American Compassion*, 86.

The closest present-day analogy is the extensive social ministries often operated by inner-city churches—though without access to the lightly taxed private wealth that enabled the earlier programs to flourish—for their own members, with an emphasis upon nonprofessional mutual assistance. Most Americans cities have an array of church-based programs, serving their black and Hispanic communities, which have been almost invisible until recently to those who discuss and those who formulate urban policy.[69] Much of the interest in funding faith-based social service organizations is based upon the belief that the institutions that are created and sustained by the poor can deliver some types of services—especially those that aim at a fundamental change of life-direction—more effectively than can secular, middle-class agencies, much less government itself.

It has also been argued that policies that facilitated and funded the creation of schools by inner-city churches could lead not only to more effective education but also to revival of the civil society as parents and others learn to work together in the interest of children.[70]

To the extent that a faith-based social service organization or school abides by professional norms in determining whom to employ and how they define and carry out their services, it is likely to encounter little difficulty from government regulation . . . but it may experience profound shifts in its religious character. In Britain, as the welfare state developed after World War II,

> the role of religious nonprofit agencies gradually diminished as the state assumed primary responsibility for the delivery and regulation of public welfare. Religious agencies also faced increasing secularizing pressures from the emerging social work and health care professions that dominated public welfare. Social work professionals stressed "objective" and "scientific" criterion [sic] that they often believed excluded or made irrelevant a religiously informed point of view. Christian agencies, which in many cases shared the ideological presuppositions of the profession, fueled the secularization process by redefining their work in more "acceptable," i.e. nonreligious, terms.[71]

Problems arise when government seeks to require that nonpublic care providers—schools or youth programs or services to the elderly or counseling and job-preparation programs—conform to procedures that have been prescribed for their analogues in the public sector. The requirements of "the contracting regime make it difficult . . . to sustain an alternative, non-

---

[69] See, for example, the stirring account of one Brooklyn church in Freedman, *Upon This Rock*.

[70] For a summary of this argument, based upon the analogy of post-Communist developments in Eastern Europe, see Glenn, "Free Schools."

[71] Monsma and Soper, *The Challenge of Pluralism*, 145.

professional model of service delivery."[72] Detailed regulations may be thought necessary in government-operated programs, where no assumptions can be made about the values, motivations, and character of staff, but impose crippling restrictions on faith-based programs that rely more upon a shared understanding that upon elaboration of procedures. A fundamental mission shift occurs when "even nonreligious charities accepting public funds have been forced to treat all of their clients bureaucratically, within the parameters set by law and regulation, rather than dealing with each human being on an individual basis."[73]

Of course faith-based programs must be scrupulously careful not to rely upon good will alone to protect the interests of those whom they serve; they must have in place appropriate safeguards. Indeed, they should have a keen enough sense of human sinfulness to take the need for such measures particularly seriously.

A distinction should be made, however, between procedures that seek to protect confidentiality or ensure that children are not subject to abuse, procedures to provide accountability for the use of public funds, on the one hand, and procedures that define the nature of appropriate treatment, on the other. The former, while burdensome, are in large measure necessary; the latter may intrude in a damaging way upon the freedom of the organization to carry out its mission. "Service contracts," Loconte notes, "are short on purple prose but long on prescriptive protocols: treatment guidelines, staffing ratios, credentialing requirements, discrimination statutes, and so on."[74] By all accounts it is essential to the success of Teen Challenge to talk with drug addicts about their relationship with God, and the organization successfully resisted the attempt by Texas state officials to require it to adopt a medical/psychological model of treatment—a model that, ironically, seems to be distinctly less effective in bringing about real change in the lives of addicts.

This is no mere jurisdictional dispute; it goes to the heart of professional self-definition as it has emerged over the past century. A decision by a public regulatory agency, that forms of service falling outside the norms of the professions to which they are usually entrusted are not only valid but deserving of recognition and support, threatens much that social workers and psychologists have labored to accomplish in the interest of their own status as well as to benefit those they serve. As Lubove describes the early development of social work as a profession, "the persistent efforts of caseworkers to establish a scientific knowledge base and methodology, to limit the area of intuition, moralism, and empirical insight . . . showed the extent

---

[72] Smith and Lipsky, *Nonprofits for Hire*, 85.
[73] Olasky, *Renewing American Compassion*, 110.
[74] Loconte, *Seducing the Samaritan*, 55.

to which the goal of rationality permeated the subculture."[75] To surrender this "goal of rationality" and allow a place for faith and for moral appeals in the treatment of clients is more profoundly threatening to these semisecure professions than is the recent interest in healing prayer for physicians, secure as they are in the scientific basis of medicine accumulated over the last hundred years. While much has been learned about human behavior over the same period, the scientific basis—and the professional status—of social work and psychology are far less secure than is that of medicine, and faith-based programs like Teen Challenge are for them a fundamental challenge. "Casework rooted in a psychiatric explanation of human behavior was a key, presumably, to a knowledge base and helping technique more 'scientific' and hence more professional"[76] than moral exhortation, and the claim of its unique validity will not be surrendered lightly.

The concept of professionalism and the norms that are its primary justification are, in turn, a fundamental challenge to faith-based schools and agencies. On the one hand, most would be reluctant—and foolish—to admit that they were *not* going to conform to norms that are understood to be a guarantee both of quality and also of protection for the client or pupil. On the other, these norms are commonly based upon assumptions about human nature that run contrary to those upon which the faith-based institutions were founded.

It is one thing for particular assumptions about human nature to shape schools and programs that compete with others based upon different assumptions, and quite another for them to become the basis for a privileged model of education or social service. The gravest danger of all arises from efforts to impose a single approach as uniquely valid. Donald Erickson contends, for example, that "the mental health movement was a powerful force behind the spread of the idea that schools should bear responsibility for the global personality development of children. Public officials who assented to that view could easily have slipped into the assumption that the state must require all schools, public and private, to make the same 'mental health' contributions to children. (A basic problem here, of course, is widespread disagreement as to the school conditions that are healthful mentally.)"[77] The recent controversy over "Outcome Based Education" arose from state efforts to require that schools promote certain "approved" attitudes and personality characteristics in their pupils through statewide testing for such attitudes and characteristics.[78]

[75] Lubove, *The Professional Altruist*, 121.
[76] Ibid., 220.
[77] Erickson, "Bad Fences," 229.
[78] See Glenn, "Outcome-Based Education."

It is not the existence of and government support for schools based upon what could be called counterreligious viewpoints that leads to controversy, but the effort to impose such viewpoints uniformly within a context of mandatory school attendance and government monopoly of tax-supported schooling. Parents protest when they have no affordable alternative.

While, as we have seen, government and professional norms may sometimes be in conflict, it is more common for them to form a united front of universalistic values and perspectives against the stubborn particularities of religious and other voluntary communities and thus against the amateur citizen, whether client or parent or board member of a nonprofit organization.

Nor is this concern about the consequences of uniformity for freedom of conscience a new development. Presbyterian theologian J. Gresham Machen called, in 1934, for protecting the distinctiveness of Christian schools against "a drab uniformity which is the most un-American thing that could possibly be conceived!" Underlying efforts to standardize education, he had argued earlier, "is the theory of the behaviorists—that the human race has at last found itself out, that it has succeeded in getting behind the scenes, that it has pulled off from human nature those tawdry trappings in which the actors formerly moved. . . . present-day education to a very large extent is dominated by exactly this theory, in one form or another . . . by persons who have not the slightest notion what the ultimate source of their ideas in the field of education really is or what the result of them will be, but who are putting them into practice all the time."[79]

Professional norms typically require that the social worker or mental health professional or teacher "be *impersonal* and *objective* (limit the relationship to the technical task at hand, avoid emotional involvement) and *impartial* (not discriminate, give equal service regardless of personal sentiment)."[80] Parsons describes the great importance of the norms surrounding the relationship between male doctors and their female patients.[81] But norms like "affective neutrality" may prevent the sort of personal engagement that can bring about life-changes or see an adolescent through a crucial stage of development. It may be that the effectiveness of faith-based organizations is precisely that they encourage such engagement, and that for them to adopt affective neutrality as the basis for their relationship with those in need or with pupils would be to denature them.

Does this mean that the social work and the teaching and counseling carried out within faith-based organizations must be in conflict with professional norms, or that they have nothing to learn from the professions as

---

[79] Machen, *Education, Christianity, and State*, 83, 89.
[80] Wilensky, "The Professionalization of Everyone?" 140.
[81] Parsons, *The Social System*, 457–58.

they have developed over recent decades in a highly secularized form? By no means, but they should "Test everything; hold on to what is good" (1 Thess. 5:21). Treating pupils and clients decently, skillfully, and always with their best interests in mind is entirely consistent with religious convictions.

The Salvation Army experiences this tension in a heightened form, since it is at the same time an Evangelical church with unapologetic faith-statements and moral teaching, and also a large social agency that employs thousands of staff, including many professionals, who are not members and who, in some unknown number of cases, do not believe what the Army believes. Salvation Army leadership is very much aware of the need to keep these two sides—social service to any in need without religious criteria and gathered Christian fellowship—in a fruitful and faithful relationship, and they have increased their efforts to hire staff who, even if not members of their small (eighty-three adult members) denomination, nevertheless share its Christian confession. One divisional social service director—an Evangelical but not himself a Salvationist—reports,

> It is our practice here . . ., when we advertise to hire professional staff always to bill ourselves as a "Christian social service agency." As part of the hiring process we hand candidates a copy of our mission statement and ask them to describe in writing how they would integrate it into their daily work. These two perfectly legal practices result in self-screening out of many who do not share our perspective and have resulted in our being able to hire a professional staff almost all of whom support the Army's spiritual mission.[82]

Making the right employment decisions is essential to the preservation of the distinctive character of a faith-based school or agency, as we will see in chapter 6. There is a prior issue, however, that cannot be addressed by the administrators of these organizations in the first instance: defining the nature of professional practice that takes place within religious institutions, and learning how to prepare teachers, social workers, and other professionals who will be *fully as professional* as their counterparts working in nonreligious settings *but in a different way* that reflects an understanding of human needs and potential informed by theological anthropology.

There has not yet been sufficient discussion of how valid professional norms can best serve as *one of* the benchmarks for the work of faith-based schools and agencies, and how staff can best be trained and supported to work in these organizations in ways that further their whole mission. Despite the hundreds of programs for professional training in Catholic and Protestant institutions in the United States and other countries, one has the impression from the literature that most tend to mimic secular programs, with an added dose of personal piety thrown in. Alternative forms

---

[82] Letter to the author from Howard Green, March 16, 1998.

of professional certification may be necessary to maintain distinctive institutions providing services in a distinctive way, as we will see in chapter 7,
but they must rest upon careful reflection on how faith-based practice is
distinctively different.

Summary

The development of the professions of social work, teaching, and school
administration is closely entwined with the extension of government activity in these areas, and the organized professions make use of government
to support their monopoly position.

There has been a marked shift, in the norms governing social service
and education, from an emphasis upon moral considerations to a disparage-
ment of the exercise of moral judgment on the part of the professional.

The nature of professional training is such that those who undergo it
are likely to adopt a distinctive way of understanding human nature and
the goals of professional practice, and a detached style that is very different
from that practiced—with positive results—in many religious and quasi-
religious organizations.

Professionalization, while it may raise the standards of service or teaching in significant respects, may also distance nonprofit organizations or
schools from those they serve and from their communities.

Imposition of professional norms upon a faith-based school or agency,
by government requirements or, more subtly, by acceptance of professional
norms, may lead to a fundamental shift in its way of understanding and
living its mission.

Much needs to be done within the faith communities to define more
clearly sets of standards for professional practice in education and social
work that are at least as high as the secular standards, but are not
based upon the same worldview and assumptions about the goals of human
development.

6

EMPLOYMENT DECISIONS

A S JUSTICE BRENNAN pointed out in 1987, "Determining that certain activities are in furtherance of an organization's religious mission, and that only those committed to that mission should conduct them, is . . . a means by which a religious community defines itself."[1]

These decisions affect most decisively whether a faith-based agency or school will maintain its integrity of mission. It is safe to say that an organization whose staff are all thoroughly and consciously committed to furthering the same mission and have thought through what that means for teaching, counseling, and other services will have little difficulty using public funds when the terms on which they are provided are acceptable, and rejecting public funds when they are not. It is also safe to say that the most careful protections in law and government procedures will not protect a faith-based organization from *self*-betrayal.

Government can affect the employment decisions of a faith-based organization—whether it receives public funds or not—in two ways. One is through requiring that staff be hired who possess certain qualifications taken to demonstrate that their training is equivalent to that of staff in comparable secular organizations. For example, as we have seen in chapter 2, states may require that teachers in faith-based schools hold state certification. This in turn may require professional training that is intended to inculcate values and beliefs that are in conflict with those represented by schools with religious understandings of the goals of human development. This was discussed in chapter 5.

The other way in which government may affect crucial employment decisions is through enforcement of antidiscrimination requirements in a way that prevents a faith-based organization from using criteria important to its mission. This can be especially difficult when a staff member who has already been hired and whose work is in other respects satisfactory violates some fundamental norm of the organization and its sponsoring church or association. In that case the offense—typically sexual behavior, expressed opinions, or religious activities or lack thereof—stands out as the only basis upon which the organization bases a negative action toward the employee. Such action under those circumstances would typically be considered for-

---

[1] Corporation of the Presiding Bishop v. Amos, 483 U.S. 327 at 342.

bidden discrimination on the part of a secular organization, and the question arises whether a faith-based organization should be allowed to play by different rules.

A Tale of Two Cities

In 1980, Mayor Koch of New York issued Executive Order 50, requiring organizations funded by the city not to discriminate in hiring on the basis of race, creed, color and many other factors, including "sexual orientation and affectional preference." The city insisted that if private agencies received city money, they must observe the city's employment guidelines; Mayor Koch told reporters, "If the city were to not follow this policy and provide religious groups with an exception to the rules, regulations and laws, we would be creating a new discrimination" (*New York Times*, March 3, 1984, sec. 1, p. 1).

In March 1984 the Salvation Army—the first organization to balk at the requirement—was warned by the city that seven contracts worth $4 million for child care services would not be renewed. In support of the objections of its local district, the national organization stated, "The Salvation Army has been established to provide humanitarian services consistent with the values and goals of the Christian faith." The local commander insisted that the organization "did not 'practice discrimination.' But he said it had to keep control over 'certain positions where there is a transmission of certain principles that The Salvation Army holds important.' An 'overt' homosexual, he said, would not qualify as the head of a day-care center." He reported a "very positive" and "spontaneous" reaction from the public; about 150 people had donated more than sixteen thousand dollars (*New York Times*, April 22, sec. 1, pt. 2, p. 25). The disparity between the amount in public funds lost and the amount in private funds contributed, however, illustrates the extreme difficulty faced by such organizations if they take a stand against government requirements.

Subsequently, the Roman Catholic archdiocese (with almost sixty contracts with the city worth $82 million annually) and the Orthodox Jewish organization Agudath Israel (about $1.5 million in city funds a year), threatened to cancel city contracts if forced to abide by the executive order. In May 1985 Archbishop O'Connor told reporters that the Archdiocese of New York was prepared to operate social programs (day care programs, adoption services, centers for the elderly and job-training centers) without any government money if the state's highest court upheld Mayor Koch's authority to bar job discrimination against homosexuals in all programs covered by city contracts. Insisting that the church did not discriminate against homosexuals, he said the issue was the right of the archdiocese to determine its own hiring policies; he supported "efforts to fight discrimination as long as it is clear that this does not include condoning homosexual activity or the teaching of homosexuality" (*New York Times*, May 20, 1985, B3).

Despite this brave language, it turned out that Catholic agencies had already signed eighteen city contracts—for foster care and Head Start—with provisions against discrimination on the basis of sexual preference. They did so with fingers crossed, insisting that as religious organizations they had a right to act on these decisions on the basis of their beliefs—but the City's lawyers did not agree. The Salvation Army, less willing to compromise or perhaps to risk being held to a commitment it could not in good conscience make, signed a "phase-out" contract, intending to end its involvement with the city within six months. All three organizations went to court to oppose enforcement of the executive order.

In June 1985 the New York Court of Appeals ruled that Mayor Koch had exceeded his authority by ordering a requirement that only the city council—which had consistently voted down similar measures for fourteen years—could enact. A year later the council did so, but with the significant difference: religious groups were accommodated by allowing them to hire or refuse to hire people based on whether they "promote the religious principles" of those organizations (*New York Times*, June 21, 1986, sec. 1, p. 32). In effect, the resistance of the three religious organizations had been successful in defending their zone of autonomy—comparable to that under federal law—to make hiring decisions on the basis of their own religious teachings.

A parallel situation played out differently a decade later across the country. In January 1997, controversy erupted in San Francisco over a city ordinance that required city contractors that provided their employees with health insurance benefits for their wives or husbands to extend that coverage to unmarried couples. The Catholic archbishop demanded that Catholic Charities—holder of $5.6 million in contracts with the city to provide a variety of social services—be exempted in the name of religious freedom, since recognizing domestic partners would violate Catholic "religious and ethical tenets." Ironically, one of the consequences of the controversy between the archdiocese and the city was the cancellation of a grand opening ceremony for a new Catholic Charities forty-five-bed facility for people with HIV. Within weeks, however, the archdiocese agreed to an arrangement allowing employees of Catholic Charities to "designate a legally domiciled member of the employee's household as being eligible for spousal equivalent benefits"; homosexual activists hailed this as a capitulation

Major Gaines of the Salvation Army—providing alcoholism, housing, and food programs with $3 million in city funds—told a reporter that "we're looking at the new ordinance with the intent to comply" (*San Fran-*

cisco Chronicle, January 31, 1997, A19). A year earlier the city's board of supervisors had held up a sixty-five-thousand-dollar federal grant for mattresses and kitchenware to serve the homeless because of a letter by a Salvation Army officer stating that homosexual behavior was "contrary to the teachings of the Bible and presents a serious threat to the integrity, quality and solidarity of society as a whole." Major Gaines, the local director, quickly repudiated that position and "ordered all officers and key staffers to attend group meetings on AIDS and how to be more sensitive to gays, their needs and lifestyle" (*San Francisco Chronicle*, January 5, 1996, A22). In the wake of the more recent threat, the local Salvation Army agreed to work to hire more homosexuals and to review its policies toward homosexuality. The bold defiance of a decade before was seen no more . . . at least in San Francisco.

Licit Employment Discrimination on the Basis of Religion

Government does not and may not take religious convictions or other matters of belief and opinion into account in making its own employment decisions; this seems to be one of the reasons why religious schools tend to be more coherent—and thus more effective—than are public schools. In contracting with nonprofit organizations, federal, state, and local government agencies include provisions forbidding discrimination in any hiring done under the contract; this proviso can create difficulties for faith-based organizations when it is applied to behaviors that they consider sinful or contrary to the nature of their mission.

Quite apart from government funding, under Title VII of the federal Civil Rights Act of 1964 it is "an unlawful employment practice for an employer . . . to fail or refuse to hire or to discharge any individual, or otherwise to discriminate against any individual with respect to his compensation, terms, conditions, or privileges of employment, because of such individual's race, color, religion, sex, or national origin" (42 USCS at 2000e2).

But, as Stephen Monsma has written, "If the teachers or other staff of a nonprofit agency cannot be hired on the basis of their faith commitments, the religious character of that nonprofit would be destroyed."[2] The importance of allowing such "discrimination" in the interest of the First Amendment right to the free exercise of religion has been recognized by Congress and by the Supreme Court *in principle*; as we will see, its application

---

[2] Monsma, *When Sacred and Secular Mix*, 126.

in practice has by no means always protected faith-based organizations sufficiently.

There is probably no aspect of a faith-based organization's operation that is as important to the continued integrity of its mission as decisions made about hiring staff and about disciplining or firing staff who turn out not to support the distinctive character of the organization. Curiously, those who make these decisions for faith-based organizations are sometimes remarkably casual about inquiring about the religious convictions of those who work or seek to work for them. Often they seem apologetic about taking religion into account, sharing the common American attitude that religion is "a person's own business." Monsma found, for example, that only 9 percent of the Catholic and mainline Protestant child care agencies in his sample reported that they employed only staff in agreement on "religious orientation," as did 14 percent of the Jewish and 32 percent of the Evangelical organizations. In no case did a majority of the agencies say that they gave preference to coreligionists.[3] The prospect for maintaining their religious character intact seems dim for most of these agencies, if the survey responses are a true reflection of their hiring practices.

This casualness about the religious factor in hiring may also reflect fear of litigation or government intervention in response to charges of discrimination. While staff of such organizations do not enjoy all of the constitutional protections that apply in public institutions—since the U.S. Constitution applies to action by government and its agents—they are protected under state and federal antidiscrimination laws. The prohibition of racial and ethnic discrimination in services under Title VI of the federal Civil Rights Act applies only to programs and activities receiving federal funding, but the employment nondiscrimination provisions of Title VII apply to private employers as well.

There is a significant exception to Title VII, however, designed to protect the integrity of faith-based organizations through allowing them to discriminate on the basis of religion in deciding whom to hire. This reflects a recognition on the part of Congress and the federal courts that, if the distinctive character—and thus the effectiveness—of a program is to be preserved, the staff must believe in it. The logic behind this is expressed in a 1985 case, *Rayburn v. General Conference of Seventh-Day Adventists*, about the selection of clergy:

> The right to choose ministers without government restriction underlies the well-being of religious community. . . . perpetuation of a church's existence may depend upon those whom it selects to preach its values, teach its message,

---

[3] Ibid., table 7, p. 75.

and interpret its doctrine both to its own membership and to the world at large.[4]

Teachers, like ordained ministers for their churches, have the responsibility of interpreting and representing in their own persons the message of the school that employs them, and they do so without direct supervision and in relation to children whose judgment is unformed. A school whose intended "message" is explicitly religious needs to ensure that this message is supported by each of its teachers. The same is true of counselors and others who work in faith-based social agencies.

But does a school or agency have a right—whether legal or moral—to tell staff what they must believe or express, or to use personal convictions as the basis for decisions affecting employment? There seems to be a good deal of unclear thinking about this question. Although nonpublic schools, especially those of a religious character, might appear to offer less freedom of expression to teachers than do "neutral" public schools, the distinctive ethos of a school does not necessarily represent a limit on the teacher's freedom of expression, correctly understood. The greatest educational freedom will presumably be experienced by teachers whose employment is in schools—whether public or nonpublic—that match their own convictions about education. A Spanish study of educational freedom points out that "[a]n educational program that is definite and stable will permit a larger degree of identification than will a program in which there can be no single established and permanent orientation, as is the case in public schools, which, as Martínez López-Muñiz points out, 'must be open to all tendencies of thought and all standards of conduct which are allowed by law.' "[5]

The freedom of nonpublic schools to express a distinctive ethos and character is thus the guarantor of the freedom of those teachers who wish to teach in a way consistent with that ethos and character; public school teachers are not free to do so. As a result, "the internal pluralism of public schools is not a model which guarantees in itself the right to education in its full sense, nor the freedom of those who teach; in this way they are denied the possibility of adhering voluntarily to a specific educational project." It is therefore possible to speak of "the *collective* freedom of teaching or, what is the same thing, the right to direct the school that belongs to the sponsor of the school" and that supports the freedom of teachers *to the extent that they work in a school that corresponds to their own convictions about education.*[6]

---

[4] *Rayburn v. General Conference of Seventh-Day Adventists*, 772 F.2d 1164, at 1167–68.

[5] De los Mozos Touya, *Educación en libertad y concierto escolar*, 248.

[6] Martínez López-Muñiz, "El art. 27 de la Constitución," 29.

The Right to a Shared Vision of Service

Collective freedoms, collective rights are unfamiliar concepts to most Americans, rooted as these concept are in a pluralistic understanding of society for which American individualism has left little room. It may be that the experience of living under totalitarian or authoritarian regimes has encouraged many European thinkers to rediscover the importance of protecting civil society institutions within which freedom may be experienced and the virtues that make freedom possible may be developed. Since a school is a collective enterprise, there is little possibility of enjoying educational freedom as a purely individual right; education with a distinctive character is possible only through association with others who seek the same sort of school, and this in turn implies the exclusion of any who are not willing to support that goal.[7]

It is therefore a matter of considerable consequence to teachers as well as to those who operate faith-based schools and to parents who choose them, that those who make the hiring decisions be able to employ criteria that will sustain the distinctive character of the school. It is here that government interference could have the most damaging effect. In general, European governments allow faith-based organizations that receive public funds to use religious criteria in their hiring. For example, "voluntary aided" schools in Britain, almost all sponsored by the Anglican and Roman Catholic churches, have control over hiring and generally seek to employ coreligionists.[8] In choosing a school for their children, parents have a right to confidence that the school will be "as advertised," and teachers have a right to work in a school where there is a shared vision of education.

There is reason to believe that it is not just the relative or complete autonomy of most religious schools that gives than the advantage in effectiveness that American and European researchers have documented, but also the moral coherence that they derive from a shared ethos. "Consensus on goals, high expectations for students and the like could be reflections of the cultural aspects of schools rather than their rational aspects, tied more closely to social organization and to a community of values . . than to role compliance within a bureaucratic structure."[9]

If there are some advantages possessed by nonpublic schools that have a religious identity, and especially in how they serve students who are in some way at risk, the advantage does not—in the United States—consist

---

[7] An apparent exception, "home schooling," in fact confirms the point: Burke's "little platoons" shrunk to their smallest scale in the family.

[8] Monsma and Soper, *The Challenge of Pluralism*, 46.

[9] Cibulka, O'Brien, and Zewe, *Inner-City Private Elementary Schools*, 179.

in superior financial resources or more highly educated staff. Quite the contrary. The National Center for Education Statistics reports that (in 1993–94) 42 percent of the public school teachers but only 30 percent of the private school teachers had earned master's degrees. This is at least partially explained by the fact that the average salary range for least to most experienced teachers was $34,200 to $54,900 in public schools, and $22,000 to $32,000 in private schools. Similar disparities exist between the salaries of human service workers in the public and private sectors, estimated (for Massachusetts) in one study in the range of 12 to 29 percent. And yet teachers and direct-care workers who do not work for government commonly report themselves as more satisfied with their work. Why?

Perhaps it is because they believe in the organization for which they work, and that their coworkers share with them a clear sense of why they are committed to it. Smith and Lipsky suggest that "when workers cannot be presumed to be motivated by bureaucratic incentives, other mechanisms to insure conformity to organizational tasks must operate. For workers such mechanisms include a sense of well-being derived from the value and importance placed on their work. . . . volunteers and workers who are not primarily motivated by income considerations have a certain power in the organization. . . . Thus many workers in nonprofit agencies must be considered at least in part volunteers, who take at least some of their compensation in nonmonetary form because of the satisfaction which it provides them."[10]

In apparent confirmation, an American government report found that 36 percent of the private school but only 11 percent of the public school teachers pronounced themselves "highly satisfied" with their jobs. An important element of this satisfaction seems to be that they feel more sense of control over significant aspects of their work. For example, 59.2 percent (versus 34.9 percent of public school teachers) reported they had a great deal of influence over discipline policies, and 55.7 percent (versus 34.3 percent) over curriculum.[11]

The smaller average size of American private schools—those in central cities averaged 191 pupils, contrasted with 516 in the public schools—undoubtedly helps to create a calmer and more purposeful climate. Students in grades 6–12 reported feeling more secure in private schools, though these are by no means inviolate havens: 32 percent reported they had witnessed incidents of robbery, bullying, or physical attack, contrasted with 58 percent of those attending assigned public schools.[12] Perhaps the most significant difference, however, is one of *attitude*, which no doubt reflects

---

[10] Smith and Lipsky, *Nonprofits for Hire*, 125–26.
[11] Choy, *Public and Private Schools*, 10–13, 16.
[12] Ibid., 8, 14, 18.

a large element of self-selection among those families who make the sacrifices to send their children to private schools. While 46.4 percent of central-city public secondary teachers reported serious apathy among their students, this was true of only 10.7 percent of the central-city private secondary teachers; 32.5 percent of the former but only 5.4 percent of the latter complained of "disrespect for teachers."[13]

It seems obvious that motivated students, a relatively safe and undistracted environment, and a size that allows the students and adults to know one another well would more than offset the public school advantage in resources such as computers and master's degrees. A further advantage enjoyed by the faith-based private schools has already been mentioned: clarity about goals and shared values. The NCES study found that 71.4 percent of the teachers in the small (less than 150 students) private schools agreed that "colleagues share beliefs and values about [the]central mission of school," compared with 40.8 percent of those in small public schools. In large schools, with more than 750 students, both numbers dropped, to 49.4 percent in the private and only 26.2 percent in the public schools.[14]

Thinking of the importance, to individuals, of being able to associate freely with others who share their convictions, especially in an activity as value-laden as education or human services, is a useful corrective to the common assumption that individual rights must always necessarily trump group rights. In some—perhaps many—cases, individual interests can be satisfied only by providing scope and stability for the groups within those interests can find satisfaction.

The assumption that individual rights must prevail is gaining ground even in the Netherlands, with its more pluralistic social and political order. There is a substantial amount of government interference with employment practices of faith-based schools—despite explicit constitutional protection of their distinctive character—much of it deriving from uneasy attempts to balance the demands of nondiscrimination with those of freedom. This has been understood as a question of individual rights (to admission to a school, or to employment in a school) versus group rights (to maintain a school of a distinctive character, resting on judgments that are at some points exclusive). A law adopted in 1994 forbids discrimination on the basis of race, sex, and other characteristics including homosexuality and marital status; this seems to forbid a faith-based school from not hiring a teacher on the basis of being gay or an unwed mother, even if the school is in effect the agent of a group of families who believe strongly in traditional sexual morality. On the other hand, the law makes an exception for the right of nonpublic schools to make demands that are essential to car-

[13] Ibid., 19.
[14] Ibid., 21.

rying out their mission, provided that these demands are not based upon making distinctions on the basis of race, sex, homosexuality, or marital status. So what does that mean? The courts will have to figure it out, Postma concludes.[15] On the other hand, four years after the much-contested passage of this law there had been no cases arising that challenge the right of a faith-based school to take sexual behavior into account in making employment decisions. Whether this reflects self-selection into nonreligious schools on the part of gay teachers, or indifference on the part of the leadership of some faith-based schools, it is impossible to say.[16]

Apart from nondiscrimination, many decisions about salaries and working conditions of Dutch teachers are determined through national negotiations within the context of those for all public employees, so that the board of a nonpublic school has little discretion in relation to its staff, once hired, except to require them to support the distinctive mission of the school. In 1992 the government, for budgetary reasons, even placed restrictions upon the choices they could make in hiring, requiring that first preference be given to teachers on half-pay. If the board decides that none of those available match the mission of the school, this decision is reviewed by a standing commission the majority of whose members do not belong to the same religious tradition as the school. Thus the freedom of the board of a faith-based school to make this fundamental decision has been limited.[17]

The issue has also arisen in Spain. Publicly funded nonstate schools must comply with government requirements as to materials and programs, the methods that must be employed, the levels to reach for graduates, and the means of evaluation of graduates. There has been considerable controversy over whether these requirements trespass upon the right of those operating nonstate schools "to define their distinctive character and to ensure effectively that this is carried out as necessary in the educational process."[18] This "distinctive character" (*carácter propio*) is significant since it may form the basis for selecting particular teachers and for insisting that teachers not undermine the mission of the school; for example, a teacher mocking Catholic doctrine would be dismissible from a Catholic school, though he or she could not be dismissed for refusing to endorse such doctrine contrary to conscience. (But note that a school's distinctive character must be consistent with Spain's constitutional principles of "liberty, equality, justice, pluralism.")

The issue of the autonomy of nonstate schools was brought before Spain's Constitutional Court, which ruled that the government could set

---

[15] Postma, *Handboek*, 131, 147–48.
[16] Source: discussion with several Dutch authorities on education law, December 1998.
[17] Postma, *Handboek*, 142–44.
[18] Riu i Rovira de Villar, *Todos tienen el derecho*, 53.

standards but should do so with careful respect to the constitutional guarantee of educational freedom. While nonstate schools were required to "conform to the minimums set by the public authorities with respect to the content of the various subjects, the number of hours of instruction, etc.," they were free to do so in a way that gave expression to the educational concepts on the basis of which the school had been established.[19] A later ruling of the court confirmed that teachers could be required to conform their teaching to the distinctive character of the school, and found unconstitutional a provision of Spain's comprehensive education law that gave the authorities scope to rule on the appropriateness of this distinctive character.[20] As in the Netherlands, the legal situation around this issue in Spain remains unsettled.[21]

The American Congress, in adopting the Civil Rights Act's Title VII forbidding employment discrimination, stipulated in section 702 that it "shall not apply . . . to a religious corporation, association, educational institution, or society with respect to the employment of individuals of a particular religion to perform work connected with the carrying on . . . of its activities." Further on in the same statute Congress provided that (1) it was not unlawful to use religion, sex, or national origin as a criterion when it was "a bona fide occupational qualification reasonably necessary to the normal operation of that particular business or enterprise," and (2) that religion could be used as an employment criterion by an educational institution "owned, supported, controlled, or managed by a particular religion" or having a curriculum "directed toward the propagation of a particular religion." Obviously, Congress was concerned to make this "religious exemption" from nondiscrimination requirements broad and explicit; indeed, this exemption was strengthened in 1972 to ensure that it would cover all of the activities of a religious organization, and not just those activities religious in themselves.

The Supreme Court ruled in 1979 that laws regulating labor-management relations could not be enforced upon religious schools; several recent decisions have been based upon this precedent. There have been few cases involving teachers in religious schools, but it seems clear that the burden is upon the school to show that enforcement of labor laws would require "inquiry into the religious function of the school."[22]

In a unanimous 1987 decision involving a Mormon gymnasium facility in Salt Lake City, the Supreme Court upheld the exemption for discrimina-

---

[19] Ruling of the Tribunal Constitucional on February 13, 1981, rpt. ibid., 107.

[20] Ibid., June 27, 1985, rpt. ibid., 134–37.

[21] Source: discussion with several Spanish authorities on education law, December 1998.

[22] *National Labor Relations Board v. Catholic Bishop*, 440 U.S. 490; see Mawdsley, "Emerging Legal Issues," 612; *DeMarco v. Holy Cross High School*, 797 F.Supp. 1142 (1992).

tion on the basis of religion even for employment that was not in any obvious respect religious. The plaintiff was a building maintenance employee who lost his position in 1981 because he was not a member in good standing of the Church of Jesus Christ of the Latter-Day Saints. The federal district court had found that section 702 was unconstitutional as applied to employment in a secular capacity. The judge pointed out in his decision that section 702 granted a benefit to religious organizations that was not equally available to other organizations; this had "the primary effect of advancing religion," one of the criteria for an unlawful establishment of religion articulated by the Supreme Court in the so-called *Lemon* test.

In reversing this decision, the Supreme Court held that the 1972 amendment broadening the religious exemption was justified because, in the words of Justice White's majority opinion,

> it is a significant burden on a religious organization to require it, on pain of substantial liability, to predict which of its activities a secular court will consider religious. The line is hardly a bright one, and an organization might understandably be concerned that a judge would not understand its religious tenets and sense of mission. Fear of potential liability might affect the way an organization carried out what it understood to be its religious mission.[23]

In a concurring opinion, Justice Brennan noted that "the particular character of nonprofit activity makes inappropriate a case-by-case determination whether its nature is religious or secular." In words from which we have already quoted, he went on to articulate the importance of treating the First Amendment guarantee of the free exercise of religion as requiring government to respect the ways in which religious communities understand what is central to them and what is not:

> For many individuals, religious activity derives meaning in large measure from participation in a larger religious community. Such a community represents an ongoing tradition of shared beliefs, an organic entity not reducible to a mere aggregation of individuals. Determining that certain activities are in furtherance of an organization's religious mission, and that only those committed to that mission should conduct them, is thus a means by which a religious community defines itself. Solicitude for a church's ability to do so reflects the idea that furtherance of the autonomy of religious organizations often furthers individual religious freedom as well.[24]

For courts to become involved in determining whether an activity is religious or secular would result, Brennan warned, "in considerable ongoing government entanglement in religious affairs," as well as "a risk of chilling"

---

[23] *Presiding Bishop v. Amos*, 336.
[24] Ibid., 342.

the nonprofit activities of religious organizations. After all, "churches often regard the provision of such services as a means of fulfilling religious duty and of providing an example of the way of life a church seeks to foster."[25]

What about nonteaching staff of a confessional school? The guidance counselor or the principal have responsibilities that require in some sense interpreting or representing the beliefs and values of the school, but what about the school secretary, or the custodian? It seems likely that *if the school is authentically (not just residually) religious*, it will be allowed to insist upon hiring or continuing to employ only staff who at least do not in any way contravene its message. A federal appeals court found in 1991 that "Congress intended the explicit exemptions in Title VII to enable religious organizations to create and maintain communities composed solely of individuals faithful to the doctrinal practices, whether or not every individual plays a direct part in the organization's 'religious activities' [that is,] persons whose beliefs and conduct are consistent with the employer's religious precepts."[26]

In a case the following year involving a Muslim receptionist employed by a Presbyterian nursing home who insisted upon wearing a head-scarf or *hijab* on certain days, the federal district court found that the sponsoring organization "may determine for itself what environment it seeks to provide in its agencies. . . . The employees' action, attitudes, and appearances are obviously an important element in creating that environment. . . . Plaintiff is free to exercise her religion, but she may not do so on PMI premises in a way that PMI deems is contrary to its interest. The [Title VII] exemption merely allows PMI to operate its retirement home as it sees fit without any conflicting religion by symbol or otherwise garbling its message of Christianity."[27]

While the language of the federal statute and the decisions upholding and applying it seem to offer strong protection to the ability of faith-based organizations to shape their mission and preserve their integrity through hiring decisions, the legal situation is by no means unambiguous. For example, the freedom to create and operate distinctive schools comes into conflict with the freedom of conscience of teachers when a teacher expresses views that disagree with the religion or philosophy upon which the school that employs her is based. Title VII of the Civil Rights Act, as we have seen, explicitly exempts schools controlled by churches and other religious organizations from some nondiscrimination requirements. Similarly, the Spanish courts have held that "the ethos or distinctive character of the school acts as a limit upon the teaching activity of the teacher, since 'the

[25] Ibid., 343–44.
[26] *Little v. Wuerl*, 929 F.2d 944, at 950, 951.
[27] *EEOC v. Presbyterian Ministries, Inc.*, 788 F.Supp. 1154, 1156 (1992).

freedom of the teacher does not allow him to direct open or surreptitious attacks against the ethos' of the school,"[28] and the French Constitutional Court in 1977 confirmed the duty of teachers in nonpublic schools that receive public financial assistance to respect the distinctive character of their employers, as a necessary condition of the practical realization of educational freedom. Another ruling in France in 1993 found that respecting the distinctive character of the school may be imposed as an obligation upon teachers, so long as their freedom of conscience is respected.[29]

This last point is important, and the school's control of the messages conveyed by teachers is not easily exercised in instances when the teacher chooses to argue that her freedom to teach has been violated. A teacher can be required not to criticize or undermine the ethos and distinctive character of the school but cannot be required to say or teach anything that she does not believe. The right to protect the distinctive character of the school does not mean that the teacher in a private school must become an apologist for the school's ethos. In contrast with public school teachers, those in publicly funded private schools in France are not barred from expressing strongly held views, but they may be required not to express such views if they conflict with the ethos of the school. On the other hand, they may not be required to express support for that ethos against their own convictions.

American jurisprudence makes a distinction between schools that are under the direct control of a religious organization and schools that, although autonomous, are based upon a religious ethos; the former may take religion into account in personnel decisions, the latter must demonstrate that they are pervasively and not just residually religious in character. This distinction is a way for the courts to avoid difficult decisions about the extent to which a set of beliefs is "sincerely held" by a school that is not controlled by a church, but it is blind to the fact that such a school may well be more authentically distinctive—and more distinctively religious— because its ethos and character have been worked through rather than borrowed from an institutional connection. The leading case addressing this question involved nonpublic schools in Hawaii whose founding document a century ago required that they hire Protestant teachers and teach morality. As we have seen in chapter 2, the court of appeals concluded that the Kamehameha Schools were not sufficiently religious to be entitled to use religion as a basis for making hiring decisions.

A distinguished historian commented that this decision was of a piece with a general "assault on private institutions that want to preserve their religious traditions."

---

[28] De los Mozos Touya, *Educación en libertad y concierto escolar*, 300.
[29] Georgel and Thorel, *L'enseignement privé en France*, 206.

The issue of hiring is crucial to a college's or university's existence as a religious institution—even those that are relatively open. The University of Notre Dame, for instance, tries both to be open to wide diversity and to maintain a strong Catholic identity. As a Protestant at Notre Dame, I value that openness. But if the university had to drop all consideration of religion in its academic hiring, the overwhelming majority of professors and administrators would eventually have a profile of beliefs just like that of every other major university in the country. Notre Dame would cease to be a distinctly Catholic university, at least so far as its fundamental academic tasks were concerned. Religiously defined institutions are caught in a vise. For several decades, to qualify for Government aid, they have had to prove that their overall function and teaching are essentially secular. Now they have to prove that they are essentially religious if they are to maintain their religious identities in hiring. Those who value diversity and the rights of minorities should apply those principles in thinking about religiously based education. Diversity in American life should include room for diversity among institutions. If we are serious about multiculturalism, it does not make sense to deny a place for the institutions of religious subcultures. . . . Religious discrimination is so often mentioned in the same breath as racial and sexual discrimination that people come to think of them as equivalents. Yet the parallels take us only so far. Discrimination on the basis of religion can indeed be an immense evil. But if religion is central to the purpose of an institution, that organization cannot survive without the freedom to insure that at least some of its employees share its purposes. People who share a religious heritage should have the right to perpetuate that heritage through their educational institutions without penalty or prejudice. If they do not, then it is their values and practices—their religious freedoms—that are being trampled.[30]

To the extent that a well-considered distinctiveness contributes to the quality of education as well as to the exercise of freedom by parents and teachers, it would seem that the convenience of an easily applied label, based upon a formal organizational connection, should be eschewed. The fact that a school or an agency wears a "Catholic" or a "Jewish" label should not provide it with a higher level of protection from government interference than another—like many Evangelical and Fundamentalist schools—that is independent but resolutely religious. The difficulty that Justice Brennan was attempting to avoid in the case discussed above, of course, was that of government engaging in close scrutiny of a faith-based organization's beliefs and practices to determine whether it qualifies to be exempted from such close scrutiny! For the court to hold that the Kamehameha Schools were not religious enough to qualify for the exemption

[30] Marsden, "Church, State, and Campus," 23.

involved a judgment that the liberal Protestant expressions of religion (including a disinclination to engage in proselytizing) are somehow less religious for that reason. The court's dilemma is obvious: if religion is not to serve as a cover-all pretext, it must be shown to have some compelling power for those who claim to act in its name. At what point does liberal religion dwindle away to vague sentiment, or to no religion at all?

Most judges are less willing than was the Ninth Circuit in *Kamehameha* to inquire into how sincere and theologically grounded is the basis for a religious school's personnel decisions. A Christian school that did not re-hire a pregnant teacher because of a religious belief that mothers should stay at home with their children was found not guilty of sex discrimination in 1985 because the Sixth Circuit was reluctant to see the state seeking to regulate "the ideological resources of the school" and to evaluate "the subjective sectarian decision to determine if it was made or if the real reason for dismissal was some form of prohibited discrimination" (*Dayton Christian Schools v. Ohio Civil Rights Commission*, 766 F.2d 932 at 960).

The *Kamehameha* decision illustrates how fragile is the protection offered by the Free Exercise Clause of the First Amendment and by the provision in the Civil Rights Act permitting faith-based organizations to discriminate in employment on the basis of religion—and thus seek to ensure consistency in the message and the manner of their work.

The primary lesson that can be learned from *Kamehameha* is that the legal autonomy of faith-based organizations depends in part upon their own moral autonomy, the extent to which they consciously express a distinctive character. The possession and expression of a clearly defined ethos is the best defense against the tendency of government to extend its reach. Stephen Monsma found, in his survey of child-service agencies, that those that were the highest on his "religious practices" scale were most positive about the general effects of receiving public funds; only 13 percent reported that they had been forced to curtail any religious practices as a result of government pressure, though almost 40 percent had come under some pressure to do so.[31]

Ironically, then, agencies or schools that have not been hiring on the basis of religion would be at some risk in starting to do so, because a court might hold that this is obviously not an important requirement of their beliefs and practices. Those that have been consistent in making religion a criterion for hiring, at least by exacting some sort of promise to act and teach or counsel in ways consistent with the religious mission of the school or agency, would have a better chance of having employment or disciplinary actions on the basis of religion upheld.

---

[31] Monsma, *When Sacred and Secular Mix*, 90–93.

On the other hand, those schools or agencies that have been consistent about protecting their religious mission through hiring coreligionists, and insisting upon standards of private life in their employees, are thereby making it less likely that they will qualify for government funding under American law. As Monsma points out, "both [Justice] Blackmun in the *Roemer* opinion and [Justice] Brennan in his *Grand Rapids* opinion mentioned . . . that one mark of pervasively sectarian organizations is that they take religion into account in hiring decisions."[32] Only by adopting a policy of religion-blind hiring can a faith-based organization make the case, it seems, that it is capable of carrying out secular activities deserving of public funds.

Required Qualifications

As we have noted in chapter 5, in Massachusetts "numerous state contracts for counseling, therapy, rehabilitation, and education sustain layers of requirements for caregivers." A Catholic Charities official told Loconte that, in such programs, "[e]very staff member is independently licensed, either as a psychologist, psychiatrist, or as an independent clinical social worker." Similarly, although the Salvation Army insists upon its status as a church, religion is not a criterion for employment in its social service programs. "We have a drug clinic, and that needs a licensed clinician. We have a day-care center that needs a masters-level program in child development. Those criteria will always be first and foremost." The director of one of the Salvation Army's local day-care centers is Jewish, and there is only one Salvationist among eight employees of a drug treatment center that also includes an Islamic counselor.[33]

The right of government, in making contracts with faith-based organizations, to attach requirements for the formal qualifications of staff seems unchallenged. Even the Civil Rights Act exemption that we have been discussing would seem to do no more than to protect the right to decide between two certified or licensed applicants on the basis of criteria relevant to the well-established religious mission of the organization, not to evade the qualifications issue altogether. Nor would the Charitable Choice provision of the new welfare law prevent government from setting requirements for staff that are reasonably related to ensuring that they are qualified to do the work for which government is paying.

Even in those cases in which no public funds are involved but a compelling public interest is at stake, such as the education of children, the courts have been reluctant to strike down state requirements of state-certified

[32] Ibid., 125.
[33] Loconte, *Seducing the Samaritan*, 62–63, 79–80.

teachers. Instead, they have sometimes found that "as applied" to a particular situation—home schooling or a faith-based school—such requirements infringed upon First Amendment–protected liberties.

As we have seen in chapter 5, the training leading up to professional qualifications is often deliberately designed to socialize the trainee into a set of beliefs and values that may be in conflict with those of the faith-based agency or school that may hire her. It is for this reason that faith-communities may seek to maintain their own professional training programs that meet state requirements within the context of their own understanding of the purposes of human life and the nature of the needs to be met by social workers, teachers, and other professionals.

The availability of such alternative teacher preparation institutions—fully funded by the state, unlike in the United States—has been an important means of maintaining the character of religious schools in the Netherlands and other countries. It is in Belgium that the concern for the basis upon which teachers have been trained is carried to what may be its logical conclusion, with limits upon the proportion of teachers in "neutral" state schools who may be graduates of Catholic teacher-training institutions, lest these schools surreptitiously become Catholic through hiring too many teachers who have received Catholic training.[34]

American First Amendment jurisprudence has encouraged faith-based agencies and colleges to separate their secular from their religious functions, in order to receive public funding for the former, and the recent *Agostini* decision (see chapter 4) could encourage schools with a religious character to do the same. Grave dangers lie that way, as Monsma has pointed out. Through the process of separating secular from religious functions, it becomes impossible to apply religious criteria to the former. "[A] trap snaps shut . . . If a religious nonprofit agency or institution is performing certain secular functions that are clearly and cleanly separable from its religious functions, what rationale does it have to defend its practice of hiring only fellow religious believers to perform those supposedly secular functions? Or on what basis can one justify introducing any religious values or practices at all[?]"[35] By acting secular to obtain government funds, a faith-based organization makes it legally difficult—perhaps impossible—for it *not* to make hiring decisions on the basis of strictly secular criteria.

The danger is that, before long, the culture of an organization with a religious identity will be such that it no longer even seems desirable to take the measures required to preserve its religious character. St. Francis House, a shelter for homeless men and women in Boston, "makes little effort to

[34] De Groof, *Le pacte scolaire*, 70.
[35] Monsma, *When Sacred and Secular Mix*, 152.

recruit other Franciscans as staff. . . . with a staff of 60, St. Francis employs few 'overtly religious people.' " Catholic Charities' day care program in the same city "offers no religious instruction for its children. Youth intervention programs avoid discussion of religious topics. Education and parenting programs for pregnant teens, though pro-life, are short on references to distinctive Catholic religious teaching."[36] Nor is this loss of nerve by any means limited to Catholic institutions.

Summary

The most crucial aspect of maintaining the integrity of any organization with a mission is to control with great care the hiring and discipline of staff. Without such controls, the organization is likely to lose its focus with or without government interference.

Faith-based organizations that receive public funds are under increasing pressure to implement nondiscrimination requirements forcing them to employ staff who, by their expressed views or behavior, are likely to give messages contrary to those intended by the employer.

Absent public funding, faith-based organizations are protected in their right to make employment decisions based upon criteria relevant to their religious character, provided that they do so consistently and can show the connection between decision and character.

The Charitable Choice provision of the new federal welfare law also protects such decisions, even when a faith-based organization receives public funds.

State requirements of specific professional qualifications are not readily evaded, even though the preparation required to receive such qualifications may include professional socialization tending to make the employee less likely to sustain the mission of the faith-based school or agency.

Groups that wish to continue to provide education or social services with a distinctively religious flavor should give priority to professional training and socialization within the framework of their chosen perspective . . . whose application to practice at a professional level may need to be thought through more clearly than in the past.

Faith-based organizations should beware of separating secular from religious functions in order to obtain public funding for the former, since this can make it impossible to apply religious criteria to employment and thus protect the nature of their mission.

[36] Loconte, *Seducing the Samaritan*, 78, 85.

INTERLUDE

THE SALVATION ARMY

By Emily Nielsen Jones and Charles L. Glenn

A S POLICYMAKERS explore how education and social services can become more effective by greater use of nonprofit providers, faith-based organizations stand to gain much in terms of financial support and public recognition. Many in the religious community view the recent political favor toward faith-based organizations with skepticism. Some, like Beth Kidd, director of Place of Promise, a residential treatment center for the homeless in Boston, want nothing to do at all with government funding, as they fear it will lead to inevitable infringement on their autonomy and corruption of their spiritual character: "Our identity is the most important thing to us. . . . We are an organism, a living body of Christ, not an organization and we don't expect the government to fund the preservation of our identity." Kidd told journalist Joe Loconte that refusing government contracts gives her center "the freedom to challenge people to reform destructive attitudes and behaviors—a freedom that her state-paid colleagues tell her they don't always have."[1]

Others, like John Samaan, director of the Boston Rescue Mission, another homeless center in Boston, are more optimistic, guardedly intrigued by the potential of access to public funding. "We [Christians]," he told us, "pay taxes like anyone else and should not be discriminated against in [government] contracting, but we also should be careful about not becoming too beholden to the government."[2]

Given the organizational drift and secularization of so many religious organizations that differ little from their secular counterparts after coming to depend upon public support, these concerns are not unfounded. What should religious nonprofits make of their newfound political popularity? What impact will the resulting "embrace" of government have on the distinctive character of these organizations? This interlude explores the effects of cooperation with government and acceptance of public funding upon one of America's most popular and active nonprofit social service agencies.

[1] Loconte, *Seducing the Samaritan*, 22, 28.
[2] Source: notes of the January 14, 1997, "Ambiguous Embrace" luncheon meeting.

Comparing the Salvation Army with organizations like the YMCA and the American Red Cross, which have over time shed their religious commitments, the former stands out as an example of how to accept government support without abandoning religious character. Not that the Salvation Army has been unaffected by the struggles and accommodations so typical in the experience of faith-based nonprofits in the United States. By contrast with the rescue missions affiliated with the International Union of Gospel Missions, the present-day Salvation Army seems rather professionalized. The 250 local missions affiliated with the IUGM typically rely entirely upon private donations and eschew entanglement with government, though their annual revenues of $350 million make them the sixth-largest nonprofit in the United States.[3]

Government contracting and support from the general public through United Way and other charitable contributions, as well as through government grants and contracts, have been a mixed experience for the Salvation Army. On the one hand, the Army has dramatically expanded its outreach to the poor in a variety of different program arenas, growing to become the country's largest social service agency, while retaining its founding identity as a Christian ministry. On the other, even the most ardent Salvationist would acknowledge that the Army's popularity with the public and government funders has not been without cost.

The requirements of government contracting, coupled with the trend toward professionalization of care, have altered the character of some of the Salvation Army's social programs, diluting the distinctive qualities that arguably have been key to its effectiveness in changing lives. The stated mission of the Army has remained relatively constant over time, yet its social service wing has gradually evolved from a grassroots, personal ministry into a large, institutionalized operation increasingly detached from the religious life of its members. With only eighty-three thousand adult members, the Salvation Army has nearly twenty thousand people on probation or parole assigned to them and provides help to thirty million (counting those who seek help repeatedly) a year.[4] Many of its social service programs have taken on a life of their own as the public and the government have pumped millions of dollars into the Army's coffers to support its work with the poor. For some Salvation Army leaders, their organization's remarkable success in the social service arena seems a mixed blessing.

Since its early days on American soil, the Salvation Army has relied heavily on the support of people outside its religious community to finance its

---

[3] IUGM president Dick McMillen, testimony before the House Subcommittee on Housing and Community Opportunity on June 26, 1997, in *Rescue Magazine*, August 1997, 6–7.

[4] Letter to the author from Lt. Col. Paul E. Bollwahn, National Social Services Consultant, Salvation Army, February 11, 1998.

work among the poor. Its experience suggests that the underlying issue for faith-based charities is not whether the government is or has been hostile to religious conviction—clearly, long overdue policy changes must be made to protect the religious integrity of organizations providing services through public funding—but rather how an organization responds to the external forces and secular assumptions that impinge on its work and life.

Compared with other nonprofits with a history of religious affiliation, the Salvation Army has been relatively resilient in the face of the external influences that can weaken or eliminate religious distinctiveness. A significant shift *has* occurred in the character of its social programs, however, as the Army has accommodated itself to the contemporary social service establishment. More insidious than any governmental interference has been the Army's rapid rise to popularity in this country, and the subtle and gradual internal accommodations that have accompanied its evolution from a ragtag missionary crusade to a large-scale, national operation.

Despite the Salvation Army's high visibility and broad popular support in the United States,[5] few Americans think of it as an evangelical Protestant church. According to Roger Green, a professor at Gordon College and himself a Salvationist, this is a uniquely American phenomenon that continues to baffle the leadership of the Army. In other countries, such as Canada, the Salvation Army has a strong and visible presence first and foremost as a church, and secondly as a Christian-based charitable organization. In the United States, where church membership in the Army is low relative to other denominations, the religious activities of the Army are obscured by its popularity as the country's largest charitable organization. When people think of the Salvation Army in America, they think of thrift shops and Christmas bell ringers next to red kettles; they do not think of an evangelical church whose primary mission is to "win souls for Jesus Christ"!

Even the tens of millions of Evangelicals who have little loyalty to the traditional denominations do not usually see the Salvation Army as a church that they might choose to join. In fact, the Salvation Army has not shared in the explosive growth of Evangelical denominations and independent congregations that do not enjoy its high visibility and general acceptance, even though it has many of the characteristics that sociologists of religion believe are associated with such growth.[6] No doubt the high level of personal commitment and discipline required, the sense of being always

---

[5] "For the third consecutive year, The Salvation Army was ranked as the top philanthropic organisation in the United States, according to statistics compiled by the *Chronicle of Philanthropy* in its November 2, 1995, issue. The Salvation Army topped all U.S. charities in private contributions." *Salvation Army Year Book*, 228.

[6] See Finke and Stark, *The Churching of America*; Smith, *American Evangelicalism*.

on duty for the Kingdom, the prospect of being in fellowship with street people, is unattractive to Christians who are quite comfortable in the pews of an entertaining megachurch.

How Did the Salvation Army Become Different?

What differentiates the Salvation Army's social service programs from those run by government agencies and secular nonprofits? As an organization that began as a missionary effort during the spiritual revivals and humanitarian movement of the late nineteenth century, the Salvation Army has been motivated by a distinctive theological mission rooted in the Wesleyan holiness tradition, an outgrowth of Methodism.

To understand the nature of the impact of government contracting on the evolution of this organization, it is necessary to understand the founding inspiration that continues to give the Salvation Army its unique evangelical raison d'être.

Although an inextricable component of Salvation Army mission today, social work among the poor was not part of the original mission of the Salvation Army. Gradually, Booth's followers in the East London Revival Society found their way into the business of social outreach among the poor as they lived out the practical implications of their holiness theology. In 1878, they "solemnly convened a 'War Congress' and issued a declaration of war: 'The Christian Mission has met in Congress to make War. It has glorified God for the conquests of 1877–8. It has organised a salvation army to carry the blood of Christ and the fire of the Holy Ghost into every corner of the world.' "[7] It was not until 1890, though, with the publication of Booth's *In Darkest England and the Way Out*, that the Salvation Army became well known for its commitment to social outreach as a goal alongside evangelism.[8] The book was a tremendous success and was read with great interest not only by Salvationist officers, but also by other Christian and secular leaders in the social reform movement of that time, selling 115,000 copies in the first year of publication and another 100,000 the following year. "Within months of its appearance £100,000 [a very large amount at the time] was raised to support the program."[9] Widely read in America as well, the book proved to be a major impetus behind the development of a structured Salvation Army social service program in the United States.

---

[7] Himmelfarb, *Poverty and Compassion*, 219.
[8] McKinley, *Marching to Glory*, 70.
[9] Himmelfarb, *Poverty and Compassion*, 220.

In Darkest England articulated a theological justification for a twofold mission that embraced both spiritual and social redemption. Booth's intention was not to write an abstract religious treatise—though the book is permeated with theology— but rather a motivating piece to be read by the public at large. In fact, one of Booth's key advisors, who did a good deal of the actual writing of the book, was a secular journalist. He viewed *In Darkest England* as a persuasive tract to enlist new support in the larger cause of social reform.[10]

If the goals of social reform were ambitious, Booth's goal was even more so: the eradication of all social oppression and, ultimately, the ushering in of the Kingdom of God on earth. "The ultimate end, Booth explained, was the saving of the soul, but to save the soul, one had first to save the body. There was no point in giving a tract to a sinking man; he had to be put on firm ground and given the means of life."[11] Booth firmly believed that his crusade was divinely blessed and that he thus had an appointed responsibility to lead the larger society in the cause of social redemption. His agenda would require the support of all of society, not just his devout followers. Social reformers, secular and Christian alike, were invited to join his crusade: "All that I want is to have the work done. . . . If you have any better plan than mine for effecting this purpose, in God's name bring it to the light and get it carried out quickly. If you have not, then lend me a hand with mine, as I would be only too glad to lend you a hand with yours if it had in it greater promise of successful action than mine."[12]

In Darkest England provided the springboard to launch the Salvation Army full force into the work of social reform. The Salvation Army to this day has been vested with an enlarged sense of responsibility to society that far outstrips the social efforts of other Protestant churches. While few would fault the Army for being too charitable, it might be faulted for having an overinflated estimation of its own capacity to achieve sweeping social objectives. While Booth recognized that there were other organizations involved in social reform, his vision placed the Salvation Army at the helm of social reform and frequently trivialized the role of other organizations. The world needed the Salvation Army to fulfill a role that no one else was able to fill: "seeing that neither Governments, not Society, nor individuals have stood forward to undertake what God has made appear to us to be so vitally important a work, and as He has given us the willingness, and in many important senses the ability, we are prepared . . . to make a determined effort not only to undertake but to carry it forward to a triumphant success."[13]

---

[10] Green, "Historical Salvation Army Perspective," 57.
[11] Himmelfarb, *Poverty and Compassion*, 221.
[12] Quoted by Green, "Historical Salvation Army Perspective," 67.
[13] Ibid., 68.

Booth called for an elaborate network of institutions to meet the needs of the "submerged tenth," including "colonies" for the unemployed. "An unemployed man might enter a city colony where he would receive food and shelter in return for work until he was able to return to private employment; if he could not or would not find employment, he would be transferred to a farm colony, where he would have a second opportunity for rehabilitation; and if that failed, he would be helped to emigrate to an overseas colony."[14] With such an ambitious social vision, it is not difficult to see how the Salvation Army's evangelistic purpose has frequently been overshadowed by its ever expanding social responsibilities. William Booth implanted within the Salvation Army a social conscience that would not rest until all of society was perfected. While we cannot know what Booth would have thought of the professionalization and institutionalization of service that has crept into the Salvation Army—as an admirer of the British Army, perhaps he would have found much to his liking!—his broadening of the Army's mission to encompass secularly motivated social reform set the stage for future tension between maintaining a distinctively Christian character and expanding social ministry to meet any need arising in the larger society. Nor were his many critics unaware of this difficult tension: "One of Booth's most bitter critics, T. H. Huxley [1890], quoting his statement that he was 'primarily and mainly' interested in saving the soul, accused him of using social work as a mask for his proselytizing mission. . . . Others had the opposite objection, complaining that the Army was essentially a 'philanthropic and humanitarian agency in which religion is entirely subservient to social organization.' "[15]

The Army began in the United States in 1879–1880 as a missionary project, and soon after the turn of the century it became an actor on the national scene. The Army's practice of being ready to respond to any need it encountered frequently brought it into informal disaster relief work. In 1906 the Army had its first experience with large-scale emergency relief, a role it would continue for years to come, when an earthquake and fire devastated the city of San Francisco. With more than four hundred thousand people homeless and the city's fire department and other public services incapacitated, the Army stepped into the breach, and Salvationists from all over the area rallied to offer assistance to refugees, raising funds and distributing food and bedding. The Army's services came to the attention of the city after the Army used its small fleet of industrial home wagons to rescue hundreds of injured people from encroaching flames. The military governor sought the help of the Army to staff the refugee camps around the city. By the end of the crisis, the

[14] Himmelfarb, *Poverty and Compassion*, 221.
[15] Loconte, *Seducing the Samaritan*, 22, 28.

Army had fed more than thirty thousand people and given beds to more than nine thousand. In characteristic Salvationist style, the material services offered to the refugees were accompanied by cheerful singing and evangelistic testimonies. The Army's ready service in the San Francisco earthquake disaster made headlines across the country and helped to popularize its name. Salvation Army emergency relief services have subsequently been provided in countless other disaster situations around the country.

The public's growing fondness for the Salvation Army, and its willingness to lend financial support to the Army's work, was reinforced during World War I. This was a critical turning point, marking its transition from a small fledgling missionary venture to a large-scale popular charity. The Salvation Army was quick to offer its services to help in this time of need, serving as one of seven "auxiliary welfare agencies" authorized to operate refreshment huts at military training camps and with the American forces at military training camps and in France. Along with the YMCA, the Salvation Army set up canteens for soldiers. The canteens were an enormous success and were fondly remembered by veterans after the war for their homey atmosphere and personalized service. In contrast to the efficient and bureaucratic procedures of the YMCA huts, the Army huts were staffed by friendly Salvation Army volunteers, mostly women, who provided warm hospitality and nonessential creature comforts such as baked goods, singing and games, and reading rooms, all of which helped solidify the image of an organization with a personal touch.[16]

Even at this early date, there were signs that the Army's social work was overshadowing its evangelistic activities. The Army itself acknowledged that "the public accorded it only 'passive acceptance' so far as its evangelical crusade was concerned and that much of its spiritual work lapsed 'into comparative obscurity, from which there seemed to be no escape.' " While the traditional crusade-style meetings continued, "Few knew the Army for what it was, and few cared."[17]

The Army's visibility and popularity with the public increased as it expanded its humanitarian activities during the depression (when it "was caring for 20 percent of the homeless and transient population of the United States—more than any other agency")[18] and World War II. By the end of that war, the Army's social service programs were expanding rapidly, creating new organizational pressures at a time when the membership of the Army began to decline relative to the national population; "the number of

---

[16] Ibid., 152.
[17] Ibid., 147.
[18] Ibid., 210.

officers actually declined in the 1950s."[19] Many old-timers had a difficult
time adjusting to the more bureaucratic and professionalized atmosphere
that began to change the ethos of their ministry. Older officers still clung
to their traditional view of the Salvation Army as primarily a "great crusade
for souls"; many grew frustrated with the increasing administrative responsibilities that consumed their time and distracted their attention from direct ministry. As the early pioneers of the movement passed from the scene,
it became increasingly difficult to maintain the fervor that had given the
Army's programs their unique evangelistic flair. This was particularly true
of the social welfare programs that gradually began to lose the simplicity
and personal stamp that had endeared the Salvation Army to the public.
Although the Army remained committed to evangelism, its overt religious
activities began to decline during the fifties and sixties. Between 1950 and
1965, the number of street meetings fell by almost 50 percent, and by 1980
the Army conducted just one-tenth as many outdoor evangelistic meetings
as it had in 1950.[20]

For an organization with such a decidedly evangelistic mission, not to
mention an uncontemporary, somewhat quirky militaristic subculture, the
Salvation Army has enjoyed an unusual level of popularity in this country.
Within ten years of its founding in the United States, the fledgling missionary movement was well on the road to gaining respectability in the American mind. With corps in forty-three states by 1890 (the year of *In Darkest
England*), the Salvation Army had begun to lay the groundwork for what
would eventually become a major national social welfare operation. By the
first decade of the twentieth century, "Salvation Army corps had become
clearly established in the public mind as centers of many kinds of social
relief activities" rather than as an evangelistic religious movement.[21] In general, the Army's religious crusades have historically been viewed with indifference, amusement, or disdain, despite the public's love affair with the
Army's work among the poor; every year, a wide segment of the American
public throws money in its red kettles. Individual contributions, primarily
from non-Salvationists, make up almost half of the Army's annual revenue.[22] According to one recent survey, two out of three Americans believe
that the Salvation Army is more effective in providing social welfare services to the poor than is the government.[23]

[19] Ibid., 250.
[20] Ibid., 253, 258.
[21] Ibid., 140.
[22] Salvation Army, *1994 National Annual Report*.
[23] *U.S. News and World Report*, April 24, 1995.

The Salvation Army's Self-Understanding

Although the external circumstances of its program delivery have changed throughout its history, the Salvation Army's self-understanding and presentation to the public have remained surprisingly consistent over the course of its history in the United States. Unlike most Protestant denominations, the theological identity of the Salvation Army has not been splintered or liberalized by the larger societal forces of secularization and materialism. Nor has the Salvation Army followed the pattern of so many charitable organizations that have shed their Christian affiliation over time. The current mission statement (1991), an abbreviated version of one issued in 1982 after the Army's Centennial Celebration, conveys its continuing self-understanding as first and foremost an evangelical Christian ministry: "The Salvation Army, an international movement, is an evangelical part of the universal Christian Church. Its message is based on the Bible, its ministry is motivated by the love of God. Its mission is to preach the gospel of Jesus Christ and to meet human needs in His name without discrimination."[24]

Although the words have been changed, this mission statement continues to embody the missionary spirit that drove the early growth of the Salvation Army. Since its early beginnings, the Salvation Army has avoided calling itself a church, although it is now legally incorporated as such. Rather, it has seen itself as a movement, a missionary crusade, to live out the full Christian message, untainted by the formalities and narrow vision of mainstream denominational Christianity. The banner motto of the Army—"Holy War against Sin and Suffering"—captures well its twofold mission of spiritual transformation and social uplift. In theological terms, the Salvation "War" involves helping people come to the realization of the gravity of their sinful condition and leading them to a salvation experience offered through the resurrection of Christ. Departing from the Calvinist doctrine of "divine election," founder William Booth believed that salvation was available to everyone, and was only limited by human sin and lack of will; "Christ is the Deliverer for time as truly as for eternity," he insisted.[25]

The task of the Salvationist is to carry on the redemptive work that Christ began on earth by spreading the message of Christ to all who are willing to hear, particularly to those most neglected by society. For the Salvationist, individual conversion is only the beginning of the total salvation experience, to be followed by sanctification through active participa-

---

[24] *Salvation Army Year Book*, title page.
[25] Quoted by Green, "Historical Salvation Army Perspective," 63.

tion in a Christian fellowship and service to others. Salvationists have historically seen their evangelism and social relief work as part of God's cosmic plan to redeem the world and usher in the Kingdom of God here on earth. The primary hindrance to the triumph of God's plan is not just individual sin, but also social sin, which keeps masses of people "imprisoned for life in a horrible dungeon of misery and despair." Founder William Booth insisted that universal social redemption is necessary for Christ's message to be made available to all: "The Scheme of Social Salvation is not worth discussion which is not as wide as the Scheme of Eternal Salvation set forth in the Gospel. The Glad Tidings must be to every creature, not merely an elect few who are to be saved while the mass of their fellows are predestined to a temporal damnation. . . . It is now time to fling down the false idol [the Calvinist teaching of predestination], and proclaim a Temporal Salvation as full, free, and universal, and with no other limitations than the 'whoever will' of the Gospel."[26]

Aiming for the goals of both individual and social redemption, the Salvation Army's "war" has historically been waged on the two fronts of evangelism and social action. As a more recent restatement of Booth's theme has it,

> Evangelism is concerned with transformation on the personal level, and social action on the socio-economic level. Evangelism is an announcement of the Kingdom's presence and an invitation to accept citizen status. Social action is also an announcement of the Kingdom's presence, but in this case by supporting and participating in the social change for which that presence calls. Without both ways to witness, the proclamation of the gospel is hindered. Evangelism without social action is flight from the world and refusal to accept the reality of the Kingdom's transforming presence in the midst of this world which God loves. Social action without evangelism is flight from the personal depth of the gospel and refusal to take seriously Jesus' unmistakable command to his followers to become "fishers of men." People used to suggest to William Booth, "You know, General, we can do with your social operations, but we can't do with your religion; we don't want it." The General would reply, "If you want my social work, you have got to have my religion; they are joined together like the Siamese twins, to divide them is to slay them."[27]

The Army's evangelistic ministry, although it has evolved somewhat in form and style over time, continues to retain the informal, crusadelike quality of its early history. Historically, evangelistic crusades were conducted in open-air settings, typically on a street corner, where Salvationists knew

---

[26] William Booth, *In Darkest England and the Way Out* (1890), quoted by Green, "Historical Salvation Army Perspective," 61–62.

[27] Needham, *Community in Mission*, 62–63.

they could attract a crowd. Over the last half century, reliance on the traditional open-air meeting format has declined dramatically, yet the Army has
not lost its commitment to evangelism. As part of the new directions initiated by the Second Century Advance initiative, local corps (what other
Christian denominations would call churches or parishes) were encouraged
to "explore all evangelistic opportunities" that might be more conducive
to outreach than the traditional street corner format.[28] Evangelistic outreach is still considered a primary responsibility of the local corps and is a
regular feature of the Sunday meetings as well as special outreach events.

On the social service front, the Army's methodology and program emphases have evolved dramatically since its founding. Though motivated
by otherworldly ideals, the Salvation Army quickly became well known in
America for its practical work among the poor. The familiar red soup kettles on the streets in December are reminiscent of the Army's early "soup
and soap" practical approach to charity. In order to reach the needy of a
city, Salvationists would often begin their work by setting up a soup ministry on the street or in a public place. As their presence grew, the local corps
generally responded in a variety of ways to the perceived needs around
them. Even as the Army became more and more institutionalized, its programs were known for their personalized and down-to-earth quality. It is
precisely this characteristic that has endeared the Salvation Army to the
American public.

Today, many of the Army's programs, particularly street ministry initiatives sponsored by local Salvation Army Corps Community Centers,
continue to pride themselves on being warm, personable expressions of
Christian love. However, due to forces of bureaucratization and professionalization, the Army's larger, more institutionalized programs have lost a
measure of the down-to-earth, homey quality of earlier days. It may be—
but an outsider cannot really judge—that some of its power to change lives
through personal relationships with unabashed believers has been lost as
well. This is not to romanticize amateurism, but to suggest that there are
some forms of healing beyond the reach of professional technique.

Charity has never been viewed by the Salvation Army as an end in itself
and in fact often served as a prelude to evangelistic efforts—handing a
person a bowl of soup went hand in hand with presenting the Gospel message—and as an essential dimension of faithful discipleship. In fact, over
the course of its history, the Salvation Army has retreated from some service areas after it had accomplished its social purpose or when a program
no longer seemed compatible with evangelism. For example, in the early
part of this century it opened a number of match factories to offer immigrants a safe working environment and a fair wage. These factories prolif-

---

[28] McKinley, *Marching to Glory*, 297.

erated and thrived, but when the government took action to correct the problem by implementing safety and fair-wage regulations in commercial factories, the Army closed its own factories since their purpose had been achieved. In some cases, successful programs have been terminated when it became clear that they were not fulfilling the organization's spiritual goals.

The best example in recent years of the Salvation Army's tendency to phase out of a service niche was the decision to close the William Booth Hospital in Flushing, New York, which over time had become just like any other well-run, successful hospital and was employing and serving primarily Jewish staff and patients—a respectable institution and a worthy cause, but not the vision of William Booth![29] Many other Booth Memorial Hospitals around the country have also been closed or sold, not due to financial or operational problems, but because they had become virtually indistinguishable as a Christian enterprise.

Closing successful ministries is not easy, and it has become more difficult for the Salvation Army to face such decisions. "Once a program gets started, it can take on a life of its own. And with plenty of money at its disposal, it is hard to close. This diminishes its flexibility."[30] Financial stability is without question a welcome asset for any organization, yet programs can become so stable and ossified that their original purpose is lost. The Salvation Army has broadened its scope so widely that many of its programs have taken on a momentum of their own. Decisions like closing the match factories or the hospitals are difficult to make when government funding creates financial incentives to maintain programs.

Elements of the Salvation Army's Persistence as a Faith-Based Organization

One of the more obviously distinctive marks of the Salvation Army is its quasi-military culture. With a flair for the dramatic, the Army has decorated itself with proud symbols and colorful customs that have attracted the attention of the American public. The particular devices have changed over time, but the overarching atmosphere has remained a constant. Both in external form as well as internal structure, the Salvation Army is imbued with a sense of heritage and separateness, an ethos of organized purpose. Booth himself claimed that he "received more practical help from the regulations of the British Army than . . . from all the methods of churches" in structuring his religious crusade. The use of the military analogy of a "holy

[29] Interview with Roger Green, May 19, 1997.
[30] Ibid.

war" has provided both theological as well as practical benefits to the Salvation Army. This military theme has served as a "constant reminder that there were many battles yet to fight" to achieve God's purposes here on earth.[31] It has been the rallying motto of the Salvation Army throughout its history and has provided an overarching spiritual motivation for service. The use of uniforms and military titles has helped to foster a spirit of enthusiasm as well as a cohesive sense of identity that has contributed to the distinctive character of the organization. Although the dress code has relaxed over time (the bonnet and high-collar tunic were made optional in 1981), remnants of the traditional uniform have persisted and continue to be worn with pride by many officers.[32]

Organizationally, the military theme has expressed itself in the Salvation Army's extremely hierarchical leadership structure, an organizational approach that has proved effective in maintaining continuity from one generation to the next, and in keeping a large organization moving forward toward a vision. Founder William Booth himself firmly believed that the Army's authoritarian and efficient organizational structure made it uniquely suited to take the lead in the work of social redemption, writing that "so far from resenting the exercise of authority, The Salvation Army rejoices to recognize it as one great secret of its success, a pillar of strength upon which all its soldiers can rely, a principle which stamps it as being different from all other religious organizations founded in our day."[33]

The Salvation Army in the United States is divided into four territories that report directly to International Headquarters in London and are coordinated by a national commander and support staff based outside Washington. Each territory is divided into divisions made up of separate local congregations, or corps, and division-wide programs and institutions. Each corps is led by a commanding officer, an ordained minister, who is appointed by the Army (not called by the local congregation, as in most Protestant churches) and who oversees at least one social worker and the overall spiritual life of the congregation. In the face of changing external influences, this hierarchical organizational model has served the Army well as it has striven to live out a distinctive value system while adapting to meet the needs of the surrounding society.

The Army's formal social service programs are administered at the local level. This social service operation has become so massive that it has acquired a life largely independent from the more strictly denominational officer chain of command. Two informal organizational subcultures have

[31] McKinley, *Marching to Glory*, 48.

[32] Ibid., 295.

[33] Booth, *In Darkest England*, quoted by Green, "Historical Salvation Army Perspective," 56.

developed, one made up of ordained clergy, the other primarily of lay professionals. While there is a formal connection between the Army's religious and social service arms, the difficulty of integration between the two has been a growing concern among the Army's leadership, which firmly believes that social outreach should remain closely tied with the Army's religious life.

Nevertheless, the fact that the Salvation Army's social service arm still has formal ties with a practicing church has helped it to maintain a Christian identity and subculture, particularly when compared with some faith-based organizations with no formal parent church relationship. The very different paths taken by the Salvation Army and the YMCA can be attributed in part to the Army's strong organizational structure: "The dual redemptive mission of The Salvation Army would succeed through proper management where other less authoritarian or individualistic enterprises had failed."[34]

Most of the Protestant social movements, like the YMCA, which began during the social reform era of the late nineteenth and early twentieth centuries were organized more democratically. Many began as collaborative efforts involving a variety of different denominations. In contrast, the Salvation Army's "second mission" was officially initiated from the top down, culminating with Booth's *In Darkest England and the Way Out* (1890), a document that laid out a rationale and a plan for social ministry among the poor. One consequence is that the Salvation Army has been able to preserve its original mission to a greater extent, though by no means unchanged. "The YMCA," by contrast, "started out to improve the 'spiritual, mental and social condition of young men,' but has developed into an organization that is more interested in recreational and cultural development than it is in the spiritual."[35]

While there are many factors that buttress or undermine the founding philosophy of an organization, the Salvation Army's hierarchical governance system and its deliberate effort to keep its social services under the auspices of its church leadership have been instrumental factors in helping to preserve a distinctive Christian ethos.

Threats to the Salvation Army's Distinctive Mission

As we have seen in the cases of the match factories and the Booth Memorial Hospitals, the Salvation Army historically has not shied away from shutting down programs even when the funds to operate them were available. In

[34] Green, "Historical Salvation Army Perspective," 56.
[35] Smith and Lipsky, *Nonprofits for Hire*, 164.

recent years, there have been fewer examples of the Army pulling out of service areas that, for whatever reason, are no longer conducive to its spiritual goals. With a secure and growing stream of funding from governmental sources, Salvation Army programs have acquired an institutional stability that has created an organizational ethos very different from that of the Army's earlier days. The distinctive character of the Army's programs has been to some extent diluted by dynamics associated with professionalism and institutionalization. It is no longer a spontaneous movement run exclusively by Salvationist church members and volunteers. To a still strongly Evangelical grassroots ministry that continues to provide help with much of the inspired amateurism of a century ago, the Salvation Army has yoked—somewhat uneasily—a variety of large-scale professional services.

Much of this expansion continues to be supported by unrestricted gifts from the general public; only 15 percent of the Salvation Army's funding nationwide comes from all levels of government, and another 7 percent from the United Way.[36] In most spheres of the Army's work, therefore, it is not necessary to avoid religious themes. There are cases of overzealous government interference—"in 1989 a Salvation Army homeless shelter in New Britain, Connecticut, was refused a $7,000 government grant by the Department of Housing and Urban Development because it had a picture of Jesus in its facility"[37]—but these seem to be the exception rather than the rule.

Although the Army's social services have grown exponentially, church membership has remained relatively constant; the most recent official report shows 3,645 active officers (ordained ministers) in the United States, and 83,690 "soldiers" or committed members aged fourteen and over, against 39,377 lay employees.[38] Surely no other Christian denomination has almost half as many lay employees as it has members! According to Roger Green, this has completely changed the character of the organization from one dominated by a ministry mindset to one dominated by the client-professional relationship: "The corps [of Salvationists] has grown, but not at the same rate as the social services. There are more clients than members."[39]

As the organization has responded to new needs and challenges in society, it has entered into a vast array of different service areas. Today, the Army's social services have proliferated to include thrift stores, rehabilitation centers, senior citizen centers, group homes, day camps, day care centers, after-school programs, correctional visitation, hospice work, private

[36] Bollwahn, letter, February 11, 1998.
[37] Monsma, *When Sacred and Secular Mix*, 129.
[38] *Salvation Army Year Book*, 230.
[39] Interview with Roger Green, May 19, 1997.

residential homes, disaster relief, and special Christmas and Thanksgiving programs. Given the wide scope of these activities, it is not surprising that few people today know that the Salvation Army is a practicing church. The social service wing has taken on an institutional life of its own distinct from the Salvation Army as a church, bearing less and less resemblance to the Army's earlier signature approach of explicit faith proclamation in serving the poor and needy.

Although tension between the social and evangelistic emphases of the Army is nothing new, the challenges involved in maintaining a healthy harmony between the two have become increasingly acute since the 1970s, when the Salvation Army became a major government contractor. Between 1960 and 1980, the Army brought to bear its impressive organizational efficiency and willingness to undertake tasks that other organizations found unattractive on just about every new social need identified in American society. The War on Poverty of the 1960s created new opportunities for service and partnership with government. By the late eighties, the Salvation Army was the largest private provider of beds in the country as a contractor in the Federal Emergency Food and Shelter Program.[40]

Shifts in the character of the Army's social programs over the past three decades can in part be attributed to external pressures associated with government contracting. The temptation of government funding and the strings that it brings with it are often blamed as the main culprit of the "mission shift" and loss of religious distinctiveness of many charities. But overt conflicts with government have been surprisingly infrequent. Salvationists report an amicable working relationship with government officials, who by and large dismiss the organization's religious identity as separate from the public services that it renders. More insidious than governmental infringement have been the internal pressures within the Army itself associated with balancing its dual identities as both a social service agency and a church. Many within the Salvation Army have simply accepted the terms on which they receive government funding. They do not have sufficient distance to recognize the subtle and unconscious shifts that have occurred in the character of their programs as a result of the lure of doing more good through government funding.

With a successful track record of service, the Salvation Army is recognized among government officials as a strong candidate for providing services under contract. The Army's success in winning contracts has opened doors into an array of new service areas, yet this has changed the dynamics surrounding the founding of new programs. In the past, it was the perceived need of people in the surrounding community that prompted the Salvation Army to create a new program. Today, the reality of social service

[40] McKinley, *Marching to Glory*, 301.

contracting is that government Requests for Proposals (RFPs) often are the primary impetus. As the number and size of the Army's contracts with the government increased, particularly during the 1980s, it experienced greater pressure to submit its local programs to accrediting and licensing procedures that have changed the character of its programs. Increasing governmental regulations and reporting requirements have also added tremendously to the Army's operating costs, diverting both financial and human resources away from program delivery.

Institutionalization as a result of large-scale government grants and contracts has changed the landscape of social service delivery by nonprofit organizations and has made maintaining an explicitly Christian ethos an uphill battle for the Salvation Army and other faith-based charities.

By accepting funds from the government, the Salvation Army in effect asserts that its ministries are not "pervasively sectarian." This requirement asks the organization either to abandon its greatest strength or to be less than candid about how it carries out its work. Secular absolutists assume that "counseling and assisting frightened, hurt, confused victims of domestic violence is a purely secular activity. This assumption is false. When churches such as the Salvation Army engage in such activities they are seeking to live out their sense of Christian compassion, and for any sincere Christian believer, healing the hurts suffered by a victim of domestic violence has physical, emotional, and spiritual dimensions. But legally the Salvation Army—and countless other religious nonprofit agencies—can only receive public money on the subterfuge that that money is going to fund secular activities."[41]

The Salvation Army in fact does play the game of government contracting, while continuing to view its social service programs as a Christian ministry. While it "manages to keep religion close at hand as it helps the needy, . . . it must push explicit expressions of faith to the periphery."[42] The Army makes Bible studies, prayer meetings, and church services available to clients of publicly funded programs, but contracting requirements prohibit it from infusing the program itself with religious belief. As a result, according to some staff, there is "little difference between sectarian [like Salvation Army] and non-sectarian nonprofits" beyond the religious "extras" that supplement the Army's core social services.[43]

The effects of *professionalization* may be even more difficult to evade. Like most reputable social service organizations, the Salvation Army has been affected by the trend toward employment of formally qualified staff who are judged by professional norms of competence. In the past, the

---

[41] Monsma, *When Sacred and Secular Mix*, 157.
[42] Loconte, *Seducing the Samaritan*, 87.
[43] Interview with Karen Phillips, March 12, 1997.

Army's outreach was fueled by volunteers and clergy, and service was seen primarily as an expression of moral and spiritual values. Between 1951 and 1961, the number of paid staff working for the Salvation Army doubled, and the growth has continued. Today, the majority of the staff running the Army's social service programs are paid employees, most of whom are not members of the Salvation Army church. Many, in fact, do not even consider themselves Christian believers and are hired with the understanding that they cannot be expected to personally endorse the Salvation Army's central religious beliefs. "By default, masses of people are hired who are not in sympathy with the Army's religious mission."[44] Or, as another Salvationist put it, "God is not an evident part of the present-day social work theorist's ontology."[45]

There are different perspectives within the Salvation Army about whether or not this is a problem. The leadership tends to believe that Christian commitment is central to the effectiveness of Army programs: "We are in this because we are called by God to serve as his ministers. That's the strength of the Salvation Army. We're all in this because we want to serve the Lord and preach the Gospel. And when the Army quits doing that, we've lost the mission."[46]

This commitment has led to a difficult confrontation with the question of hiring. Antidiscrimination provisions are ordinarily included in contracts with all levels of government (see chapter 6). As General Wiseman, the head of the Salvation Army from 1974 to 1977, wrote more recently, "In order to ensure the future effectiveness and integrity of Salvation Army social services extreme care should be exercised in selection of personnel, both Salvationist and non-Salvationist. They should be people of quality who readily accept the basic theological assumptions which undergird our ministry."[47]

But this is easier said than done. Typical is the account of one of the Boston officers: "We've been working diligently over the last year to really make an effort to hire only Christian, born-again, saved staff. Now that hasn't been done universally, and probably even around our division we have a number of caseworkers who aren't Christians. They are good people, they're well educated, they're compassionate, they're caring—they can fulfill that aspect of the Salvation Army mission. And we would say to those employees [that] if you're willing, to say to individuals, 'Here is a list of our [religious] services if you're interested,' and beyond that they would pull the captain [ordained minister] in."[48] Like many other officers in the

---

[44] Interview with Roger Green, May 19, 1997.
[45] Read, "Deacons and Samaritans," 175.
[46] Interview with Major Gil Reunders, January 1997.
[47] Wiseman, "Call to Renewal and Change," 281–82.
[48] Interview with Major Gil Reunders, January 1997.

Salvation Army, Reunders sees hiring non-Christians as an unfortunate necessity that should be minimized as much as possible.

Social service administrators, on the other hand, tend to place more emphasis on professional credentials. According to the social service coordinator for the Army's Massachusetts Bay Area centers, professional credentials are the primary focus of the Salvation Army's screening process for prospective staff: "We have a drug clinic, and that needs a licensed clinician. We have a day care center that needs a masters-level program in child development. Those criteria will always be first and foremost."[49] Karen Philips, director of social services for the Massachusetts Division, echoed this sentiment: "My first qualification is can the person I'm hiring do the job. Never has our Christian faith in any way been compromised by having to interview and hire people who can do the job."[50]

In general, people on the social service side believe that a "holistic," "caring" attitude is sufficient to uphold the Army's Christian philosophy of service. Non-Christian social workers at a minimum must be able to make referrals when issues pertinent to faith arise: "Where you need professionals, have them; where you need more than that, you pull in the [ordained] officers."[51]

While hiring competent and caring staff is good policy for any social service agency, it is hard to make the case that this differentiates Salvation Army programs from their secular counterparts. What social service organization does not claim to treat clients with warmth and compassion? Opinion within the Salvation Army has shifted in recent years toward the importance of hiring Christians as much as possible to strengthen the Christian dimension of its programs. The extent to which this is possible is uncertain, given the ambiguity surrounding state nondiscrimination laws. The Personnel Council of the Army issued a Personnel Policy Statement to assist officers in responding to questions regarding the role of religious faith in the screening of prospective employees. Like the law itself, this statement is vague and open-ended, yet it reflects the Army's efforts to do no less than the law allows in terms of taking religious convictions into account in whom it hires and how it provides humanitarian services: "The Salvation Army has been established to provide humanitarian services consistent with the values and goals of the Christian faith. In this context, employment decisions made by The Salvation Army will be in accordance with the applicable federal, state and local law, with the understanding that The Salvation Army does not waive or otherwise relin-

[49] Loconte, *Seducing the Samaritan*, 79–80.
[50] Ibid., 81.
[51] Interview with Karen Phillips, March 12, 1997.

quish any rights in the free exercise of religion guaranteed by the Constitution of the United States."[52]

Nor is this a uniquely American problem. In Britain, as in the United States, the Salvation Army is the largest charitable organization, "with an annual budget of over 10 million pounds, close to two-thirds of which comes from the government . . . the Salvation Army proposed its own equal opportunities policy that states that any managing position be filled by a practicing Christian."[53]

A chorus of scholarly voices has arisen within the organization calling for a return to the traditional Salvation Army approach to service that goes beyond simply hiring more Christian social workers. Many, including Major Philip Needham, have spoken out about the negative consequences of professionalization and have advocated bringing all of the Army's outreach efforts under the umbrella of the local Salvation Army churches.

> In our attempt to professionalize our services—and who can question the desirability in doing so?—we have too often placed those services in the hands of workers who have no identification with our basic mission or who have no stake in our fellowship. A non-Christian social worker may do very effective social work, but it is not a genuine expression of the Army's Gospel-motivated mission. A non-Salvationist Christian social worker can do social work from a Christian perspective and minister to the soul as well as the body, but he will usually not work intimately with the corps, not be able effectively to utilize the resources and strengths of the soldiery in his helping, and probably not relate his ministry well to other ministries and programs within the corps.[54]

In 1973, the Salvation Army officially restructured itself to strengthen the tie between the corps and social outreach and renamed the "corps" (the local church) the "Corps Community Center," symbolizing a renewed emphasis on officer and "soldier" (nonordained members) involvement in meeting needs.[55] Today, the Corps Community Centers (CCC's) are a hub for programs such as youth drop-in centers, after-school tutoring, Alcoholics Anonymous, and feeding the elderly. The extent of rank-and-file involvement in the CCC's varies, but the general sentiment in the Army is that this model provides Salvationists with meaningful opportunities to serve both the spiritual and the physical needs of their communities. Since the early eighties, the leadership of the Army has worked to develop administrative guidelines to strengthen the capacity of the CCC's for service.

[52] Salvation Army, *Personnel Policy Statement*, February 25, 1997.
[53] Monsma and Soper, *The Challenge of Pluralism*, 146.
[54] Needham, "Toward a Re-Integration," 147–48.
[55] McKinley, *Marching to Glory*, 286.

Despite such efforts, however, a major part of the Salvation Army's social outreach, in terms of dollars and human resources, remains separate from the CCC's in large institutionalized programs.[56] Some Salvationists advocate cutting back these programs to a scale that can be maintained by the available supply of qualified workers who are committed Christians. There has been a renewed effort to recruit at Christian colleges to increase the ratio of Christian to non-Christian staff, but even the most strategic recruitment strategy has not yielded enough well-qualified believers to fill the Army's large staff requirements.

Professionalism and religious distinctiveness are not inherently incompatible, and the Army remains committed to both. In other countries, such as Canada, there seems to be less tension between the two. Roger Green describes a Salvation Army hospital in Canada, located in a town with a large, active Salvation Army Corps, conveniently located right next to the hospital. The hospital is staffed with fully qualified professionals, not all of whom are Christian, and has a reputation for excellence. In addition to professional service, patients at Scarborough have Salvation Army church services piped into their rooms, and a host of programs run by officers and laypeople from the corps next door. The hospital has a chapel with regular services. Lay Salvationists can be seen mingling with patients in the halls and in rooms on regular visitations. Prayer is as much a part of the hospital routines as pills and shots. On a recent visit, Green saw the chief hospital administrator on his knees praying with a patient in the chapel. In addition to high professional standards, prayer and love and hope permeate the building.

Government expectations can also be a problem in maintaining a distinctive character in social programs that are funded under government contracts that must meet bureaucratic norms of procedural standardization. As Loconte has pointed out, a "secular medical model of treatment" has become the assumed standard of government social service.

Although not explicitly hostile to religious conviction, at least in principle, most government officials uncritically accept the notion that social service delivery can and must be free of any particular spiritual outlook. They tend to view an organization's religious affiliation as irrelevant to social service delivery, if not actually problematic. As a result, there is an implicit bias against programs that are too explicitly religious. Given the lack of clarity surrounding the "not pervasively sectarian" legal principle that has governed government contracting with faith-based organizations, they are subject to on-the-spot decisions by low-level bureaucrats who generally lack the legal sophistication to understand where the law ends and their own biases begin. As one Salvationist complained, "powerful secular

[56] Ibid., 313–15.

humanist departments in welfare, health and education lay down the law according to materialist concepts and keep nongovernmental agencies in line by funding policies."[57] General Wiseman warned, "Under increasing pressure from secularized societies it is possible the Army will be tempted to compromise principles in order to maintain existing operations."[58]

Nor is this problem limited to the United States; "I read a letter from a socialist minister of health," reports an Australian Salvationist, "expressing disapproval of reference to Christian conversion in a report of a government-funded Salvation Army alcoholic treatment programme."[59]

Given the Salvation Army's explicit statement of faith, which accompanies all its funding proposals, it is intriguing that it has been able to maintain a positive relationship with government. Most Salvation Army officials report noninvasive, amicable relations with officials. Most seem to have few complaints about overt religious discrimination on the part of government bureaucrats and generally do not seem to think that government contracting has negatively affected the religious character of their programs. Their primary complaint echoes that of nonreligious social service providers: too many regulations, too much paperwork. Whether their perception is accurate is another issue. When the issue is probed further, some express frustration with the ambiguity surrounding the legality of using religious criteria in hiring. While the official policy of the Salvation Army has been that it does not "discriminate on the basis of religion" in employment, in practice there is confusion about how this can be reconciled with upholding the Salvation Army's explicitly religious mission. "In my experience," we were told, "I've always sensed from leaders I've worked under that we've got to be careful because we don't want to lose our government funding. So we kind of tip toe around and [are] very careful in all that we do and say and in what we write and certainly you never think to ask them about anything on a religious side. In many cases, we don't have any idea if a person is a Christian or not. And that's what we are trying to turn around now." Subtle accommodations are frequently made to appease government officials: "The way we usually get around [the nonsectarian principle] is if there is a designated room that is used for counseling, we may not have any [religious] pictures up there, but we will not take down a picture or a cross in a lobby."[60]

Although the Salvation Army has not been immune from accommodation to the demands of the secularizers, it has shown an unusual ability— compared with many publicly funded organizations with a religious iden-

[57] Carpenter, "Secular Humanism," 36.
[58] Wiseman, "Call to Renewal and Change," 278.
[59] Carpenter, "Secular Humanism," 39.
[60] Interview with Major Gil Reunders, January 1997.

tity—to draw a line to preserve its religious integrity. As Reunders explained, "Our mission doesn't fade because we have seen that what makes programs work is a relationship with Jesus Christ. That's the difference in all that we do and that's the bottom line." Having a clear sense of this "bottom line" helps the Salvation Army to resist intrusion from government and secular funders. "Some people read those contracts and feel that you need to take everything down, and we just don't. That's the identity of who we are, so if you come into our lobby, you see a cross."[61]

Resisting the Lure of Popularity

What explains the popularity of the Salvation Army in this country? Its early popularity can be attributed in part to the wave of social reform activity that began at the close of the nineteenth century in response to growing urbanization. At this time, Protestant denominations generally began to shift their focus from foreign missions to urban evangelization and social reform. Immigration and urban poverty were viewed as threats to the moral stability of America's cities. Many in mainstream denominations supported the Salvation Army and viewed it as part of a larger movement to Christianize and reform America's urban areas. Yet this alone does not explain why a fringe, ragtag missionary crusade would gradually become an American icon. Its evolution into a very large and popular social welfare organization can be attributed to an interplay of factors: the self-sacrificing zeal of its members, the hierarchical organizational structure, the social reform mood of the country, and maybe even a little divine favor! The overarching theme, though, of the Army's growth has been its willingness and ability to partner with the public to achieve common social objectives. Throughout its history, the Salvation Army has worked cooperatively with groups and individuals outside of its immediate circle of faith as it has grown in popularity. The Army's vision has always been larger in scope than the limited resources of its membership could sustain. Early in its history in the United States, the Army came to rely on the financial support of non-Salvationists—including wealthy benefactors as well as those who threw change into the kettles—to carry out its social programs.

Popular acceptance has been both a blessing and a curse for the Army. On the one hand, the Army has received generous funding from outside sources to expand its programs and extend its social outreach; on the other, it has continually had to struggle with how to preserve the spiritual character of its programs while positioning itself to have wide appeal among people who for the most part do not share its evangelical motivation. On

[61] Ibid.

his eighty-first birthday, General Booth described the inseparable relationship between the Army's spiritual and social mission this way: "Social service is only the expression of life which abides in the soul and forces into activity the desire to take on the burdens of humanity. It is only when we get more soul into our lives that we are able to do any good. . . . All the social activity of the Army is the outcome of the spiritual life of its members. All social service must be based on the spiritual or it will amount to little in the end."[62]

As they expanded fund-raising efforts with government, local United Funds, and foundations in the 1980s, Salvation Army leaders recognized that their organization was becoming increasingly vulnerable to outside influences. In order to protect its mission from being compromised by its funding arrangements, they adopted an official statement in March 1981 that "any agency, government or private," that contracts with the Salvation Army should "clearly understand that The Salvation Army is an international religious and charitable movement" and is a "branch of the Christian Church." Over the course of the eighties, a series of official guidelines were developed to govern its relationships with government and secular funders. For example, the Salvation Army and the United Way signed an agreement entitled "Working Together" in 1983. In 1987, National Headquarters released a document entitled "Guidelines for Relationships between the Salvation Army and Other Groups and Organizations."[63] While these efforts did help Army administrators to navigate the waters of government contracting, they did not remove the threat of litigation over the Army's religious purposes and especially over its criteria for hiring staff under external grants and contracts.

Not that this is a new issue; an obituary for William Booth in the *Christian Advocate* in 1912 noted that "of late years there has appeared to be a larger emphasis on social ministries than upon distinctly evangelical effort." Four years before that a well-known American Salvationist had warned that "unless care is taken, there is danger that our Field Operations will become fully absorbed in the Charity and Relief work, to the exclusion of the Spiritual side of things."[64]

This concern was echoed more recently after the Salvation Army's Centennial Celebration in 1980. A series of new organizational goals was adopted, the first of which was to affirm the Army's "spiritual commitment" and to remind the world that "the main purpose of all Salvation Army social services continues to be to lead people to Christ."[65]

[62] Quoted by Robinson, "The Whole Gospel," 8.
[63] McKinley, *Marching to Glory*, 310.
[64] Colonel Holz (1908), quoted ibid., 140.
[65] Ibid., 289–90.

Although theologically connected in the mind of a good Salvationist, the relationship between the Army's evangelistic efforts and its social service work is far more complex and problematic in practice than in theory. This despite the confident words of the Army's national specialist on social services: "I believe social work and evangelism are different but when synthesized, work together to form a seamless ministry. We needn't worry when rendering social casework services with a motive of being part of a redemptive continuum that the Holy Spirit is not fertilizing the seeds planted. Too many mistakes are made when we operate on God's behalf as a committee of one, in essence a Christian vigilante, prematurely righting wrongs, solving peoples' problems and generally frustrating that which takes a process of the individual under the guidance of the Holy Spirit to resolve."[66]

This formulation expresses confidence that God can work through ministries of service, including some that are highly "professional," because of the context through which those services are provided, even when nothing is said explicitly by staff. In a speech to fellow Salvationists, Lieutenant Colonel Bollwahn was more explicit about fellowship with a faith-based congregation as the culmination of work with individuals drawn to the Army by their needs: "The Army made a bridge to reach this individual. As we continue with him, we will create more bridges to wholeness. Will we, the corporate 'we,' create a bridge to the center or heart of our denominational fellowship? . . . Perhaps the most humanizing and spiritually influencing treatment we can provide—for a person who is ready—is a welcome to be a member of a regular congregation."[67]

It is difficult to be confident, however, that services provided by a non-Christian staff member according to strictly professional norms in a context that has been purged of religious references to meet government requirements (or the fear of them) would have such a result.

A more traditional formulation of the organization's strategy for changing lives is that "the uniqueness of Salvation Army models of recovery [from addictions] is the pervasive foundational belief in personal triumph through Jesus Christ. . . . The reality of forgiveness of sin, the power to be justified, and the grace that nurtures physical, emotional and spiritual restoration is the glue and the energy of Salvation Army programming." State evaluators have been known to comment on "the obvious value of the strong spiritual component, acknowledging its vital contribution to individual success."[68]

---

[66] Letter to the author from Lt. Col. Paul E. Bollwahn, National Social Services Consultant, July 8, 1997.

[67] Bollwahn, "Building Bridges," 8–9.

[68] Bollwahn, "Personal Triumphs."

One example of the Salvation Army's commitment to integrating faith and professional standards is a well-designed self-study guide, by an officer with a doctorate in psychology, on faith-based counseling skills. This suggests a model of practice "*both* fully professional *and* fully consistent with an evangelical approach to Christian values and religious experience."[69] The counselor is advised to wait patiently for the right opportunity, perhaps after many sessions, to introduce explicit scriptural references or to offer to pray with a client.[70]

The effort to maintain a balance between spiritual and social efforts is by no means unique to the Salvation Army. As Major Ray Peacock stated in 1983, "One of the most important debates of the 20th century involves the relationship between evangelism and social action. Are they of equal importance, or does one take precedence over the other?"[71] For religious organizations like the Salvation Army that place an emphasis on social redemption, the challenge is particularly acute. The Army's Centennial Celebration prompted an organization-wide dialogue, called the Second Century Advance Initiative, which highlighted above all else the importance of not letting service overshadow the Army's larger theological purpose. Many officers warned that the Army's social service wing was in jeopardy of losing its Christian witness and called for deliberate action to make sure that social services did not obscure the Army's religious mission. They asked:

> Should The Salvation Army's emphasis be that of a balanced ministry between evangelism and social responsibility, the whole gospel to the total human personality? If so, is it possible for that balanced ministry to involve an equal partnership between evangelism and social responsibility, or is prioritization inevitable . . . ? should The Salvation Army . . . withdraw from areas of ministry in which there is little or no room for fulfilling the evangelistic mandate because of government or secular restrictions? Is it possible to maintain a Christian social services program without the bulk of workers in that program being persons who have experienced an individualistic [*sic*] reconciling conversion?[72]

The new objectives that emerged from the Second Century Advance Initiative were "first and foremost spiritual in nature," due in large part to the results of a nationwide survey "which showed that while the army was the most popular charity in the United States, relatively few Americans, even among religious donors, realized that it was a religious organization."

[69] Letter from John R. Cheydleur, May 1998.
[70] Cheydleur, *Faith-Based Counseling Skills*.
[71] Quoted by Robinson in Waldron, *Creed and Deed*, 6.
[72] Ibid., 4.

The new program that emerged generated a wave of enthusiasm in the organization to stress the Christian ideals and mission of the Army to the larger public. The first "Battle Objective" called for "affirming spiritual commitment" based on a "Bible-based growth program" for the local corps and for reminding the world that "the main purpose of all Salvation Army social services continues to be to lead people to Christ."[73] The concern for balance continues: "More than ever, there is a concern about keeping the spiritual and the social emphases integrated. There is a feeling that the pendulum has swung so far toward social services and away from maintaining its religious mission."[74]

Because the Salvation Army has been and still is a church, with a very clear evangelical identity, many in the Army have taken for granted the Christian nature of its social service programs. According to Roger Green, the Salvation Army has "not historically been a theologically reflective movement," but this has changed in the recent past. In the 1980s, a chorus of voices rose up within the Salvation Army in reaction to what was perceived as a lack of theological knowledge and preparation on the part of both officers and social service administrators. In the fifties and sixties, leadership training had taken on a more practical quality, with many officers receiving professional training in such fields as social work and education. While this may have strengthened their professional credentials to provide services, many were ordained during this time period with limited theological training. These professionally trained ministers were vulnerable to secular philosophies that pervaded schools of social work at the time, and uncritically accepted "the social work line" that social services could and should operate free of religious or philosophical worldviews. While most ministers in the Salvation Army at this time remained firm in their Christian conviction, their lack of theological sophistication contributed to a gradual shift toward what some have seen as a "do-goodism" ethic that, on the surface at least, satisfied their Christian social conscience as well as the "nonsectarian" requirement of government contracting.[75]

The eighties and the nineties were a time of heightened interest in the Salvation Army's theological roots. Officers and laypeople within the Army began to pursue scholarly inquiry and to publish articles and books exploring how to live out the Salvation Army's distinctive theological heritage more fully. On the membership level, there was widespread interest in these writings and a growing concern about the importance of proclaiming the Gospel in all that the Army does, including its social services. After the Centennial Celebration, the Second Century Advance called for "prepara-

---

[73] McKinley, *Marching to Glory*, 289–90.
[74] Interview with Karen Phillips, March 12, 1997.
[75] Ibid.

tion of a document which explicitly states the basic Biblical presuppositions underlying our social work" for use in "orientation and in-service training." *Basic Biblical Propositions*, written by Major Peter Hoffman, was released in February 1988, affirming the Salvation Army's "redemptive and social ministry," based on the "Scriptural position regarding the responsibility of God's people to care for other human beings."[76]

The theological discussions begun after the Centennial continue today and have cumulatively strengthened the Army's ability to evaluate its programs against a theological framework. The Salvation Army's ability to articulate a clear philosophy of service and its capacity for introspection and self-criticism are critical assets that have helped to safeguard its religious character to a large degree from both the internal and external pressures that are a reality for all faith-based organizations.

As policymakers begin to include religious organizations in their plans, careful consideration should be given to how to establish a genuine partnership that preserves the special qualities that make them capable of effective transformation of lives. As Amy Sherman points out, "People of faith, of course, are concerned about the threat of secularization. But others ought to be worried as well, for the dilution of a ministry's religious distinctiveness may remove the very element that makes it so effective in addressing social problems."[77] Although the pressures of secularization and standardization—which to a large degree have gone hand in hand with public funding—are real and powerful, the Salvation Army's story demonstrates that there is much that an organization can do internally to preserve its religious integrity while operating in what continues to be a precarious legal and regulatory environment.

Even though it has staunchly defended its identity as an evangelical organization, the Salvation Army is not immune to the dynamics that have prompted so many other service organizations to shed their Christian conviction. Will the Salvation Army take the wide road of the YMCA and Catholic Charities, or will it go through the narrow gate of keeping its evangelistic message as the center of its work? Compared with smaller, grassroots faith-based organizations that receive little or no public funding, the Army has a more difficult task of remaining true to its mission—indeed, of coming to a renewed understanding of that mission.

What differentiates the Salvation Army from like-minded organizations is the enormous scope of its work and the popularity it enjoys. Yet these assets are also the primary source of the Army's vulnerability as an organization striving to live out a Christian witness in a secular culture. The reality of the Army's current circumstances is an implicit tension between

[76] McKinley, *Marching to Glory*, 299.
[77] Sherman, "Thy Neighbor's Keeper," 43–46.

size and religious integrity, particularly given the limited number of qualified social workers who are evangelical Christians. In the past, the Army's
Christian distinctiveness has been compromised somewhat as it has grown
in size and scope. The key to becoming more distinctively Christian in its
social work lies in the Army's willingness to reflect on its theological vision
of service. As Major Philip Needham wrote in a thoughtful essay on "rein-
tegrating" the organization's mission, "there can be no true Christian evangelism without a social ministry, and no true Christian social service without evangelism. . . . In the case of the marriage of evangelism and social
service, the larger purpose is to proclaim the Kingdom of God in the world
and to help people to enter it."[78]

But he goes on to warn, "Social service is a spillover of the mutual caring
ministry within the Christian fellowship. If social service derives from any
other source, it is not Christian social service."[79] If that fellowship becomes
too attenuated, if the active congregational life becomes overshadowed by
the work of paid staff who have no connection with the congregation, if
the message becomes unclear or compromised, it is difficult to see how the
work of a faith-based organization can preserve its distinctively religious
character.

There is much to admire about the work of the Salvation Army, but
equally admirable is the seriousness with which it is grappling with how to
maintain its distinctive character and mission in the "ambiguous embrace"
of government and of the contributing public.

[78] Needham, "Toward a Re-integration," 141.
[79] Ibid., 146.

7

LOSS—AND RECOVERY—OF NERVE

[M]any faith-based charities seem all too willing to accommodate
themselves to the secularizing demands of government authorities
. . . , even to the point of compromising their own religious identity.
Evidently they believe that their contribution to the public good
comes mainly by way of delivering services more efficiently than
government bureaucracies. This, however, is a major failure to
appreciate what in fact is the principal contribution of these faith-
based charities, namely, that they deliver such services not merely
more efficiently but also more effectively. That is the case because
they deliver these services in a qualitatively different manner, one
that addresses matters of the heart by drawing on spiritual and
moral resources that are beyond the competence of government.
(Luis Lugo, "Equal Partners")

AS LUIS LUGO points out, government interference is not the only
threat to the integrity of faith-based organizations. They are also
faced with the more subtle danger of self-betrayal, voluntary
abandonment of their original purpose. This may happen as a result of a
kind of "loss of nerve" on the part of staff and even of boards and sponsoring organizations, as they become less clear about whether the beliefs and
values upon which the organizations were founded are still relevant to present circumstances. Professional norms (discussed in chapter 5) may play a
part, but so may broader forces of secularization that have penetrated even
into the churches.

It is, after all, a feature of modernity that religious convictions become
privatized, "values and meanings lose their connection with tradition and
become vaguer, more general, more abstract, morally free-wheeling."[1] Nor
is this effect limited to those who stand outside the churches and religious
organizations, but often affects clergy, lay leaders, board members as well.
When those who set the direction for an organization with a traditional
religious identity no longer can see how that identity should affect its mission, the legal and other safeguards that we have discussed are useless.
"There is nothing from a governmental level that we can do to prevent
you from corrupting yourself," the legislative director for Senator Ash-

---

[1] Adriaansens and Zijderveld, *Vrijwillig initiatief en de verzorgingsstaat*, 13.

croft, who sponsored inclusion of Charitable Choice in the new federal welfare law, told representatives of faith-based agencies. "The only thing we can do is insure that religious entities have equal access to the process in getting contracts. Now, if the money becomes more important than the religious mission, there's nothing that I can do legislatively to prevent that."[2]

There is ample reason to believe that many such agencies—and schools with a religious identity—have become substantially conformed to secular models. Robert Whelan found, in his recent study of (mostly religious) nonprofit charitable agencies in England, that "[t]he belief that lives can— or even should—be changed is scarcely in evidence. The charitable sector is thus unable to offer any real alternative to the welfare state, at a time when there is widespread dissatisfaction with the *status quo*." He attributes this failure to the wholesale abandonment of the religious perspectives that inspired the creation of these organizations.

> [I]t is this sense of "otherness" which seems to be missing, this spiritual per-spective on material needs which should separate church-based from statutory programmes of assistance. In short, the churches no longer present an alterna-tive. They seem to be content to provide services in much the same way as the state, taking taxpayers' money and reporting to local authorities and govern-ment departments.

By way of evidence, he cites a 1985 report by the Church of England, in which there are few mentions of *either* charity or evangelism. The report "contains long lists of demands on national and local government, whilst making almost no mention of any contribution required from the church as an institution or from individual Christians."[3]

As we saw in chapters 5 and 6, it is above all through the appointment of staff who do not share the convictions upon which the organization was founded that mission shift is likely to occur, abetted by overexpansion to take advantage of the availability of public funding. Whelan was told by one believing Christian active in social welfare work that "in an eagerness to meet the ongoing needs of the area or get a particular project off the ground, there is always a temptation to go for what seems to produce the greatest practical benefit. This often involves appointing people with en-thusiasm and expertise but with little if any Christian conviction. It is justified on the grounds that they will be influenced towards Christianity by the rest of the team. Usually the reverse is the case. Many Christian organizations have done this and have moved away from a biblically-based

---

[2] Loconte, *Seducing the Samaritan*, 125.
[3] Whelan, *The Corrosion of Charity*, 93, 98, 83.

mission so that in the end the Christian content is reduced to a general desire to do good to others."

As a result of such well-intentioned choices, Whelan concluded, "[a]s the organisations have expanded they have acquired large staffs most of whom enter via the social work sector rather than through church channels. . . . Often those adhering to the original spiritual vision of the founder find themselves outnumbered by those who have no particular religious beliefs, or at least no essentially religious view of social welfare work."[4] This is the phenomenon with which the Salvation Army and other faith-based nonprofits in the United States are contending.

Even more damaging in its effects is the abandonment of such a vision on the part of religious leaders themselves. One of the effects of postwar theological reflection among Protestants was a valuing of the "secular" for its own sake, often inspired by a rather shallow reading of Dietrich Bonhoeffer's prison writing. Books like Cox's *The Secular City* and Robinson's *Honest to God* became best-sellers and required reading by those rising to leadership in the mainline Protestant churches.[5] The more the secular sphere was seen as rich in signs of grace, the less urgent and even credible was it to seek to bring a revelation-based understanding to bear upon social problems. Religious people should just roll up their sleeves and join in the world's work—especially the struggle for racial and economic justice— without any pretensions to special insights or agendas. A "servant Church" should not seek to impose itself upon the World.

This line of thinking was consistent with the anti-imperialism fervor that was sweeping the postwar world, and soon found a welcome in the Catholic circles as well through a superficial reading of the documents of Vatican II.

A dramatic example is provided by the precipitous abandonment of foreign missionary efforts by the mainline Protestant denominations. While in some cases—the missions in China and Cuba, for example—this was the result of expulsion by Communist regimes, in many others it resulted from loss of conviction that evangelistic missions were a good thing. This, in turn, reflected an uneasiness about the idea that non-Christians should be encouraged to become Christians. Was that project not, after all, a form of cultural imperialism if not actually the handmaiden to political imperialism itself? Were we so sure that our beliefs were better than those held by other peoples? Would it not be better simply to offer practical assistance

---

[4] Ibid., 12, 76.

[5] As in another connection in chapter 4, I can give personal testimony. In the late sixties I worked on social justice issues for the national Episcopal Church and the National Council of Churches and can recall no occasion when a Christian perspective was suggested that varied from the dominant progressive agenda.

such as medical care unaccompanied by explicit evangelism or expectation
that those to whom assistance was provided would come to share our religious beliefs? Was such "self-emptying" not in fact a more authentically
Christian posture in relation to a world that should no longer be defined
as being "in darkness" without the Gospel?

And so the missionary enterprise faded away among mainline Protestants, and soon even the medical and educational missions failed in many
cases for lack of new recruits. The Peace Corps—a government agency—
came to seem a more legitimate expression of American idealism and good
will than programs under voluntary denominational auspices. Tocqueville
would have been baffled! In retrospect, it is clear that the provision of
assistance unrelated to evangelism was simply a transition to complete
abandonment of the missionary enterprise. Indeed, some of the churches
in developing nations "planted" by earlier generations of missionaries and
unaffected by liberal self-doubt began to send missions to other countries
. . . including the United States!

But as the mainline denominations abandoned the mission field, there
was an increase in overseas activity by evangelical groups who made no
apologies for seeking to "win souls," and who experienced considerable
success. Perhaps the most notable feature of this development for our purposes is that the evangelical groups *also* began to provide very extensive
medical, educational, and relief services but without the slackening of religious witness so evident among the mainline denominations: organizations
like World Vision make no apology for believing in proclamation of the
Gospel *and* provision of practical assistance and development aid. Monsma
found that four of the twelve "conservative Protestant" aid agencies that he
surveyed reported they encouraged religious commitments by those being
served, in contrast with only one of twelve "mainline Protestant" agencies.
Seven of the former but none of the latter reported that they integrated
"voluntary worship services or other religious activities" into their relief
and/or development programs.[6]

Nor is the association of development aid and evangelism fortuitous,
since there is reason to believe that the changes in attitude and behavior
associated with religious conversion lead also to improved health, prosperity, and community life. David Martin reports on research conducted
among an indigenous people in Mexico, which found that

> [t]hose Mayos who became Protestant, which effectively means Pentecostal,
> initiated a major change of life, notably by gaining freedom from the fiesta
> system and from the obligation of *fiesteros* to give away huge quantities of food.
> To reject the obligations of the fiesta helped them get together more money for

[6] Monsma, *When Sacred and Secular Mix*, 76.

consumer goods and the education of their children. They also saved money by their rejection of all entertainment, especially drinking. Yet the rejection of waste and indulgence was not a rejection of wealth. Pastors encouraged their congregations to work hard, educate their children and improve their material conditions. It was not accounted a reproach to own a tape recorder or a car.

Martin concludes that, throughout Latin America, "Pentecostalism provides a substitute society, and within that society cares largely for its own, by way of schools, orphanages, homes for the elderly and informal employment exchanges."[7]

By detaching the assistance they provided from any expectation of personal change—or from the power to change as a result of religious experience—the mainline efforts in development assistance may have been reducing the effectiveness of the assistance itself.

The parallel with what has occurred in domestic social service is obvious. Roy Lubove, Gertrude Himmelfarb, and others have traced how a movement to "redeem" the poor faltered and then changed its character entirely as the result of a loss of conviction that society has a right to ask those who receive its assistance to change their behavior. "It was the welfare state that finally brought about the divorce of morality from social policy. The divorce was finalized when the services and benefits provided by the state were made available to everyone regardless of merit or even need. And it was legitimized when it became a moral principle to eschew moral distinctions and judgments. There was an ethical theory implicit in this policy of moral neutrality: it was the theory that society was responsible for social problems and that therefore society (in the form of the state) had the moral responsibility to solve those problems."[8]

This assumption is reflected in social work textbooks, which insist upon a "nonjudgmental attitude." Payne quotes one introductory textbook as instructing future social workers, "The person's worth is validated equally by his or her decision to achieve potential or to permit it to lie unused, by a decision to achieve or merely vegetate." Another stresses that "social workers should not judge clients' behavior by imposing a moral value on it." This emphasis, Payne concludes, encourages social workers "to be complacent about programs that validate and reinforce destructive lifestyles, such as income support for unwed mothers or for alcoholics and drug addicts."[9]

This is in striking contrast with the assumptions motivating social work in the nineteenth century, when those seeking to help the poor made no

---

[7] Martin, *Tongues of Fire*, 211, 258.

[8] Himmelfarb, *Poverty and Compassion*, 384.

[9] Payne, "Absence of Judgment," 52–53.

apologies for stressing the need to change their hearts and their lives. Nor were they shy about associating these changes with religious conversion; indeed "the underlying causes and long-term needs *were* religious, early nineteenth-century charity workers consistently argued."[10] This did not mean that professions of religious faith were made the condition of receiving assistance; that would have been inconsistent with the evangelical charity workers' understanding of the nature of grace and of conversion, while for Catholic and Jewish charity workers extending assistance to their coreligionists was a matter of serving those already within the faith-community rather than seeking conversion. In the 1890s, "Church-based organizations generally did not discriminate along religious lines; the Home for Crippled Children, for example, announced that 'the home is distinctly Protestant, but no child is debarred on account of race, nationality or religious belief.' "[11]

Professional norms have many positive effects, as we have pointed out in chapter 5, but they can create serious problems for faith-based social agencies or schools. The problems are of two kinds. First, to the extent that they are codified by government as staffing requirements for approval of an organization's right to operate, or to receive public funds, professional norms may make it difficult for a faith-based organization to preserve its distinctive character. Second—and equally dangerous—the norms may come to be accepted by those who give direction to the organization as representing a better definition of good practice than that to which the school or agency was originally dedicated. This leads to a loss of nerve, a "pre-emptive capitulation"[12] that surrenders to the world even before its demand is made, a "seduction of the Samaritans" in Loconte's evocative title.

Changing the mission of an organization is not necessarily a bad thing, of course; needs may change, and so may the understanding of what constitutes effective service. We are familiar with the phenomenon of mission shift in the business world and among charitable organizations: polio largely vanquished, the March of Dimes changed its focus to birth defects. "Mission creep" is another matter: when an organization drifts away from its original purpose without taking stock of what is being lost or weighing the prospects of carrying out the new mission effectively.

There are many nongovernmental social service agencies that make no mystery of their willingness to respond to shifts in what government chooses to fund: they are in a sort of nonprofit "business" in which the

[10] Olasky, *Tragedy of American Compassion*, 30.

[11] Ibid., 81.

[12] It was Luis Lugo who introduced me to this marvelous phrase, in the context of our collaboration through the Center for Public Justice.

customer is always right. If government wishes to switch from community-based supervision and treatment of adolescent offenders to their incarceration in secure facilities, the director of one such NGO told us, his agency is prepared to modify its way of working with youth . . . and presumably the philosophy behind it as well. The "ambiguous embrace" is in such cases an altogether comfortable one. But for agencies or schools founded in order to embody a distinctive understanding of human nature, the danger is very real. "The main threat of this expansion to the voluntary sector," Wuthnow concludes, "has thus not been the absorption of previously voluntary services into monolithic agencies of the state, but a more subtle reorientation of the aims and aspirations of voluntary associations."[13] Community-based agencies can be changed in fundamental ways without that being the intention of either government or agency leadership.[14]

For those social agencies and organizations (and, potentially, schools) that are religious, the cost may be especially high, not only for themselves but also for those they might have served better if they had remained more consistently true to their original understanding of their mission. Amy Sherman tells us, "Secular experts may be able, for example, to instruct churches in techniques for helping substance abusers quit drinking and drugging. But as one former addict who had repeatedly relapsed during his time in government-sponsored recovery programs explained, 'Those programs generally take addictions from you, but don't place anything within you. I needed a spiritual lifting.' "[15] Something has to be put in the place of drugs or alcohol at the center of the addicted person's life, and—without reducing faith to a form of therapy—it is clear that religious experience and community based upon shared belief can have a powerful effect.

The Importance of Maintaining Distinctiveness

One of the most convincing accounts of the role of a distinctive worldview in making an organization effective is the study of why Catholic high schools are effective, by Anthony Bryk and his colleagues. Drawing upon a nationwide, longitudinal study of student outcomes correlated with a wide variety of background and schooling factors, they also looked closely at school characteristics including the role played by a well-defined educational mission based upon religious convictions. They rejected the contention of enthusiasts for educational markets, that autonomy and lack of

[13] Wuthnow, "Tocqueville's Question Reconsidered," 291.
[14] Gonzalez Borrero, "Management of Hispanic Nonprofit Organizations," and Estrada, "Survival Profiles."
[15] Sherman, *Restorers of Hope*, 217.

bureaucratic constraints are sufficient to explain the demonstrated success of faith-based schools, especially with the most vulnerable pupils, writing that "we believe that the structural features of Catholic schools, divorced from their traditions, would likely produce a set of school consequences quite different from those described in this book."[16]

At one time, Catholic schools may have had a taken-for-granted character. Catholic parents were expected to send their children, and they were staffed by members of teaching orders whose Catholic identity was beyond question. That is no longer the case, in the United States or in the Western democracies that provide public funds for Catholic schools, like Britain, France, Australia, and the Low Countries. "The days when a steady stream of Catholic parents automatically sent their children to Catholic schools have long since passed. For most families, Catholic and non-Catholic alike, the decision to enroll a child is a deliberate act."[17] Nor is there anything like an adequate supply of teaching sisters and brothers, and the relatively low salaries paid by American Catholic schools would make it difficult to attract and retain competent teachers who could not feel committed to a school's mission.[18]

The difficult financial circumstances of most faith-based schools in the United States may, paradoxically, have helped to generate a strong sense of commitment and community that can be lacking in comparable schools in other countries that provide full funding. In Britain, where Catholic, Anglican, and Jewish schools are government-funded, there is a "reluctant private sector"—reluctant in the sense that they *want* to receive public funds—of Evangelical and Muslim schools that do not receive public funds, but may be all the more clearly profiled as a result.[19] "The parents who founded these schools want to see spiritual values enshrined in them, not the materialist values that now prevail in our society. Many materialists do not understand this because they themselves attach little importance to, or even deny, the spiritual."[20]

The effectiveness of faith-based schools that are clear about what they stand for—perhaps because they have been marginalized by public policy decisions—may well be related to community formed around a vision for education. "Teachers consider themselves much more efficacious, enjoy

---

[16] Bryk, Lee, and Holland, *Catholic Schools*, 17.

[17] Ibid., 165.

[18] In 1993–94, the average salary for Catholic school teachers was $21,652, compared with $34,189 in public schools (in "conservative Christian" schools it was $15,823, suggesting an even greater need for nonmonetary rewards!) (National Center for Education Statistics, *Private Schools*, 93).

[19] Tasker, "Developing Third Sector Alliance," xii.

[20] Hodgetts, "Third Sector Alliance," 57.

their work more, and have higher morale if they teach in schools that are organized communally. The level of teacher absenteeism is also somewhat lower. Similarly, students are less likely to cut class, be disorderly, be truant, and drop out if they attend schools that are high on the community index."[21] In the government survey of schools in 1993–94, the greatest disparity in responses between public and nonpublic school teachers was on whether their schools were communities. On a scale of 1 to 10, public school teachers gave their schools an average of 5.7, and nonpublic teachers 8.4 (9.0 in "conservative Christian" schools).[22]

The significance of community is, for Bryk and associates, absolutely central to the ability of Catholic high schools to work effectively with youth.

> We expect that a communally organized school indirectly engenders positive academic outcomes for students through the increased efforts of teachers and students. . . . Schools organized as communities exhibit a set of common understandings among members of the organization. These include tenets about the purpose of the school, about what students should learn, about how teachers and students should behave, and—most important—about the kind of people students are and are capable of becoming. Such educational concerns in turn reflect more fundamental beliefs about the nature of the individual and society. Not any set of values will do. . . . Such a commitment requires regular public expressions of concern and action toward the common good as well as a shared understanding of the nature and importance of the common good.[23]

The voluntary nature of the community created in faith-based schools— perhaps especially when some sacrifice is involved on the part of parents and teachers—helps to reduce the conflict over behavior and discipline that plague so many public schools.

> On the organizational side, a voluntary community enjoys a base of moral authority. Such authority depends on the consent of those influenced by it, and it is made possible by the commitment from both teachers and students to a particular school. The presence of moral authority is important because much of what happens in schools involves discretionary action. Great effort may be required within public bureaucracies to secure basic agreements on issues that are intrinsically matters of judgment. In a voluntary community . . . many potentially contentious issues never develop into conflicts, because communal norms define a broader realm of "what is appropriate here."[24]

[21] Bryk, Lee, and Holland, *Catholic Schools*, 283.
[22] National Center for Education Statistics, *Private Schools*, 104.
[23] Bryk, Lee, and Holland, *Catholic Schools*, 276–77.
[24] Ibid., 314.

But none of this happens by accident, they point out; to the contrary, "school administration also takes on a distinctive character: tending to the meaning-inducing quality of school life becomes a deliberate aim, on a par with concerns about the efficient organization of instruction." And the school's guiding ethos is not simply plucked out of thin air. "For school leaders, charting such a course involves continuous navigation through a sea of dilemmas. The religious tradition provides much guidance. It stabilizes what schools will and will not do, and affords a sense of sureness about the importance of these endeavors."[25]

Although studies of the "Catholic school effect" commonly focus on positive effects as indicated by academic outcomes, Bryk and his associates insist that the "social interactions of schooling are not simply a mechanism for accomplishing some other aim; they are education itself." Schools that have a strong community life that in turn is based upon shared convictions convey important lessons about life, lessons that are especially consequential for adolescents. But schools cannot be neutral; "*all* education conveys religious understandings, that is, a set of beliefs, values, and sentiments that order social life and create purpose for human activity. These may be comprehensive ideals that ennoble the person and reach out broadly to others, or they may narrowly focus only on advancing material self-interest."[26]

This is a compelling and attractive description of a system of schooling centered upon education in the fullest sense, and not upon instruction and social adjustment alone. We might question whether most Catholic education leaders would endorse the recasting of their ethos in essentially humanistic terms; indeed, the authors express some concern lest the tendency within the Catholic Church toward a greater stress upon Christian doctrine, symbolized by the development of a universal catechism, somehow derail what they see as an entirely positive development away from doctrine. Concerned to draw some encouragement for public schooling from the successes of Catholic schools, they seek to minimize what is stubbornly Catholic about the latter and thereby drift free, in their final pages, from what until that point has been a thoroughly realistic account of what works and what does not, suggesting that "there is no reason why schools organized like Catholic schools could not (and should not) be major components in such a system. That religious orders founded Catholic schools and that these schools continue to benefit from a religious tradition offers no particular barrier to the creation of 'secular schools' espousing a similar

---

[25] Ibid., 315, 317.
[26] Ibid., 291, 341.

set of humanistic beliefs and social principles, and maintaining a similar organizational order."[27]

Bryk and his associates are describing schools that are free to set their own agenda with minimal interference by government. A very different sort of research provides insight into the experience of faith-based institutions that rely upon public funding.

When Sacred and Secular Mix

To what extent and in what ways are faith-based social agencies affected by the receipt of public funding and the "strings" that come with it? We are fortunate to have available an excellent quantitative study of this question by political scientist Stephen Monsma. Monsma surveyed three types of nonprofit organizations nationwide in late 1993 and early 1994: colleges, international relief agencies, and child and family service agencies; our discussion will be confined largely to the third group. He received 286 completed surveys—handled so as to be anonymous—from these social agencies, a 49 percent response rate. The surveys asked a long series of questions about the services provided by the agency, its religious character (if any), the ways in which that religious character is expressed in the work of the agency, the extent to which the agency receives public funding, and any constraints or difficulties associated with such a relationship with government. In his analysis, Monsma then sorted the responding agencies into three groups depending upon whether the responses indicated they were pervasively religious, residually religious, or completely secular.[28]

Receipt of public funding—including grants and loans, purchase-of-service contracts, in-kind contributions, and "grants to individual users of a nonprofit's services" through a voucher or other mechanism—was almost universal (90 percent) among the child-serving agencies.

> Among the child service agencies receiving public funds, the most frequent form of public money was purchase of service contracts, with 90 percent of them receiving some government funds of this type. Typically these agencies provide residential care and other services for children who are under state supervision or control due to their having been neglected or abused or being children and youths in the juvenile justice system. State or local governments then purchase residential care and other forms of education and counseling help for these children. . . . The second most frequent form of government funds was grants of

[27] Ibid., 327.
[28] Monsma, *When Sacred and Secular Mix*, 201–28.

TABLE 7.1

Nonprofit Organizations' Secular-Religious Nature and Receipt
of Public Funds

Public Funding	Secular (%)	Religious in Past (%)	Religious (%)
None	5	0	18
1% to 19%	9	7	19
20% to 39%	4	7	12
40% to 59%	9	10	9
60% to 79%	22	15	17
80% to 100%	51	61	25
N	92	41	137

Source: Adapted from Monsma, *When Sacred and Secular Mix*, table 3, p. 68.

in-kind materials, with 41 percent reporting receipt of this type of assistance. Usually this consists of food or surplus government property.[29]

Smith and Lipsky make a careful distinction among those nonprofits that have a long history of good works and institutional stability (and often a substantial endowment), those that were founded opportunistically in recent decades in response to government's need to find service providers with which to contract, and those that were organized by activists to meet some immediate need—often of advocacy more than service-delivery—and only later if at all turn to government funding.[30] Our research in Boston uncovered a number of small Catholic agencies that have deliberately not sought public funding because they are consciously in opposition to public policy on such issues as abortion and homosexuality. These are usually the expression of the vision of a handful of founders and have no intention of growing substantially larger. On the other hand, Catholic Charities and other umbrella organizations have over the decades absorbed a number of such groups, obtained public funding for their work, and perhaps unintentionally contributed to their secularization as a result.

Monsma notes that "there was a tendency for the younger organizations to receive larger proportions of their budgets from government sources. Their founding and the defining of their missions may have taken into account the increase in public funds available starting in the 1960s. . . . A supplementary explanation could be that the younger nonprofits have not had the time that older organizations have had to develop strong alternative sources of funding."[31]

As table 7.1 demonstrates, secular and formerly or residually religious agencies are substantially more dependent upon public funding than are

[29] Ibid., 65–66.
[30] Smith and Lipsky, *Nonprofits for Hire*.
[31] Monsma, *When Sacred and Secular Mix*, 67.

TABLE 7.2
Nonprofit Organizations' Religious Traditions and Receipt of Public Funds

Public Funding	Jewish (%)	Catholic (%)	Evangelical (%)	Mainline (%)
None	38	5	27	5
1% to 19%	46	5	16	14
20% to 59%	17	24	18	23
60% to 100%	0	67	39	59
N	24	21	44	44

Source: Adapted from Monsma, *When Sacred and Secular Mix*, table 5, p. 73.
Note: Because of rounding, not all columns total 100%.

those whose directors describe them as unapologetically religious, and "many more religious agencies get by without any government funds than is the case among their secular counterparts."[32] Since other strongly religious agencies *do* receive large amounts of public funding, it appears likely that the pattern of relatively less dependence on government is the result of decisions by the agencies themselves rather than of government unwillingness to fund them. This is one of the possibilities that Monsma set out to explore in more depth.

One of his findings was that Catholic and Evangelical organizations in all three spheres surveyed, despite many reasons for conflict with government because of their moral teaching, by no means hold back when it comes to receiving public funds. This is especially true of Catholic child-serving agencies, as demonstrated by table 7.2.

Such figures do not tell us much, of course, unless we are able to assess the extent to which these organizational affiliations find expression in a distinctive character. We would want to know how typical is the child service agency director who wrote to Monsma, "Religious life goals [are] built right into individual service plans which are agreed to by client, state and agency staff." Or another who told him that since most of the clients come from some sort of a religious background, to develop treatment plans with no reference to religion would not be good therapy.

One of the striking—and counterintuitive—results is that Catholic agencies are distinctly more "liberal" in the sense of leaving religion to one side than are mainline Protestant agencies, much less the more conservative Protestant agencies. This is surely correlated with their heavy dependence upon public funds, though the survey results cannot tell us which came first. That is, have Catholic agencies become indistinct in their religious identity as a result of doing so much business with and for government, or

---

[32] Ibid., 69.

TABLE 7.3
Religious Practices of Faith-Based Child Service Agencies

Religious Practices	Jewish (%)	Catholic (%)	Evangelical (%)	Mainline (%)
Staff Make Informal References to Religious Ideas with Clients	61	50	82	74
Require Religious Activities	0	14	57	45
Encourage Religious Commitments by Clients	4	9	73	26
Give Preference in Hiring Staff on the Basis of Religious Orientation[a]	43	0	45	13
Only Hire Staff in Agreement on Religious Orientation[a]	14	9	32	9

Source: Adapted From Monsma, *When Sacred and Secular Mix*, table 7, p. 75.
[a] Agencies could be counted in one or the other of the last two rows, not both.

had they already moved in that direction and as a result found it natural to undertake to provide public services with little denominational character?

Monsma developed a "religious practices scale" by assigning variable weight to the responses to this set of questions; he found that those agencies that rated highest on the scale "reported receiving significantly lower proportions of their budgets from public sources than did the less religious agencies." He concluded, that

> religion is indeed a factor in reducing the dependence of child service agencies on public funds is supported by the responses given to a question asked of all agencies that indicated they received no public money. . . . Of the thirteen agencies that receive no government funds and rank high on the RPS, eleven reported it was a policy not to accept government funds, and only two said that was just the way things had worked out. But of the eleven agencies that score medium or low on the RPS and receive no public money, only four said not accepting public money was a policy and seven said it was the way things had happened to work out. . . . Whether due to fear of government control, other available sources of money, or other causes, it appears the religious nature of some child service agencies have [*sic*] led them to avoid public funds.[33]

The final question of concern to us in Monsma's important study is the influence of government funding upon the religious character of the services provided. Here we must proceed with some caution, since it may be that faith-based agency administrators completing the survey were reluctant to report compromises about which they did not have a clear conscience. The survey results are in fact quite unexpected. For example,

[33] Ibid., 78–79.

when asked *why* they refrained from any of the religious practices listed in the survey, 17 percent of the religious child service agencies replied that they *ought not to* include religious practices in their work, 10 percent that they were legally prevented from doing so, and 73 percent that they *had no desire to* do so. This seems to confirm the counterintuitive conclusion of the policy review conducted in this book, that government interference may be less significant than loss of conviction or lack of clarity about the significance in practice of religious convictions, insights, and actions. It may be that, for some of these agency directors, a deep personal faith is the motivation for their work and has made a great difference in their lives, but they do not see how it could make a difference in the lives of their clients, or they feel it would be unprofessional to do anything about that. They may be inhibited by a sense that there would be something indecent about taking advantage of a client's vulnerability to promote their religious viewpoint. These are honorable motivations, and the training material used by the Salvation Army shows how delicately such matter must be approached.[34] But, by dismissing the inclusion of religious elements in their work, are they limiting what their agencies can accomplish? Are they conceding that they will provide services in a manner identical to that of secular agencies? Many of the faith-based agencies were not taking full advantage of their opportunities to be distinctive, apparently because "self-imposed concepts of what is and is not proper seems to be limiting their religiously based activities. . . . Certain cultural, professional, or legal norms may—perhaps even unself-consciously—be leading the heads of religious nonprofits to conclude they do not want to engage in certain religious practices, even practices normally associated with the religions traditions of which their nonprofits are a part."[35] They have experienced a loss of nerve.

We must not exaggerate. More than three-quarters of the directors of child service agencies reported that they engaged in some religiously based practices openly and directly, not subtly and indirectly. Nearly as many reported that, of the religious practices their agencies did not engage in, they refrained from engaging in them because they had no desire to do them, not because they felt they ought not to or could not do them.[36] It may be that in many cases these directors are exercising thoughtful—even theologically informed—judgment about which religious practices are compatible with their mission, and which are not.

On the other hand, "30 percent of the heads of the 122 religious agencies receiving public funds reported government officials as having questioned

---

[34] Cheydleur, *Faith-Based Counseling Skills.*
[35] Monsma, *When Sacred and Secular Mix*, 104.
[36] Ibid., 86–89, 91.

or pressured them with regard to their religiously motivated practices," and many spoke of "a generalized suspiciousness or hostility from government officials toward religious practices."

When asked about the overall effects of government funding and supervision, the directors of distinctively religious agencies were more positive than those of either the secular agencies or of the residually religious agencies. "It is especially noteworthy that the religious agencies ranking highest on the Religious Practices Scale cited the most positive effects," and they were less likely to complain that government support made them "less flexible and more 'bureaucratic' " than were the directors of either the secular agencies or the formerly religious agencies.[37] This finding could be extremely significant for public policy, suggesting that the more distinctively religious social agencies—and schools—may be the most successful in resisting assimilation to a failed model of standardized government provision. In this connection, Coleman and Hoffer's finding that Catholic high schools are more successful with at-risk youth than are private nonreligious high schools takes on a new significance.[38] The success is perhaps due not only to the fact that they are not subject to bureaucratic control—the heart of Chubb and Moe's controversial argument for vouchers[39]—but also to their religious character.

It is clear that those faith-based agencies that choose to include religious practices as part of their service to clients are often able to do so without outside interference, but a potential problem arises from the arbitrary nature of government toleration of such religious practices in the agencies that it funds. Monsma comments that "restrictions on hiring practices, religious exercises, required behavior standards, and more—are ones that would result in the serious compromise of their religious autonomy, if suddenly they were uniformly applied to all religious nonprofits receiving public funds. Even today, the hit and miss quality of the restrictions that have been imposed poses a threat to their religious autonomy."[40]

Whether some government official overseeing a grant or contract ever chooses to raise an issue about a religious practice, agencies may grow more cautious and thus more secular in order to avoid the possibility. According to Monsma, "the extent to which organizations unconsciously position themselves to receive public funds by slowly toning down or giving up some of their distinctive religious practices is unknown. They may even rationalize their doing so under the cause of raising their professional or

---

[37] Ibid., 93.
[38] Coleman and Hoffer, *Public and Private*, 213.
[39] Chubb and Moe, *Politics, Markets*.
[40] Ibid., 99.

academic standards, embracing greater diversity, or better serving a diverse constituency."[41] Whatever the immediate reason, the long-term effect is to reduce the distinctiveness and flavor that they are able to offer to the social service mix.

Recovering Identity: The Dutch Debates

In no other nation to such an extent as in the Netherlands is there a lively discussion over how the distinctive identity or "signature" of individual schools can be expressed and further developed within a highly regulated framework of government mandates. Countless articles, conferences, and debates have taken place in recent years over how the shared vision of staff, parents, and governing bodies can find expression in every aspect of the life of a school, and whether and to what extent public schools can legitimately become as individually distinctive as private schools.

While these debates have not been unique to the Netherlands, they have been especially thoughtful there, perhaps because there is more variation in publicly supported schooling than, say, in France or Spain, where almost all nonpublic schools are Catholic. In the Netherlands, just over 30 percent of elementary pupils attend Catholic schools, and almost as many attend Protestant schools (of several varieties), while another 10 percent attend a rich variety of other nonpublic schools of many types. For example, hardly had the first publicly financed Muslim schools been established than rival Muslim schools of different shades of Islam demanded and were accorded recognition. The same process occurred with Hindu schools, and there are long-established networks of Waldorf (Rudolf Steiner), Montessori, Dalton, and other schools employing distinctive pedagogies. Postma provides a list of nineteen recognized varieties of nonpublic elementary schools, and seven at the secondary level.[42]

It has come to be conventional wisdom in recent years, as a result of a good deal of research in the Netherlands, that there are three considerations that parents have in mind in selecting a school, pretty much in this order: the quality of the school, the ease of getting to the school, and the sector to which a school belongs. What this actually means is by no means clear because we don't know what parents mean by quality. Among the issues of quality may well be the commitments, the ethos upon which a school is based. Those considerations cannot simply be relegated to the third category, the formal identification of a school as Protestant or Catholic or neutral, for they are often deeply implicated in decisions about the

---

[41] Ibid., 165.
[42] Postma, *Handboek*, 128–29.

quality of the school. In order to convince parents of the value of a school, it's necessary that those doing the convincing have a clear idea of what the school is about, what it is trying to do, and that idea cannot simply be an abstract notion or a label, but must be expressed in the life and organization of the school if it is to be convincing.[43] This is a special challenge for public schools, because they are required to be accessible by pupils of any group within the society and to teach in a way that respects a wide diversity of views; there has thus been extensive discussion in the Netherlands of what it might mean for public schools to have a distinctive character.[44]

The task of defining clearly the mission of a school is in some respects surprisingly more difficult for a Protestant or Catholic school, under conditions of widespread pluralism, than it is for a public school. While the public school may define its mission in terms of the encounter between diverse traditions and beliefs and positions without making a decision to support one or another, the Protestant or Catholic school must decide what it means to be a Christian school under contemporary conditions. This is not so easy because members of these churches hold many varying views about how to apply their religious convictions. It is one thing to hold to certain theological propositions; it is quite another to decide how they apply to addressing a variety of issues in daily life and in the work of a school. The nature of the Catholic or the Protestant school, which must be defined somehow in positive terms, may become more difficult to express than the nature of the public school, which is often defined in negative terms, by the *absence* of a worldview.[45] It can no longer be assumed that a shared belief in fundamental theological principles (even to the extent that such agreement exists) will translate automatically into agreement on how a school should set about its work.

Even the possession of a clearly defined *ethos* does not guarantee a *common culture* among teachers and pupils or a *distinctive character* expressed in the program and organization of the school. The ethos may be shared only on an intellectual level but not result in a common culture among the participants; that is, they may agree on the words but have very different feelings, norms, and habits in their daily work. And the ethos may not be worked through in the details of school organization and program that make up its distinctive character.

In thinking about the mission of a school, according to a recent report prepared by a Dutch Protestant organization concerned with school iden-

---

[43] Nuis, "Onderwijs als maatschappelijk goed," 11.

[44] Glenn, "Het unieke van het Nederlandse systeem," and "Het Nederlandse onderwijsbeleid."

[45] But see Braster, *De identiteit van het openbaar onderwijs*, for a thorough exploration of this interesting question.

tity, it is possible to think about fundamentals, principles, and goals, but that can be an unwieldy task and beyond the scope of many teachers. There can also be a less structured account, a collection of expressions of what the school stands for. For example, that children are brought into contact with the Bible, with the narratives of the dealings between God and human beings, with the way of Jesus. Such an approach stresses concern about values like freedom, justice, wholeness, contrasts pairs of concepts like right and wrong, true and false, sense of responsibility and dependency, offers an orientation toward the transcendent, what is beyond even our spirituality, and encourages devotion and love. Schools may define their mission in terms of a perspective on life and society, on the place of children, the relationship between preparation for social roles and personal development. These can be building stones for a school mission that in interaction with school practice can gradually be crystallized and given expression. "In interaction" because it's not very sensible to write a beautiful-sounding school mission without giving a lot of thought to how that will be visible in school practice. It is in fact better to begin with practice. The school team should identify their strengths, the aspects of education they want to be sure not to fail to address. Starting from that point there can be a gradual building up in stages of perspectives that at the conclusion of planning can be discussed and explored.[46]

The report emphasizes that an effective working through of the school's identity must begin with thinking about practical situations in which the identity might come to expression in the distinctive character of the school. In working through such situations, it is possible to begin to arrive at a common mind on the part of those engaged in the school about what the identity of the school is. In talking about how to deal with particular situations in school life, it becomes clear what meaning they assign to the formal commitments that, otherwise, might have little real meaning. In other words, it is not just that the ethos of a school is worked out in its distinctive character; the elaboration of a distinctive character may also shape the school's ethos.

In-depth discussion of the school's situation, collection of diverse opinions from the staff, provide the opportunity to have those views begin to work, and lead to new insights and to perhaps some changes in opinion or in ideas about how one ought to express the life of the school. Gradually a school team can reach the point of being ready to draft a statement of their vision for education. In most cases, of course, they are not able to operate with complete freedom in developing any kind of school mission because there are prior commitments to the ethos that gives the school its primary identity. A Protestant school is not free to become Catholic or

[46] Unie voor Christelijk Onderwijs, *De verzuiling voorbij.*

Muslim simply because the teachers decide it would be a good idea; presumably, in deciding to work at a particular school, teachers were aware of these prior commitments. As they work through the question of how the school should deal with particular kinds of situations, they do so on the basis of at least a general understanding of what it means to be a Protestant school, for example, in what kind of relationship that means that one must stand to the authority of Bible and to individual conscience and so forth and so on. The same would apply to teachers working in a Muslim or Catholic or humanist school. A fundamental direction would be given, but the practical outworking of that would be a task that the school team would address as a part of their process of arriving at a common mind. In fact, unless they *do* engage in such a process of reflection and application, the formal identity of the school is likely to remain an undelivered letter.

Inevitably this question of the mission of a school leads to another: to what extent a school ought to seek to shape its pupils to have particular values and a particular relationship with society and indeed with religious and other traditions. The Dutch minister of education issued a call several years ago for schools to address more vigorously the question of the *formation* of pupils in this sense, leading to an important debate over whether it is appropriate for schools to seek to do more than simply instruct, whether schools can legitimately, in a free society, seek to shape those who are subject to their authority. As usual in such debates, those who have thought more carefully about the issue have pointed out that every school, whether it wishes to or not, helps to form the attitudes and the values of its pupils; the only question is whether this will be done in a conscious and intentional way, or whether it will simply happen unintentionally. This shaping of pupils occurs in the common life of the school, it occurs between teachers and pupils in the way discipline is handled, in the instruction itself, in every aspect of school life. The influence of society of course is also very much present within the school, but some schools may function in ways that reinforce the values (whether good or bad) that are operating in the wider society, while other schools may cause pupils to gain some distance from the values of society, again either for good or for ill.

An example of differences in the underlying ethos of schools may be helpful. Supporters of humanistic education in the Netherlands stress the importance of schools helping pupils to learn how to make decisions for themselves. Supporters of Protestant education, on the other hand, regard this as wishful thinking based upon a view of human nature that denies its potential for evil. Simply leaving pupils to make decisions as best they can, helping them perhaps only with the process of decision making, leaves them utterly vulnerable to the influence of the values abroad in society. It is not as though pupils are likely to invent authentically original values for themselves; during the stage when they tend to reject whatever their parents stand for, they are very likely to simply act on the basis of the values that are presented to them in the media and by their peer group. In order to equip young people to be decision makers, it is important to provide them with an alternative way of understanding the world and arriving at decisions, so that they will not be overwhelmed by the influence of what seems absolutely taken for granted. The school is to help pupils to learn to see with eyes that are not dazzled by the images presented to them by the wider society.[47]

This is a curious reversal; religiously based schooling has usually been thought of as being somehow anchored in conventional thinking in contrast with the free-spirited questioning and criticism of all that is taken for granted that might be found in public or humanist schools in which, as Bowers has put it, "emancipation is to be attained by organizing the learning environment in a manner that will eliminate any serious encounter with the manifestations of tradition."[48] Protestant and Catholic educators in the Netherlands insist that it is their own form of schooling that is critical and unconventional, and that the weakness of public schooling is its acceptance of the existing state of things and the framework of meaning that leads to that acceptance. Public schooling, from that perspective, does not give pupils a basis from which they are in a position to criticize the existing situation in the world around them. It is naive to expect that pupils can, out of their own guts, so to speak, bring forth reasonable and coherent grounds for being critical of and finding alternatives to the materialism and indifferent cruelty of the wider society.

A well-considered distinctiveness is, from this perspective, *more* conducive to equipping pupils to be responsible decision-makers than is the uniformity called for by some public school advocates. At elementary school age, what most pupils need is the security of being part of a world that makes sense; they must learn to love what is noble and hate what is base, as Aristotle tells us, before they learn to reason about it. It is not at this stage in development appropriate to place heavy emphasis on the idea that all values and social norms are somehow relative and based upon cultural differences; it is instead important to socialize children at this age into a coherent structure of values and norms. Only after that is clearly established are they equipped to begin to handle the diversity of values and norms that they must come to terms with in order to live in a pluralistic society. This process should be occurring at the level of secondary, not elementary education. Socialization occurs not only through the explicit content of courses, but just as much through the underlying ways in which the school itself operates. The need to create a school climate that is safe

[47] Ibid.
[48] Bowers, "Culture against Itself," 476.

and respectful of those involved is not simply a precondition for the educational mission of the school, but is itself a very important part of that mission. In creating the identity of the school it is essential that these questions of how the school lives, its *climate*, be clearly and effectively addressed.

But a school or social agency climate that does not rest upon openly discussed convictions is likely to be as passing as the weather, affected by a staff member's departure or a new government requirement. As Bryk and his associates noted, there are great advantages to the participants in a school if they can all have reference to a tradition that does not constantly have to be renegotiated.

Being Explicit about Identity

"One of the most effective ways for religious agencies to resist increasing government control," Monsma and Soper concluded in their study of five democracies, "is to strengthen their distinctive religious nature." They were told by one of their Dutch informants that it was easier for distinctively Christian organizations to resist pressure to merge with other organizations as a result of budget cuts than for organizations with vague identities.[49] This parallels our finding in chapter 6, that religiously distinctive schools and agencies retain more control over the hiring decisions with which they protect that distinctiveness, in a "virtuous circle."

But legal considerations are not the primary reason why a faith-based organization should seek to retain its distinctive character. Much more important, according to many observers of faith-based agencies and schools, is the contribution to their effectiveness of an explicit religious foundation. Amy Sherman notes that "these days it's fashionable to assert that successful social programs are those with a 'spiritual component.' While there is truth to this claim, it is important to note that there is a difference between ministries with a spiritual component and those that are distinctively Christian." The effective church-based programs that she describes "lead people to Jesus, not to a 'spiritual encounter.' In so doing, they provide people a moral anchor, a transcendent referent by which to judge their choices." In this way, they can "hold new converts accountable to the objective truths in God's Word. In the typical 'spiritually sensitive' post- modern approach, individuals design their own methodology of recovery, believing that the god they have fashioned for themselves will bless their efforts. Such spirituality leaves humans in charge, trusting in their ability to decipher a way out of their predicaments. Postmodern spirituality does not challenge people to conform their behavior to an objective stan-

---

[49] Monsma and Soper, *The Challenge of Pluralism*, 79.

dard of morality; it encourages them to do whatever they feel helps them."[50]
This self-referential strategy, she concludes, lacks the power of an approach
that asserts the existence and authority of objective standards for living and
for relationships.

A similarly explicit religious message is foundational for the Salvation
Army and Teen Challenge, as we have seen.

Nor is all the interest in drawing upon a specific tradition and set of
convictions confined to the Evangelical camp. In Catholic education circles
(as the study by Bryk and associates suggests) there is intense concern to
identify what is distinctive about schools and colleges that, perhaps somewhat residually, call themselves "Catholic." "In the thirty years since the
end of the Second Vatican Council," McLaughlin writes, "Catholic education has faced a continual demand for the clarification of the precise respects in which it is, or should be, *distinctive*."[51] The concern is to ensure
that religion is not confined to a halfhearted course but rather permeates
the entire curriculum and school life. "Catholic education," Groome argues, "intends to inform and form the very being of its students, to mold
their identity and agency—who they are and how they live." Nor, he insists,
can this be achieved without effort, even struggle. "This characteristic is
not to be taken for granted; in fact it is counter-cultural to much of modern
education."[52] McLaughlin agrees that "Catholic education . . . is an enterprise which is in significant respects conducted 'against the grain of the
world.' " To say precisely how it should be done, however, is no simple
matter; "the lack of a coherent modern statement of a Catholic philosophy
of education deprives the Catholic educational community of important
resources with which to confront questions of distinctiveness."[53]

Although American Jews are in many respects the strongest supporters
of public schools and opponents of arrangements like vouchers to allow
poor parents to choose nonpublic religious schools, there is a very large
Jewish social welfare network on nonprofit organizations, many of which
receive public funds, and a growing number of Jewish day schools that, so
far at least, do not. The government report cited above identified over
650 Jewish private schools in 1993–94, enrolling altogether about 185,000
pupils, and there is now a concerted effort to create many new schools.
"Even parents in the more liberal Conservative and Reform denominations
have joined Orthodox parents in being drawn to such schools." There are
nineteen Reform Jewish day schools, serving a community that has long
enjoyed a romance with public schooling; Reform leaders "once spoke out

[50] Sherman, *Restorers of Hope*, 58–59.
[51] McLaughlin, "Distinctiveness of Catholic Education," 136.
[52] Groome, "What Makes a School Catholic," 121.
[53] McLaughlin, "Distinctiveness of Catholic Education," 138–39.

against [Jewish] schools in the belief that they were an affront to the Reform ideal of living as much as possible within the larger society."[54] For an earlier generation of assimilation-oriented Jewish immigrants and their children "the public school was . . . not only enthusiastically but truly fanatically supported."[55]

Jewish schools are an especially interesting case because their religious character is not just a means—even a very important means—of enabling them to educate effectively, but is their primary reason for existence. It does not appear that most parents who choose these schools are rejecting the public schools so much as looking for something that public schools cannot provide. A recent study concluded that "Jewish day schools are the best vehicle for implementing Jewish involvement and are the only type of Jewish education that stands against the very rapidly growing rate of intermarriage."[56] According to some observers, it is only now that non-Orthodox Jews have been so thoroughly assimilated into American society that they are free to emphasize their religious differences without the implication that this makes them outsiders. Thus "they could start thinking of establishing separate schools only when they reduced their claims to difference from all-encompassing ethnic-cultural to more limited religious dimensions."[57]

Fieldwork in several Jewish schools near Boston by my students made it clear that the nature and goals of Jewish education are still very much under negotiation. As with Catholic and Protestant schools in the United States and in the Netherlands, and as with the Salvation Army and other faith-based social service providers, the questions of character and identity are recurring and not resolvable by attaching a label or adopting a mission statement. Translation into the stuff of daily life and work, of treatment or pedagogy, of expectations and hopes, is supremely difficult. And it will not be accomplished without steering carefully between absorption by the welfare state and marginalization. Smith and Lipsky conclude wisely, "To combat totalitarianism from above, voluntary associations must achieve some success in solving societal problems, even if this means large bureaucracies and instrumental programs. But to combat the withdrawal of individuals from public life itself, voluntary associations need to remain small, informal, personal, and diverse. . . . Only in this way can the individual be drawn into a community of others who reflect together about their fundamental values and engage the public sphere in discourse about those values."[58]

---

[54] Archer, "Breaking for Tradition," 36–42, 38–39.
[55] Rauch, "Jewish Day School," 140.
[56] Avi Chai Foundation research cited by Archer, "Breaking for Tradition," 41.
[57] Rauch, "Jewish Day School," 141.
[58] Smith and Lipsky, *Nonprofits for Hire*, 305.

Summary

Professional norms and oversight by government may threaten the integrity of faith-based schools and agencies, but an even great threat is posed by loss of conviction on the part of staff and those who direct their activities. Secularization may also weaken the support that such organizations had drawn from their religious communities.

Such loss of conviction undermines precisely those qualities that can make a faith-based organization unusually effective.

Stephen Monsma's research shows how extensive is the participation of faith-based organizations in government funding programs, and that those that are most distinctively religious report relatively few problems as a result. He warns, however, that many are self-censoring beyond what is necessary or appropriate, and that government forbearance could end in unpredictable ways.

The Dutch discussions over the religious identity of schools (see also the interlude on neocorporatism) illustrate how complex the task of maintaining this identity can be, even in a policy context that provides ample protections and full funding. It is not a matter, as many American Christians assume, of simply adopting a curriculum that makes use of the Bible and stresses traditional values. Professional norms should be engaged, not avoided. As the director of an urban rescue mission told Amy Sherman, "I think our program should exceed what the secular realm does; we shouldn't try to get by on less because we're Christians."[59]

The task of working through how a school or an agency should translate its religious identity into the details of its life and work is an ongoing one. It cannot be completed once and for all, nor can it be imposed from without—though, as we saw in the case of the Salvation Army, a connection with a hierarchical organization may help to ensure that the task is taken seriously.

[59] Sherman, *Restorers of Hope*, 175–76.

8

RECOMMENDATIONS

> More than efficiency in provision is involved in program
> sponsorship. It is consequential whether governmental norms,
> market practices, or community associations govern social
> welfare provision in the broadest sense.
> (Smith and Lipsky, *Nonprofits for Hire*)

THIS STUDY began with seven questions:

1. Should government make a greater use of faith-based organizations to provide social services and education?

2. May the United States government make a greater use of faith-based organizations without overstepping the limits set by the First Amendment?

3. If it makes a greater use of faith-based organizations to provide social services and education, how should government behave to avoid spoiling their distinctive character and contribution?

4. What measures should government take to ensure that making a greater use of faith-based organizations does not lead to negative consequences, such as a decline in the quality and general availability of services or an increase in discrimination?

5. Should faith-based organizations seek government support for their social and educational ministries?

6. In accepting government support, how should faith-based organizations protect themselves from interference with their core mission and distinctive character?

7. How can faith-based organizations reconcile professional norms with the maintenance and expression of their core mission and distinctive character?

This chapter draws together what we can learn from the experience of faith-based agencies and organizations in the United States that receive public funds, from that of faith-based schools in the United States that do not but are regulated by government, and from that of other Western democracies that have lower barriers to cooperation between government and the faith-based schools and agencies.

1. Should Government Make a Greater Use of Faith-Based Organizations to Provide Social Services and Education?

Put another way, is it appropriate and desirable to have what has been called a "growing 'welfare economy' outside the 'welfare state,' "[1] not under the direct administration of government but providing public services? Should staff of nongovernmental agencies be making decisions that affect the eligibility of poor applicants for welfare benefits, for example, or the access of their children to free child care? Can a charter school, typically with a self-perpetuating board made up of parents and teachers, be considered a "public school" even though not subject to a school board elected by the general public?

There are two good reasons for making a greater use of nonprofit organizations of all kinds, including those with a religious character, and one that, though often advanced, is not so good. The not-so-good reason is that this will save money, since (for example) the per-pupil cost in Catholic and Evangelical schools is typically about half that of public schools. Economist Estelle James, who has studied the phenomenon of private schools and human service agencies in many countries, concludes that "the cost-reducing rationale, although plausible in the short run, may be more questionable in the long run, as fees and donations fall, professional staff members replace volunteer labor, and government standards are imposed as subsidies grow. . . . In the long run NPOs can be relied on for the large-scale delivery of social services only if they are heavily subsidized by government; and then they are likely to be subject to the same procedures and costs as government agencies."[2] Smith and Lipsky agree, writing that "in the long run, lower wages paid by private agencies should be seen as a temporary and transient feature of privatization. The dynamics of privatization contain within them pressures that will eventually surface to reduce or end wage disparities.[3] And this is only just: staff who choose to work in faith-based schools and agencies should not be required to make a financial sacrifice for doing so. Government neutrality should not have the result of making it more costly to act on the basis of belief than of nonbelief.

Respect for a Pluralistic Social Order

The first good reason for government to support work in the public interest carried out by faith-based agencies and schools is that it shows respect

[1] Hood and Schuppert, *Delivering Public Services*, 2.
[2] James, *Nonprofit Sector*, 7, 15.
[3] Smith and Lipsky, *Nonprofits for Hire*, 197.

for the appropriate relationship between a unitary state and a pluralistic society. It is worth recalling T. H. Marshall's wise comments, in 1949, about appropriate limits on the services that should be rendered by government agencies:

> perhaps the most important field in which their action is inappropriate is that where variety is a result, not merely of differences of need, but of differences of taste, belief and deep conviction as to the ways and means by which the need should be met. The history of education is shot with conflict arising from the fact that a state service cannot identify itself with a denominational religious faith. A statutory service for marriage guidance must meet similar difficulties, because a moral code is involved about which there is no unanimity of opinion. . . . As the State takes over more and more the task of providing material assistance, the function of the voluntary organizations will increasingly . . . be one of education. Not education in the prescribed subjects of the classroom, but education for living. . . . This function will remain theirs because it is one in which the State cannot safely meddle. But its retention in their hands will be justified only if they preserve freedom and variety within themselves.[4]

Both in England and in the United States, of course, these limits have increasingly been overstepped. As we will see in section 7, below, Marshall's final point is also important. That is, it is not enough for the state to respect diversity by supporting a variety of approaches to human services and education, if those who provide them do not make their own efforts to retain and express their distinctive character.

There are some spheres of life into which the state had better not meddle, except under highly exceptional circumstances. One is the family, another is the internal life of religious congregations, a third the relationship between a counselor and the one being counseled. Rightly considered, the relationship between pupils and the teacher to whom their parents entrust them should be able to claim equal privilege, but we have grown accustomed, in the United States, to seeing education as a state function of no more inherent mystery than collecting tolls.

The pluralist understanding of the social and political order that some derive from neo-Calvinist, others from Catholic sources, is in fact among our legacies from America's founding era. This understanding "sees a variety of social structures as having ontological status and, as such, possessing rights that all governments should recognize." On the basis of this understanding, "the pluralist creatively seeks to develop political processes and public policies that will not merely tolerate faith communities and associations and their individual members, but will integrate them fully—as reli-

---

[4] Marshall, *Class, Citizenship*, 357.

gious structures and persons—into the life of the body politic."[5] In our diversity, appropriately structured, James Madison and others believed, is our strength. At no point is it more necessary to protect the independence of civil society institutions from the state than when it comes to the shaping of values and ways of understanding the world.

In short, government should entrust the care and education of children and adults to the greatest extent possible to civil society institutions that reflect the diverse nature of the society, though without falling into the error of prejudging which institutions individuals will choose to turn to in their need or to educate their children. Because a person is Laotian or Jewish does not necessarily mean that she will turn to a Laotian or a Jewish social agency or school, but, within the limits of practicality, it is a good thing if that choice is available for those who want it.

Concern for Effectiveness

But if respect for *freedom* argues for providing services through civil society institutions, so does a concern for *effectiveness*. This is not to say that a private nonprofit is always more effective in providing services than is its government counterpart, but there does seem to be some tendency in that direction. Indeed, the same teacher or social worker may be more effective in one setting than in another. Wuthnow points out that "it makes a difference not only that a function such as religion or health or education is provided but also how (in which sector) that function is provided. The difference it makes may have more to do with the values that are expressed and dramatized than with the services actually rendered."[6] Something about the nature of institutions that are based upon shared values and voluntary association makes them able to have a more profound effect upon those they serve than do their counterparts that function on the basis of bureaucratic criteria and procedures.

It should be clear, therefore, that what we are talking about is not "privatization" in the usual sense of entrusting human services and education to the mercies of the market. Economic arguments are indeed made for the superior efficiency of market allocation of resources and of straight-out competition,[7] but efficacy in education or counseling is not the same thing as efficiency. It is true that the line between for-profit and nonprofit sectors is not as clear as is often assumed, but as Alan Wolfe appropriately points out, although "the market is a fantastically sensitive device for responding to changes in preference, . . . that is also what makes it problematic as a

---

[5] Monsma, *Positive Neutrality*, 198, 176.
[6] Wuthnow, "The Voluntary Sector," 8.
[7] Van Mierlo and Gerrichhauzen, "De toekomst van het particulier initiatief," 206.

moral code organizing obligations among strangers."[8] Good education, good programs for at-risk adolescents, good counseling and crisis intervention need to be able to make reference to forms of obligation (to oneself and to others) that are beyond the reach of market rationality.

A review of the growing role of "paragovernmental organizations" in providing public services in Europe concluded that "most countries are experimenting to some degree with ways of changing the 'classic' rule structure of core government bureaucracies into something more PGO-like."[9] That is, government itself is seeking to emulate some of the strengths—flexibility, responsiveness—of organizations that function in the quasi market of nongovernment public services. What it cannot do, however, is to emulate the intensity of those organizations that are based upon religious conviction, nor can it match their ability to communicate moral earnestness and a sense of the purposes of human life.

2. May the United States Government Make a Greater Use of Faith-Based Organizations without Overstepping the Limits Set by the First Amendment?

This is not the place to argue over constitutional law, but two points bear repeating. The first is that government, under our constitutional order, is to be *secular:* neutral with respect to religious and other forms of belief and opinion. It should not favor choices made on the basis of religious conviction, but neither should government make it more difficult to choose on that basis rather than on some other way of orienting oneself in life. But, unfortunately, as legal scholar Stephen Carter has pointed out, "in our sensible zeal to keep religion from dominating our politics, we have created a political and legal culture that presses the religiously faithful to be other than themselves, to act publicly, and sometimes privately as well, as though their faith does not matter to them." Neutrality should mean evenhandedness. "If neutrality means that the government cannot take steps to treat religious schools better than other schools, it surely means as well that the government cannot take steps to treat religious schools worse."[10]

A more sensible approach is taken by most other Western democracies, which simply treat decisions made on a religious basis as equivalent to any other decisions: no better, no worse. So if a group proposes to start a school in the Netherlands, the question government asks is whether the school meets the various criteria for public funding such as curriculum, compe-

[8] Wolfe, *Whose Keeper?* 103.
[9] Hood and Schuppert, *Delivering Public Services*, 248.
[10] Carter, *The Culture of Disbelief*, 3, 200.

tence of staff, and above all whether a sufficient number of parents indicate their intention of enrolling their children. Whether the school to be religious or not basically does not matter.[11] Parents have a right to public funding for a school in which they have confidence, and, if the school of their choice has a religious character, that does not constitute governmental preference for religion. What is at stake is freedom of conscience, not support for religious institutions. American policymakers would be sensible to take the same position.

The second point is that it is desirable to administer public funding in such a way that the decisions about the level of funding (if any) that goes to a particular school or agency is determined by the decisions of parents or clients and not by government. Education vouchers are an example: government does not allocate any funding directly to one school or another, but waits to see what decisions are made by parents and then funds accordingly on a per capita basis. There is a growing body of legal precedent indicating that such arrangements avoid the "entanglement" of government with religious organizations and protects its neutrality.

3. If It Makes a Greater Use of Faith-Based Organizations to Provide Social Services and Education, How Should Government Behave to Avoid Spoiling Their Distinctive Character and Contribution?

During the late sixties and the seventies, in the United States, government eagerly funded a wide range of nonprofit organizations to provide a variety of services (ironically, at the very same time that the federal courts were cutting away at public funding for nonpublic schools). At first, public funding came with few strings attached, under a variety of federal antipoverty initiatives that stressed grassroots initiative; quite a bit was stolen, more was wasted. The second wave of funding came from the states, as they deinstitutionalized mental hospital patients and sought to provide a wide range of services through nonprofits, many of which were newly founded for that purpose. In contrast with the federal funding, state funding tended to be much more tightly controlled; the state was not interested in funding experiments in community action, but in purchasing services; "state contracts are usually negotiated for very specific programs that allow nonprofit agencies little leeway."[12]

Overregulation is an almost irresistible feature of government arrangements with external service-providers, and one that can undermine the very

---

[11] Note that this is a recent development since my *Choice of Schools*.
[12] Smith and Lipsky, *Nonprofits for Hire*, 10.

purpose of turning to civil society institutions to provide public services. Officials may start with good intentions of making use of the flexibility and responsiveness of nongovernmental agencies, but recoil when it appears they will be held accountable for any problems that ensue. It is a fundamental rule of bureaucratic self-preservation that you can never be blamed if something went wrong when you were following prescribed procedures, and so it is tempting to impose ever-more-elaborated requirements upon external providers, as we are already seeing with charter schools. Handing over operational responsibility to nongovernmental organizations starts enthusiastically, but

> when it comes to concrete issues (court cases, urgent political demands, major scandals), such commitment is likely to weaken. Legislatures will start to demand day-to-day accountability. Political chiefs will become impatient with any obstacles placed in the way of carrying out their "orders of the day" in relation to their perception of that day's political needs. Law courts, which are never very friendly to "managerial" ideas if managerialism means more arbitrary decision-making, will continue to want core bureaucracies to observe stringent procedures in making decisions. Audit offices will want extensive documentation to be preserved, so that failures and shortcomings can be fully uncovered. . . . pressures of this kind often serve to make PGOs [paragovernmental organizations] more core-government-like over time, and perhaps may trigger off another progression towards even more autonomous PGOs; that is, under pressure from courts and audit offices, enterprises originally set up as independent from core government may come over time to resemble core government bureaucracies.[13]

Concerns have been expressed all over Western Europe that the growing role of government, its "continuously swelling arsenal of complicated requirements with respect to the organization and quality of education," will not only do harm to educational freedom but also limit the creative problem-solving that school staff and boards would otherwise undertake. As a Belgian legal scholar notes, "the education apparatus [of government] has obtained for itself an actual power, by which it no longer acts as a stimulator for the sake of pedagogical goals in a supple administrative climate—in accordance with the overall legal framework established by government—but sometimes constitutes itself as detailed norm-giver and unavoidable arbiter."[14]

"The character of the government/agent relationship [with external service-providers] is said to be changing" in Britain. "Informal relations of trust have been giving way to more formal, contractual relations based on

---

[13] Hood and Schuppert, *Delivering Public Services*, 249.
[14] De Groof, *De Grondwetsherziening van 1988 en het onderwijs*, 162.

explicit objectives and clear criteria of accountability. As a result, there is a distinct danger that the much-vaunted flexibility and innovativeness of the voluntary organizations might be compromised."[15]

Much depends upon the mechanism used to support and oversee provision of services by nonprofits. Payment or reimbursement for a service provided by a voluntary agency to an individual generally involves fewer measures of control than do direct grants or subsidies to the agency.[16] Whether in the form of a voucher or a third-party payment (in which case the client in effect "charges" the service to government rather than paying for it with a voucher), such arrangements can avoid the extensive entanglement usually associated with contracts, categorical grants, or subsidies. Government must still have some process for ensuring that publicly funded services are provided only by approved agencies, clinics, or schools, but there is no need for a public official to review budgets or make decisions between competing providers.

Of course, excessive supervision and interference can creep back in even with a voucher system, as it has under the contract-for-services system, which at one time was considered a model of hands-off management.

> For a while, contracting appeared to be a model for a marriage of the best of the public and nonprofit sectors. The public sector would provide the financing and the nonprofit sector would deliver the services. Hence service could be provided flexibly on a broad scale while still retaining community oversight, volunteer involvement, and alternative service programs. Yet contracting over time has evolved into quite a different policy strategy, with extensive government intervention in the affairs of nonprofit agencies, a shift of many nonprofit agencies from the informal to formal care systems, greater homogeneity of services within particular service categories, a diminished role of the board of directors in agency governance, and destabilization among nonprofit agencies."

As a result, although "supported by some as a device to reduce the size and influence of government, privatization as contracting instead has resulted in unprecedented involvement of government in the affairs of nonprofit organizations."[17]

What's more, contracting—and other arrangements between government and nonprofits—can create problems with accountability.

> [S]ervice outcomes are often very difficult to define and to measure. . . . This is why outputs—i.e., activities that easily lend themselves to quantification, such as the number of interviews, meals served, and hospital days are usually

---

[15] Beckford, "Great Britain," 40.
[16] Kramer, "Use of Government Funds," 229.
[17] Smith and Lipsky, *Nonprofits for Hire*, 215, 204.

substituted for outcomes. . . . Demands for information can be a particular problem for a small voluntary agency because it lacks the administrative resources to comply. . . . The fact that purchase of service arrangements may be more disadvantageous to a small agency is ironic because small size, flexibility, and informality are supposed to be the advantages of a voluntary organization. . . . to compete successfully and to comply with governmental regulations, the small agency must become more bureaucratic and must lose the very qualities that made it a desirable service provider.[18]

Measuring outputs is a poor way of ensuring accountability in education or the human services. For example, a school may report upon the number of students graduated or promoted to the next grade, but this says nothing about what they have actually learned or are capable of accomplishing. On the other hand, actual outcomes are notoriously difficult to measure in the human services, and more difficult than is often assumed in education—witness the heated controversies over standards and testing in the United States over the past decade and more.

Perhaps the essential quality for government officials in this respect (as in others) is a good measure of humility, a recognition that they do not know everything about how the services in question should be provided, nor can they measure or even specify other than in general terms the outcomes desired. Even more important, they cannot and should not specify the process by which the results are obtained, much less the worldview that should inform that process. The state's interest, after all, is in outcomes, whether demonstrated competencies or steady employment or improved social functioning. How these outcomes are achieved—extreme cases aside—should not be a concern of government officials.

One might wish that both Christian and secular groups would abandon claims to provide the only responsible form of education; ironically, it seems to be the secularists who are now the more intolerant in the United States. While the Christian Coalition, speaking for the so-called religious Right, expresses its support for the secular public school system while asking public funding for religious alternatives, many secularists question whether a faith-based school can ever provide an education fit for a free society.[19]

After all, one of the reasons why government should turn to nonprofit organizations, and especially those with some distinctive grasp on reality (whether religious or not), is because it recognizes the limits of its own competence. "Government . . . 'purchases' the greater responsiveness of

[18] Kramer, "Use of Government Funds," 233–34.
[19] Reed and Simonds, "Agenda of Religious Right"; Dwyer, *Religious Schools*.

the voluntary sector when it makes outright grants to nonprofit organizations or lets contracts with few strings attached."[20]

But this requires, as well, that government allow voluntary agencies the freedom to do what they know how to do best, and respect the religious basis of those for which that is fundamental. It must not penalize faith-based agencies or schools for being true to their founding commitments or ask them to pay for public support by abandoning those commitments. A democratic pluralism that "welcomes religion as a strong, robust force into the public realm, would expect religiously based schools to be 'pervasively sectarian.' "[21]

"How has it come about," Olasky asks, "that any activity funded by the government must be conducted as if atheism were the established religion? Why should we tolerate such bias against a vital dimension of our existence that has demonstrably made a difference in the lives of millions?" Why should faith-based schools and social agencies be expected to deny the core of their identity in order to continue to play the role that in fact they invented and have modeled for hundreds of years, in the new situation created by the expanded welfare state?

4. What Measures Should Government Take to Ensure That Making a Greater Use of Faith-Based Organizations Does Not Lead to Negative Consequences, Such as a Decline in Quality and Availability of Services or an Increase in Discrimination?

If schools and social agencies are encouraged to develop or to maintain a distinctive character—and some do so based upon religious understandings of their mission—the resulting diversity is likely to expand the range of approaches to education and social services that are considered legitimate. Problems arise when faith-based organizations insist upon their own definitions of effective practice, and these fall outside or directly violate the norms set up by the professions. As Olasky points out, "serious religious groups ... attribute their effectiveness not to niceness but to spiritual transformation brought about by worship, teaching, and theological advocacy," activities falling outside the norms of professional practice. Medicine can tolerate faith healing, but less secure professions are less tolerant of rivals to their interpretation of sound practice. As a result, "government

---

[20] Smith and Lipsky, *Nonprofits for Hire*, 218.
[21] Monsma, *Positive Neutrality*, 239.

funds may be used by religious groups that have set up religionless programs, government look-alikes that are rarely effective—but any program
that communicates to clients the need for religious conversion, no matter
how effective, faces a ban."[22]

On the other hand, as the faith-healing analogy suggests, there are dangers in the provision of services—especially to those who are vulnerable—
on the basis of untrained enthusiasm and undisciplined conviction. Free
societies find it difficult to judge to what extent nonprofessionals should
be prevented from providing "professional" services, especially as more and
more spheres of human interaction become professionalized. You can't sue
your brother-in-law for practicing law without a license when he gives you
bad advice, or your minister for malpractice when his spiritual counsel
doesn't produce a closer walk with God . . . or at least you can't do it yet!
The United States has, in general, leaned toward allowing considerable
scope for amateur provision of services, provided that no misrepresentation
of credentials is involved. Parents may teach their children at home, for
example, or send them to private schools with uncertified teachers, neither
of which is allowed under most circumstances in Western Europe.

Accountability

Perhaps the most difficult issue in this whole discussion is that of the appropriate scope, focus, and limits of government oversight of education and
human services. There is a natural inclination to apply the same criteria
and close controls that are used by government for its own operations,
but this method of preventing abuses within a bureaucracy, if applied to
nonprofits, would cripple their "potential virtues of autonomy, flexibility,
user-responsiveness and subsidiarity."[23]

American public policy tends to provide close supervision of what happens in public schools and very little supervision, in most states, of what
happens in nonpublic schools. If the reason for government involvement
is really concern for the education of all the nation's children, it is difficult
to see why such heavy-handed oversight is needed for some schools and so
little for others. Surely the fact that public funds are involved should not
be the decisive consideration; if that were all that were at stake, a financial
auditing system would be sufficient. The fact that government at all levels
is heavily involved in setting standards for the content of education—in
public schools—suggests that much more is at stake: a set of Enlightenment
beliefs about reshaping humanity through education. This agenda should
at last be seen as inconsistent with a free society; no elite, however well

---

[22] Olasky, *Renewing American Compassion*, 129, 128.
[23] Hood and Schuppert, *Delivering Public Services*, 254.

intentioned, should be able to use compulsory schooling to manipulate other people's children without their permission.[24]

It would be possible to argue that government should regulate nonpublic schools much more than it does now. There are efforts, usually sponsored by the professional education associations that are the primary representatives of the interests of public education, to treat them like public schools. This was the source of a major political crisis in France, in 1984; the new Socialist government sought to conform nonpublic schools to the public system, in "a single great unified system."[25]

One wonders how public education leaders have the nerve to claim that nonpublic schools should conform to their own floundering model. "Must a private school meet all of the requirements imposed on public schools before it can be considered capable of offering an adequate education? Yet it is public education that has come under severe condemnation during the past 30 years for poor performance."[26]

A better case can be made that the flourishing state of nonpublic education absent state regulation argues for setting the entire educational system free of the sort of detailed specification of inputs and process that so hobble our public school systems, particularly in large cities. Millions of parents have been making decisions about nonpublic schools for many years, with no serious problems resulting from this largely unregulated process. "Since the right to choose was given to parents and not the state, . . . they, rather than the state, should initially be allowed to pass judgment on the acceptability of the choice."[27] Why not trust teachers and principals in public schools to act as honorably as do those in the great majority of private schools, and trust parents to choose public schools with as much seriousness as millions now choose private schools?

With government support inevitably comes a measure of government supervision and control, not just in order to ensure that funds are spent appropriately but also because, from the perspective of policymakers, "the State cannot waive its right to inspect and approve a service whose efficient discharge is a matter of public policy." This was the case, T. H. Marshall tells us, even in England, despite having "evolved a system or tradition by which the grant of public money is not necessarily accompanied by the exercise of public control." In 1949, as the British welfare state took shape, he warned that "we should not . . . assume that, as the sums increase, the control will not increase also."[28]

[24] Glenn, *Myth of Common School*.
[25] Ibid., 264–70.
[26] Randall, *Private Schools and Public Power*, 92.
[27] Ibid., 93.
[28] Marshall, *Class, Citizenship*, 353–54.

The Dutch constitution allows different requirements for the quality of public and subsidized nonpublic schools, but their standards must be equally high. The Dutch hold, reasonably, that nonpublic schools need not be modeled on public schools, but that public authorities can appropriately supervise whether they are producing equivalent results. Government can also ensure that nonpublic schools function in a way consistent with the public interest, though Postma points out that this is such a wide-open concept that it should be invoked very cautiously.[29] The requirement of adequate quality applies to all schools, as it should, whether or not they receive public funding. In fact, as we have seen, almost all Dutch schools are fully funded by the government, whether operated by government or by private associations.

In the Netherlands, as in most of its European neighbors and in the United States,[30] schools are accountable for meeting a great variety of government requirements specifying the number of hours different subjects must be taught, the qualifications and duties of staff, and the reports that must be filed. They are not, however, accountable for particular outcomes, except implicitly and indirectly. That is, if their pupils fare badly on the nationwide tests, government officials might take that as a signal that extra attention was needed, but it is the pupils who bear the direct consequences of poor performance in abridged access to further educational options. There are no negative consequences for the funding of the school they have attended—indeed, commonly they receive additional funding if their pupils are doing poorly.

Problems with Accountability

The difficulty with holding schools accountable is that every approach that has been tried has unanticipated consequences that create new problems. As a result, a carefully calibrated cocktail of approaches should be used, with no one element allowed to overpower the others. It has seemed to many of us concerned with educational policy that clear *outcome standards* that were limited to the essentials and could be measured in valid and unburdensome ways would make it possible to give much more autonomy to schools and teachers. Or *professional standards* could be raised and thus make it unnecessary for the state to intervene except in cases of manifest failure and abuse.

[29] Postma, *Handboek*, 109–13.

[30] As we have seen, this oversight applies equally to public and nonpublic schools in most of Europe, but unequally in the United States, where lack of public funding has in practice resulted in much less government oversight.

Democrats in Congress have promoted "delivery standards" that would require that the inputs provided to schools—facilities, materials, teacher qualifications and experience—be somehow equalized (and more than equalized to respond to the greater needs of some groups of pupils). The weakness of the delivery standards approach—aside from the fact that one cannot imagine how it could be achieved in an educational system with more than fifteen thousand autonomous school districts—is that we do not know what inputs and what levels of inputs are essential for the education of every child, and what inputs are essential or desirable for some children but not for others. Simply to try to make every school as much like every other school as possible is not a formula for effective and responsive education. Better to provide an appropriate level of funding to every school (adjusted for circumstances and the nature of the enrolment) and let the decisions about how it will be used be made by those on the scene, as in charter schools.

Raising professional standards and working conditions is very desirable—American teachers are less qualified and less respected (though not, at least when experienced, less well paid) that those in most comparable societies—but that is insufficient to ensure accountability. Most teachers are not likely to press for fundamental instructional change, even when given considerable autonomy through "school-based management."[31] After all, many observers have pointed out that schools tend to be operated for the benefit, not of the children, but of the adults who work in them.

The limits of the professionalization strategy and of a focus on resources has convinced many education reformers that clear outcome standards are essential, together with valid means of determining whether schools have enabled their pupils to meet these standards, and consequences for staff—not just for pupils!—when the standards are not met. The same logic has led to a stress on outcomes for social service providers as well. "Rather than holding contractors to process standards (such as what kinds of professional degrees staff members must hold), which tend to force conformity on providers, governments should strive to hold contractors accountable to outcomes."[32]

It is important to distinguish between "output" standards, such as that a family was removed from public assistance or an individual was placed in

---

[31] Hannaway, "Management Decentralization."
[32] Smith and Lipsky, *Nonprofits for Hire*, 228.

a job or a student graduated from high school, and "outcome" standards that tell us whether the family remains self-supporting or the individual becomes a successful employee or the student has learned what she needs to do well in work or further study. Outputs are easy to measure, outcomes very difficult.

Unfortunately, as Americans have recently learned, it is easier to talk about accountability for educational results than to put a system in place that provides sufficiently reliable and valid information to serve as the basis for holding staff accountable. The same limitations have been experienced in designing an accountability system for social services; if anything, this is more elusive. In both spheres, it is inherently difficult to specify all of the desired outcomes with sufficient precision, and this can involve value judgments that are highly controversial. To be fair to staff, these outcomes would have to adapted in some way to the starting point of those they are working with, to measure the "value added" by the school. An inner-city school may be doing extremely well to achieve test results that would be a source of embarrassment to a suburban school. On the other hand, do we really want to have different expectations for pupils based upon their social class background? That can be an unkind kindness, leading to failure to provide them the opportunity to learn much of what other pupils learn. Care must be taken either way.

PEER ACCOUNTABILITY

Standards, like good professional training and adequate resources, are an important element in the accountability mix, but incapable of sufficient precision and scope to stand alone. Three other control elements have important parts to play and are not sufficiently employed by American policy. One is *peer accountability,* as widely employed for accreditation in American secondary and higher education. While it should not stand alone, since it can lend itself to mutual back-scratching, there is considerable merit to a process that brings practitioners into direct contact with each other and with each other's work. Not much in how a school or agency operates can be hidden from a team of visitors who are themselves experienced in the same sort of operation. And a peer accountability system can take into account the distinctive character of the institution under review by ensuring that some of the members of the review team are sympathetic to its goals and methods. Evaluation by peers has solid advantages, "especially for judgements of quality, for which no simple performance statistics can be devised, and in which whatever decision is made will be open to prima facie challenge."[33] It is more difficult to dismiss

---

[33] Hood and Schuppert, *Delivering Public Services,* 257–58.

the criticisms of a group of peers than those of a government official who "really doesn't understand"!

GOVERNMENT INSPECTORS

There does seem also to be a place for *government-appointed inspectors* who have a stable relationship with a group of institutions and can advise, praise, and admonish as occasion indicates. In Britain, Germany, Belgium, the Netherlands, France and other countries with strong education systems, the school inspector plays an important role. Some are especially concerned with probationary teachers, others have special assignments such as the schooling of immigrant children. Typically, they have no direct authority over the schools they inspect, but their reports may be the basis for outside intervention and are generally taken very seriously.[34]

INFORMED CHOICE

A third control mechanism that can supplement the five already mentioned in a powerful way is *informed choice* by parents and other "consumers" of services.[35] This is not to call for a pure "market" in education or social services, but to suggest that people (including poor people) are quite capable of judging whether they and their children are being treated with respect and concern and—with information on the virtues of the available alternatives—of making sound choices.[36] What sort of information addresses their primary concerns, and how best to make it available, are complex questions that cannot be answered here, but we do not have to imagine the answers. After all, millions of urban parents over the past several decades have taken advantage of "controlled choice" and magnet schools, and what we can learn from those experiences has by no means been exhausted.[37]

Equity Effects

A related concern that government should take into account is whether the way in which services—including especially education—are provided has the result of exacerbating social class and other differences within the soci-

---

[34] Braster, *De inspecteur en de school;* for discussion of school inspectors and other accountability devices in twenty-five countries, see Glenn, "Common Standards."

[35] For a justification of the metaphor of parents as education consumers, see Ballion, *Les consommateurs d'école.*

[36] Glenn, McLaughlin, and Salganik, *Parent Information.*

[37] The studies included in Peterson and Hassel, *Learning from School Choice,* are far superior to those in Fuller, Elmore, and Orfield, *Who Chooses?*

ety. Nonprofit organizations tend to focus upon serving particular groups of clients and responding very well to their needs, while government places primary value on equity and universal coverage. As a result,

> the absence of equity considerations as the driving force within nonprofit agencies is more and more difficult for government officials to tolerate. Consequently, government administrators strive, through regulation, negotiation, and coercion, to make the services and clients of nonprofit agencies funded by government compatible with the government's goal of targeting for equity and effectiveness. . . . Imposition of these criteria can conflict with the norms of the traditional and new community nonprofit agencies, which seek to be responsive to the individual within the parameters established by agency mission and the likelihood of successful treatment outcomes.[38]

When government funds religious and ethnic organizations to provide social services, this is often justified by pointing to the special ability of these organizations to reach particular groups of clients and to gain their confidence. Minority organizations, in particular, are presumed to have a superior ability to reach out to those sharing their ethnicity. It is not necessary that all services supported with public funds be available to all comers, provided that all who need or want those services have access to equivalent services. "Programming in the name of diversity of approaches and responsiveness to clients is acceptable if it can be shown that certain kinds of selectivity would increase effectiveness, and that similar services were available to those who would be otherwise eligible."[39]

Providing social services though such groups is common in the United States, but proposals that government fund *schools* run by the same sorts of sponsors are adamantly (and, so far, successfully) opposed on the grounds that this would be socially divisive and a betrayal of the mission of public education. In fact, however, reaching poor families and gaining their confidence is at least as important in education as it is in social services, and public schools are conspicuously failing to do so. How many urban teachers have ever been in the homes or the churches of their pupils, have ever eaten a meal with their families?

But won't there be a lot of bizarre developments if we open the door to sponsorship of publicly funded schools by groups or institutions of a religious character? Here's where the experience with social services is instructive: there is little reason to believe that public funding of thousands of faith-based agencies and organizations to provide counseling, day care, services for the elderly, and dozens of other services has resulted in abuse either of the purposes for which the funds were intended or of the consciences of clients.

---

[38] Smith and Lipsky, *Nonprofits for Hire*, 141–42.
[39] Ibid., 220.

If that were a danger for education, we would expect it to have appeared already in the largely unregulated world of nonpublic education. But according to Peter Cookson (no friend of vouchers), "there is little evidence that school choice automatically leads to the foundation of bizarre schools. In fact, most alternative [that is, unconventional] public schools have been founded by public school educators who have a deep commitment to children and find that the conventional public school system stifles creativity. . . . there is little evidence from the private sector that parents will choose schools that advocate hatred or follow policies that are not in the best interest of children."[40] Similarly, Vance Randall reports that "there is no empirical evidence . . . that parents with children in private schools or private schools themselves have harmed the children by providing an inadequate education. . . . This study has not found, in the review of court cases or readings, any documented evidence that attendance at a private elementary or secondary school has ever harmed a student, educationally or physically."[41]

Would public funding of nonpublic schools create new social class inequities? Nonpublic schools in the United States do serve a rather more affluent population than that served by public schools, though this is usually exaggerated by those who take elite "independent" schools to be typical of the nonpublic sector; in fact these represent a little more than 10 percent of all the private school pupils in the country. More typically, the families who use nonpublic schools cannot afford to live in the suburbs with the high-flying public schools; it is, after all, much less expensive to send a child to Phillips Andover Academy—even without the scholarships often provided to low-income students—than to the public high school in Andover, which requires students to be residents of that expensive community. Contrary to a widespread impression, it is the public schools in affluent suburbs and not private schools—except for the minority of "prep schools"—which represent the elite option in American education. "In 1988 roughly 70 percent of all eighth-graders with family incomes above $75,000 . . . attended public schools, whereas 6 percent attended prep schools."[42]

Experience shows that direct public provision of schooling and of social services does not prevent social class or racial differentiation in whom is served, where, and how adequately, nor does private provision necessarily increase it. As economist Estelle James's comparative international studies have shown, "Provision of services by NPOs often leads to social segmentation along cultural or ideological lines, given their source of demand and entrepreneurship. However, it need not stratify along economic (class)

[40] Cookson, *School Choice*, 124–25.
[41] Randall, *Private Schools and Public Power*, 90.
[42] Powell, *Lessons from Privilege*, 92.

lines. Indeed, in Holland and Sweden NPOs and government agencies serve much the same socioeconomic mix; contrary to the American situation, private schools and other services do not 'cream' and are not 'elite.' "[43]

In the United States, researchers have found that nonpublic schools and classes are—counterintuitively—less segregated by race than are public schools. In 1992, "more than half (54.5 percent) of public school students were in classes with fewer than 10 percent minority students or more than 90 percent minority students. Fewer private school students, 41.1 percent, were in these highly segregated classes."[44] This can be explained in part by the fact that attracting clients or pupils on the basis of religious considerations may have the effect of drawing from a more diverse population than does drawing them on the basis of residential areas or of reputation. Religious identification tends to be more diverse than most other social groupings, and middle-class parents who will take their children out of a school with a growing proportion of poor or minority children if school quality is the only consideration, will often stay with a faith-based school that has a strong community ethos.

Equity arguments are frequently used against public support for nongovernmental providers with a religious identity, because of their preference for serving clients or families who share their premises about the goals of human life, or who share their ethnic or racial identification, as in the case of "Afro-centric" schools. The grounds for the objection tends to shift: is it concern about those who would not be served by a particular institution, or concern that those who are served would somehow be excluded from the mainstream? The socializing function of schools makes religious or ethnic identification a particularly difficult issue in education; it has been more easily accepted in social services. The "Charitable Choice" solution seems wise: fund faith-based organizations and allow them to choose their staff, board members, and methods, but protect the rights of conscience of their clients and ensure that alternate providers are available. Government support for race-based organizations, while more common, in fact raises graver questions that go beyond our present scope.[45]

Financial Accountability

One necessary dimension of public support for nonpublic providers of services is to ensure that funding is not misspent. Government itself makes it very difficult for its officials to make purchases, employ even temporary staff, or let contracts. To require nonpublic grantees or contractors to put

---

[43] James, *Nonprofit Sector*, 10.
[44] Greene, "Civic Values," 97.
[45] Glenn, "Minority Schools on Purpose."

in place equally elaborate procedures would be inconsistent with their scale and style and would almost guarantee that they become as inflexible and ineffective as government itself. On the other hand, any financial scandals involving public funds are followed by demands for tightened controls. This was, as noted above, a weakness of many of the programs funded during the War on Poverty and helped to discredit the overall effort. It cannot be assumed that every organization that proclaims a high-minded purpose is being operated for that purpose alone, and many nonprofits have weak structures of internal accountability. They are particularly susceptible to self-serving manipulation by their staff. "The rules of the charity or voluntary association form of enterprise are built on the assumption that the members of the association are primarily other-regarding rather than opportunistic, or that members can effectively keep the directorate in check. However, if those assumptions are not fulfilled in practice—if the company, charitable enterprise or voluntary association is no more than a public bureaucracy clad for reasons of convenience in mufti (as it were); if there is no competition in practice, no altruistic ethic, perhaps no real 'members' in an independent sense—such organizational forms are far more vulnerable to producer group opportunism."[46]

This is often the case with advocacy groups that claim to represent constituencies but are in fact self-appointed. They may take positions on public issues—like the opposition of civil rights organizations to parent choice of schools—which are directly contrary to those of their rank and file. The Ford Foundation provided many millions of dollars to establish Latino advocacy organizations, including the National Council of La Raza, the Mexican American Legal Defense and Educational Fund, the Puerto Rican Legal Defense and Educational Fund, and the Southwest Voter Registration Education Project, which managed to function without accountability to a grassroots membership; this may in fact have impeded the emergence of real political mobilization among Latinos, as it has obscured the policy discussions around immigration and bilingual education.[47]

One of the many advantages of vouchers and other arrangements that put the power to purchase services from nongovernment organizations with public funds in the hands of individuals is that they greatly reduce the potential for financial abuse. Each parent who hands over a voucher for schooling or day care knows whether her particular child is being served, and will notice if the level of service provided is conspicuously below what other parents are receiving from other centers or schools. By contrast, it is very difficult for government officials to keep track of the

[46] Hood and Schuppert, *Delivering Public Services*, 12–13.
[47] See Geyer, "The Death of Citizenship," 59–71, 62; for an unrepentant inside account, see Nicolau and Santiestevan, "Looking Back."

quality of performance: they can count the number of beds that are filled in a homeless shelter, but not whether those sheltered are treated with respect and concern.

Alternative Modes of Service and Control

In brief, reliance upon nonprofit organizations and agencies to provide public services requires methods of ensuring accountability that differ from those used within government. This can be hard for some officials to accept, since "it is assumed that public services—services provided collectively to some public, or on the basis of government's legal authority—are provided by public sector bureaucracies in a uniform 'civil service' mould."[48] As we have seen, the uniformity that may be a virtue in government provision of services is inconsistent with the strengths of nonprofits, and especially those with a religious identity.

A combination of accountability measures should replace the approach characteristic of internal government management. Clear *outcome standards* (not out*puts*) and ways of measuring their accomplishment, *professionalization of staff*, and—within reason—*delivery standards* that ensure that adequate resources are available should be combined with *peer review, government-appointed inspectors*, and *informed choice* by those they seek to serve.

5. Should Faith-Based Organizations Seek Government Support for Their Social and Educational Ministries?

There is considerable resistance to the idea of accepting government support in Evangelical circles, largely for the reasons discussed in the preceding chapters. This hesitation is shared by some involved with Catholic social ministries who believe that Catholic Charities has made too many compromises with government regulators in order to qualify for funding. While most supporters of Catholic schools believe that vouchers would be to their benefit, there are some who are concerned that, even without public funding, many Catholic schools have lost much of their distinctiveness. It is among Evangelicals, however, that the strongest reservations seem to exist. In some circles relics of anti-Catholic sentiment lead them to oppose school vouchers because they would benefit parochial schools, but it is safe to say that their primary concern is that with public funding would come unacceptable new requirements. Many who have sacrificed long to create and support faith-based schools or person-to-person ministries believe that

---

[48] Hood and Schuppert, *Delivering Public Services*, 1.

something essential would be lost if they entered into any sort of association with government.

The primary issues at the moment center on how government regulators might interpret antidiscrimination requirements to interfere with how they select staff (especially around the question of homosexuality and other "lifestyle" issues) and to forbid the explicitly religious aspects of their work.

Faith-based organizations providing human services have an additional concern: that the sudden interest in their taking on some of the tasks that government has performed in the recent past may simply be asking them to take over responsibility for functions that they are not equipped to carry out. Some of those in policy circles concerned to "end welfare as we know it" have spoken too lightly about religious congregations and other nonprofit organizations taking over responsibilities that are far beyond their capacity. And some of these responsibilities would change the nature of the relationship between these groups and those in need. Determining eligibility for cash benefits, for example, is not a task that many faith-based organizations are eager to take on. "If people say they are hungry, or homeless, or have been recently assaulted and are fearful for their safety, nonprofit organizations are inclined to accept such testimony as sufficient. Government officials . . . cannot tolerate such an accepting attitude."[49]

Although these concerns are all reasonable, there are also good reasons why faith-based organizations—especially those that recognize the biblical mandate to care for the poor and vulnerable—should respond positively to opportunities to obtain public funding for aspects of their work, always provided that they can do so on terms consistent with their distinctive character. There are some things that government does well, but others that it does not, and those who are in a position to do a more effective job for the benefit of those in need should not hold back.

As Lamar Alexander pointed out in his introduction to the report of the National Commission on Philanthropy and Civic Renewal, "the era of big government is now proclaimed to be over mostly because we have come to realize that government can't solve the moral problems that worry us the most today. Government may replace income by offering Food Stamps, but government is not so good at helping someone get on his or her feet and stay there, to find and keep a job, to reject drugs, to develop willpower, or to love a child."[50] Government can often do very well tasks that require applying universal criteria in an evenhanded way, but it does not do so well at responding to individuals in their infinite particularity. As Osborne and Gaebler put it in an influential book, "the third sector [contrasted with government and the market] tends to be best at performing tasks that gen-

[49] Smith and Lipsky, *Nonprofits for Hire*, 123–24.
[50] National Commission on Philanthropy and Civic Renewal, *Giving Better*, 9.

erate little or no profit, demand compassion and commitment to individuals, require extensive trust on the part of customers or clients, need hands-on, personal attention . . . and involve the enforcement of moral codes and individual responsibility for behavior."[51]

While there are certainly structural barriers to opportunity for poor families, for the handicapped and the addicted, for those whose race or national origin makes them subject to discrimination, it has become increasingly obvious that the choices people make have a major effect upon their life chances. Faith-based organizations are especially well equipped to affect how people make choices. In an important new study of the relationship between poverty and school achievement, Susan Mayer concluded that "parental income is not as important to children's outcomes as many social scientists have thought. This is because the parental characteristics that employers value and are willing to pay for, such as skills, diligence, honesty, good health, and reliability, also improve children's life chances, independent of their effect on parents' income. Children of parents with these attributes do well even when their parents do not have much income."[52]

In many cases, faith-based human service agencies and congregations help to develop the characteristics that enable children or adults to take advantage of the opportunities available. They cannot substitute for income maintenance and other functions that government is best equipped to carry out, but they can do much that government cannot. If public funding will enable them to expand greatly the number of those they can help, and if it offered on terms that respect the distinctive character of the program, it should be treated as a "Macedonian call" (Acts 16:9) to "come over and help us"!

Research on Catholic schools, as we have seen, shows that they can be especially effective with groups of pupils who are not well served by the urban public schools. Bryk and his associates found that "the achievement advantage of white over minority students . . . increases in public high schools during the last two years of schooling, whereas the minority gap actually decreases in Catholic schools." In general, "students' personal and academic background play a more substantial role in the public sector in determining subsequent academic experiences."[53] But hundreds of inner-city Catholic schools have been forced to close for financial reasons in recent years, and most are in jeopardy; it would be a shame for them to refuse public funding that would enable them to continue to serve poor and minority children effectively.

---

[51] Osborne and Gaebler, *Reinventing Government*, 46.
[52] Mayer, *What Money Can't Buy*, 2–3.
[53] Bryk, Lee, and Holland, *Catholic Schools*, 247, 256.

Less visible, but also often dramatically effective, are the "independent neighborhood schools," many of them faith-based, that serve thousands of inner-city children; these schools are only just beginning to be recognized for their contributions to building community as well as educating children. It seems highly likely that, if public funds were available, these schools would proliferate and also enrich their educational offerings. In so doing, they would help to rebuild the distressed civil society of our inner-city areas.[54] Given their commitment to serve poor and working-class children and adults well, community-based schools and agencies should not be shy about accepting public funds *if* offered on terms that respect their distinctive character.

6. In Accepting Government Support, How Should Faith-Based Organizations Protect Themselves from Interference with Their Core Mission and Distinctive Character?

"If offered on terms that respect their distinctive character" is a big "if," of course. Government is always driven toward the application of uniform criteria, but the genius of nonprofits—especially those with a religious or ethnic community orientation—is that they respond to the way in which individuals or groups of individuals are different and do not fit into uniform molds. "Both government and private agencies may seek to be responsive to clients' individual needs, but government agencies are more constrained than private agencies in this regard, because challenges on the grounds that all clients are not receiving the same services are more potent in the public sector."[55]

To the extent that nonprofits are forced or influenced to conform to the model set by government-provided social services or education, something valuable may be lost. What we could (fashionably) call "institutional biodiversity" would undoubtedly be reduced. "Uniformity has the effect of diminishing the extent to which the voluntary sector functions as a laboratory of innovation once a service area has been established as appropriate for government funding."[56]

Nonprofit organizations that were founded primarily in order to provide services under contract with government know what they are getting into and usually have no hesitation changing their priorities or their modes of work when government's expectations change. The situation is quite

---

[54] Institute for Independent Education, *Road to Success;* Glenn, "Free Schools."

[55] Smith and Lipsky, *Nonprofits for Hire*, 122.

[56] Ibid., 135.

different when the way an organization works is closely bound to the self-understanding upon which it is based and the purposes for which it was set up. In such cases, mission shift could be disastrous—but may be difficult to resist if the organization has become overly dependent upon public funds. Marvin Olasky warns that "repeatedly, the lure of governmental funds has made it hard for organizations to remain dedicated to compassion that is challenging, personal, and spiritual. . . . one goal of those who care about mediating structures should be to change Washington's rules so that religious charities are freed from discrimination not only overt but subtle as well."[57]

One of the community-oriented agencies discussed by Smith and Lipsky is the Ecumenical Social Action Committee, started to meet various community needs in Jamaica Plain, a Boston neighborhood. In 1971, sixteen out of the seventeen board members were neighborhood church lay activists and pastors; I was one of them. But over time the work became more and more professionalized, as our staff angled for government funds to carry out ambitious—and useful—projects. "By 1985 only nine out of 25 board members had church links, and the president and vice-president were corporate executives."[58] ESAC survived, but it was no longer able to mobilize grassroots support from churches, or to represent authentically to government the organized community life of the neighborhood.

Holding On to the Vision

What can we learn from the experience of ESAC and hundreds of other faith-based agencies and organizations that have lost their distinctive character and become handmaids of government and secular foundations? One lesson is the importance of constantly referring back to the founding vision of the organization, its mission, in making decisions related to practice and to priorities. This means that the mission-statement must be concrete and specific, not simply a set of high-sounding intentions, and it should make clear what the organization is *not*.

Resisting Temptation

A second lesson is that the organization must be willing to say no to opportunities to do good or to expand its staff and visibility, if these will seduce it from its fundamental mission. Sometimes government or other funding sources will seek to hire a nonprofit agency to carry out tasks that it would like to see done, but that have little to do with the agency's real competence

---

[57] Olasky, "Corruption of Religious Charities," 104.
[58] Smith and Lipsky, *Nonprofits for Hire*, 78, 93.

or fundamental purpose. A community-based Hispanic agency in Boston came to grief over a generous contract to manage services to children at risk: its organizational structure was not sufficiently developed to keep track of the complex and sensitive tasks involved. A rather informal structure was one of its strengths in relating to its constituency, but proved inadequate when the organization took on inappropriate responsibilities. Children came to grief through its inefficiency, which seemed to illustrate the generalization that "Hispanic nonprofits . . . for both ideological and practical reasons, have resisted developing strong management and organizational systems for fear of becoming too bureaucratic."[59]

Style of Service

In particular, faith-based organizations must not grow apologetic about the demands that they make upon those whom they serve, since that is in fact part of their strength. "Church-based homeless shelters that offer spiritual challenge as well as material help have a hard time competing against government-financed shelters, especially when the latter do not conclude that some lifestyles, such as alcoholism or drug addiction, are inferior to others."[60] Addicted men and women will naturally prefer to take advantage (literally) of shelters that make no demands upon them, but it continues to be valid for churches to provide an alternative for those who are ready to submit themselves to loving discipline in order to change their lives.

Employment Decisions

A third and absolutely crucial lesson is that the organization must insist upon its distinctive mission in making employment decisions. This becomes increasingly difficult as an organization's complexity requires professional management, since it goes against both professional and managerial norms to hire people on the basis of their beliefs rather than their competence alone. But an organization that does not take great care over the composition of its staff in relation to the beliefs and values that are intended to inform its work will soon find that they have been frittered away.

Can a school or agency qualify as sufficiently religious to enjoy the exemption from the prohibition on discrimination based upon religion, without thereby being disqualified, as too "pervasively religious," from participating in government-funded programs. This is something of a Catch-22; it appears that faith-based programs qualify as providers of educational and

[59] Gonzalez Borrero, "Management of Hispanic Nonprofit Organizations," 117.
[60] Olasky, "Corruption of Religious Charities," 93.

social services only by disclaiming any intention of being resolutely religious but, in so doing, they may no longer be entitled to choose staff on the basis of religious commitment and so many drift further and further away from their original character . . . and from what made them especially effective. Or they can insist upon religious distinctiveness and reinforce it through hiring coreligionists, but thereby be disqualified from consideration for government contracts or many foundation and United Fund grants.

While the recently adopted Charitable Choice provision of federal welfare legislation may ease this dilemma for faith-based social agencies, it does nothing for religious schools. The Supreme Court has held that schools with any religious connection whatsoever must—sight unseen—be considered "pervasively religious" and thus ineligible for public funding. The Kamehameha Schools in Hawaii could presumably not receive public funds because, as schools with a religious identity, they are presumed to be pervasively sectarian, but they (as we have seen) cannot discriminate on the basis of religion in its hiring policies to preserve their religious identity because they are not sectarian enough!

Standing Up to Government

Government requirements can be resisted, often with success. After all, government may come to be as dependent upon faith-based organizations as they are upon public funding, if not more so. Much of what the Salvation Army does, for example, could not be done by government officials and would be unattractive to for-profit organizations operating by market calculation. The federal welfare reforms of 1988 and 1996 have depended heavily "upon the development in the fifty states of nonprofit organizations able to supply job training, remedial education, job finding, and child care. Indeed, when public officials—state, local, and federal—want to provide social services today, they expect to seek out nonprofit organizations to provide them."[61]

Nor is it always necessary for faith-based agencies to act as though they were secular and to compete on the basis of cost efficiency alone. After all, "when it comes to purchasing the care and control of drug addicts, the safety and nurturing of children, the relief of hunger and the regulation of family life (through child protective activities) from private agencies, other values than efficiency are at stake,"[62] and some faith-based agencies and organizations are well positioned to provide what is most needed. At least

---

[61] Smith and Lipsky, *Nonprofits for Hire*, 213.
[62] Ibid., 11.

they can do so if government officials get over their nervousness about organizations whose underlying motivations may seem to them irrational and even dangerous, and if the organizations themselves do not compromise away what gives them their flavor in order to assuage this nervousness.

What we have called the "civil society strategy" depends, for its effects, upon the extent to which the faith-based and community-based nonprofits are successful in incarnating a form of service or education that government cannot do as well—*not* becoming a pale reflection of or a cheaper substitute for what government itself does.

7. How Can Faith-Based Organizations Reconcile Professional Norms with the Maintenance and Expression of Their Core Mission and Distinctive Character?

Professionalization is in many ways a very good thing, offering enhanced skills and also norms that can protect the interests of vulnerable clients and schoolchildren. But it can easily result in substituting purposes, methods, and understandings of human life that are inconsistent with those that the agency or school is intended to represent. And, in so doing, it may in fact make the agency or school less effective in some important ways. For example, if volunteers are effectively crowded out of the provision of social services, there may be a loss of person-to-person connections that can make all the difference in turning a client's life around.

To prevent such negative effects from professionalization, at least the following measures seem necessary.

Involved Boards

The board of a faith-based or community-based institution should ensure that it does not surrender responsibility for articulating its purposes and for ensuring that those purposes are faithfully translated into action. It has become received wisdom in the field of "administrative science" that boards should set global policy but stay out of how it is carried out. Certainly board interference with operational details can be a problem, but in fact those details tend to *become* the policy as it is actually experienced, and they require regular and careful attention if a faith-based agency or school is not to become conformed to the norms of its secular counterparts.

And this implies, in turn, that great care must be taken in appointing new board members. Organizations that receive public funding often come under considerable pressure to make their boards more "representative," and even those that do not seek support from government may hope to increase their contributions by adding board members with access to corporate and personal wealth. Those motivated by generosity or public-spiritedness to serve on a board and raise money for a school or social agency may not take with sufficient seriousness the premises upon which its work is based. For example, they may be uncomfortable with what seems to be a judgmental attitude toward pupils or clients who will not abide by the expectations that make it possible for the organization to function . . . and to change lives.

Professional Self-Understanding

Also crucially important, though more remote from the daily life of faith-based organizations, is the self-definition of the professions, which in turn shape how their staff have come to understand the goals and requirements of their jobs. There is major intellectual work to be done by those who train staff for faith-based schools and agencies. Too often they accept the norms prevalent in their professions with an added dose of personal piety that does little to sustain a truly alternative approach. If it is true that agencies and schools that proclaim their religious identity actually are in some fundamental way different than their secular counterparts because they rest upon a different understanding of human "nature and destiny," it should be possible to articulate that and make it the basis for professional training as well as practice. If there is no such difference, the rationale for making greater use of their capacity to serve the public good becomes very shaky, and it is unlikely they will be capable of resisting accommodation to the norms of government and of secular professionalism.

Peer Accountability

Peer accountability, while it can create pressures to conform to professional norms, can also sustain an alternative, faith-based approach to education or social service if there is a peer network organized institutionally to validate that approach. A good examples of such a network is the "Unie" in the Netherlands, which for more than a century has worked with Protestant schools to help them to sustain and express their religious character. Several such networks function in the same way in the United States, setting standards for Evangelical Protestant schools and their staff that are accepted voluntarily by those schools that choose to seek membership, and that are backed up by training programs focused upon how particular sets of faith-commitments can be expressed in curriculum and school life. Recognition by these networks is valued and serves the participants both in recruiting staff and students and also in dealing with state education officials. The corresponding Catholic networks are somewhat more hierarchical, but function in much the same fashion, and there are several networks of Jewish schools. In social service, the International Union of Gospel Missions is a good example of mutual support and accountability in preserving a distinctive focus.

Putting Them Together

A strong and engaged board, then, clarity about the distinctive understanding of human nature and its needs upon which the organization is based, professional norms that are congruent with that understanding, training that supports those norms, and peer support. Faith-based schools and agencies that exemplify those qualities are well positioned to maintain their integrity and expand the reach and quality of their services in partnership with government.

REFERENCES

Adriaansens, H. P. M., and A. C. Zijderveld. *Vrijwillig initiatief en de verzorgingsstaat* (Voluntary initiative and the welfare state). Deventer: Van Loghum Slaterus, 1981.

Akkermans, P. W. C. *Onderwijs als Constitutioneel Probleem* (Education as a constitutional problem). Alphen aan den Rijn, Netherlands: Samsom, 1980.

Anheier, Helmut K. "West Germany: The Ambiguities of Peak Associations." In *Between States and Markets: The Voluntary Sector in Comparative Perspective*, ed. Robert Wuthnow. Princeton: Princeton University Press, 1991.

Aquina, Herman. "PGOs in the Netherlands." In *Delivering Public Services in Western Europe: Sharing Western European Experience of Para-government Organization*, ed. Christopher Hood and Gunnar Folke Schuppert. London: SAGE Publications, 1988.

Arons, Stephen. *Compelling Belief: The Culture of American Schooling*. Amherst: University of Massachusetts Press, 1986.

Asimov, Nanette. "Many Private Schools Wary of Prop. 174 Despite Its Allure." *San Francisco Chronicle*, October 21, 1993, A19.

Baer, Richard A., Jr. "The Supreme Court's Discriminatory Use of the Term 'Sectarian.' " *Journal of Law and Politics* 6, no. 3 (1990).

Ballion, Robert. *La bonne école* (The good school). Paris: Hatier 1991.

——. *Les consommateurs d'école* (The school consumers). Paris: Stock, 1982.

Barber, Bernard. "The Sociology of the Professions." *Daedalus* 92, no. 4 (1963).

Batty, Dave. *Philosophy of Teen Challenge*. Springfield, Mo.: Teen Challenge National Office, 1994.

Becker, J. W., and R. Vink. *Secularisatie in Nederland, 1966–1991: De verandering van opvattingen en enkele gedragingen*. Rijswijk, Netherlands: Sociaal en Cultureel Planbureau, 1994.

Beckford, James A. "Great Britain: Voluntarism and Sectional Interests." In *Between States and Markets: The Voluntary Sector in Comparative Perspective*, ed. Robert Wuthnow. Princeton: Princeton University Press, 1991.

Berger, Peter L., and Richard John Neuhaus. *To Empower People*. 1977. In *To Empower People: From State to Civil Society*, ed. Michael Novak. Washington, D.C.: American Enterprise Institute, 1996.

Bicknese, Aaron T. "The Teen Challenge Drug Treatment Program in Comparative Perspective." Ph.D. diss., Northwestern University, 1999. Typescript.

——"Teen Challenge Drug Treatment in Comparative Perspective: A Crossroads Monograph Proposal." 1996. Typescript.

Bischof, Günter, and Anton Pelinka, eds. *Austro-Corporatism: Past, Present, Future*. New York: Transaction, 1995.

Bishop, John H. "Signaling, Incentives, and School Organization in France, the Netherlands, Britain, and the United States." In *Improving America's Schools: The Role of Incentives*, ed. Eric A Hanushek and Dale W. Jorgenson. Washington, D.C. National Academy Press, 1996.

Blumenfeld, Samuel L. *Is Public Education Necessary?* Boise, Idaho: Paradigm, 1985.

Bollwahn, Paul E. "Building Bridges." July 24, 1995. Typescript.

———. "Personal Triumphs." N.d. Unpaginated typescript.

Bowers, Charles L. "Culture against Itself: Nihilism as an Element in Recent Educational Thought." *American Journal of Education,* August 1985, 465–90.

Brager, George. "The Indigenous Worker: A New Approach to the Social Work Technician." *Social Work,* April 1965.

Brandl, John E. "Governance and Educational Quality." In *Learning from School Choice,* ed. Paul E. Peterson and Bryan C. Hassel. Washington, D.C.: Brookings Institution, 1998.

Braster, J. F. A. *De identiteit van het openbaar onderwijs* (The identity of public education). Groningen: Wolters-Noordhoff, 1996.

———. *De inspecteur en de school* (The inspector and the school). Rotterdam: Erasmus Universiteit Subfaculteit der Sociaal-Culturele Wetenschappen, Vakgroep Onderwijssociologie en Onderwijsbeleid, 1987.

Brown, Dorothy M., and Elizabeth McKeown. *The Poor Belong to Us: Catholic Charities and American Welfare.* Cambridge: Harvard University Press, 1998.

Bryk, Anthony S., Valerie E. Lee, and Peter B. Holland. *Catholic Schools and the Common Good.* Cambridge: Harvard University Press, 1993.

Bryson, Joseph E., and Samuel H. Houston Jr. *The Supreme Court and Public Funds for Religious Schools: The Burger Years, 1969–1986.* Jefferson, N.C.: McFarland, 1990.

Budziszewski, J. "Politics of Virtues, Government of Knaves." *First Things,* June–July 1994, 38–44.

Burger, Steve. "125 Years of Rescue Missions." *Rescue Magazine,* October 1997.

Burtchaell, James Tunstead. "The Alienation of Christian Higher Education in America." In *Schooling Christians,* ed. Stanley Hauerwas and John H. Westerhoff. Grand Rapids, Mich.: Eerdmans, 1992.

Carpenter, George. "Secular Humanism and Social Holiness." In *Creed and Deed: Toward a Christian Theology of Social Services in the Salvation Army,* ed. John D. Waldron. Oakville, Ontario: Salvation Army Triumph Press, 1986.

Carpenter, Joel A. *Revive Us Again: The Reawakening of American Fundamentalism.* New York: Oxford University Press, 1997.

Carr-Saunders, A. M., and P. A. Wilson. *The Professions.* Oxford: Oxford University Press, 1933.

Carter, Stephen L. *The Culture of Disbelief: How American Law and Politics Trivialize Religious Devotion.* New York: Basic Books, 1993.

Cawson, Alan. "Corporatism." In *The Blackwell Encyclopaedia of Political Thought,* ed. David Miller. Oxford: Basil Blackwell, 1987.

Center for Public Justice. *A Guide to Charitable Choice.* Washington, D.C., 1997.

Centre for Educational Research and Innovation. *Education at a Glance: OECD Indicators.* Paris: Organisation for Economic Cooperation and Development, 1993.

Chavez, Stephanie, and Jodi Wilgoren. "Private Schools Polarized over Voucher Issue." *Los Angeles Times,* Orange County ed., October 18, 1993, A1.

Chevallier, P., B. Grosperrin, and J. Maillet. *L'Enseignement français de la Révolution à nos jours* (French education from the Revolution until today). Paris: Mouton, 1968.

Cheydleur, John R. *Faith-Based Counseling Skills.* N.p., n.d.

Choy, Susan P. *Public and Private Schools: How Do They Differ?* NCES 97–983. Washington, D.C.: National Center for Education Statistics, 1997.

Christian College Coalition. *Resource Guide for Christian Higher Education.* Washington, D.C., 1995.

Chubb, John E. "The Performance of Privately Managed Schools: An Early Look at the Edison Project." In *Learning from School Choice,* ed. Paul E. Peterson and Bryan C. Hassel. Washington, D.C.: Brookings Institution, 1998.

Chubb, John E., and Terry M. Moe. *Politics, Markets, and America's Schools.* Washington, D.C.: Brookings Institution, 1990.

Cibulka, James G., Timothy J. O'Brien, and Donald Zewe. *Inner-City Private Elementary Schools: A Study.* Milwaukee: Marquette University Press, 1982.

Colarelli, Nick J., and Saul M. Siegel. *Ward H: An Adventure in Innovation.* Princeton, N.J.: Van Nostrand, 1996.

Coleman, James S., and Thomas Hoffer. *Public and Private High Schools: The Impact of Communities.* New York: Basic Books, 1987.

Commission of the European Communities. *Structures of the Education and Initial Training Systems in the Member States of the European Community.* Brussels: Eurydice European Unit, 1991.

Coons, John E. "Intellectual Liberty and the Schools." *Journal of Law, Ethics, and Public Policy* 1 (1985).

Coons, John E., and Stephen D. Sugarman. *Education by Choice: The Case for Family Control.* Berkeley and Los Angeles: University of California Press, 1978.

————. *Scholarships for Children.* Berkeley: Institute of Governmental Studies Press, 1992.

Coughlin, John J. "Common Sense in Formation for the Common Good—Justice White's Dissents in the Parochial School Aid Cases: Patron of Lost Causes or Precursor of Good Mews." *Saint John's Law Review* 66:261–327.

De Groof, Jan, *De Grondwetsherziening van 1988 en het onderwijs: De schoolvrede en zijn toepassing* (The constitutional revision of 1988 and education: The "school peace" and its application). Brussels: E. Story-Scientia, 1989.

————. *Le pacte scolaire: Coordination et annotations.* Brussels: E. Story-Scientia, 1990.

————. "The Overall Shape of Education Law: Status of Comparative and Supra-National Education Law." In *Subsidiarity and Education Aspects of Comparative Educational Law.* Leuven, Belgium: Acco, 1994.

Delattre, Edwin J. *Character and Cops: Ethics in Policing.* Washington, D.C.: American Enterprise Institute for Public Policy Research, 1989.

Dewey, Douglas D. "An Echo, Not a Choice." *Policy Review,* November–December 1996, 28–32.

Dewey, John. "Can Education Share in Social Reconstruction?" 1934. In *The Later Works,* vol. 9, *1933–1934.* Carbondale: Southern Illinois University Press, 1986.

————. "Intelligence and Morals." 1908. In *The Middle Works,* vol. 4, *Essays on Pragmatism and Truth, 1907–1909.* Carbondale: Southern Illinois University Press, 1977.

Dewey, John. "Toward a National System of Education" (1935). In *Later Works*, vol. 11, *Essays and "Liberalism and Social Action," 1935–1937*. Carbondale: Southern Illinois University Press, 1987.

Doek, Jaap E. "Relations in Child Protection." In *Rethinking the Balance: Government and Non-governmental Organizations in the Netherlands*, ed. Tymen J. van der Ploeg and John W. Sap. Amsterdam: VU Press, 1995.

Dwyer, James G. *Religious Schools v. Children's Rights*. Ithaca, N.Y.: Cornell University Press, 1998.

Education Commission of the States. *Alternative Routes for Teacher Certification*. Denver, February 1995.

Ensign, Forest Chester. *Compulsory School Attendance and Child Labor*. Iowa City, Iowa, 1921; rpt. New York: Arno Press and New York Times, 1969.

Erickson, Donald A. "Bad Fences Make Bad Neighbors: A Look at State Regulation of Private Schools." In *Religious Schooling in America*, ed. James C. Carper and Thomas C. Hunt. Birmingham, Ala.: Religious Education Press, 1984.

Esbeck, Carl Howard. "A Constitutional Case for Governmental Cooperation with Faith-Based Social-Service Providers." *Emory Law Journal* 46, no. 1 (1997).

———. *The Regulation of Religious Organizations as Recipients of Governmental Assistance*. Washington, D.C.: Center for Public Justice, 1996.

Esch, *see* Van Esch.

Estrada, Leobardo F. "Survival Profiles of Latino Nonprofit Organizations." In *Hispanics and the Nonprofit Sector*, ed. Herman E. Gallegos and Michael O'Neill. New York: Foundation Center, 1991.

Fernandez, Alfred, and Siegfried Jenkner, eds. *International Declarations and Conventions on the Right to Education and the Freedom of Education*. Frankfurt am Main: Info3-Verlag, 1995.

Finke, Roger, and Rodney Stark. *The Churching of America: Winners and Losers in Our Religious Economy*. New Brunswick, N.J.: Rutgers University Press, 1992.

Formicola, Jo Renée, and Hubert Morken, eds. *Everson Revisited: Religion, Education, and Law at the Crossroads*. Lanham, Md.: Rowman and Littlefield, 1997.

Freedman, Samuel G. *Upon This Rock: The Miracles of a Black Church*. New York: Harper, 1994.

Freund, Paul. "Public Aid to Parochial Schools." *Harvard Law Review* 92 (1969): 1680.

Fuller, Bruce, and Richard F. Elmore, with Gary Orfield, eds. *Who Chooses? Who Loses? Culture, Institutions, and the Unequal Effects of School Choice*. New York: Teachers College Press, 1996.

Garvey, Gerald J., and John J. DiIulio Jr. "Sources of Public Service Overregulation." In *Deregulating the Public Service: Can Government Be Improved?* ed. DiIulio. Washington, D.C.: Brookings Institution, 1994.

Geel, *see* Van Geel.

Gendt, *see* Van Gendt.

Georgel, Jacques, and Anne-Marie Thorel. *L'enseignement privé en France* (Private education in France). Paris: Dalloz, 1995.

Gerrichhauzen, L. G., and J. G. A. van Mierlo. "Het particuliere bestuursstelsel, een bestuurskundige analyse" (Private administrative structure, an administrative science analysis). In *Het Particulier Initiatief in de Nedelandse Verzorgingsmaatschap-*

pij: Een bestuurskundige benadering, ed. van Mierlo and Gerrichhauzen. Lochem and Ghent: Uitgeversmaatschappij De Tijdstroom, 1988.

Geyer, Georgie Anne. "The Death of Citizenship." *American Experiment Quarterly* 1, no. 1 (1998): 59–71.

Glenn, Charles L. *Choice of Schools in Six Nations*. Washington, D.C.: U.S. Department of Education, 1989.

————. "Common Standards and Educational Diversity." In *Subsidiarity and Education: Aspects of Comparative Educational Law*, ed. Jan De Groof. Leuven, Belgium: Acco, 1994.

————. "Controlled Choice in Massachusetts Public Schools." *Public Interest* 103 (spring 1991): 88–105.

————. *Educational Freedom in Eastern Europe*. 2d ed. Washington, D.C.: Cato Institute, 1995.

————. "Free Schools and the Revival of Urban Communities." In *Welfare in America*, ed. Stanley Carlson-Thies and James W. Skillen. Grand Rapids, Mich.: Eerdmans, 1996.

————. "Letting Poor Parents Act Responsibly." *Journal of Family and Culture* 2, no. 3 (1986).

————. "Minority Schools on Purpose." In *Changing Populations, Changing Schools: 94th Yearbook of the National Society for the Study of Education*, part 2, ed. Erwin Flaxman and A. Harry Passow. Chicago: National Society for the Study of Education, 1995.

————. *The Myth of the Common School*. Amherst: University of Massachusetts Press, 1988.

————. "Het Nederlandse onderwijsbeleid: Een benadering vanuit de Angelsaksische wereld" (Dutch educational policy: A consideration from the Anglo-Saxon world). In *"Een onderwijsbestel met toekomst": 75 jaar onderwijspacificatie 1917–1992*. Amersfoort, Netherlands: Unie voor Christelijk Onderwijs, 1992.

————. "Outcome-Based Education: Can It Be Redeemed?" In *Curriculum, Religion, and Public Education: Conversations for an Enlarging Public Square*, ed. James T. Sears with James C. Carper. New York: Teachers College Press. 1998.

————. "Religion, Textbooks, and the Common School." *Public Interest* 88 (summer 1987): 28–47.

————. "Treatment-Oriented Agencies and Growth-Oriented Agencies." Harvard Graduate School of Education, April 1969.

————. "Het unieke van het Nederlandse systeem" (The uniqueness of the Dutch system). *Inzicht* 125, no. 2 (1991).

————. "What Would Equal Treatment Mean for Public Education?" In *Equal Treatment of Religion in a Pluralistic Society*. Grand Rapids, Mich.: Eerdmans, 1998.

Glenn, Charles L., Kahris McLaughlin, and Laura Salganik. *Parent Information for School Choice: The Case of Massachusetts*. Boston: Center on Families, Communities, Schools and Children's Learning, 1993.

Gonzalez Borrero, Maria. "The Management of Hispanic Nonprofit Organizations." In *Hispanics and the Nonprofit Sector*, ed. Herman E. Gallegos and Michael O'Neill. New York: Foundation Center, 1991.

Green, Roger Joseph. "An Historical Salvation Army Perspective." In *Creed and Deed: Toward a Christian Theology of Social Services in the Salvation Army*, ed. John D. Waldron. Oakville, Ontario: Salvation Army Triumph Press, 1986.

Greene, Jay P. "Civic Values in Public and Private Schools." In *Learning from School Choice*, ed. Paul E. Peterson and Bryan C. Hassel. Washington, D.C.: Brookings Institution, 1998.

Greenwood, Ernest. "Attributes of a Profession." In *Professionalization*, ed. Howard M. Vollmer and Donald L. Mills. Englewood Cliffs, N.J.: Prentice-Hall, 1966.

Groome, Thomas H. "What Makes a School Catholic." In *The Contemporary Catholic School: Context, Identity, and Diversity*, ed. Terence H. McLaughlin, Joseph O'Keefe, and Bernadette O'Keeffe. London: Falmer Press, 1996.

Haase, David L. "Coats Hears from Religious Groups about Ways to Lend a Hand to Poor." *Indianapolis Star*, September 29, 1995, E10.

Hannaway, Jane. "Management Decentralization and Performance-Based Incentives: Theoretical Considerations for Schools." In *Improving America' s Schools: The Role of Incentives*, ed. Eric A Hanushek and Dale W. Jorgenson. Washington, D.C.: National Academy Press, 1996.

Hargreaves, David H. "Diversity, Choice, and Excellence: Beyond the Comprehensive School." In *Freeing Education: Steps towards Real Choice and Diversity in Schools*, ed. Fiona Carnie, Martin Large, and Mary Tasker. Stroud, U.K.: Hawthorn Press, 1996.

Hartocollis, Anemona. "Religious Leaders Map Plans to Use New Law for Publicly Financed Charter Schools." *New York Times*, December 29, 1998, A17.

Havel, Václav. *Living in Truth*. London: Faber and Faber, 1987.

Herrick, Thaddeus. "Christian Drug-Abuse Group Wins Fight with State." *Houston Chronicle*, December 1, 1995, 42.

———. "Welfare from the Streets; San Antonio Preacher Reflects Gingrich Reforms." *Houston Chronicle*, March 6, 1995, A1.

Hersey, Cliff. "Professed Out Loud and Honestly: The Challenge of Post-secondary Education in the United States." Ed.D. diss., Boston University, 1997.

Hess, Catherine B. "Research Summation." Rehrersburg, Pa.: Teen Challenge Training Center, n.d.

Hess, Frederick M. "Policy Churn and the Plight of Urban School Reform." In *Learning from School Choice*, ed. Paul E. Peterson and Bryan C. Hassel. Washington, D.C.: Brookings Institution, 1998.

Hill, Paul T., Lawrence C. Pierce, and James W. Guthrie. *Reinventing Public Education*. Chicago: University of Chicago Press, 1997.

Himmelfarb, Gertrude. *The Idea of Poverty: England in the Early Industrial Age*. New York: Random House, 1983.

———. *Poverty and Compassion: The Moral Imagination of the Late Victorians*. New York: Random House, 1992.

Hodgetts, Colin. "Third Sector Alliance: Schools That Want to Join the State System." In *Freeing Education: Steps towards Real Choice and Diversity in Schools*, ed. Fiona Carnie, Martin Large, and Mary Tasker. Stroud, U.K.: Hawthorn Press, 1996.

Hodgkinson, Virginia A., Murray S. Weitzman, Stephen M. Noga, and Heather A. Gorski. *A Portrait of the Independent Sector: The Activities and Finances of Charitable Organizations*. Washington, D.C.: Independent Sector, 1993.

Hodgkinson, Virginia A., Murray S. Weitzman, with others. *From Belief to Commitment: The Community Service Activities and Finances of Religious Congregations in the United States, 1993 Edition: Findings from a National Survey*. Washington, D.C.: Independent Sector, 1993.

Hoefnagel, H. J. M. "Developments in Dutch Education Policy and Responsibility for Education." In *Subsidiarity and Education Aspects of Comparative Educational Law*, ed. Jan De Groof. Leuven, Belgium: Acco, 1994.

Hood, Christopher, with Marco Allegra, Herman Aquina, Rune Premfors, Allan Rosas, and Gunnar Folke Schuppert. "Institutional Arrangements for Five Public Services in Six Countries." In *Delivering Public Services in Western Europe: Sharing Western European Experience of Para-government Organization*, ed. Christopher Hood and Gunnar Folke Schuppert. London: SAGE Publications, 1988.

Hood, Christopher, and Gunnar Folke Schuppert, eds. ." *Delivering Public Services in Western Europe: Sharing Western European Experience of Para-government Organization*. London: SAGE Publications, 1988.

Humboldt, Wilhelm von. *The Limits of State Action*. 1792. Ed. and trans. J. W. Burrow. Indianapolis: Liberty Fund, 1993.

Institute for Independent Education. *On the Road to Success: Students at Independent Neighborhood Schools*. Washington, D.C., 1991.

Jach, Frank-Rüdiger. *Schulvielfalt als Verfassungsgebot* (School diversity as a constitutional requirement). Berlin: Duncker and Humblot, 1991.

James, Estelle, ed. *The Nonprofit Sector in International Perspective*. New York: Oxford University Press, 1989.

James, Thomas, and Henry M. Levin, eds. *Comparing Public and Private Schools*. 2 vols. New York: Falmer Press, 1988.

Jenkner, Siegfried. "Das Recht auf Bildung als Menschenrecht und seine Realisierung in beiden deutschen Staaten" (The right to education as a human right and its realization in both German states). *Pädagogik und Schule in Ost und West* 4 (1990).

———, ed. *Das Recht auf Bildung und die Freiheit der Erziehung in Europäischen Verfassungen* (The right to education and freedom of education in European constitutions). Frankfurt am Main: Info3-Verlag, 1994.

Jorgenson, Lloyd P. *The State and the Non-public School, 1825–1925*. Columbia: University of Missouri Press, 1987.

Kellner, Hansfried, and Peter L. Berger. "Life-Style Engineering: Some Theoretical Reflections." In *Hidden Technocrats: The New Class and New Capitalism*, ed. Hansfried Kellner and Frank W. Heuberger. New Brunswick, N.J.: Transaction, 1992.

———. "Het onderwijsbestel in hoofdlijnen" (The educational system in outline). In *Onderwijs: Bestel en beleid*, ed. J. A. Van Kemenade. Groningen: Wolters-Noordhoff, 1981.

Kemenade, *see* Van Kemenade.

Kemerer, Frank R. "The Use of Government Funds by Voluntary Social Service Agencies in Four Welfare States." In *The Nonprofit Sector in International Perspective*, ed. Estelle James. New York: Oxford University Press, 1989.

Kemerer, Frank R., Joe B. Hairston, and Keith Lauerman. "Vouchers and Private School Autonomy." *Journal of Law and Education* 21, no. 4 (1992): 601–28.

Kirby, Gretchen G., LaDonna A. Pavetti, Karen E. Maguire, and Rebecca L. Clark. *Income Support and Social Services for Low-Income People in Massachusetts*. Washington, D.C.: Urban Institute, December 1997.

Koekebakker, Olof. *Immigrant in Europa*. Utrecht: Nederlands Centrum Buitenlanders, 1990.

Koppejan, J. "Ontstaan en groei van het reformatorisch onderwijs" (Origin and growth of reformed education). In *Belijden en opvoeden: Gedachten over de christelijke school vanuit een reformatorische visie*, ed. M. Golverdingen et al. Houten: Den Hertog, 1989.

Kosmin, Barry A., and Seymour P. Lachman. *One Nation under God: Religion in Contemporary American Society*. New York: Crown, 1993.

Kramer, Ralph M. "The Use of Government Funds by Voluntary Social Service Agencies in Four Welfare States." In *The Nonprofit Sector in International Perspective*, ed. Estelle James. New York: Oxford University Press, 1989.

Lambert, J. "School Legislation in Germany." In *Subsidiarity and Education Aspects of Comparative Educational Law*, ed. Jan De Groof. Leuven, Belgium: Acco, 1994.

Langouet, Gabriel, and Alain Leger. *Public ou privé: Trajectoires et réussites scolaires* (Public or private: Trajectories and academic success). Paris: Publidix, 1991.

Leclerc, Gérard. *La bataille de l'école: 15 siècles d'histoire, 3 ans de combat* (The school battle: 15 centuries of history, 3 years of combat). Paris: Denoel, 1985.

Lelièvre, C. "Considerations historiques" (Historical considerations). In *Public ou privé: Trajectoires et réussites scolaires*, by Gabriel Langouet and Alain Leger. Paris: Publidix, 1991.

Lenaerts, Koen. "Subsidiarity and Community Competence in the Field of Education." In *Subsidiarity and Education Aspects of Comparative Educational Law*, ed. Jan De Groof. Leuven, Belgium: Acco, 1994.

Leune, J. M. G. "Besluitvorming in het onderwijsbestel" (Decision making in the educational system). In *Onderwijs: Bestel en beleid*, ed. J. A. van Kemenade. Groningen: Wolters-Noordhoff, 1981.

Lieberman, Myron. *Education as a Profession*. Englewood Cliffs, N.J.: Prentice-Hall, 1956.

———. *Privatization and Educational Choice*. New York: St. Martin's Press, 1989.

Lijphart, Arend. *The Politics of Accommodation: Pluralism and Democracy in the Netherlands*. Berkeley and Los Angeles: University of California Press, 1968.

Lines, Patricia M. "Private Education Alternatives and State Regulation." *Journal of Law and Education* 12, no. 2 (1983): 189–234.

Loconte, Joe. "Paying the Piper." *Policy Review* 93 (January–February 1999): 30–36.

———. *Seducing the Samaritan: How Government Contracts Are Reshaping Social Services*. Boston: Pioneer Institute, 1997.

Loury, Glenn C. "Professors and the Poor: Discussion at a Poverty Conference." In *One by One from the Inside Out: Essays and Reviews on Race and Responsibility in America*. New York: Free Press, 1995.

Lubove, Roy. *The Professional Altruist: The Emergence of Social Work as a Career, 1880–1930*. Cambridge: Harvard University Press, 1965.

Lugo, Luis E. "Equal Partners: The Welfare Responsibility of Governments and Churches." Washington, D.C.: Center for Public Justice, 1996.

Machen, John Gresham. *Education, Christianity, and the State*, ed. John W. Robbins. Hobbs, N.M.: Trinity Foundation, 1995.

Madiot, Yves. "Le juge et la laïcité" (The judge and secularity). *Pouvoirs* no. 75: *La laïcité* (1995).

Manuel, David. "Teen Challenge: Conquering Drugs." *Saturday Evening Post*, December 1987, n.p.

Marsden, George. "Church, State, and Campus." *New York Times*, April 26, 1994.

———. *The Soul of the American University*. Oxford: Oxford University Press, 1994.

Marshall, T. H. *Class, Citizenship, and Social Development*. Garden City, N.Y.: Doubleday Anchor, 1965.

Martin, David. *Tongues of Fire*. Oxford: Blackwell, 1990.

Martínez López-Muñiz, José Luis. "El art. 27 de la Constitución: Análisis de su contenido, doctrina jurisprudencial. Tratados internacionales suscritos por España" (Article 27 of the Constitution: Analysis of its content [and] jurisdictional doctrine. International treaties signed by Spain). In *Aspectos jurídicos del sistema educativo*. Madrid: Consejo General del Poder Judicial, 1993.

Marwijk Kooy-von Baumhauer, *see* Van Marwijk Kooy-von Baumhauer.

Mawdsley, Ralph D. "Emerging Legal Issues in Nonpublic Education." *West's Education Law Quarterly* 2, no. 4 (1993): 605–20.

Mayer, Susan E. *What Money Can't Buy: Family Income and Children's Life Chances*. Cambridge: Harvard University Press, 1997.

McConnell, Michael M. "Equal Treatment and Religious Discrimination." In *Equal Treatment of Religion in a Pluralistic Society*, ed. Stephen Monsma and Christopher Soper. Grand Rapids, Mich.: Eerdmans, 1998.

McKinley, Edward H. *Marching to Glory: The History of the Salvation Army in the United States, 1880–1992*. Grand Rapids, Mich.: Eerdmans, 1995.

McLaughlin, Terence H. "The Distinctiveness of Catholic Education." In *The Contemporary Catholic School: Context, Identity, and Diversity*, ed. McLaughlin, Joseph O'Keefe, and Bernadette O'Keeffe. London: Falmer Press, 1996.

Mees, Rudolf. "Financing Free Education." In *Freeing Education: Steps towards Real Choice and Diversity in Schools*, ed. Fiona Carnie, Martin Large, and Mary Tasker. Stroud, U.K.: Hawthorn Press, 1996.

Mellor, William. "Teen Challenge: Overcoming Substance Abuse by Spiritual Renewal." In *Philanthropy, Culture, and Society*, October 1996, 1–8.

Meyer, Heinz-Dieter. "Fröbel oder 'Head' Start?—Religion und Wissenschaft in der frühkindlichen Erziehung in Deutschland und den USA. 'Säkularisierung' auf demPrüfstand." In *Religion und Politik*, ed. Heinz-Dieter Meyer, Michael Minkenberg, Ilona Ostner, Jahrbuch für Europa- und Nordamerikastudien 2. Bonn: Leske und Buderich, 1998.

Meyer, Heinz-Dieter, Silke Tollmien, Andreas Flegel, Oliver Schwarz, and Suzanne Moeller. "Welfare between Charity *(Nächstenliebe)* and Bureaucracy: German Public and Church-Affiliated Pre-schooling Compared." Draft, 1996, and
subsequent addenda.

Mierlo, *see* Van Mierlo.

Mill, John Stuart. *On Liberty.* 1859. Ed. David Spitz. New York: W. W. Norton,
1975.

Miller, David. "Welfare State." In *The Blackwell Encyclopaedia of Political Thought.*
Oxford: Basil Blackwell, 1987.

Monchambert, Sabine. *La liberté de l'enseignement* (Educational freedom). Paris:
Presses universitaires de France, 1983.

Monsma, Stephen V. *Positive Neutrality: Letting Religious Freedom Ring.* Westport,
Conn.: Greenwood Press, 1993.

———. *When Sacred and Secular Mix.* Lanham, Md.: Rowman and Littlefield, 1996.

Monsma, Stephen V., and J. Christopher Soper. *The Challenge of Pluralism: Church
and State in Five Democracies.* Lanham, Md.: Rowan and Littlefield, 1997.

Mozos Touya, Isabel de los. *Educación en libertad y concierto escolar* (Educational freedom and school contracts). Madrid: Editorial Montecorvo, 1995.

Musil, Jiří. "Czechoslovakia in the Middle of Transition." *Daedalus* 121, no. 2: *The
Exit from Communism* (1992).

National Center for Education Statistics. *Private Schools in the United States: A Sta-
tistical Profile, 1993–94.* NCES 97–459. Washington, D.C.: U.S. Department of
Education, 1997.

National Commission on Philanthropy and Civic Renewal. *Giving Better, Giving
Smarter.* Washington, D.C., 1997.

National Institute on Drug Abuse. *An Evaluation of the Teen Challenge Treatment
Program.* Washington, D.C.: U.S. Department of Health, Education, and Welfare, 1977.

Needham, Philip. *Community in Mission: A Salvationist Ecclesiology.* London: International Headquarters of the Salvation Army, 1987.

———. "Toward a Re-integration of the Salvationist Mission." In *Creed and Deed:
Toward a Christian Theology of Social Services in the Salvation Army,* ed. John D.
Waldron. Oakville, Ontario: Salvation Army Triumph Press, 1986.

Neuhaus, Richard J. Foreword to *Welfare Reformed: A Compassionate Approach,* ed.
David W. Hall. Phillipsburg, N.J.: P and R Publishing, 1994.

———. *The Naked Public Square: Religion and Democracy in America.* Grand Rapids,
Mich.: Eerdmans, 1984.

Nicolau, Siobhan O., and Henry Santiestevan. "Looking Back: A Grantee-Grantor
View of the Early Years of the Council of La Raza." In *Hispanics and the Nonprofit
Sector,* ed. Herman E. Gallegos and Michael O'Neill. New York: Foundation
Center, 1991.

Nuis, A. "Onderwijs als maatschappelijk goed" (Education as a social good). In
Marketing en public relations in het openbaar onderwijs. Almere: Vereniging voor
Openbaar Onderwijs, 1993.

Olasky, Marvin. "The Corruption of Religions Charities." In *To Empower People:
From State to Civil Society,* ed. Michael Novak. 2d ed. Washington, D.C. American
Enterprise Institute Press, 1996.

———. *Renewing American Compassion.* New York: Free Press, 1996.

———. *The Tragedy of American Compassion*. Wheaton, Ill.: Crossway Books, 1992.

Olsen, Darcy. "The Advancing Nanny State." Policy Analysis No. 285. Washington, D.C.: Cato Institute, October 23, 1997.

Osborne, David, and Ted Gaebler. *Reinventing Government*. Reading, Mass.: Addison-Wesley, 1992.

Parsons, Talcott. *The Social System*. New York: Free Press, 1964.

Partin, Malcolm O. *Waldeck-Rousseau, Combes, and the Church: The Politics of Anticlericalism, 1899–1905*. Durham, N.C.: Duke University Press, 1969.

Payne, James L. "Absence of Judgment." *Policy Review*, November–December 1996.

Peterson, Paul E. "School Choice: A Report Card." In *Learning from School Choice*, ed. Peterson and Bryan C. Hassel. Washington, D.C.: Brookings Institution, 1998.

Peterson, Paul E., and Bryan C. Hassel, eds. *Learning from School Choice*. Washington, D.C.: Brookings Institution, 1998.

Piveteau, Didier J. "Catholic Education in France." In *Catholic Education in the Western World*, ed. James Michael Lee. Notre Dame, Ind.: University of Notre Dame Press, 1967.

Ploeg, *see* Van der Ploeg.

Postma, Andres. *Handboek van het Nederlandse Onderwijsrecht* (Handbook of Dutch educational law). Zwolle: W. E. J. Tjeenk Willink, 1995.

———. "The Principle of Subsidiarity in Dutch Educational Law." In *Subsidiarity and Education Aspects of Comparative Educational Law*, ed. Jan De Groof. Leuven, Belgium: Acco, 1994.

Powell, Arthur G. *Lessons from Privilege: The American Prep School Tradition*. Cambridge: Harvard University Press, 1996.

Quade, Quentin. *Financing Education*. New Brunswick, N.J.: Transaction, 1996.

Randall, E. Vance. *Private Schools and Public Power: A Case for Pluralism*. New York: Teachers College Press, 1994.

Read, James E. "Deacons and Samaritans: Christian Reflections on Professional Social Work." In *Creed and Deed: Toward a Christian Theology of Social Services in the Salvation Army*, ed. John D. Waldron. Oakville, Ontario: Salvation Army Triumph Press, 1986.

Reed, Ralph E., Jr., and Robert L. Simonds. "The Agenda of the Religious Right." *School Administrator*, October 1993.

Reichley, A. James. *Religion in American Public Life*. Washington, D.C.: Brookings Institution, 1985.

Riu i Rovira de Villar, Francesc. *Todos tienen el derecho a la educación* (Everyone has a right to education). Madrid: Consejo General de la Educación Catolica, 1988.

Ritzen, J. M. M. "Onderwijs en economie" (Education and economy). In *Onderwijs: Bestel en beleid*, ed. J. A. Van Kemenade. Groningen: Wolters-Noordhoff, 1981.

Robinson, Earl. "The Whole Gospel." In *Creed and Deed: Toward a Christian Theology of Social Services in the Salvation Army*, ed. John D. Waldron. Oakville, Ontario: Salvation Army Triumph Press, 1986.

Rodríguez-Fraticelli, Carlos, Carlos Sanabria, and Amílcar Tirado. "Puerto Rican Nonprofit Organizations in New York." In *Hispanics and the Nonprofit Sector*, ed. Herman E. Gallegos and Michael O'Neill. New York: Foundation Center, 1986.

Sacken, Donal M. "Regulating Nonpublic Education: A Search for Just Law and Policy." *American Journal of Education*, May 1988, 394–420.

Salamon, Lester, and Helmut K. Anheier. *The Emerging Nonprofit Sector: An Overview.* Manchester: Manchester University Press, 1996.

Sandin, R. T. *The Search for Excellence: The Christian College in the Age of Competition.* Macon, Ga.: Mercer University Press, 1982.

The Salvation Army Year Book. London, 1997.

Sap, John W. "From Opponents to Responsible Partners." In *Rethinking the Balance: Government and Non-governmental Organizations in the Netherlands,* ed. Tymen J. van der Ploeg and Sap. Amsterdam: VU Press, 1995.

Schoten, *see* Van Schoten.

Scott, W. Richard. "Professional Employees in a Bureaucratic Structure: Social Work." In *The Semi-Professions and Their Organization: Teachers, Nurses, Social Workers,* ed. Amitai Etzioni. New York: Free Press, 1969.

Senate Report on the Adolescent Family Life Act. Senate Report no. 97-161, 1981.

Shain, Barry Alan. *The Myth of American Individualism.* Princeton: Princeton University Press, 1994.

Sherman, Amy L. *Restorers of Hope.* Wheaton, Ill.: Crossway Books, 1997.

———. "Thy Neighbor's Keeper." *Reason,* August–September 1997.

Simonse, Joop. *De teloorgang van het kerkelijk clubhuiswerk: Het verhaal van een secularisatieproces* (How church settlement house work went astray: The account of a process of secularization). Ten Have/Baarn, Netherlands: Passage, 1997.

Skillen, James W., and Rockne M. McCarthy, eds. *Political Order and the Plural Structure of Society.* Atlanta: Scholars Press, 1991.

Smith, Christian. *American Evangelicalism: Embattled and Thriving.* Chicago: University of Chicago Press, 1998.

Smith, Stephen Rathgeb, and Michael Lipsky. *Nonprofits for Hire: The Welfare State in the Age of Contracting.* Cambridge: Harvard University Press, 1993.

Sociaal en Cultureel Planbureau. *Sociaal en Cultureel Rapport 1996.* Rijswijk, Netherlands, 1996.

———. *Sociale en Culturele Verkenningen 1997* (Social and cultural explorations, 1997). Rijswijk, Netherlands, 1997.

Spencer, Herbert. *The Man versus the State.* Indianapolis: Liberty Classics, 1982.

Spotts, Frederic. *The Churches and Politics in Germany.* Middletown, Conn.: Wesleyan University Press, 1973.

Stark, Rodney, and William Sims Bainbridge. *The Future of Religion.* Berkeley and Los Angeles: University of California Press, 1988.

Struik, L. A. "De openbare school en de 'algemeen bijzondere' school." In *Schoolbestuur,* September 1985.

Summers, Anita A., and Amy W. Johnson. "The Effects of School-Based Management Plans." In *Improving America's Schools: The Role of Incentives,* ed. Eric A. Hanushek and Dale W. Jorgenson. Washington, D.C.: National Academy Press, 1996.

Tasker, Mary. "Developing a Third Sector Alliance." In *Freeing Education: Steps towards Real Choice and Diversity in Schools,* ed. Fiona Carnie, Martin Large, and Mary Tasker. Stroud, U.K.: Hawthorn Press, 1996.

Teen Challenge National Training and Resource Center. *Research on the Effectiveness of Teen Challenge.* Springfield, Mo., n.d.

Thielicke, Helmut. *Theological Ethics*, vol. 2, *Politics* (1958–59). Ed. William H. Lazareth. Philadelphia: Fortress Press, 1969.

Thompson, Roger D. *Teen Challenge of Chattanooga, TN: Survey of Alumni.* Chattanooga: Teen Challenge, 1994.

Timmins, Nicholas. *The Five Giants: A Biography of the Welfare State.* London: Fontana Press, 1996.

Tobin, William J. *A Summary and Analysis of the New Final Rule for the Child Care and Development Fund.* Falls Church, Va.: William J. Tobin and Associates, 1998.

Tocqueville, Alexis de. *Democracy in America.* Ed. J. P. Mayer, trans. George Lawrence. New York: Harper and Row, 1988.

Toren, Nina. "Semi-professionalism and Social Work: A Theoretical Perspective." In *The Semi-professions and Their Organization: Teachers, Nurses, Social Workers*, ed. Amitai Etzioni. New York: Free Press, 1969.

Tyack, David. *The One Best System: A History of American Urban Education.* Cambridge: Harvard University Press, 1974.

Tyack, David, and Elizabeth Hansot. *Managers of Virtue: Public School Leadership in America, 1820–1980.* New York: Basic Books, 1982.

Unie voor Christelijk Onderwijs. *De verzuiling voorbij* (Beyond pillarization). Amersfoort, Netherlands, 1994.

Valente, William D., with Christina M. Valente. *Law in the Schools.* 4th ed. Columbus, Ohio: Merrill, 1997.

Van der Ploeg, Tymen J. "Introduction to the Dutch Model of Government–Nongovernmental Organizations." In *Rethinking the Balance: Government and Nongovernmental Organizations in the Netherlands*, ed. van der Ploeg and John W. Sap. Amsterdam: VU Press, 1995.

Van der Wouden, Ries, Marieke Ruinaard, Rick Kwekkeboom, Elisabeth ter Borg, Peter Voogt, and Wiert Wiertsema. *Evaluatie sociale vernieuwing: Het eindrapport* (Evaluation of social renewal: Final report). Rijswijk, Netherlands: Sociaal en Cultureel Planbureau, 1994.

Van Esch, Wil, Miek Laemers, and Gerrit Vrieze. "Vooral professionele eisen bepalen de identiteit van een school" (Primarily professional demands determine the identity of a school). *Didaktief*, December 1992.

Van Geel, Tyll. *Authority to Control the School Program.* Lexington, Mass.: D. C. Heath, 1976.

———. *The Courts and American Education Law.* Buffalo, N.Y.: Prometheus Books, 1987.

Van Gendt, Rien. *Educational Financing and Policy Goals for Primary Schools.* Paris: Organisation for Economic Cooperation and Development, 1979.

Van Kemenade, J. A. *De Katholieken en hun onderwijs: Een sociologisch onderzoek naar de betekenis van katholiek onderwijs onder ouders en docenten* (Catholics and their education: A sociological investigation of the significance of Catholic education to parents and teachers). Meppel, Netherlands: Boom, 1968.

Van Marwijk Kooy-von Baumhauer, Liesbeth. *Scholen verschillen: Een verkennend vergelijkend onderzoek naar het intern functioneren van vijfentwintig scholengemeenschappen vwo-havo-mavo* (Schools differ: An exploratory comparative investigation of the internal functioning of twenty-five secondary schools). Groningen: Wolters Noordhoff, 1984.

Van Mierlo, J. G. A., and L. G. Gerrichhauzen. "De toekomst van het particulier initiatief in Nederland" (The future of private initiative in the Netherlands). In *Het Particulier Initiatief in De Nedelandse Verzorgingsmaatschappij: Een bestuurskundige benadering*, ed. van Mierlo and Gerrichhauzen. Lochem and Ghent: Uitgeversmaatschappij De Tijdstroom, 1988.

Van Schoten, A. P. M., and H. Wansink. *De nieuwe schoolstrijd: Knelpunten en conflicten in de hedendaagse onderwijspolitiek* (The new school struggle: Bottlenecks and conflicts in contemporary educational policy). Utrecht: Bohn, Scheltema and Holkema, 1984.

Viteritti, Joseph P. "Choosing Equality: Religious Freedom and Educational Opportunity under Constitutional Federalism." *Yale Law and Policy Review* 15, no. 1 (1996): 113–92.

Waldron, John D. *Creed and Deed: Toward a Christian Theology of Social Services in the Salvation Army*. Oakville, Ontario: Salvation Army, 1986.

Weber, Max. *The Theory of Social and Economic Organization*. Ed. Talcott Parsons, trans. A. M. Henderson and Talcott Parsons. New York: Free Press, 1964.

Weiss, Manfred, and Cornelia Mattern. "The Situation and Development of the Private School System in Germany." *Social Change and Educational Planning in West Germany*, ed. Hasso von Recum and Weiss. Frankfurt am Main: Deutsches Institut für internationale Pädagogische Forschung, 1991.

Wetenschappelijk Instituut voor het CDA. *Ruimte voor kwaliteit* (Room for quality). Deventer: Van Loghum Slaterus, 1989.

Wever, Douglas. *The Teen Challenge Therapeutic Model*. Adopted by the Teen Challenge National Board of Directors, June 7, 1993. Springfield, Mo.: Teen Challenge National Office, 1993.

Whelan, Robert. *The Corrosion of Charity: From Moral Renewal to Contract Culture*. London: IDEA Health and Welfare Unit, 1996.

Wilensky, Harold L. "The Professionalization of Everyone?" *American Journal of Sociology* 70, no. 2 (1994): 137–58.

Winter, David. "Rendering unto Caesar: The Dilemma of College-Government Relations." In *Making Higher Education Christian*, ed. Joel Carpenter and Kenneth Shipps. Grand Rapids, Mich.: Eerdmans, 1987.

Wiseman, Clarence D. "Call to Renewal and Change." In *Creed and Deed: Toward a Christian Theology of Social Services in the Salvation Army*, ed. John D. Waldron. Oakville, Ontario: Salvation Army Triumph Press, 1986.

Wolfe, Alan. *Whose Keeper? Social Science and Moral Obligation*. Berkeley and Los Angeles: University of California Press, 1989.

Wouden, *see* Van der Wouden.

Wubbenhorst, William. "POS Reform in Massachusetts." Typescript prepared for the Center for Public Justice, 1996.

Wuthnow, Robert. "Tocqueville's Question Reconsidered: Voluntarism and Public Discourse in Advanced Industrial Societies." In *Between States and Markets: The Voluntary Sector in Comparative Perspective*, ed. Wuthnow. Princeton: Princeton University Press, 1991.

———. "The Voluntary Sector: Legacy of the Past, Hope for the Future?" In *Between States and Markets: The Voluntary Sector in Comparative Perspective*, ed. Wuthnow. Princeton: Princeton University Press, 1991.

INDEX

NEW FORUM BOOKS

New Forum Books makes available to general readers outstanding original interdisciplinary scholarship with a special focus on the juncture of culture, law, and politics. New Forum Books is guided by the conviction that law and politics not only reflect culture but help to shape it. Authors include leading political scientists, sociologists, legal scholars, philosophers, theologians, historians, and economists writing for nonspecialist readers and scholars across a range of fields. Looking at questions such as political equality, the concept of rights, the problem of virtue in liberal politics, crime and punishment, population, poverty, economic development, and the international legal and political order, New Forum Books seeks to explain— not explain away—the difficult issues we face today.